d Sea

Arctic Circle

Grímsey

Rauðinúpur   Hraunhafnartangi
Raufarhöfn
page 274
Fontur

Kópasker   Hólaheiði
Öxarfjörður   Þórshöfn
Langanes
Bakkaflói

Flatey
Ólafsfjörður   page 232
Hrísey   Skjálfandi
Grenivík   Húsavík
Dalvík   85   Ásbyrgi   Bakkafjörður
Jökulsárgljúfur
Eyjafjörður
Tröllskagi   Þjóðgarður Vatnajökull   Vopnafjörður
(Vatnajökull National Park)
page 240   Vopnafjörður   Héraðsflói
87   Dettifoss
kárjökull   Akureyri   Dimmifjallgarður   Smárfjöll   page 284
1387   Reykjahlíð
Mývatn   85   94   Borgarfjörður
26   page 262   Eystri
821   8   Egilsstaðir   Seyðisfjörður
1   page 296   Neskaupstaður
Frjóská   Þjóðgarður Vatnajökull   Eskifjörður
(Vatnajökull National Park)   Fljótsdalsheiði   Reyðarfjörður   Reyðarfjörður
752   Lögurinn   Stöðvarfjörður
Sprengisandur   Ódáðahraun   1
Skjálfandafljót   Askja
ofsjökull   Þjórsá   Djúpivogur
Tungnafells-   Papey
Jökull

Hámarinn   Vatna   page 196
1573   Grímsvötn   1
Þjóðgarður Vatnajökull   Höfn
Þórisvatn   (Vatnajökull National Park)   Snæfell
26   Tungnaá   1383
Langisjór   page 198
Laki   Skaftafell
812
208   1
Kirkjubæjarklaustur   Skeiðarársandur   Ingólfshöfði   ATLANTIC

OCEAN

N

Iceland

0   40 km
0   40 miles

INSIGHT GUIDES
ICELAND

APA PUBLICATIONS L

Part of the Langenscheidt Publishing Group

✻ INSIGHT GUIDE
ICELAND

Editorial
Project Editor
Alexia Georgiou
Picture Editor
Tom Smyth
Publishing Manager
Rachel Fox
Series Manager
Rachel Lawrence

Distribution
UK & Ireland
**Dorling Kindersley Ltd,
a Penguin Group company**
80 Strand, London, WC2R 0RL
customerservice@dk.com

United States
Ingram Publisher Services
1 Ingram Boulevard, PO Box 3006
La Vergne, TN 37086-1986
customer.service@ingrampublisher
services.com

Australia
Universal Publishers
PO Box 307
St Leonards, NSW 1590
sales@universalpublishers.com.au

New Zealand
Brown Knows Publications
11 Artesia Close, Shamrock Park
Auckland, New Zealand 2016
sales@brownknows.co.nz

Worldwide
**Apa Publications GmbH & Co.
Verlag KG (Singapore branch)**
7030 Ang Mo Kio Ave 5,
08-65 Northstar@AMK
Singapore 569880
apasin@signet.com.sg

Printing
CTPS-China

©2011 Apa Publications GmbH & Co.
Verlag KG (Singapore branch)
All Rights Reserved

First Edition 1992
Sixth Edition 2011
Reprinted 2013

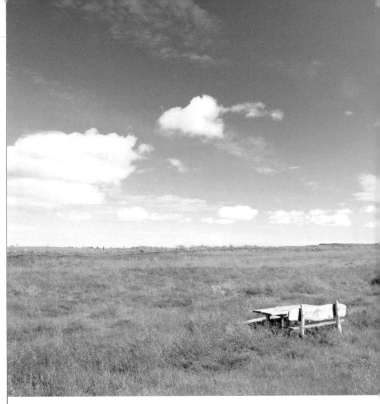

ABOUT THIS BOOK

The first Insight Guide pioneered the use of creative full-colour photography in travel guides in 1970. Since then, we have expanded our range to cater for our readers' need not only for reliable information about their chosen destination but also for a real understanding of the culture and workings of that destination. Now, when the internet can supply inexhaustible (but not always reliable) facts, our books marry text and pictures to provide those much more elusive qualities: knowledge and discernment. To achieve this, they rely heavily on the authority of locally based writers and photographers.

Insight Guide: Iceland is structured to convey an understanding of the island nation and its people as well as to guide readers through its myriad attractions:

◆ The **Features** section, indicated by a pink bar at the top of each page, is a series of illuminating essays that cover the natural and cultural history of the country, as well as daily life, environmental issues and the arts.
◆ The main **Places** section, indicated by a blue bar, is a complete guide to all the sights and areas worth visiting. Places of special interest are coordinated by number with the maps.
◆ The **Travel Tips** listings section, with a yellow bar, provides full information on transport, hotels, activities from culture to shopping to sports, an A–Z section of essential practical information, and a handy phrasebook with Icelandic words and expressions. An easy-to-find contents list for Travel Tips is printed on the back flap, which also serves as a bookmark.

LEFT: the tranquillity of the East Fjords.

The contributors

This new edition of *Insight Guide: Iceland* was commissioned and co-ordinated by Insight Guides editor **Alexia Georgiou** at Insight Guides' London office, edited by **Naomi Peck** and updated by **Fran Parnell** – who also expanded several of the chapters and penned the Why Is Iceland So Broke? mini feature.

It builds on the excellent foundations of previous editions of the book, such as the 2008 edition, produced by Insight Guides' Managing Editor **Tom Le Bas**, for which **James Proctor**, former BBC Scandinavia correspondent, supplied new features on Food and Drink, Environmental Protection and Whaling. Proctor also provided much of the new text for the tint panels and tips in the Places section.

Of particular note is **Tony Perrottet**, editor of the original edi-

tion of *Insight Guide: Iceland*, who also wrote the chapters on The Southwest, Vestmannaeyjar, The Southeast, Akureyri and Surroundings, Grímsey, Lake Myvatn, The Northeast, and The East Fjords. **Rowlinson Carter** wrote the detailed coverage of Iceland's history from its murky beginnings through to the mid-20th century, while **Bernard Scudder** contributed the chapters on Modern History, Harvesting the Sea and Reykjavík. **Anna Yates** wrote Forged by Fire, Honed by Ice, the text for the photo features on Life on the Land and The Great Outdoors, A Naturalist's Paradise, and the chapters on The Reykjanes Peninsula and Snæfellsnes and the West, and the essay on Flowers among the Lava. **Alda Sigmundsdóttir** wrote the Embracing the Night essay. **Arthúr Bollason** contributed the photo feature on the Saga Characters, while **Doreen Taylor** wrote the photo features on Iceland's Sea Birds and Natural Wonders. **Gary Gunning** contributed the essay on the Politics of Fishing. **Birna Helgadóttir** wrote The Icelanders, Living with the Environment, Language and Literature, and Icelandic Hauntings. The West Fjords was written by **Catherine Harlow**, and the chapters on Húnaflói and Skagafjörður and The Interior by **Julian Cremona**.

Much of the stunning photography is the output of **Ming Tang-Evans**. Out-of-house designer **Tracey Vosvenieks** worked on the layout. Thanks also go to **Sue Pearson**, who proofread the guide.

Map Legend

▬ ▪ ▬	International Boundary
▬ ▬ ▬	State Boundary
▬ ▪ ▬	National Park/Reserve
▬ ▬ ▬	Ferry Route
	Glacier
✈ ✈	Airport: International/ Regional
🚌	Bus Station
❶	Tourist Information
✝ ✝ ✝	Church/Ruins
✝	Monastery
☾	Mosque
✡	Synagogue
🏰	Castle/Ruins
∴	Archaeological Site
⋂	Cave
1	Statue/Monument
★	Place of Interest

The main places of interest in the Places section are coordinated by number with a full-colour map (eg ❶), and a symbol at the top of every right-hand page tells you where to find the map.

Contents

LEFT: Goðafoss waterfall, in the Akureyri region.

Maps

Inside front cover: Map of Iceland
Inside back cover: Map of the main bus routes in Reykjavík.

THE BEST OF ICELAND: TOP ATTRACTIONS

From the ethereal, magical lightshow of the aurora borealis, a glacial lagoon and the wonders of Iceland's barren wilderness areas, to the cultural attractions of Reykjavík

△ Visitors often come to Iceland in the darkest winter months simply to try and observe the **Northern Lights**. The country's high latitude and clear skies create fine conditions for the uncanny lightshow of the aurora borealis, though the spectacle can never be guaranteed. *See page 203*

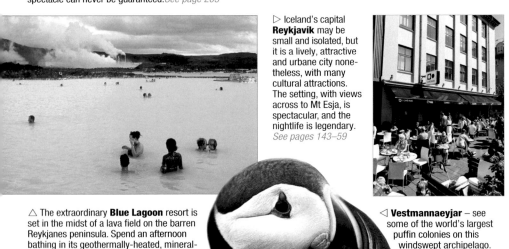

▷ Iceland's capital **Reykjavík** may be small and isolated, but it is a lively, attractive and urbane city none-theless, with many cultural attractions. The setting, with views across to Mt Esja, is spectacular, and the nightlife is legendary. *See pages 143–59*

△ The extraordinary **Blue Lagoon** resort is set in the midst of a lava field on the barren Reykjanes peninsula. Spend an afternoon bathing in its geothermally-heated, mineral-rich waters and you will emerge relaxed, reenergised and already planning your next trip to Iceland. *See pages 163–4.*

◁ **Vestmannaeyjar** – see some of the world's largest puffin colonies on this windswept archipelago. *See page 188*

◁ Almost wiped off the map by the volcanic eruption of 1973, **Heimaey** is a quintessential Icelandic fishing port with an attractive harbour and two looming volcanic peaks. Situated on the friendly Vestmannaeyjar islands off the southwest coast. *See page 185*

▽ Iceland is perhaps the best place for **whale-watching** in Europe. Catch a glimpse of one of these majestic creatures off Húsavík, on the north coast. *See page 334*

▽ **Jökulsárlón** glacial lagoon features on a hundred postcards, but nothing prepares you for its ethereal beauty. Glinting blue icebergs, calved from the mighty Vatnajökull icecap, float through the lagoon on their way to the sea. *See pages 200–210*

▷ Two natural wonders, **Geysir and Gullfoss** make a must-see countryside excursion for those on short city breaks. Geysir gave its name to all the world's geysers, although these days it is outperformed by its neighbour Strokkur. Nearby, the dramatic double waterfall Gullfoss is awesome in its elemental power. *See pages 176–7*

◁ **Ísafjörður** is the remote capital of the beautiful West Fjords region, notable not just for its setting but also for its restored 18th-century timber buildings. It is also the jumping-off point for wilderness hikers seeking to explore the deserted Hornstrandir peninsula. *See page 218*

▽ **Þórsmörk**, one of Iceland's most spectacular and inaccessible wilderness areas, is sealed off by a trio of glaciers, surging rivers and steep mountainsides covered in tiny birch trees. *See page 179–80.*

THE BEST OF ICELAND: EDITOR'S CHOICE

Stunning scenery, tumbling waterfalls, geothermal baths, outdoor pursuits and exciting nightlife – not to mention the charms of Europe's most northerly city... here are our recommendations for Iceland's unmissable attractions

ABOVE: riding the Icelandic horse, a sure-footed breed.

UNIQUELY ICELANDIC

● **Horse-riding** The one-of-a-kind Icelandic horse is a sturdy, calm-natured breed. Farms across the country offer visitors anything from a one-hour sortie to a seven-day trek. *Page 333*

● **Geothermal swimming pools** Emerging from a hot tub into the frigid polar air is a memorable experience. *See page 335*

● **Þingvellir** Revered by Icelanders, this beautiful natural amphitheatre is the birthplace of nation. *See page 171*

● **Independence Day** On June 17th Reykjavík and other places put on street parades, street theatre and music events. *See page 330*

● **Pickled shark and brennivín** Iceland's traditional foodstuffs are eaten with gusto during the pagan festival of Þorrablót. *Pages 119 and 329*

LEFT: taking the waters at Jarðböðin nature baths.

SPECTACULAR SCENERY

● **The coast around Vík** Black volcanic sands, pounding Atlantic surf and jagged rocks give Iceland's southern tip a gothic majesty. *See page 181*

● **Skaftafell** Part of Europe's biggest national park area, this is prime hiking country, dominated by glaciers. *See page 199*

● **Snæfellsnes** The mystical volcano here was the entrance point to the planet's interior in Jules Verne's *Journey to the Centre of the Earth*. *See page 210*

● **West Fjords** Towering cliffs and remote fjords in Iceland's sub-arctic northwest. *See pages 217–25*

● **Jökulsárgljúfur National Park** The impressive Dettifoss waterfall and Jökulsá Canyon are reasons to make the trip to this area in the far northeast. *See page 275*

● **Herðubreið** This towering peak rises over the plain of the eastern interior, with the Herdubreidarlindur valley an oasis of green amid desert-like surroundings. *See page 307*

BELOW: the Snæfellsnes peninsula, whose focus is the Snæfellsjökull glacier.

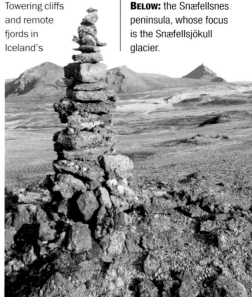

SIGHTS IN REYKJAVÍK

● **Hallgrímskirkja** Visible from most points in the city, climb the tower of this striking modern structure for breathtaking views. *See page 151*
● **National Museum** Recommended to anyone wishing to understand Iceland's past. *See page 151*
● **National Gallery** A light and airy space in which to admire Icelandic and foreign art. *See page 149*
● **Culture House** Explore the medieval past, brought vividly to life in the saga manuscripts. See also the **Saga Museum**. *See pages 149 and 153*
● **Árbær Open-Air Museum** An eye-opening experience, showing how

people lived in the not-so-distant past. *See pages 154–5*
● **Laugardalur** Reykjavík's main leisure complex features a magnificent open-air swimming pool with the full range of geothermally heated hot tubs and plunge pools. *See pages 153–4*

ABOVE: Reykjavík nightlife.
BELOW RIGHT: razorbills.

ABOVE: Skaftafellsjökull, a finger of the Vatnajökull icecap.

VOLCANOES AND GLACIERS

● **Krafla and Leirhnjúkur** Tempt fate in one of Iceland's most explosive areas, full of craters, bubbling mudpots and smoking new lava. *See page 267*
● **Hveravellir** In Iceland's barren interior, these remarkable brilliant-blue hot springs are surrounded by outlandishly coloured rocks. *See page 299*
● **Vatnajökull** Europe's largest icecap and its glaciers dominate the southeast. Snowmobile tours are

possible in summer. *See page 199*
● **Laki and Lakagígar** Site of the largest eruption in recorded history, today spongy green moss covers the otherworldly crater row. *See page 197*
● **Svínafellsjökull glacier walk** Strap on crampons and stride up a glacier on an unforgettable ice walk *See page 199*

BIRDWATCHER'S PARADISE

● **Lake Mývatn** Waterfowl breed at this volcanic lake. *See page 261–7*
● **Látrabjarg bird cliffs** Spectacular sea cliffs, home to thousands of sea birds. *See page 224*
● **Grímsey** Small island known for its abundant

birdlife. *See pages 253–7*
● **Króksbjarg** and **Bakkar cliffs** A haven for kittiwakes and fulmars. *See page 234*
● **Skeiðarársandur** World's largest breeding ground for great skuas. *See page 198*

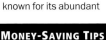

MONEY-SAVING TIPS

● **Cheap Sleeps** There are 36 youth hostels around Iceland (www.hostel.is) offering comfortable budget accommodation. Also, some hotels and guesthouses have cheap dormitories with either made-up beds or mattresses for sleeping bags.

● **Tourist Information** Local tourist offices are often located in

the town hall or library. Many are closed during the winter.

● **Money-saving passes** The bus station BSÍ (www.bsi.is) sells a host of bus passes and tickets that will save you money on journeys around the island. They are usually valid from 15th May to 31st August. Most popular is the **Full-Circle Passport**, entitling holders to a

circular trip on the Ring Road either clockwise or anticlockwise, with unlimited stops. The **Full-Circle & Westfjords Passport** extends the loop to take in Iceland's isolated northwest. Another attractive ticket is the **Beautiful South Passport**, allowing unlimited travel on seven of Reykjavík Excursions' southern bus routes over a period of 3, 5, 7, 9 or 11 days. *See pages 315–16.*

AN EXTRAORDINARY ISLAND

Iceland offers not only a wealth of natural wonders, from glaciers to geysers, but also a rich mine of history and literature

The reason for hereness seems beyond conjecture,
There are no trees or trains or architecture,
Fruits and greens are insufficient for health
And culture is limited by lack of wealth.
The tourist sights have nothing like Stonehenge,
The literature is all about revenge.
And yet I like it if only because this nation
Enjoys a scarcity of population…
— W.H. Auden, *Letters from Iceland*

Iceland has come a long way since the English poet Auden penned these facetious lines in 1936. From an isolated agricultural society that many people thought had scarcely progressed beyond the Middle Ages, there has emerged a high-tech welfare state with one of the highest standards of living in the world. Yet at least one thing hasn't changed since Auden's visit: Iceland still has a scarcity of population (around 318,000) that leaves it with some of the greatest wilderness areas in Europe.

In fact, Iceland may be the ultimate nature trip. It has virtually no pollution and all energy is either geothermal or hydroelectric. Drinking water comes from pure glaciers; fish is caught in unpolluted waters; even the lamb and cattle graze in fields untouched by fertiliser. Most Icelanders now live in and around the capital, Reykjavík, leaving huge swathes of the volcanically active island – one of the most recently formed on earth – quite deserted. Dotted by steaming lava fields, icecaps, glaciers, hot pools and geysers, the Icelandic landscape has an elemental rawness that nobody who sees it can easily forget.

Perhaps not surprisingly, the people who live on this extraordinary island are an eccentric breed. Speaking Europe's oldest language, little changed since the days of the Vikings, accustomed to the endless light of summer and Stygian gloom of the long winters, the Icelanders can be as extreme as their homeland. Rather shy, they will rarely be the first to talk to strangers. But once their traditional reserve is broken through, they can be among the most friendly and hospitable people in Europe.

Which may all help explain why Iceland exerts such a powerful hold over travellers, compelling them to return again and again. ❑

PRECEDING PAGES: East Fjords, Heradssandur; lightning flashes through a cloud of volcanic matter erupting from Eyjafjallajokull volcano, April 2010; Reykjavík skyline. **LEFT:** Dettifoss waterfall. **ABOVE:** Asmundur Sveinsson sculpture at Keflavík.

FORGED BY FIRE, HONED BY ICE

Iceland is one of the youngest landmasses in the world, geologically speaking. As a result, its inhabitants are used to living with change and disruption

In geological terms, Iceland is a mere baby. No more than 20 million years have passed since volcanoes on the floor of the far northern Atlantic Ocean began to spew lava, laying the foundations of what would become Iceland. Today it is still one of the most volcanically active spots on earth – giving geoscientists the chance of observing a land still in the making.

Movements of the earth's crust

According to the theory of plate tectonics, the earth's surface comprises a number of plates (seven major and dozens of minor plates), which "float" on the mass of magma beneath. The Andes and the Himalayas are evidence of massive collisions of tectonic plates, which have folded the earth's crust up to form great mountain ranges.

Volcanoes and earthquakes are symptoms of this vast movement, occurring at the boundaries where tectonic plates meet. These boundaries can be convergent, where the edge of one plate is forced underneath another and great slabs of the earth's surface are "lost"; or divergent, where the plates tear apart and magma rises to the surface from below, forming new crust. Iceland straddles a divergent boundary, the Mid-Atlantic Ridge, where the Eurasian and North American tectonic plates are being pulled apart. Thus, the island is literally being torn in two, at a rate of around 2cm (nearly an inch) a year, with lava rising from the earth's centre to fill the gap.

Volcanic belt

The Mid-Atlantic Ridge, running clear across the island from southwest to northeast, is marked

by a belt of volcanic craters, hot springs, steam springs, solfataras (areas of high-temperature activity) and earthquakes. This belt extends to a width of about 40km (25 miles) in the north, and up to 60km (40 miles) across in the south, and covers about a quarter of the country.

Not surprisingly, Iceland's rocks are almost all volcanic (predominantly basalt). The oldest rocks, from the Tertiary pre-Ice Age period, are the plateau basalts of the East and West Fjords. Slightly inland are younger grey basalts from the interglacial periods, generally appearing as open moorland with less evidence of glaciation. Further in towards the present-day volcanic zone is the palagonite formation, from subglacial erup-

---

LEFT: the solfatara, or volcanic vent, of Hverir near Lake Mývatn. **RIGHT:** on Vatnajökull, largest icecap in Europe.

tions in the last part of the Ice Age. Typical of these belts are tuff ridges and table mountains, the soft rock often extensively eroded by wind and water. Iceland's youngest rocks occur in and around the present-day volcanic zone.

The northwest and the east of Iceland are no longer volcanically active. Most of the rest of the island, however, conceals a seething mass of volcanic and geothermal activity. There are over 100 volcanoes in Iceland; 35 of these have been active over the past 10,000 years (recent history in geological terms!). In the past few centuries Iceland has experienced an eruption every five years on average. Most are minor, short-lived and cause minimal damage, like the photogenic eruption of Mount Hekla in 1991 – "tourist eruptions", in local parlance. Others can cause a little more trouble, like the 2010 eruption under the Eyjafjallajökull glacier. The resulting ash cloud, which reached a height of 10km (6 miles), brought airplanes across Europe to a standstill for six days in April, with an estimated cost to the airline industry of £2.2 billion.

In the shadow of disaster

Despite an apparently flippant attitude towards volcanoes, Icelanders do not forget the threat they live with. The catastrophic eruption of Lak-

THE BIRTH OF SURTSEY

The ultimate "tourist eruption" was the formation of the island of Surtsey, which began on the ocean floor just southwest of the Vestmannaeyjar (Westman Islands) in 1963 *(see pages 190–191)*. In addition to the spectacle of lava and ash, the Surtsey eruption produced voluminous clouds of steam as cold seawater met hot lava and instantly boiled. By the end of the eruption, the new island was 2.8 sq km (1 sq mile) in area – erosion has now reduced this to about 1.57 sq km (½ sq mile). The new islet was a welcome gift to scientists, a natural laboratory which offered them a chance to observe the processes by which virgin land is colonised by plants, birds, insects and mammals.

agígar in the late 18th century poured out the largest lava flow ever produced by a single volcano in recorded history, with a volume of about 12 cubic km (3 cubic miles). As if that were not enough, it also emitted noxious gases which poisoned livestock and crops, blocked out the sun, and led to a disastrous famine. About one-third of the population died.

In 1973, the subterranean peril was brought home with a vengeance, when a new volcano flared up on Heimaey in the Vestmannaeyar. It buried one-third of the town under lava and ash *(see the panel on page 187)*.

Evidence of subterranean unrest has been felt since the mid-1970s around Mount Krafla near Lake Mývatn, an area free of volcanic activity for over two centuries. A massive eruption, which lasted from 1724 until 1729, laid waste three farms, before the lava flow halted at Reykjahlíð church, where the congregation was praying for deliverance. Two centuries later, the earth began to move when construction started on the geothermal power station below Mount Krafla; many people concluded that man's interference with the forces of nature had set off a reaction within the earth. Mount Krafla has erupted several times since 1975, most recently in 1984, although the lava has never threatened Reykjahlíð.

It has been estimated that one-third of all the lava that has erupted on earth in recorded history

the country's mountain ridges to knife-edges.

Although Iceland emerged from its glacial pall about 10,000 years ago, it remains a land of glaciers and icecaps – curiously, they are believed to have been formed not in the Ice Age but during a cold spell around 500BC, reaching their largest size during the "Little Ice Age" of AD 1500–

> *Vatnajökull, up to 1km (3,200ft) thick and 8,300 sq km (3,200 sq miles) in area, is not only Europe's largest icecap, it is also bigger than all the rest put together.*

has come from Iceland. As any visitor will soon discover, almost all of it is scoria, a type of basalt that is full of tiny air bubbles and is consequently very light. Loose, sharp and difficult to cross, scoria also creates unusual and haunting formations. A small amount is smooth, hard "ropy" lava.

Caps of ice

In spite of its subterranean heat, Iceland has largely been shaped by cold. In the Ice Age, glaciers gouged out the plunging fjords which cut into the coastline on the north, east and west, and sharpened

LEFT: the 1973 eruption of Eldfell which threatened to engulf the town of Heimaey.
ABOVE: the eruption of Grímsvötn in 1996.

1900. Ice covers around 11 percent of the island's 103,000 sq km (40,000 sq miles). However, since 1990, all of Iceland's glaciers have been in retreat; land is currently being revealed that has been covered in ice since the 16th century.

Contrasts between heat and cold are nowhere so striking as in the glaciers that sit atop volcanoes. Some seem extinct: the volcanic crater on which the cone-shaped Snæfellsjökull glacier rests, for instance, has not erupted for 700 years.

Melting glaciers

Eruptions from subglacial volcanoes often cause more damage than those from open-air volcanoes. Hot lava melts the ice, triggering sudden floods – *jökulhlaups* – with unpredictable results.

Mount Katla, the volcano lying dormant under the glacier Mýrdalsjökull, is Iceland's largest caldera, at 80 sq km (30 sq miles). When Katla erupts, the *jökulhlaup* can be 200,000 cubic metres (7 million cubic ft) of water a second.

In 1996 a volcano in the Bárðarbunga-Grímsvötn fissure erupted beneath Vatnajökull, melting huge quantities of ice and scattering ash over a 100-km (60-mile) area. Meltwater from the eruption flowed into a sub-glacial caldera, which began to fill. On 5 November 1996, the water in the caldera spilled over the brim, resulting in a massive flood across the sand plain south of the glacier that swept away roads and bridges. It deposited icebergs the size of apartment blocks, which, as they melted, turned the sands into pits of quicksand.

Meltwater from the glaciers flows out into winding rivers, which swell whenever warm weather melts the glacial ice or when volcanic activity begins beneath the glacier. Unlike the crystal-clear rivers fed by rain or underground streams, glacial rivers carry silt from the glacier, so they are generally brownish and murky in colour. Unbridged rivers are one of the main dangers to travellers in the highlands, as the water can rise with alarming rapidity.

Iceland is no stranger to earthquakes. The stretching and straining of the earth's crust at the

South Iceland Quakes

Every 100 years or so a major earthquake brings destruction to southern Iceland. In 1784 the South Iceland Quake, estimated at 7.5 on the Richter scale, destroyed houses, farms and a cathedral. In 1896, southern Iceland was agitated by violent tremors and in 1912 a category 7 earthquake shook the region. In June 2000, three quakes, measuring 6.5, 5.5 and 6.6, struck over the course of three days, and in May 2008 another one measuring 6.3 hit Selfoss – footage can be seen at the Folk Museum in Eyrarbakki *(see page 170)*. Experts warn that although some tension on the earth's crust has been relieved, the "big one" is yet to come.

junction of tectonic plates inevitably produces sudden movements under pressure. Strict building regulations ensure that all man-made structures can withstand major earthquakes.

Using geothermal heat

Living on a "hot spot" implies coexistence with natural risks. Yet the heat in the earth has also brought its own inestimable benefits. In a cold climate, what could be more valuable than endless natural hot water?

All spouting springs (geysers) in the world owe their name to the Great Geysir in Iceland's southwest, which used to spout to a height of 60 metres (196ft). The geyser spent most of the 20th century in a dormant state, but earthquakes in Southern

Iceland in 2000 gave it a fresh burst of life; it now erupts several times per day to a height of around 10 metres (33ft). Nearby Strokkur (meaning "churn") erupts every few minutes to a height of about 30 metres (100ft), and several more spouting geysers can be seen around the country.

Natural hot water bubbling irrepressibly out of the earth has been prized by the Icelanders ever since they settled the country. Ingólfur Arnarson named Reykjavík ("smoky bay") after seeing clouds of steam rising from springs in today's Laugardalur valley. These springs became the community's public laundry in later centuries, when housewives would trudge the 3km (2 miles) from Reykjavík

Nesjavellir and Hellisheiði; the latter is now the world's largest geothermal power station. Today 85 percent of Iceland's atmospheric heating is from geothermal sources, and almost every community has its own geothermally warmed open-air swimming pool.

At Svartsengi in the southwest, superheated water (two-thirds of which is brine) from far beneath the earth's surface passes through a heat-exchange process to provide fresh water for heating, and generate electricity. A bonus is that the hot lake formed by the run-off water has developed into a popular spa, the Blue Lagoon (Bláa Lónið, *see pages 163 and 164*). Rich in salt

along Laugavegur ("hot spring road") carrying their washing. The laundry springs can still be seen in Laugardalur, by the Botanical Gardens *(see page 154)*, where one "washbasin" remains.

In 1930, geothermal energy was first piped from the springs to the town to heat a swimming pool and a school. Developing technology has made it possible to look further and drill deeper for hot water, and high-efficiency insulation means that water can be piped long distances. Reykjavík's main sources of geothermal energy lie about 30km (18 miles) from the city, at

LEFT: geothermal power production, Reykjanes Peninsula. **ABOVE:** feeling the heat: one of the thousands of tourists who visit Mývatn every year.

and other minerals, the waters of the lagoon are reputed to be beneficial for skin conditions.

Harnessing glacial rivers

The water that tumbles over precipices from Iceland's glaciated mountains and rivers is transformed into hydroelectric power (HEP); another valuable resource. The first HEP plant opened in Iceland in 1904, and today hydroelectric power stations supply 73 percent of Icelanders' electricity.

Whatever the changes their society is undergoing, the Icelanders still live very close to nature. They take for granted an untamed, unpolluted environment that is still growing, still changing, where eruptions and earthquakes are accepted as part of the tenor of life. ❏

DECISIVE DATES

4th century BC
Pytheas, a Greek explorer, reports sightings of an island which he called "Ultima Thule".

c. 6th or 7th century AD
Irish monks (pictured right) start to settle on "Thule", forming small communities.

mid-9th century
A Norwegian, Hrafna-Flóki, tries to settle in the West Fjords. Foiled by the harsh winter, he calls the land Ísland (Iceland).

VIKING SETTLEMENT
874
Ingólfur Arnarson (the "First Settler", statue pictured below left) and his foster brother Hjörleifur Hróðmarsson settle on Iceland in the southwest and on the south coast respectively.

25,000. Creation of the Alþingi parliament, a central authority presided over by a law-speaker.

10th century
Erik the Red (pictured right) settles on Greenland and persuades numerous Icelanders to follow.

CONVERSION AND FEUDING
984
Þorvaldur Koðránsson the Well-Travelled starts to convert Iceland to Christianity often using violent means. Later Olaf Tryggvason, King of Norway, sends his chaplain Þang-brand to continue conversions.

1000
Christianity is adopted as Iceland's official religion at the annual Alþingi meeting.

930
By 930 many other Norwegian chieftains and their families have followed and the population stands at an estimated

1163
The "Stone-Throwing Summer" of violent clashes between different groups of Vikings.

1179
Birth of Snorri Sturluson, diplomat and saga writer.

1230–64
The Sturlung Age of feuds between private armies and political factions.

1241
Murder of Snorri Sturluson on the King of Norway's orders.

1262
The Alþingi agrees to allow King Haakon of Norway to collect taxes.

DISASTER AND DECLINE

1389
An eruption of Mount Hekla is followed by smallpox and other epidemics.

1397
Scandinavian union of Norway, Denmark and Sweden transfers the sovereignty of Iceland from Norway to Denmark. Denmark, following Norway's example, prohibits Iceland from trading with any other countries, and agrees to send supply ships in exchange for fish.

1469
England and Denmark go to war over England's illegal trading with Iceland.

1526
A feud between the Roman Catholic bishops of Iceland's two sees, Ögmundur Pálsson of Skálholt and Jón Arason of Hólar, leads to a duel at the Alþingi.

1541
Denmark sends two warships to impose a new Lutheran church code through the Alþingi; former rivals Jón and Ögmundur both resist, but Ögmundur is exiled to Denmark, dying aboard ship.

1548
Bishop Jón is summoned by the king to Copenhagen, but instead stays in Iceland and continues his rebellion against the Protestants.

LEFT TOP: the Irish monks arrive over the seas. FAR LEFT: statue of Ingólfur Arnarson. LEFT: Erik the Red. TOP: ceremony at the Þingvellir plains, first gathering place of Iceland's parliament. RIGHT: illustration from the sagas.

1550
King Christian III of Denmark orders Jón's arrest; after being captured, he is beheaded along with two of his sons.

1627
3,000 pirates land on Heimaey in the Vestmannaeyjar (Westmann Islands), killing many of the inhabitants and taking others captive.

1662
Denmark divides Iceland into four commercial trading districts which are not permitted to trade with each other, only directly with Denmark. This is reinforced by a Danish naval blockade.

1783
Eruption of Laki volcano in southern Iceland kills approximately 10,000 Icelanders; most deaths are due to the ensuing "Haze Famine".

1800
The Alþingi is abolished on the orders of the Danish king.

A REVIVAL OF FORTUNE

1801
At the Battle of Copenhagen, the British fleet destroys the Danish Navy and confiscates the entire Danish merchant fleet.

1809
"Revolution" led by Jorgen Jorgensen, a Danishman serving in the British Navy, who liberated Iceland, declaring it independent. The revolution is quashed the same year by another member of the British Navy, and Jorgensen is jailed in England.

1811
Birth of Jón Sigurðsson, the force behind the movement for Icelandic independence from Danish rule.

1830
Iceland allowed two seats among 70 on an advisory body to the Danish crown.

1843
Royal degree signed by King Christian VIII *(pictured below)* reinstates a consultative Alþingi of 26 representatives,

with 20 elected members and six chosen by the crown.

1854
Trade monopoly with Denmark ended.

1874
Denmark gives the Alþingi autonomy over domestic affairs, but retains a veto over all it does.

1879
Death of Jón Sigurðsson.

1881–95
Benedikt Sveinsson, a campaigner for independence, calls for real self government every year at the Alþingi; attempts to pass the proposal are foiled by the royal veto.

THE 20TH CENTURY AND BEYOND
1904
Iceland is granted home rule.

1911
Founding of Reykjavík University.

1915
Introduction of total prohibition.

1918
Denmark makes Iceland a sovereign state with its own flag, still with the king of Denmark as its head of state, and agrees to hold further negotiations on Iceland's status in 1940.

1940
With Iceland occupied by Britain and Denmark by Germany, there is no communication between them. The Alþingi announces that it has taken over the governing of Iceland.

1941
Iceland requests full independence from Denmark.

1944
Following a plebiscite at which the termination of the union with Denmark and a new constitution are approved, Iceland becomes a republic on 17 June. This date is celebrated each year as Independence Day *(pictured below)*.

1949
Iceland becomes a founding member of NATO, abandoning its "eternal neutrality".

1951
US military return to Iceland to set up an air base at Keflavík.

1952–76
Four Cod Wars (1952, 1958, 1972, 1975) with the UK over fishing rights. In 1976 an

agreement is reached for a 320-km (200-mile) fishing limit off Iceland.

1955
Icelandic writer Halldór Laxness wins the Nobel Prize for Literature.

1963
The island of Surtsey is created by an underwater volcanic eruption off the southern coast.

2008
The worldwide economic crisis hits Iceland particularly hard; all three of the country's major banks collapse and the coun-

1973
Volcanic eruption on Heimaey island *(pictured above)* threatens to destroy it; an army of volunteers divert the lava flow, preventing complete disaster.

1980
Vigdís Finnbogadóttir, the world's first democratically elected female head of state, becomes president. She is thrice re-elected, holding office until 1996.

1986
Presidents Reagan and Gorbachev arrive in Reykjavík

for a summit to start talks to end the Cold War *(pictured below left)*.

1989
Beer Day, 1 March, celebrates the end of the ban on strong beer *(pictured right)*.

1992
Iceland walks out of the International Whaling Commission after the country's request for a limited whaling quota is rejected.

1994
Iceland enters the European Economic Area.

1996
The Grímsvötn volcano erupts under Vatnajökull, leading to a massive build-up of meltwater under the glacier, which floods out and sweeps away chunks of the Ring Road and several bridges on the south coast.

2000
Iceland celebrates one thousand years of Christianity and Leifur Eriksson's discovery of North America.

2006
Iceland resumes commercial whaling, despite strong opposition from environmental groups around the world.

try is plunged into a severe recession.

2009
Iceland applies for EU membership.

2010
In April, the ash cloud from a volcanic eruption under Eyjafjallajökull glacier brings most of Europe's air traffic to a standstill for six consecutive days.

FAR LEFT MIDDLE: King Christian VIII. LEFT MIDDLE: the fish at the centre of the Cod Wars. LEFT: Independence Day celebrations. TOP: Volcanic eruption on Heimaey island. ABOVE: Reagan and Gorbachev in 1986. RIGHT MIDDLE: Beer Day. RIGHT: the Eyjafjallajökull volcano.

ULTIMA THULE

Irish monks were the first to live on Iceland, but were soon
outnumbered by Vikings who settled and started
to farm the land

A recent visitor to Iceland overheard two farmers talking passionately in a field; they were lamenting the premature death of a young man whom they were sure would have been a great credit to the country. This sorely missed individual, it transpired, was a certain Skarphéðinn Njálsson, a character in one of the celebrated Icelandic sagas, and he had been dead for all of 1,000 years.

Various versions of this story are told by travellers to Iceland, all with the same kernel of truth: Icelanders are obsessed with their history, or at least a part of it. The period they prefer to remember is between the years 930 and 1030, when chisel-jawed saga heroes threw off the tyranny of Norway's king, created a new republic, and sailed to America way before the upstart Columbus; and after all, there is little after the 13th century on which Icelanders can reflect with pleasure. The country's recent prosperity occurred only since World War II. For the previous 600 years, Iceland was a grim, depressing place: a 19th-century English visitor complained that he never once saw an Icelander smile.

This historical roller-coaster ride has tentative beginnings, with Irish monks looking for a quiet, isolated spot to meditate, and becomes substantive with the Norwegian Viking settlement, dated at 871. These same sword-wielding Vikings, who famously reduced hapless Europeans to desperate praying, then performed an astonishing volte-face. Within generations, they took up intellectual pursuits – without ever quite putting down their swords – and created a legacy

of literature which scholars discuss in the same breath as Homer and the Golden Age of Greece.

These transformed Vikings not only wrote down their own history, but also collected and saved the oral prehistory and religion of the whole Germanic race. They wrote in their own tongue rather than in the scholarly language of Latin, on manuscripts made of calf-skin, one of the few commodities in Iceland which, like fish, was always plentiful. A great number of these manuscripts were lost or destroyed in subsequent periods of extreme hardship. Even so, those Icelandic sagas that have survived more than make up for an almost total absence of ancient monuments in the country.

LEFT: a Viking longship approaching the coast of Iceland. **RIGHT:** an early map showing the island of Thule at the world's northern edge.

The uttermost end of the earth

The cherished history of Iceland is really quite short by European standards. As far as anyone can tell, no human had yet set foot in Iceland when, for example, the Parthenon in Athens was already some 800 years old and the capital of the disintegrating Roman Empire was being moved to Constantinople.

Possibly the earliest mention of Iceland is from Pytheas, a Greek who lived in Marseilles in the 4th century BC. He explored the north personally and returned with an account of a country called Thule situated six days' sailing north of Britain and close to a frozen sea; whether this was Ice-

mately Iceland were just the ticket. The monks are unlikely to have arrived before St Patrick's celebrated missionary work in Ireland, which began in 432.

Ireland was a redoubt of Graeco-Roman learning when the Western Roman Empire crumbled. Irish chroniclers, who were familiar with earlier writers and travellers including Pytheas, tended to embellish their work with borrowed, and sometimes counter-productive, erudition. Thus the story of St Brendan's discovery of "Thule" *(see below)* is on the one hand made quite plausible by a description of a volcanic eruption which could have been Mount Hekla; but on the other

land, Greenland, Scotland, Scandinavia or Pytheas's overheated imagination has been debated for centuries. Later chroniclers *did* call the island Thule; but the country was variously known as Garðarshólmi, "Snowland" and "Butterland" before a Norwegian called Hrafna-Flóki came up with "Iceland", a name that finally stuck.

Frozen gateway to hell

It was not Scandinavians who first settled on Iceland but Irish monks driven by the desire to meditate undisturbed. They set out in coracles made of hides stretched over a framework of branches. With hardly any seafaring experience, they "sought with great labour… a desert in the ocean". The Shetlands, Faroe Islands and ulti-

ST BRENDAN IN ICELAND

St Brendan and crew were bobbing about offshore in their little boat when an inhabitant appeared: "he was all hairy and hideous, begrimed with fire and smoke". Sensing danger, St Brendan made a precautionary sign of the cross and urged the oarsmen to pull harder. "The savage man...rushed down to the shore, bearing in his hand a pair of tongs with a burning mass of slag of great size and intense heat, which he flung at once after the servants of Christ... 'Soldiers of Christ', said St Brendan, '... we are now on the confines of Hell'". He was not the last visitor to believe that eruptive Mount Hekla was the entrance to Hell.

hand credibility suffers considerably when St Brendan discovers that "Thule" is inhabited.

Sound information about Irish activities in Iceland is contained in the works of Dicuil, author of *On Measuring the Earth*, and the Venerable Bede. Dicuil quoted priests who said that between February and August it was light enough at midnight to pick lice off one's shirt.

Since the pioneering Irish communities were exclusively male, they would not have put down roots and multiplied in the usual way. The settlements were bound to wither, but was their decline in Iceland gradual? Peace of mind would not long have survived the arrival of the

hand accounts aside, concrete evidence for Irish monks in Iceland is lacking. No archaeological remains of any kind have been discovered; the surest mementoes of occupation are the "papa" (i.e. priest) place names.

Viking Exodus

According to Snorri Sturluson, the greatest of Icelandic saga writers, the Norwegians who apparently chased the Irish away were themselves fugitives. When Harald Fairhair became the first king of Norway in 872, he immediately set about mopping up the opposition, seizing the property of defeated chieftains and so forth. Of the 400

9th-century Norwegians. Ari the Learned, a 12th-century Icelandic chronicler, tells the story from the Norwegian point of view. The disembarking Vikings encountered "some Christians" who shortly afterwards "went away" because they were unwilling to live among heathens. That may be putting it mildly. Nevertheless, the Vikings were usually very candid about their atrocities, and as there is no record of anyone boasting about burying an axe in a hermit's head, scare-mongering theories about the fate of the Irish do not necessarily hold water. Second-

FAR LEFT: an episode from St Brendan's journey from Ireland to Thule: meeting a whale. **LEFT:** an illustrated saga manuscript. **ABOVE:** the Norsemen arrive.

names mentioned in the *Landnámabók (Book of Settlements)*, which lists the first Icelandic settlers, 38 are known to have been previously powerful chieftains in Norway.

Some historians believe, less dramatically, that poor economic conditions drove people abroad. Professor Munch, writing in 1859, suggested that the original settlers actually came from older Viking colonies in the British Isles, and that Scotland was therefore "the chief cradle of their race". Only a small proportion of the names in the *Landnámabók* is non-Scandinavian, and Icelanders long believed that their blood was purest Viking, but Munch's theory was quite prescient. Recent studies of mitochondrial DNA have revealed that almost half of the women who originally settled in Iceland were actually from Britain and Ireland.

The best-known story about the early Norwegians, told in the *Landnámabók*, concerns two foster brothers, Ingólfur Arnarson (the official "First Settler" of Iceland) and Hjörleifur Hróðmarsson, who spent a winter in Iceland and were so impressed that they returned with two ships piled high with household goods. They were accompanied by family, friends and 10 slaves procured in Ireland. The two brothers parted company on reaching Iceland, Ingólfur going to the southwest coast (and later to the site of Reykjavík) and Hjörleifur to the south, near present-day Vík.

him to neglect his pagan sacrifices. The rebels were tracked down to their island refuge and surprised in the middle of a meal of roast puffin. Those who escaped being killed there and then were probably mindful of the penalties meted out to slaves who rose against their masters. One Irish slave, perhaps understandably unwilling to forgive a master for castrating him (among other grievances), had tried to cut his own throat and consequently suffered the agony of a red-hot wash basin placed on his belly with predictably gruesome results. Nevertheless, he survived – but only to be buried alive in a bog. The rebellious slaves fled to cliffs

Hjörleifur was soon faced with a rebellion by his Irish slaves because they resented having to share plough-pulling duties with his only ox. Almost all the sagas carry disparaging remarks about the character of Irish slaves, and this lot were evidently no exception. They first killed the ox, blamed it on a bear and then laid an ambush for Hjörleifur and his companions when they went to hunt the bear. As the hunters fanned out, the slaves overwhelmed them one by one. They abducted the women, piled into a boat and decamped to an offshore island.

The discovery of the hunters' bodies shocked Ingólfur. Death at the hands of a slave was such a shameful fate that he could only think that his brother's Christian tendencies had caused

and threw themselves off. The island setting for this unpromising start to Icelandic history was Heimaey, one of the island group known thereafter as the Vestmannaeyjar (Westmann or "Irish" Islands).

Dividing up the island

The Age of Settlement (874–930) followed these pioneering efforts, and soon the coastline was more or less fully occupied by settlers. Iceland had not long been settled, however, when the whole cycle of emigration repeated itself and for the same reasons: either land hunger, adven-

ABOVE: a reconstruction of Erik the Red's dwelling.
RIGHT: Leifur Eiríksson sights the coast of America.

turism or falling foul of authority. Erik the Red was a prime example of the last. Already banished from Norway for murder, he was in turn banished from Iceland for more of the same. Having sailed off to the west and found somewhere else to settle, he then attempted to persuade others to join him. To succeed, he needed an attractive name for his new land, and in this he set a precedent for estate-agency hyperbole ever after. It was such a lush paradise, he told prospective settlers, that only one name would do: Greenland. Enough people believed him to fill 25 ships, but only 14 ships survived the voyage to the promised land.

Vikings in America

The Vínland sagas (the *Greenlanders' Saga* and the *Saga of Eric the Red*) credit Erik's son, Leifur, with discoveries even farther afield. Old Erik would have been a partner in his son's journey, but en route to the ship leaving Greenland he was thrown from his horse and injured a foot. Leifur's set sail, but his first port of call was a place so dismally useless that there was no point in stretching his imagination beyond "Helluland" ("Stoneland" – northern Labrador).

Conditions to the south improved, hence it was dubbed "Markland" ("Woodland"). Further still, he came across a climate so mild that it

LAYING CLAIM TO LAND

The first Viking settlers laid claim to as much land as they thought they could manage, usually by throwing the pillars of the wooden high seats (a symbol of their authority) from their longboats and making their homes wherever they washed ashore. This tradition supposedly allowed the god Thor to choose the location.

The steady influx of new settlers meant rationing the remaining land by a process known as "carrying the fire". The owner of the ship bringing a group of immigrants was a chieftain or man of substance. The rest of the party would be families and attendant slaves or "thralls". The land they were entitled to was as much as could be encircled by a ring of bonfires, with the proviso that they had

to be lit with the same torch in one day and that, when burning, they were visible from one another. The criterion for women settlers – implying that some arrived independently – was the area that a two-year-old heifer could lap in a day.

The arable coastline was gradually settled in a similar pattern to that which is seen today, with most inhabitants on the coast, especially in the southwest. The interior – "nothing but ice and fire" – was out of bounds and remained so for all intents and purposes until the early 20th century. It still remains mostly uninhabited, with only a few farmers eking out a living from the starkly beautiful but barren land.

seemed not to require winter fodder for cattle. It was clearly a worthy contender for settlement, the more so when Leifur's German foster father returned from a sortie jabbering and "rolling his eyes in all directions and pulling faces". The fellow was understandably overcome by what he saw. The 10th-century Vikings were in the habit of consuming between 10 and 18 pints of powerful mead per day, along with the odd beaker of sour milk. Leifur and the rest of the company might have been primarily mead-men, but the German recognised grapes and knew what could be done with them. It was thus that they gave the name "Vínland" to the future America.

As Freydís was soon to discover, the greatest barrier to settlement in the New World was the hostility of the natives. "They were small and evil-looking, and their hair was coarse; they had large eyes and broad cheekbones." Her crew retreated in bewilderment when attacked by these tribesmen armed with catapults, a weapon new to the Vikings. Freydís snatched the sword of a man killed by a stone and faced the attackers. Yanking out a breast, she gave it a resounding thump with the flat of her sword. The Indians were as alarmed by this as the Vikings had been by their catapults. They bolted to their boats and paddled off at speed.

The explorations of Freydís

Leifur's observations inspired a surge of voyages to this wonderful place, including one by his dreadful half-sister Freydís in a joint venture with two Icelanders, Helgi and Finnbogi. Freydís seems to have inherited Old Erik's worst characteristics – the sagas refer darkly to her "evil mind". She had married her husband Þorstein only for his money and despised him. Freydís fell out with Helgi and Finnbogi when they reached Vínland and, making the false accusation that they had insulted her, ordered Þorstein ("thou miserable wretch") to kill both of them and their party of 30 men and five women. Þorstein did as he was told but drew the line at killing the women. "Give me an axe," said the ghastly Freydís.

The lure of the land of wine was strong, but repeated attempts to follow in Freydís's wake were to prove similarly unsuccessful. Although the land was excellent, they could never live there in safety, so they made ready to leave the place and return home. Attempts continued at least until 1347, which has led to the theory that Christopher Columbus was inspired by Icelandic stories about this distant land. These stories were probably still being recounted in seafaring circles when in 1477, according to his son Fernando, Columbus called at Iceland as a crew member of an English ship.

The Icelandic commonwealth

Back in 10th-century Iceland, the displaced chieftains were determined never again to be relieved of their traditional authority by a single ruler. They entrenched themselves in their respective areas, or þings, and were called goðar, a word derived from "god". The commonwealth Alþingi, created in 930, was a parliament whose history is almost continuous to the present day. Presided over by a Speaker or Law-speaker, it was an acknowledgement that certain matters required a central authority. Legal disputes and new legislation were settled by the Lögrétta (Law Council), the nub of the parliament, composed of chieftains and their non-voting advisers. Lesser cases were dealt with by courts for each "Quarter" of the land, made up of 36 chieftains.

culture and help to explain, for example, why the language remained uniquely homogeneous without a trace of local dialects.

Although the Alþingi was the supreme spiritual and temporal authority, it was not allowed to raise a military force or to exercise police authority. Moreover, the powers of the Law-speaker were deliberately circumscribed so that the office could not be used as a springboard to monarchy; when a chieftain turned up with as many as 1,500 men to support him in a feud, there was nothing the Law-speaker could do.

The Alþingi therefore had considerable difficulty living up to its ideals. In 1012, for exam-

Every free man was entitled to attend the meetings of the Alþingi, and the occasion acted as a magnet for the entire population.

The Alþingi met for two weeks every year at Þingvellir, a point roughly in the middle of the most densely populated part of Iceland and possessing a remarkable natural amphitheatre. These annual reunions were a great influence in promoting the development of a distinctive

LEFT: an image from the Icelandic film *In the Shadow of the Raven*, set in the harsh early years.
ABOVE: longship from a 14th-century manuscript.

ple, a litigant who suspected that his case was slipping away on a legal technicality unleashed his private army. The plain of Þingvellir was strewn with corpses before proceedings could be resumed. Litigation abounded, but the law was so complicated, and the society so riddled with vendettas, that the due process of the courts was forever on a knife-edge.

Life in the longhouses

Settlers tried to recreate the conditions of pre-monarchical Norway as far as local conditions permitted. In Norway, farmsteads were a collection of separate wooden buildings, one for sleeping, another for cooking and so on. Although the *Íslendingabók* says that Iceland "was covered with wood between the mountains and the sea" at the time of the Settlement, its trees were quickly cut down for fuel and building, and timber was in short supply ever afterwards. The Icelandic farmstead was therefore a single unit, a row of rooms with common walls and a turf roof. Only the framework of the walls was timber; the rest was made up of stones and sod. While the Norwegian *stofa* or living-dining quarters were often large enough to accommodate several hundred guests, the Icelanders could not heat such a space. Buildings became smaller and the windows fewer.

Larger farmsteads able to afford the luxury of timber imported from Norway maintained the tradition of large festive halls, which also served as religious temples. In the winter a fire was lit in a hearth at the centre of the hall, the smoke being left to find its way out through shuttered apertures in the roof. The chieftain occupied a high seat at one end with the guests lining benches on either side, their backs to the wall. "The flesh of the sacrificed animals, after being boiled in a large kettle over the fire," says an 18th-century study, "was served up to these rude banqueters, who frequently amused themselves by throwing the bones at one another, the manner in which they were placed on the opposite sides of the hall being very convenient for indulging in this elegant pastime."

Farmsteads in the Middle Ages were also equipped with an early version of the sauna, water being poured over a stone stove in the bath house (*baðstofa*) to produce vapour. The early settlers evidently made full use of water from numerous hot springs to luxuriate in hot baths.

Early customs

Wool was the main clothing material used by the settlers, and was woven and coloured with mineral and vegetable dyes. According to the sagas, Skarphéðinn, the ill-fated young man whom we met at the opening of this history, made his entrance at one Alþingi in a blue mantle, blue striped trousers with a silver belt, and high shoes. His hair was combed back behind his ears, and round his head was a gold embroidered silk ribbon.

Like all young men, Skarphéðinn was addicted to what amounted to the national sports, horse-fighting (theoretically a contest between animals) and a kind of ball game called *knattleikur* (*see panel, left*).

Marriages were arranged by the male heads of families; young men could veto the decision, but brides had no say in the matter. Once accepted as a wife, the woman acquired considerable property rights and other privileges, but these did not extend to denying the husband his concubines. The law-code Grágás only cites three serious grounds for divorce; but the sagas suggest that either partner might terminate the marriage for a host of reasons, from physical abuse to cross-dressing. ❑

A VIOLENT PASTIME

Knattleikur was a ball game described in the sagas, but it is hard to work out from commentaries on play what the rules were, if any. "Þorgrímur was unable to hold his own against Gísli, who threw him down and carried the ball away. Gísli sought again to take the ball, but Þorgrímur held it fast. Then Gísli threw him down so violently that he skinned his knees and knuckles, and blood was running from his nose... Gísli took the ball in one jump, threw it between the shoulders of Þorgrímur so that he fell forwards, and said: 'The ball on broad shoulders broke, which is not to be complained of'. At the end of the game, the two players part "not as good friends as before".

LEFT: a Viking amulet incorporating Christian and pagan symbolism.
RIGHT: Vikings on the warpath.

The Coming of Christianity

Although Iceland's conversion to Christianity was at times turbulent, it ushered in a period of relative stability and a literary golden age

On the rung of government below the Alþingi, the Icelandic chieftains fought tooth and nail to preserve their individual authority. The chieftainships were in reality more like political parties than regional entities. Dissatisfied "subjects" were at liberty to switch their allegiance – and divert their taxes – to some other chieftain, even one who lived at the opposite extremity of the land. These floating constituencies acted as a slight brake on the wilder excesses of ambitious chieftains; the rough and ready equilibrium, however, was severely tested by the advent of organised Christianity.

An Irish curse

The *Landnámabók* relates that Irish monks once lived at Kirkjubæjarklaustur ("Church Farm Cloister"); and that when they vacated the land, they left behind a curse on any pagan who occupied the site. The curse seems to have delivered, at least in the case of pagan settler Hildir Eysteinsson; he dropped dead as soon as he laid eyes on his new home.

Norwegian settlers arriving from the British islands must at least have encountered Christianity, but paganism was the new country's religion of choice. Icelandic paganism was a mixture of the old Norse deities, spirits who took on the likeness of men or beasts, and fetishes which made trees and waterfalls objects of veneration. Temples were built in holy places, ritual taking the form of animal sacrifices. Only in emergencies were human sacrifices offered.

One of the more concerted efforts to introduce orthodox Christianity is related in *Kristni saga* (although this is one of the less trustworthy sagas in terms of historical accuracy). Þorvaldur Koðránsson the Well-Travelled had been baptised

Too many of the initial Christian converts in Iceland merely paid lip service to avoid paying the pagan temple tolls, which did not go down well with the chieftains for whom the tolls were a source of income.

in Germany in 981 by a Bishop Fridrek. With the bishop in tow, Þorvaldur returned to Iceland to convert his countrymen. The singing, ringing of bells, burning of incense and liturgical vestments made a favourable impression, but the number of genuine converts was disappointing.

Matters came to a head when Þorvaldur preached at the Alþingi of 984. Héðinn of Svalbarð, an arch-opponent of Christianity, engaged comedians to mimic and poke fun at the two missionaries. Forgetting himself, Þorvaldur leapt on two of the comedians and killed them. Bishop Fridrek "bore all with patience" but was outlawed from Iceland with Þorvaldur. As they were preparing to sail, Þorvaldur spotted Héðinn sawing wood nearby: his parting shot was to kill him. "Because of this violent and unchristian act, Bishop Fridrek parted from him and returned to his native country." Þorvaldur abandoned his mission and became a travelling merchant.

Viking converts

Christianity made greater advances under the influence of Olaf Tryggvason, the future king of Norway. Saga writer Snorri Sturluson describes him in *Heimskringla* as "the gladdest of all men and very playful, blithe and forgiving, very heated in all things, generous and prominent amongst his fellows, bold before all in battle"...although Snorri was basing this rather flattering description on an earlier hagiographical-style saga of the king. Olaf's early life gave no clue to the future. He was a full-blooded Viking marauder at the age of 12, terrorising the English coast with his fleet of five longships. Resting in the Scilly Isles, off England's southwest coast, he made the acquaintance of an elderly sage who put him on the True Path.

Olaf's conversion was electric and he returned to England in a different frame of mind "for England was a Christian country and he was also a Christian". Olaf applied all his former Viking energies to the conversion of his countrymen in Norway. They were, in short, given no choice. As a travelling missionary he went nowhere without a few severed heads.

News of Olaf's missionary zeal reached Iceland: "It was rumoured that the people of Norway had changed religion, that they had discarded the old faith, and that King Olaf had Christianised the western colonies; Shetland, the Orkneys and the Faroe Islands." Olaf was clearly heading their way as if Iceland were just another Norwegian colony, an offensive presumption to those independent-minded settlers.

It was one such proud Icelander, Kjartan Ólafsson, who was cajoled into entering a swimming gala while on a visit to Trondheim. He found

himself racing a powerful swimmer who was not content merely to beat him but ducked him repeatedly until he was on the point of losing consciousness. The graceless victor introduced himself as Olaf Tryggvason and suggested baptism. Kjartan thought it prudent to agree, as did other Icelanders who happened to be in Trondheim at the time. "When they accepted baptism," however, "it was usually for some ulterior motive, or because they regarded it as an interesting adventure."

Brutal methods

The personal history of Þangbrand, the chaplain to whom Olaf entrusted the conversion of Ice-

land, was not reassuring. A 14th-century saga of Olaf recounts: "[Þangbrand's] knowledge of the Christian doctrine might have made him a valuable man had not his violent temper and vicious habits rendered him unfit for so sacred a calling. He not only squandered the income of his parish, but he organised piratical raids to replenish his depleted stores, an unchristian conduct for which the king finally called him to account. Due repentance saved him from banishment, but he was sent instead as a missionary to Iceland."

Relying on his patron's proven formula of exemplary terror, Þangbrand won a few converts in the two years he spent in Iceland, but on returning to Norway in 999 he had to admit that the mission had not been a total success. Olaf

---

ABOVE LEFT: Þorgeir, the Law-speaker at the Alþingi of AD 1000, who decided in favour of Christianity.
RIGHT: a brawl between a Christian and a pagan.

was furious and ordered the seizure and execution of all heathen Icelanders in Trondheim. The expatriate colony was then quite large and, freshly baptised, they were ordered to Iceland to spread the word. Their return coincided with the Alþingi of the year 1000.

Olaf was actually using Christianity as a cloak for his territorial ambitions on Iceland, and he first had to usurp the Christian party which had been developing in Iceland of its own accord. There had even been talk of the home-grown Christians setting up an alternative government, and the arrival of the Trondheim contingent in full battle array threatened to tip the country into civil war.

A crucial decision

The *Íslendingabók*, a reliable early historical source, gives an account of the suspenseful gathering at the Alþingi. Þorgeir, the current Law-speaker, asked for time to think. He spent a day and a night in his booth, lying in silence under an animal hide as he wrestled with the prob-

> Today, the phrase *"að leggjast undir feld"*, loosely translated as *"to lie down under a hide"*, is used when someone chooses isolation to think something through.

lem. Eventually he threw off the hide and made what has been described as "perhaps the most important oration ever delivered in Iceland". His speech was a masterpiece of compromise. Although a pagan, he came down on the side of the Christians, advising all parties to back down and acknowledge that the law, and not any of them, was supreme. "It will prove true that when we sunder the law we end the peace."

The adoption of Christianity as the official religion in 1000 banned the worship of heathen gods in public, but not in private. Nor were the population required to give up their practices like exposing unwanted infants and eating horseflesh. Olaf's further plans for Iceland were never revealed because he died in battle at Svolder the same year. Olaf's Christian zealotry was his undoing. The war was the result of a grudge nursed by the wealthy Queen Sigrid of Sweden ever since Olaf first asked her to marry him and then withdrew the proposal when she declined his precondition: baptism as a Christian. "Why should I wed thee, thou heathen bitch?" he shouted, giving her a slap in the face to reinforce the point. "That," she replied icily, "may well be thy death." And so it proved.

Olaf Haraldsson, the future patron saint who succeeded to the Norwegian throne in 1016, appealed to Iceland's Christian leadership to tighten the loopholes which allowed pagan practices to continue. Their response was so satisfactory that he sent timber and a bell for a church to be constructed at Þingvellir, plus an English bishop, Bernhard the Book-wise, to speed up the conversion of the country.

One of the remaining obstacles to the establishment of orthodox Christianity was a shortage of priests. The chieftains regained a

SNORRI STURLUSON

The violence of the Sturlung Age was chronicled by Snorri Sturluson, whose family gave the Age its name. They were descendants of the saga hero Egill Skallagrímsson, and Snorri may well have written *Egils Saga*. Born in 1179, Snorri married an heiress and became a Law-speaker at the Alþingi twice. He was despatched to Norway as a diplomat, and when he returned to Iceland in 1241 against the King of Norway's wishes, he was murdered on his orders. Snorri's undisputed epitaph is the *Heimskringla*, a monumental history of the kings of Norway whose breathtaking scope is reflected in the first words: "The face of earth inhabited by man...".

measure of authority by putting up themselves or equally unqualified nominees as candidates. As the choice of bishops had to be ratified by the Alþingi, the church was for a while fully integrated in the social system, and one chieftain at least "did everything in his power to strengthen Christianity". New bishoprics were set up at Hólar and Skálholt and these gradually became known as centres of learning.

The literary Golden Age and descent into violence

Iceland enjoyed almost a century of relative peace after 1030. Long hours of darkness indoors encouraged story-telling, and the people as a whole were remarkably adept at it. An unusually large proportion of the population could read; the introduction of the Latin alphabet instead of clumsy Runic encouraged them to write as well. The Dark Ages elsewhere in Europe were characterised by clerics copying religious tracts in Latin. In Iceland people wrote in their own language – and about themselves.

The Icelandic sagas, universally acknowledged as one of the world's most important bodies of medieval literature, were first written down in the 12th century. This literary Golden Age, in which rich accounts of the religion, history, poetry, proverbs and imaginative tales of the Icelandic people were committed to calfskin, lasted for two centuries.

But this flowering of intellectual activity did not outstrip the country's tendencies towards political violence. The Alþingi of 1118 served as a reminder that government was still a hostage to the selfish machinations of chieftains. Proceedings against a notorious murderer named Mar degenerated into a bloody trial of strength between two chieftains which disrupted the Alþingi year after year. The general assembly passed numerous resolutions outlawing the culprits; they were laughed off.

The flaw in the legal system was that the Alþingi could not initiate prosecutions nor force its decisions on spirited opposition. A complicated web of murder led in 1163 to violent clashes in what became known as the "Stone-Throwing Summer". The combatants were said to have been driven to such rage that they were hurling stones so heavy that normal men, when

they tried to clean up the aftermath, could not lift them at all.

In the course of the 12th century, the country was divided between bishops aligned with the seat of Trondheim and half a dozen clans in a state of perpetual internecine warfare. At the same time economic conditions deteriorated and, as the Icelanders had no timber for shipbuilding, they were increasingly dependent on Norwegian suppliers and shippers. Matters came to a head in the so-called Sturlung Age (1230–64), notable for its bewildering combination of horrific violence and intellectual and literary endeavour, the latter having been described as the Icelandic Renaissance.

The Alþingi's impotence in the face of feuds that were tearing apart the land's most powerful families underlined the fact that anarchy had taken over. The king of Norway was as ever ready and eager to step in and the papal legate approved saying "it was unreasonable that [Icelanders] did not serve a king like every other country in the world." In 1262 the Alþingi submitted to King Haakon by granting him the right to collect taxes. In practice, submission left the Icelandic chieftains in control of their own affairs as before except that they were forbidden to wage war on one another. The people won a respite from constant upheaval, but by the end of the 13th century it was apparent that Iceland had started an unstoppable decline. ❏

LEFT: saga hero Gunnar of Hlíðarendi.
RIGHT: opposing sides lined up for confrontation at the Alþingi of AD 1000.

THE DARK AGES

A combination of absolute foreign rule, trade restrictions and a series of natural disasters led to the darkest period in Iceland's history

The terms of Iceland's submission to Norway were contained in the "Ancient Covenant" and every taxpayer was obliged to pay an annual royal tribute in the native wool. Royal officials replaced the *goðar*, and King Haakon appointed Snorri's murderer, Gissur, earl of Iceland as the Free State disintegrated. Even the weather served as a portent: it turned colder, and all over Scandinavia men dispensed with kilts and put on trousers. Temperatures continued to drop, necessitating underwear.

Gissur's "character and previous record", says Knut Gjerset, an eminent 20th-century Icelandic-American historian, "rendered him unfit to maintain peace and order, which was his principal official duty". The *Íslendinga saga* relates that in 1264 his enemies stormed his daughter's wedding, killing 25 guests while Gissur hid in a tub of whey. His revenge was to lay waste the Rangárvellir district and then invite his enemies to a peace conference. Their leader was executed, whereupon Gissur announced his retirement to a monastery. The Norwegian king decreed that Iceland would try to survive without any earls.

Imposing the law

Iceland clearly needed a new framework of government, starting with a new legal system. From 1274–6, King Magnús VI, "the Law-Mender", modernised Norway's law-code, applying it to every part of his kingdom including Iceland. The code proved so efficient that it served with very few amendments until the 19th century. The crown, now seen as part of the divine order, was made the supreme legal authority, and lawbreakers were answerable to it, not to the injured party as previously. Murder, robbery, rape, counterfeiting, forgery and seduction became capital offences, but judges were supposed to administer the law dispassionately. "For we are to hate evil deeds," the judge's manual advised, "but love men by natural instinct as our fellow Christians, but most of all their souls."

For the first time Iceland acquired a national army rather than dozens of private armies, although it was only 240 strong and the men were sent to Norway in defence of the realm against Danish and Hanseatic threats. The power of the

LEFT: a breathtaking aerial view of Laki volcano, in Skaftafell National Park.
RIGHT: an early depiction of Mount Hekla erupting.

church was strengthened, but rested increasingly in the hands of foreign bishops. Church reforms required clerical celibacy; even subdeacons who had been married for years and had several children had to give up their wives.

Public dissatisfaction in a generally peaceful era was provoked by something that would

> A violent storm in 1419 revealed the extent of illegal trade. The storm lasted only three hours, and afterwards there were 25 English ships wrecked on Icelandic soil.

haunt Iceland for centuries to come: the control of trade. Iceland had to trade to survive, and with no merchant fleet of its own the country was at the mercy of Norwegian merchants. The king was supposed to ensure that a certain number of ships called regularly to deliver essential supplies and take away the exports which paid for them. All too often the ships never came, which was especially disastrous if famine or natural disasters struck – and they did, with appalling frequency.

Years of disaster

The 14th century presaged a run of calamities almost beyond belief. Hekla erupted repeatedly; each time a pall of darkness settled over southern Iceland and the following winter was unusu-

ally severe. Heavy snowfalls thawed to become devastating floods. Hekla's 1389 eruption could be felt and heard all over the island, according to contemporary accounts: "Fire arose not only from the mountain but from the woods above Skarð, the eruption being so violent that two mountains were formed with a chasm between them. In the neighbourhood hot springs welled up, forming lakes of boiling water." Smallpox and other epidemics added to the misery.

The industrious Hanseatic merchants – by then well-established on Norway's west coast – undoubtedly could and would have traded with Iceland, but the Norwegian king set a precedent later to be slavishly followed by the Danes, declaring that trade with Iceland was a crown monopoly. Iceland thus went through the extremes of either being completely neglected or facing demands for greater quantities of the prized codfish than the population could afford.

The Scandinavian union of Norway, Denmark and Sweden effected at Kalmar in 1397 transferred the sovereignty of Iceland from Norway to Denmark. The Danes were even more remote and less interested in Iceland than the Norwegians, and, in the country, conditions deteriorated accordingly: "Our laws provide that six ships should come hither from Norway every year, which has not happened for a long time," reads a plaintive message to the Danish king, "a cause from which Your Grace and our poor country has suffered most grievous harm. Therefore, trusting in God's grace and your help, we have traded with foreigners who have come hither peacefully on legitimate business, but we have punished those fishermen and owners of fishing-smacks who have robbed and caused disturbances."

Smugglers and pirates

The unauthorised foreign traders were mostly English and their activities would be Iceland's main access to the outside world for centuries to come. They provided essential commodities in exchange for fish, which would probably have been acceptable to the Icelanders had the English not decided that they were better equipped to catch the fish themselves. This fundamental conflict of interest would continue – all the way to the notorious "Cod Wars" between

LEFT: rough seas were braved by traders around Iceland. RIGHT: monsters were said to be an additional hazard.

Iceland and England in the 1960s and 1970s.

The activities of the English traders were therefore a mixed blessing as far as Icelanders were concerned, but to King Eric VII of Denmark, who held the trade monopoly, they were an unmitigated outrage and he protested to King Henry V of England over the illegal trade.

Pirates among the English merchants – the distinction between them and merchants could not have been finer – were quick to recognise the opportunities presented by an undefended coast, and their looting of Icelandic churches was an echo of what the Vikings had done in England. Attempts to stop the pirates were generally in

vain. On one occasion, a couple of royal commissioners ordered to arrest the offenders were themselves bundled into a ship and sent to the dungeons of England.

Eric's successor, King Christian I, also tried to defend his kingdom, appointing the chieftain Björn Þorleifsson to collect customs duties from legitimate traders and to see off the pirates. Just like the commissioners before him, Þorleifsson was captured and despatched to England, along with his wife Ólöf. He managed to return to Iceland, but was killed by English pirates at Hafnarfjörður and his son captured. Ólöf paid a ransom to get her son back and then recruited an army to deal with the

WHALES, SERPENTS AND LOBSTERS

In addition to the hazards of rough seas, pirates and slave-traders, huge whales and other mysterious creatures to be found in the remote seas around Iceland featured in numerous stories during Iceland's Dark Age. The country was so cut off at this time that there were few foreigners who were able to contradict the account of 16th-century German writer and cartographer Sebastian Münster, a mixture of fact and fantasy. "In the mountain of Hecla," he wrote, "there is a great abyss which cannot be sounded and here appear often people who have recently drowned as though they were alive. Their friends beg them to come home but they reply with great sighs that they must go into Hecla and then vanish forthwith."

Münster went on to describe whales "as big as mountains... which capsize large ships and are not afraid of the sound of trumpets or of empty barrels thrown at them with which they gambol. It sometimes happens that seamen encounter a whale and if in distress cast anchor upon it thinking it to be an island... Many people in Iceland build their houses out of bones and skeletons of these whales". He also described sea serpents "200 or 300 feet long" which wound themselves around ships and "a fearful beast like unto a rhinoceros with a pointed nose and back (which) eats crabs called lobsters twelve feet long". These hefty lobsters, moreover, were said to be easily capable of seizing and strangling a man.

English. The affair escalated into a full-blown war between England and Denmark in 1469 although, ironically, the illegal traders and their customers on the spot seem to have continued their prickly but profitable dealings without even noticing.

The English traders did, however, run into stiff competition from the Hanseatic League, and the Danish kings at last found an effective weapon – to play off one against the other in what amounted to an auction for limited trading concessions.

The long decline

The auctions may have lined royal pockets but did nothing for Iceland. The cumulative effect

> *Cod was Iceland's main trading commodity; others included sulphur, tallow and sheepskin, as well as the pure white Icelandic falcon, by far the best for falconry.*

of natural disaster and stifled trade was simply too much. The most conclusive evidence of national lethargy was that literary activity ceased. The only creativity, which did not amount to much, was the lightweight balladry of wandering minstrels.

The extent to which Iceland became dispirited and defenceless is revealed by an invasion in 1627 by 3,000 Barbary pirates commanded by a "Rais Murad" who was actually a Dutchman named Jan Janszoon. Having run wild through Grindavík, Faxaflói and the East Fjords, the pirates descended on Heimaey, one of the Vestmannaeyjar (Westmann Islands) "and overran the whole island with loud yells, massacring the terror-stricken and helpless inhabitants". The youngest and strongest of the population were herded into their ships; the others into a warehouse which was then put to the torch. The local priest, a composer of hymns named Jón Þorsteinsson, was struck dead while kneeling in prayer; his wife and children and a second priest were taken to the ships, making a total of 242 captives bound for Africa.

The surviving priest was released the following spring to present the ransom demand to King Christian IV. He reported that many of the captives were already dead. The girls had been sold off to harems and the young men

LIVING CONDITIONS IN THE DARK AGES

Impoverished by years of disaster, life was harsh for most Icelanders. A text excerpt from Jón Jónsson, who was probably a sheriff living in the north of Iceland during the eighteenth or nineteenth century, brings living conditions during the Dark Ages into focus: "The living room of the common peasant farmstead was usually not covered with boards on the inside. One could see between rafters to the grass-covered roof, which soon looked like ordinary sod, and from which mildew and cobwebs were hanging. The floor was uncovered, consisting only of earth trampled hard. But during heavy rains when the roof was leaking water dripped down, and it soon became a pool of mud through which people waded. The walls along which the bedsteads were nailed fast were covered with a grey coat of mildew, and green slime was constantly trickling down the walls, especially in the winter. Bed clothes were very scarce among the poor people. Old hay, seaweed or twigs did service as a mattress, and a few blankets constituted the covering."

To make life even more wretched, there was a crippling shortage of firewood. In some houses the family slept on a platform with calves and lambs occupying the space underneath; this at least provided some heat which was conserved by keeping windows to a minimum both in size and numbers. A thin membrane – part of an animal's insides – served as glass, but it only allowed through a dim light, adding to the overall sense of living in dingy squalor.

committed to lives as galley slaves. Some of the men had become pirates themselves. It took five years to raise funds to secure the release of 37 captives, but in the end only 13 got back to Iceland.

Heimaey never recovered from the decimation of its population, and it was set even farther back by the colossal volcanic eruption in 1783 which poisoned the fish in the waters around the island. A British traveller in the early 19th century related tales of a dwindling population of barely 200 souls, whose children were dying of malnutrition because they ate nothing but the oily flesh of seabirds.

with what authority) to have concubines instead of wedded wives… It was easy for the priests to get women, so that they often got the daughters, sisters and relatives of chieftains for their helpmates. Proper and lawful agreement was entered into by both parties, so that nothing was lacking of real marriage but the name."

Feuding bishops

Old habits also affected Iceland's two bishops. Rivalry between Ögmundur Pálsson of Skálholt and Jón Arason of Hólar led to a face-off at the 1526 Alþingi between Ögmundur's force of 1,300 men and Jón's 900. Full-scale battle was

A dismal outpost

Iceland was almost oblivious of the Reformation in Europe. The people were settled, if forlornly, as Roman Catholics, and the Reformation arrived not as an intellectual awakening or rebellion against the old order but as a series of dimly understood royal decrees from Copenhagen backed by military threats.

The Church in Iceland had slipped back into old habits. "Although priests were not allowed to marry," says one of the sagas, "holy and godfearing fathers would permit them (I know indeed not

---

LEFT: spartan living conditions from the Dark Ages.
ABOVE: an artist's impression of Iceland's turbulent fall into decay.

averted by an agreement to let the issue be settled by a duel between champions. The duel was fought on an island in the Öxará River. Ögmund's man was declared the winner, but the next day his cathedral at Skálholt was mysteriously destroyed by fire. This ironically softened his feelings towards Jón because he believed the latter could only have got away with arson with God at least slightly on his side.

In Denmark and Norway, the Reformation was primarily a dynastic struggle with many nobles waiting anxiously for a pretext to despoil the rich estates of the Roman Catholic Church. That ambition extended to Church possessions in Iceland too, and in 1541 two warships were despatched to the island to push a new Church code through the Alþingi, with instructions to use force if necessary.

Bishop Ögmundur, now 80 years old and blind, mounted a spirited defence, but was dragged from his bed into a Danish ship. His captors offered to release him for a ransom: his sister's money and deeds to all his property were duly handed over, but the ship sailed with Ögmundur still aboard. He is thought to have died on the voyage.

That only left Bishop Jón, Ögmundur's former adversary and by now an old man himself. King Christian III, an arch-Protestant king, took exception to Jón's continuing defiance and summoned him to Copenhagen in 1548.

Jón ignored the summons and chose instead to raise a rebellion. The geriatric bishop led 100 men down to the Protestant stronghold of Skálholt and captured the Lutheran bishop, before marching on to the island of Viðey to attack the Danish administration there. On 27 June 1550, an exasperated King Christian outlawed the stubborn bishop and ordered his arrest, possibly after hearing that Jón had sent a request for military assistance to Charles V, Holy Roman Emperor.

Demise of the rebel

One of Jón's enemies, chieftain Daði Guðmundsson, brought the bishop's crusade to an end, defeating and capturing him in battle at Sauðafell. For several days his captors debated what to do with him. A priest suggested over breakfast one morning that he knew how the prisoner could most safely be kept. Asked to elaborate, he replied that an axe and the earth would do the trick. This suggestion was at first received as a joke, but on reflection the idea commended itself. On 7 November 1550 Bishop Jón, and two sons captured with him, were beheaded at Skálholt, providing Scandinavian Catholicism with its first and last martyrs.

News of the executions aroused bitter resentment. Three masked men carrying coffins presented themselves at Skálholt and asked for the bodies. The request was granted, bells were attached to the coffins, and the cortège moved through the countryside to the chiming of church bells. The bishop was buried at Hólar and still remains something of a national hero.

The overthrow of the Catholic party soon followed Jón's death, and the king moved in quickly on its properties. He considered using the income from the confiscated lands to build schools, but decided to keep the money himself. Thereafter, one quarter of the tithes payable to the Church were to be diverted to the royal purse, as were all fines imposed in law suits. Other reforms were progressively introduced. Adultery became punishable by death, although only on the third offence: men were hanged, women drowned. The eating of horseflesh was banned, and persistent absence from Lutheran services was punished by flogging.

The crux of the matter was that these major changes: the confiscation of the Catholic Church's property, the imposition of new taxes, and alterations to the law were all carried out without reference to the Alþingi or with any regard for the existing Icelandic procedure. The country was, in short, feeling the draught of absolute monarchy in Denmark, and things were to get a lot worse.

Crushed by foreign rule

Trade was always Iceland's Achilles heel, and absolute rule in Denmark heralded a tyrannical monopoly from 1602 worse than anything that had preceded it. Iceland was obliged to buy everything it needed exclusively from court-appointed Danish trading companies at prices fixed by the company. It was a case of paying what the company demanded or doing without. With Iceland thus held to ransom, it was no surprise that the price of imports rose by 500 percent over a period in which the prices paid for home-grown products remained static. The purchase price of Icelandic fish was barely a fifth

> *"Up till 1800," says one of the annals, "the Icelanders, both men and women, dressed according to their national style, but after that they gradually adopted Danish styles."*

of what foreign buyers would readily have paid.

In 1662 matters were made worse by the division of the country into four commercial districts. These were prohibited from trading with one another; they could deal only with Danes and on the same Danish terms. Clandestine deals with foreign vessels were made more difficult by a Danish naval blockade and more dangerous by draconian penalties. A certain Páll Torfason took a couple of fishing lines from an English ship in return for some knitted goods which the Danish merchants had previously declined, and lost the entire contents of his house. Holmfast Guðmundsson was flogged for selling fish to a near neighbour who was technically in another district.

The colonial administrators were nothing if not an extension of the arrogant court officials in Denmark. If they needed a horse, the first peasant they asked had to provide one. If it was a question of crossing a fjord, the nearest farmer was required to drop everything and get his boat out. A grumble meant a sound flogging.

Unsurprisingly, the authority of the ancient Alþingi was undermined and in 1800, on royal orders, it was abolished. The new law court which took over its political functions and the surviving bishoprics were concentrated in Reykjavík, the population of which was a mere 300. The sense of separate identity was all but lost.

Litany of wretchedness

The volcanic eruptions and earthquakes which had caused havoc in 1618, 1619, 1625, 1636, 1660 and 1693 continued practically unabated in 1727, 1732, 1755 and 1783. The last in the series, the eruption of Lakagígar (Laki), is still regarded as the worst in world history, scattering ash to every

corner of the globe. An account from a Scottish traveller, visiting 30 years after the eruption, listed the Icelanders' personal losses as 11,461 cattle, 190,448 sheep and 28,013 horses. Following the human casualties of the eruption there was famine due to the haze of smoke and ash, and a smallpox epidemic. Over 20 percent of the population died as a result of the eruption and ensuing disasters.

Summing up the misery of life in 18th-century Iceland, the Chief Justice Magnús Stephensen, a young man of 21 when Lakagígar wreaked its destruction, said Iceland experienced "forty-three years of distress due to cold winters, ice-floes, fail-

ures of fisheries, shipwrecks, inundations, volcanic eruptions, earthquakes, epidemics and contagious diseases among men and animals, which often came separately, but often in connection with and as a result of one another".

Literary rescue

In a country where "emaciated tottering skeletons" had on occasion survived famine by boiling and eating their own clothes, it is unsurprising that literary pursuits were low on the agenda. In the early 18th century, however, the scholar Árni Magnússon *(see page 87)* spent 10 years gathering up Iceland's saga manuscripts. Without his foresight, who knows how many vellums might have vanished forever. ❏

LEFT: en route to a funeral.
RIGHT: an 18th-century illustration of Mount Hekla erupting.

THE PUSH FOR INDEPENDENCE

Upheavals throughout Europe put pressure on Denmark to loosen its hold over Iceland: by 1944 Iceland had become a republic

Iceland, like Scandinavia in general, missed out on the impact of the American War of Independence and the French Revolution. It didn't even feel the whiff of liberalism which passed through Denmark at the end of the 18th century under the auspices of Dr Johann Struensee.

Struensee was a German physician who was engaged to treat the half-witted King Christian VII and contrived to run Denmark personally. He introduced freedom of the press and personal liberties including the decriminalisation of adultery. His vested interest in this particular reform was the clandestine affair he was enjoying with the young Queen Caroline Matilda, sister of England's King George III. The affair was discovered, the law repealed, and Struensee's severed head was posted on a pole to advertise that the old absolutist order was back in charge.

Denmark's misfortune, broadly speaking, was to choose the losing side in the Napoleonic Wars. The British fleet destroyed the Royal Danish Navy at the Battle of Copenhagen in 1801 and then bombarded Copenhagen itself in 1807. The entire Danish naval fleet was confiscated, along with 92 merchant vessels. With Denmark's seafaring heart torn out, poor Iceland was left more isolated than ever. British merchants were eager to take over Icelandic trade themselves, and this provided the backdrop to the most bizarre chapter in Iceland's history, the "revolution" of 1809.

An unlikely liberator

The central figure was Jørgen Jørgensen, born in Copenhagen in 1780, a son of the royal watch-

maker. A brilliant but unruly student, he found himself serving in the British Navy almost by accident as "John Johnson", and later changed his name officially to Jorgen Jorgenson. His early career was chequered, and he was actually on parole in England for gambling debts when he was taken on as an interpreter for an opportunistic and unofficial English trade mission to Iceland.

After one abortive trip, the traders landed in Reykjavík to find that the governor, anticipating their return, had plastered the town with notices prohibiting any trade with foreigners under pain of beheading. The governor, Count Trampe, was not just enforcing Danish policy; he happened to own the one Danish ship still trading with Iceland.

LEFT: 18th-century travellers stopping at a village.
RIGHT: a portrait of Jorgen Jorgenson, leader of the 1809 "revolution".

Jorgenson then came up with a bright idea: depose Trampe, reconvene the Alþingi (abolished nine years previously), declare Iceland's independence from Denmark, and make a treaty of alliance and trade with England. Some, but not all, of the English traders thought this an excellent idea. To cries of "Traitor, you'll hang for this", Trampe was marched out of his office and locked up in one of the English ships. Jorgenson could get to work.

Issuing proclamations under the self-appointed title of "His Excellency, the Protector of Iceland, Commander-in-Chief by Sea and Land", Jorgenson promised the Icelanders "peace and happiness little known in recent years" and their own national

The "revolution" quashed

The Hon. Alexander Jones's enquiries into what was going on – the flag was new to him, and he noticed that Jorgenson was building a fort at Arnarhóll – brought Iceland's "independence" to an end as perfunctorily as it had been created. "All proclamations, laws and appointments made by Mr Jorgen Jorgenson, since his arrival in this country, are to be abolished and totally null and void..."

In his memoirs, Jorgenson described the manner of his departure. He stepped into a fishing-boat and was rowed out to the departing warship by a crew of Icelanders: "So I went on

flag – three white codfish on a blue background. His Excellency was just 30 years old. Backed up by 12 armed sailors, Jorgenson "liberated" Iceland by seizing the property of Danish merchants. The Icelanders were not sure how to react. The fearsome Trampe was a prisoner, but they could not be certain that he would remain so: the price of collaboration with the English if ever he regained office did not bear thinking about.

The new regime had been in existence for just nine weeks when a second British warship, *HMS Talbot*, hove into view under the command of Captain the Hon. Alexander Jones, the son of an Irish peer and not sympathetic to revolutionary activity. Jones suspected that the British government might also have certain reservations.

board quietly, many of the poor natives shedding tears at my departure. It is true, indeed, that I left the island with regret. I had established liberty and freedom there without a drop of blood being spilt, or a single person committed to prison."

He was jailed in a convict hulk on returning to England, released, imprisoned again for more gambling debts, did some sterling work for British Intelligence (at one point disguised as an Irish pilgrim), dashed off books on such weighty topics as the geography of Persia and Afghanistan, was sentenced to the gallows for selling the bedclothes from his London lodgings, was instead transported to Australia – and there served with distinction in the police force. He died in Hobart, Tasmania in 1844.

A revival of spirit

The real price of Denmark's ultimately half-hearted alliance with Napoleon was paid at the postwar Vienna congress. Pressure from the victors forced Denmark to grant Norway its independence, albeit in a lopsided union with Sweden, and expectations rose in Iceland of a similar concession in the near future.

Visitors began to notice changes, and the foundations of Iceland's modern "cradle-to-grave" social security system caught the attention of English reformers. "We have no hesitation in saying," they reported, "that in respect to the poor, an Icelandic parish was, to say the least, equally as well managed as an English one."

Care for the poor

The basic principle was that any person incapacitated by age, infirmity or "misfortune" should in the first instance be maintained by the next of kin according to their ability to pay, the criterion being the value of their property. If circumstances required a pecking order, priority was given to a distressed mother followed by the father, children, brothers and sisters. If supporting some or all of these demonstrably exceeded a person's resources, the parish authorities stepped in.

While parishes might keep a storehouse of emergency provisions for the destitute, the responsibility for actually looking after them was passed directly to the rate-payers. Thus, the number of paupers allocated to each depended on the value of the property owned. If the alimentor (the person who paid alimony, before the term became bound up with unhappy marriage) failed to provide adequate support, the pauper could complain to the district Þing. The alimentor who left a parish to escape the burden was liable to the kind of house-arrest known as exclusion.

The English observers thought the Icelandic system clearly superior to the English in one respect. "The Icelanders… do not charge themselves with the support of the poor without taking especial care to keep the number of paupers within due limits; a care which we have grossly neglected, and are now enduring the fearful consequences of our want of foresight."

The number of paupers was controlled by, for example, not allowing a man to marry until he had the means to support a family. Nor was a slave to be freed unless the owner could provide him with an adequate plot of land. If a freed slave became destitute through the former owner's neglect, he retained his freedom but was entitled to alimony.

The English observers made further notes: "Very stringent regulations were also passed to keep the poor within their respective parishes. Clothes and shoes might be given to a pauper of another parish, but any parishioner who furnished such a pauper with victuals, except he was merely passing through the parish to go to his own, rendered himself liable to the punishment of exclusion. The Icelanders also took

LEFT: washerwomen at the hot springs in Reykjavík, 1908. **RIGHT:** a young woman in Icelandic dress photographed in the early 20th century.

ROMANTICS VS RATIONALISTS

The 18th and 19th centuries saw a revival of intellectual activity in Iceland. The rationalists, under the forceful leadership of Magnús Stephensen, railed against the lack of foreign influence in the language, which had remained virtually pristine Old Norse, saying that it smacked of darkness and superstition. They advocated an intellectual *Aufklärung* which welcomed the best that the rest of the world could offer. The romantics, on the other hand, glorified Iceland's history and language. Their champion in the 19th century, Bjarni Thorarensen, wrote the hugely popular *Eldgamla Ísafold* to the tune of *God Save the King*, and his poems were mostly about heroic saga figures.

care to make able-bodied paupers work for their living. Begging was not tolerated, especially at the Alþingi. If a beggar entered a booth on the Þingvellir plain, the booth-man might forcibly eject him, and every one who furnished such a beggar with meat, was liable to be punished with exclusion. All persons who wandered about the country for fifteen days and upwards were to be regarded as vagabonds… and punished accordingly. Besides other punishments to which they were liable, any one who thought proper might mutilate them in the manner practised in the East to qualify a man for the service of the seraglio" – this last sentence referring to castration.

Unsteady steps towards freedom

Some of these comments must have been out-of-date by the time they were written. Swift social progress was obviously being made, but Iceland still had to wait until 1830 before the ripples of Norway's 1814 independence reached its shores. Even then, the concession was merely two seats among 70 on an advisory body to the Danish crown, based in Copenhagen. Prominent Icelanders such as the jurist Baldvin Einarsson protested against such feeble representation, and the romantics pressed for restoration of the Alþingi. In 1843 King Christian VIII issued a royal decree to reinstate an Alþingi consisting of 20 repre-

A NATIONALIST HERO

Born in the West Fjords in 1811, Jón Sigurðsson, an Icelandic scholar and patriot, was educated at the University of Copenhagen. He has been called the greatest figure in modern Icelandic history. Curiously, he made his home in Copenhagen; from 1849 he merely spent alternate summers in Iceland during which time he presided over the Alþingi. His authority on Icelandic history and literature – he worked in Copenhagen on the Árni Magnússon manuscript collection, and was president of the Icelandic Literary Society – gave his nationalist movement weight and credibility in Danish eyes. He died in 1879, 25 years before the advent of Home Rule, and a further 14 from independence.

sentatives chosen by a qualified electorate and six royal nominees. The assemblies were not to be held at the old Þingvellir, as the romantics wished, but at Reykjavík, which would formally become the new capital.

Many felt that these gentle reforms did not go far enough, and believed the Alþingi should be held at Þingvellir, on lower franchise qualifications, and using Icelandic as the language of government. The nationalist cause was championed by the eclectic scholar Jón Sigurðsson, whose statue stands in Austurvöllur, the old town square in Reykjavík, opposite Parliament House. The nationalist movement demanded a totally independent national legislature and the ending of Denmark's final say over Icelandic judicial decisions.

Progress towards more substantial independence was delayed by Denmark's preoccupation with the Schleswig Holstein nightmare, a dispute with Prussia over the sovereignty of the frontier provinces, each with a divided population whose minorities refused to give in. Moreover, the Danish governor of Iceland, Jørgen Ditlev, was obstructive: he was suspected of applying for a private army to exorcise what he considered unlawful, pseudo-patriotic nonsense. While Denmark continued to turn a deaf ear to the fundamental issue of Icelandic independence, the trade monopoly was ended in 1854.

Denmark the revenue from the tax on drinks.

Under this kind of pressure, the king apparently bowed to the inevitable in 1874 by giving the Alþingi autonomy over domestic affairs, including finance. It was not quite what it seemed because he retained an absolute veto over everything the Alþingi did, but for the moment it was enough to celebrate, especially as the date coincided with the 1,000th anniversary of Iceland's settlement.

King Christian IX attended the festivities; Jón Sigurðsson was pointedly not invited, but it was said that in a private conversation afterwards the king asked him if Icelanders were satisfied with the new constitution. "As their chief wish had not been

The Icelandic exodus

With true independence still apparently unattainable, the newspaper *Norðanfari* suggested ironically in the 1870s that the only chance Icelanders had of tasting freedom was to emigrate en masse to Brazil or North America. As it was, Icelanders were soon leaving in such numbers that the newspaper changed its tune. People were asked to postpone their departure for a year or so in case things changed, and at the same time a number of teetotal societies sprang up. The aim was not so much a campaign against alcohol as to deny

The first performance of Iceland's Thousand Years by Matthías Jochumsson, the present national anthem (now known as O God of Our Land), was given at the celebrations of the granting of home rule in 1874.

granted," he replied, "how could they be?". Sigurðsson recognised full independence or nothing.

The first breakthrough

Full independence was a long time coming. Icelanders and Danes were generally talking at cross purposes. As far as the Danes were concerned, Iceland was inconceivable except as an integral

LEFT: Reykjavík in the early 19th century.
ABOVE: a 19th-century engraving depicts Icelandic everyday life.

part of the kingdom, although they were willing to tinker with semantics. One proposal would have made Christian IX "King of Denmark and Iceland" instead of just Denmark, with Iceland taken for granted. Iceland was in no mood for cosmetic compromise, and talk turned to secession, or what in the 20th century became known as a unilateral declaration of independence. After Sigurðsson's death, his successor, Benedikt Sveinsson, submitted to the Alþingi a proposal calling for real self-government every year from 1881 to 1895. It was twice passed, in 1886 and 1894, only to encounter the impenetrable stumbling block of the royal veto. The breakthrough eventually

mark by virtue of having a common king. The arrangements were ratified by a plebiscite with 12,040 votes in favour and only 897 against. This was agreed to be valid until 1943, when Iceland's status would again be open to negotiation.

"Occupation"

By the end of 1940, it became impossible for Denmark and Iceland to enter into delicate constitutional negotiations. There was no contact whatsoever between them, Denmark having been occupied by Germany and Iceland by Britain. In the latter's case, strategic considerations had taken priority over the policy of "perpetual

came in Denmark with the election of a liberal government in 1901. On 1 February 1904 Iceland received home rule.

The saga-writers would have felt at home in the first years of Icelandic home rule as the country fragmented into a political free-for-all, various factions feuding with seemingly no greater purpose in mind than advancing self-interests. Icelanders could not agree on their relationship with Denmark either, and the impasse continued until the whole question of national sovereignty in Europe was brought under microscopic scrutiny in the peace negotiations after World War I. The Danish government then took the initiative and on 1 December 1918 Iceland became a sovereign state with its own flag, linked to Den-

neutrality" which had been declared in 1915. Hitler's troops had marched into Norway and thus gained control of its immensely long Atlantic-facing coastline and ports. Iceland was a logical next step, its mid-Atlantic position being of inestimable strategic value for submarine operations and for aircraft not yet able to cross the ocean in one hop. Iceland had no military defences of its own, so Britain stepped in and "occupied" the country to pre-empt any German moves in that direction, a role later taken over by the Americans.

The British and American forces, who at times amounted to one-third of the population, were not always popular, but resentment was softened by the unprecedented prosperity that the war years brought in Iceland. The national income shot up by 60 percent on the twin strengths of construction work on American airfields and free-spending US personnel. Fish exports fetched record prices and, since they were generally paid for in dollars, Iceland had the means to import large quantities of American goods.

Not being able to communicate with Denmark to negotiate on constitutional changes, the Alþingi took a decision to act unilaterally: "Seeing that the situation which has been created makes it impossible for the king of Iceland to exercise the powers assigned to him by the constitution, the Alþingi announces that for the present it commits the exercise of these

> Total prohibition was introduced in Iceland in 1915. The move was particularly unpopular in Spain, which had traditionally paid for imports of salted Icelandic cod with surplus wine.

stitution were submitted to plebiscite in 1944 and both were approved by huge majorities. The date chosen for the formal establishment of the republic at Þingvellir was, not by accident, the birthday of the great nationalist Jón Sigurðsson, 17 June.

Denmark was then still under German occupation, and many Danes felt that what amounted to a

powers to the government of Iceland."

An Alþingi resolution made the following year went even further: "The Alþingi resolves to declare that it considers Iceland to have acquired the right to a complete breaking off of the union with Denmark, since it has now had to take into its own hands the conduct of all its affairs." It added that Iceland would become a republic as soon as it was possible to terminate the union with Denmark formally.

The termination of the union and a new con-

secession had been brought to fruition while they were hardly in a position to do anything about it. King Christian X sent a telegram of good wishes – it was only received after a ceremony which attracted no fewer than 20,000 people to Þingvellir on a cold and blustery day. The first president of the new republic, who was elected to a four-year term, was Sveinn Björnsson.

Iceland's neutrality did not save 352 seamen from death as a result of German actions at sea, but it was adhered to on principle when Iceland turned down an offer to declare for the Allies in the final months of the war. One of the first actions of independent Iceland was, on the cessation of hostilities, to demand the immediate withdrawal of the American forces.   ❑

LEFT: poet Grímur Thomsen reads to Danish King Christian IX at the 1874 National Festival.
ABOVE: a brass band greets British troops during World War II.

MODERN ICELAND

Since World War II Iceland has come of age as a
hardworking, modern society enriched by a profound
respect for its past

Iceland today has all the trappings of an
industrialised nation, with a sophisticated,
consumer-orientated society and comprehensive welfare system. It still has one of the
highest standards of living in the world in spite
of its recent financial woes. It is almost impossible to imagine that, before World War II, many
visitors thought Iceland to be barely out of the
Middle Ages.

Joining the modern world

The transformation occurred almost overnight.
Even so, Icelandic society did not abandon its
long past, but rather adapted it to the present,
replanting an ancient heritage in modern soil
where it has more or less flourished since. The
Icelandic language has been the bridge of centuries: the history of the Old Republic had been
written down in the Middle Ages using a language which modern Icelanders can and very
often do read (see page 89).

*The average Icelander works 1807 hours a
year, making Iceland one of the world's most
hard-working countries.*

The presence of first British and then American troops in Iceland during the war, although
not exactly welcome, had its brighter sides. A
frenzy of road-building and development created an economic infrastructure for the postwar period. Few can deny that the prosperity
brought by the war meant that national inde-

LEFT: Akureyrarkirkja, Akureyri's Lutheran church.
RIGHT: US servicemen at Keflavík NATO base, 1951.

pendence, declared in 1944, could be consoli-
dated in peacetime.

More controversial was what to do after the
war. Iceland's old stand of "eternal neutrality"
was abandoned in 1949 when it became a founding member of NATO. The US military had left
Iceland, but returned in 1951 to set up a permanent naval air station at Keflavík. The fact that
this made Iceland a major target in the event
of nuclear war hardly endeared the US presence
to the majority of Icelanders; nor did Icelandic
men appreciate rich American servicemen floating around the countryside. But the economic
argument was powerful: Keflavík provided jobs.
And strict controls on marines' movements,

The Politics of Fishing

Ever since Iceland gained full independence from Denmark in 1944, the country's foreign policy has been moulded by the politics of fishing

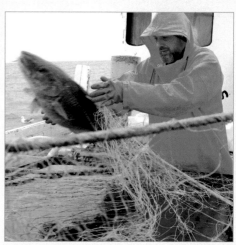

Since 1944, it is the international politics of fishing more than Iceland's role as a strategically crucial – albeit army-less – component of the NATO defence pact that have played the larger role in shaping the country's foreign policy. Indeed, the

dependence on seafood earnings is such that the republic's focussed determination to repel any perceived encroachments on its fisheries resources has brought the country into a series of long-running conflicts with even its NATO allies.

A classic example of Iceland "getting tough" with an ally are the four Cod Wars with the UK between 1952 and 1976 (see pages 113–4), centring around the extension of the fishing zone around Iceland's coast. A more recent dispute has strained relations with Norway. At issue is the fishing by Icelandic vessels of the Barents Sea "loophole", international water bounded by Norway and Russia. Norway, claiming that the fishing damages cod stocks within its own waters, has on occasion seized Icelandic vessels and levied fines on Icelandic trawler owners.

Iceland has also been involved in squabbles with Norway, Russia and the EU over catch quotas on migratory species such as redfish and herring – indeed fisheries issues loomed large in Iceland's long-standing determination to remain outside the EU. In the past, only the Social Democrats came out in favour of at least considering membership. Opponents of membership believed that Iceland's 1994 entry into the European Economic Area gave Iceland all the benefits of EU membership without any of the drawbacks.

All of the carefully considered arguments for and against were rendered void when Iceland's economy disappeared into a black hole in 2008. Such a desperate financial situation called for desperate measures, and on 16th July 2009 the new coalition government submitted an application for EU membership, with a view to adopting the euro by 2012. Financial turbulence, a weak króna and debt repayment considerations have come to dominate foreign policy, but the country's survival as a nation is still deeply dependent on seafood exports, which brought 208 billion krónur into the economy in 2009, and the fishing industry will no doubt play an important part in EU membership negotiations.

Meanwhile, the controversial return of commercial whaling in 2006 put an issue that has long been a thorn in the side of Iceland's international relations right back under the spotlight. Having halted the practice back in 1989, Iceland walked out of the International Whaling Commission in 1992: after this it always seemed likely that whaling would resume at some point. *For more on whaling and the issues that surround it, see page 115.* ❑

LEFT: fish hung up to dry in the West Fjords.
ABOVE: cod still form an important part of the catch.

rarely allowing them out from behind a huge wire fence, meant that not too many ran off with Icelandic wives.

Even so, Iceland never established an army of its own and also managed to maintain good trade relations with the Eastern bloc during the chilliest spells of the Cold War. Anti-Keflavík feeling flared up from time to time during the Vietnam war and was a popular cause on the political Left – but by the late 1970s it had become a principle which was costing rather than winning votes.

As a non-nuclear base, Keflavík kept its nose clean during the arms race against Brezhnev,

However, in March 2006, things changed for good when the US ambassador to Iceland announced that the United States had decided to substantially reduce the size of their defence force on the island. Over the proceeding months, military operations at the Keflavík base were wound down and it finally closed on 8 September. Today the old barracks are used as university accommodation, and in 2010 a deal was signed to create the world's first carbon-neutral data centre on the site. It is predicted that within the next 10 years, this hosting of millions of computer servers will become Iceland's biggest industry.

and its role largely involved escorting "stray" Soviet aircraft back out of Icelandic airspace – there were up to 200 violations some years – and monitoring submarine movements in the area. Always keeping a low profile, the US military effectively disappeared from view when a civilian passenger terminal was finally opened at Keflavík Airport in 1987. Until then, all visitors who arrived in the country by air had had to land at the US military base before being allowed to tread Icelandic soil (including Mikhail Gorbachev when he arrived for the 1986 summit, *see page 65*).

ABOVE: the Icelandic coastguard taking on the British Navy in the Cod Wars.

Riches of the sea

After World War II, the Icelandic government – with economic foresight – channelled its wartime cash-in-hand into modernising the fishing fleet, laying the foundation for a powerful industry that still exists today. Soon Iceland would be producing more income per head from fishing than Saudi Arabians did from oil.

Rich on cod income, Iceland's government grew, building an impressive system of schools, public health and social security. At the same time, Iceland's regulation of the economy had few parallels in the developed Western world. During the 1950s and 1960s, import tariffs were thrown up to protect industry, but they gradually served to foster inefficiency and higher prices for everything from fruit to toothbrushes.

It was not until the 1980s that Icelandic governments became committed, in the spirit of the times, to free-market policies. Yet throughout all of these policy changes, fishing remained the mainstay of the economy. Unfortunately, no amount of government regulation could sidestep its unpredictable nature, and fluctuations in both catches and market conditions have from time to time dealt severe blows to the virtually one-track economy.

Whenever fish catches or market prices deteriorated, the government's reaction was

blocks and detached houses that decorate streets everywhere.

The affluent society

With inflation under control and a fish-led recovery, Icelanders enjoyed one of the world's highest standards of living for over 20 years. The country was one of the most consumer-orientated countries on earth, a hangover from the high-inflation days when it paid to spend and cost a fortune to save. Icelanders were among the first to buy every new consumer durable that came onto the market, falling for any piece of wizardry that promised high-tech comfort. This

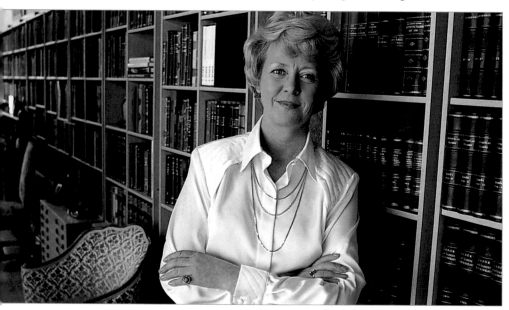

to devalue the Icelandic króna. This triggered an inflationary spiral in the 1970s. Wages were indexed to price rises, so that Icelanders joked that a foreign disaster was the best news: for example a flood in Brazil which ruined the coffee-bean harvest could push up prices in Iceland which would result in wage rises all round.

Although wage indexation was outlawed in 1983, loans did continue to be indexed, which put the brakes on one of the most popular national pastimes of the 1960s and 1970s: owing money. Before indexing, it was possible to take on huge debts and pray that inflation would go up enough to enable you to pay them back again. Generally it did, and whole generations bought or built the impressive apartment

affluent lifestyle was yanked out from under the Icelanders' feet during the 2008 economic crisis (*see page 157*).

Icelandic society is still one of the most literate in the world. Education levels are very high for both sexes: more than one-third of all 20-year-olds complete secondary grammar school, there are around 13,000 students at the University of Iceland, and another 2,000 Icelanders at foreign universities (not bad for a national population of only 318,000). More books are published and bought per head here than anywhere else in the world.

Currently, Icelandic males are at the top the world longevity tables with a life expectancy of 79.7 years. Icelandic women are also high on the list, with an average life expectancy at birth of 83.3 years. Doctors say that the reasons include an unpolluted environment and the pure food that this offers; the outrageously fresh air of an Atlantic island on the rim of the Arctic Circle; a healthy fish-based diet; and exemplary public health care. Infant mortality in Iceland is, at 2.5 deaths per 1,000 children, among the lowest in the world, and certain aspects of preventative medicine, such as early detection of female cancers, are unmatched.

Moments of glory

In recent years, Iceland has been hitting world headlines for all the wrong reasons, but it does have its quiet moments of glory. In 1980, Icelanders chose Vigdís Finnbogadóttir as the world's first democratically elected female head of state. The former theatre director, French teacher and tourist guide took the Presidency (an office outside party politics whose function is to provide a figure of national unity), and was subsequently re-elected three times. In 2009, in the wake of the financial meltdown, Jóhanna Sigurðardóttir was chosen as Iceland's new prime minister. Again, Iceland blazed a new trail: Jóhanna is the world's first openly gay head of government.

On a different front, Iceland was invaded by foreign journalists in 1986 when it became host to the historic Reagan-Gorbachev summit. As the mid-point between Moscow and New York, Reykjavík was deemed an auspicious meeting place for the leaders of the superpowers to discuss nuclear disarmament. Although the talks eventually stalled, they were symbolic of a breakthrough in East-West negotiations and stood as markers of the beginning of the end of the Cold War.

Iceland has also forged the way in genetics research. The company deCODE has made (controversial) use of Icelandic genealogical and medical records to isolate key genetic risk factors for dozens of common diseases, including Type II diabetes, cardiovascular disease and breast cancer. Stemming from this research, it has gone on to create tests that can be used to calculate an individual's susceptibility to these diseases.

LEFT: Vigdís Finnbogadóttir, president of Iceland between 1980 and 1996. **ABOVE:** Reagan and Gorbachev in Reykjavík, 1986.

Lifting a ban

On March 1 each year, Icelanders celebrate "Beer Day", in honour of the moment in 1989 that a ban on strong beer was finally abolished. Total prohibition had gone into effect in 1915; wine was legalised again in 1921, but, as a sop to the temperance lobby – which argued that because beer is cheaper than spirits, it would lead to more depravity – beer was not included in the vote.

The absurdity of the beer ban came fully to light in 1985 when the teetotal Minister of Justice prohibited pubs from pepping up legal non-alcoholic beer with legal spirits to make a potent imitation of strong beer. Finally beer

Total prohibition was introduced in Iceland in 1915. The move was particularly unpopular in Spain, which had traditionally paid for imports of salted Icelandic cod with surplus wine. Wine was legalised again in 1921.

approached legalisation in parliament – the debate and knife-edge vote were televised live and watched by huge audiences.

Keeping traditions alive

The concern at maintaining tradition does not always seem so frivolous. An ancient and homogenous culture of relatively few people is always at risk of being swallowed up by the outside world.

Symbolic of the changes wrought in Iceland has been the growth of the capital, Reykjavík – with only 5,000 inhabitants in 1901, by 2010 the figure was about 200,000 in the greater Reykjavík area, or some 63 percent of all Icelanders. The shift from country to city has completely altered Icelandic society: the generation of Reykjavík folk now around retirement age was largely born and brought up in the countryside, on farms or in fishing villages. Their children, now middle-aged, were born and bred

The leap into the modern world has been fast and furious: greater changes have taken place in the past 50 years in Iceland than in the first 1,000-plus years of settlement.

in the capital, but retained some links with the outside; and the generation now at or leaving school is thoroughbred urban, most of them brought up in the "concrete lava fields" of new residential suburbs such as Breiðholt and Árbær – whose populations alone outnumber those of the largest towns outside the capital area.

These are the first Icelanders to drift away from the "classical" colloquialisms of their ancient language, which is firmly rooted in the agricultural society of yesteryear. And they are the first to have no intimate knowledge of the mainstay industries of fishing, fish processing and agriculture – hands-on experience which in the past had given Iceland a telling edge over its international competition. This lack of basic manual skills poses a threat to Iceland's few industries, a threat whose consequences few can guess.

Recognising that language is on the front line, Icelanders' defence of their ancient Norse tongue is fierce (*see panel on page 91*). The same technological advances that are welcomed so warmly also pose the biggest threats. Satellite TV, for example, comes outside the jurisdiction of Iceland's legions of subtitlers, dubbers and professional and amateur word-coiners. Linguists say that the threats are becoming more subtle: borrowed words from foreign languages stand out instantly, but "hidden" foreignisms such as Anglo-Saxon syntax and thinking patterns are easier to slip into and more difficult to detect, yet undermine the very fabric of the language all the same.

Moreover, social scientists were astonished to discover in an opinion poll that a large majority of Icelanders still claim to believe in the existence of elves and spirits (*see pages 248–9*). Almost all Icelanders still believe in God. Even though only a small fraction go to the Lutheran church they are all still registered at birth. At one stage during the 1960s, the Norse pagan religion was revived, although it attracted little interest at the time. Over the last few years, however, perhaps owing to rising concerns over environmental issues, the congregation has crept up to 1,400 members. The religious organisation, Ásatrúarfélagið, has its own burial ground and has bought a plot of land below Reykjavík's landmark building "The Pearl" on which it intends to build a temple.

But perhaps the real achievement of modern Iceland has been to remain essentially democratic in a personal as well as a political sense. Iceland is at once a modern technological nation and a small village writ large – a place with little crime, few class distinctions and where everybody, thanks to the old Scandinavian patronymic system still in use (*see panel on page 76*), addresses one another by their first name. ❏

Left and Right: maintaining the old traditions is a preoccupation in today's globalised society.

THE ICELANDERS

Today's Icelanders, a product of their landscape and history,
are looking to the future with determination

*"Somewhere, in all these rocks and stones,
is my home."*
– Nationalist poet Pétur Gunnarsson

Probably the first thought that occurs to many visitors as they drive through the desolate lava plain that separates Keflavík airport from the capital, is: "Very impressive – but why would anyone want to live here?"

The inhabitants of a country often tend to reflect their environment. The Danes, for example, live in a flat, fertile country, and are by and large an easy-going, laid-back bunch. Their Icelandic cousins, however, do not really know how to relax and enjoy life. The visitor may be puzzled at how Icelanders can be completely uninhibited one minute, yet stubbornly taciturn the next; at how such a practical nation could produce so many poets, writers and musicians; and at how such hardworking souls, obsessed with the benefits of good honest labour, could be drowning in such a financial quagmire.

But in these tendencies towards extremes, excess and unpredictability, the Icelanders are only reflecting their homeland. Anyone would be a little crazy living in this world of glaciers and flowing magma, where the sun shines all night in summer but winter is long, dark and cold, and where its very people transformed themselves almost overnight from a near-medieval society into one with admirably high living standards.

Icelanders have a reputation for being rather dour – but this quality does not go too deep. When the days get longer and lighter and the

sun shines, however weakly, the entire nation can be seen to undergo a metamorphosis. Out come the pavement tables outside the cafés, the bottles of red wine and barbecues. Some people even manage to stop working overtime.

Medieval to modern

Icelanders have an extremely strong national identity, and a cultural heritage of which they are very proud. The constant suspicion that the outside world thinks them small and insignificant, coupled with having been isolated for so many years, sometimes makes them seem insular and absurdly patriotic. They are prone to harp on the nation's illustrious past, "cashing cheques on

PRECEDING PAGES: playing soccer in the light of the midnight sun. **LEFT:** admiring Lake Logurinn.
RIGHT: mythical characters hit the streets of Akureyri.

deeds committed 700 years ago," as writer and scholar Sigurður Norðal put it.

Yet no-one can deny that the Icelanders are a resilient bunch, having survived all sorts of calamities – both natural and induced – throughout the centuries. When the independence struggle began in the 19th century, Iceland was still deep in the Dark Ages. There were no roads and very few stone-built houses. But in a single generation, around the time Iceland gained self-government in 1918, the society moved, with no apparent difficulty, straight into the 20th century.

One of the most oft-cited reasons for the speed of this transition was the high standard of educa-

Social changes

Their fierce patriotism can give Icelanders a rather inflated view of the country's importance on the world stage. They are very sensitive to slights to their national pride, and react strongly to any real or imagined threats to the community. This characteristic can sometimes manifest itself in an unpleasant way – such as the ban on black servicemen which the Icelandic government secretly insisted on imposing when the NATO military base was established at Keflavík during the 1950s.

Iceland's racial make-up is around three parts Nordic to one part Celt. Today people are much more cosmopolitan, but before the 1960s a black

tion in the country. While the people were poor, they were never ignorant. Nearly all of them could read and write, and quite a few could speak foreign languages.

Another is the strong sense of national identity and community. They have had to learn to stick together through necessity and overcome impossible odds. Thus, in the so-called Cod Wars with Britain in the 1960s and 1970s, this country without an army took on and defeated a world power that was threatening its interests and livelihood. A similar motivation lies behind the stubborn stand on whaling (*see pages 62 and 115*). It is not so much the importance of the whale-hunt, but the questioning of Iceland's right to self-government that raises the national hackles.

> *In the pre-war years Hitler and his Nazis assiduously courted the Icelanders as an example of a "pure Aryan colony"; to the country's credit few people took any notice of this dubious flattery.*

person walking down the street in Reykjavík was invariably followed by a crowd of excited children. In fact, Icelanders are generally free of racism. In 1989, when 5,000 foreign citizens were already resident in the country (making up 2 percent of the population) a survey showed that a vast majority supported the idea of people of different races settling in Iceland. A large number of

Icelandic couples adopted Vietnamese orphans during the Boat People crisis, and few of these children have experienced anything but a warm welcome into the community.

Recently a hitherto unexplored advantage of the homogeneity of Iceland's population, teamed with genealogical records that stretch back for a thousand years, has been brought to the fore: unique opportunities for genetic research. In 1996, the first firm specialising in such research, deCODE Genetics, was founded. In its first two years deCODE grew exponentially, attracting foreign investors and generating considerable attention within the international medical community.

The genetic research issue has had a mixed response from Icelanders. While deCODE's efforts and vision have been applauded, the company is surrounded by controversy. This has mostly to do with questions such as whether a single private company should have exclusive rights to medical information; fears that the confidentiality of medical records might be violated; and wider concerns about how DNA-based risk assessment tests, created using the results of this Icelandic research, might be employed in the future.

Looking to foreign shores

One of the many paradoxes typical of Icelanders is that along with being insular, they are insatiably curious about the outside world, even to the most obscure detail. The only epic poem that has ever been written in honour of the medieval Albanian hero Count Skanderbeg was composed by an otherwise unknown Icelandic clergyman in 1861.

Icelanders lay great store by being cosmopolitan and well-travelled – "sailed", as they put it. This dates back to the days of the sagas when every self-respecting Viking started off his career by journeying abroad, returning home laden with renown and gifts from European royalty. Modern-day young Vikings and Valkyries also have the community's blessing to quit the nation's shores and try their luck at seeking fame and fortune in foreign lands. They are said to be *að gera garðinn frægan*, "winning renown for the old homestead."

The Björk phenomenon

And certainly no-one has done that with as much panache as Björk Guðmundsdóttir, who has done more to promote her home country than any advertising campaign. Björk became a household name in Iceland at age 11, when she released her first solo record. During her teens and early twenties she sang with a handful of bands before becoming a founding member of

> The world's first Basque dictionary was written by a farmer in a desolate part of northwest Iceland – he had learnt the language from Basque sailors who came to fish off the nearby coast.

The Sugarcubes. The Cubes were catapulted to stardom all over the world in 1988 with their quirky song *Birthday* – largely on the strength of Björk's inimitable vocal style. Björk launched her international solo career in the UK 1993 and has since won the widespread acclaim and respect of fans and critics alike for her unique sound and experimental style; her latest award was the prestigious Polar Music Prize in May 2010, previously won by luminaries such as Bob Dylan, Pink Floyd and B.B. King.

In May 2000 Björk added another string to her bow, and heaped yet more honour on Iceland, when she won the award for Best Actress at the Cannes Film Festival. The newcomer to acting won for her role as Selma in director Lars von

LEFT: DNA samples – Iceland is big on genetic research. **ABOVE RIGHT:** Björk, a singer who has proved herself one of Iceland's major exports.

Trier's *Dancer in the Dark*, which also took the award for Best Film.

Other cultural exports

Björk's success in the international arena has flung open the doors for other Icelandic musicians to become better known internationally. Talent scouts from every corner of the globe have made their way to this tiny north-Atlantic island to see who else might be hiding. A number of musicians and bands, notably Indie band Sigur Rós, have since landed deals with foreign recording companies. The orgy of pop and kitsch that is the Eurovision Song Contest is taken extremely

Italy, but he returned home in late 2009 to participate in a enthusiastically received retrospective of his 30-year career.

Another heavyweight figure on the Icelandic cultural scene is filmmaker Friðrik Þór Friðriksson. His film *Children of Nature*, written in collaboration with Iceland's literary golden boy Einar Már Guðmundsson, was nominated for an Academy Award in the Best Foreign Film category, in 1992. Although it did not win, it helped pave the way for Friðriksson abroad. Friðriksson has been named one of the most influential filmmakers in Europe, and his films have won awards at numerous international fes-

seriously in Iceland since it's regarded as an opportunity for Iceland to make its musical mark on the wider European continent.

In the classical sector, Icelanders have also excelled. The Iceland Symphony Orchestra has won great critical acclaim in the recent past, not least for their recordings of the works of the composer Jón Leifs. Leifs, who died in 1968 and whose unconventional – but decidedly Icelandic – sound was shunned by the establishment for decades, has recently been "discovered" by Icelanders and foreigners alike. Meanwhile, the opera singer Kristján Jóhannsson – a former Akureyri native and ex-motor mechanic – has sung in major roles at the world's top opera houses. Today he resides in

tivals throughout the world. Another respected Icelandic director, Baltasar Kormákur, has had a hand in several crowd-pleasers that have made it onto international screens, most famously the comedy *101 Reykjavík* and the recent detective film *Jar City*.

Readers with children may be familiar with the TV programme *LazyTown*, responsible for lowering childhood obesity rates in Iceland and boosting vegetable sales by 20%, and now broadcasting its healthy-lifestyle message to kids in over 100 countries. Its creator, gymnast Magnús Scheving, also stars in it as the hero Sportacus.

Icelanders are also terribly proud of their three Miss Worlds. As if to give credit to the common notion that Icelandic women are among the most beautiful in the world, two Icelandic women were awarded the Miss World title within three years of each other: Hólmfríður Gísladóttir in 1985 and Linda Pétursdóttir in 1988. Unnur Birna Vilhjálmsdóttir repeated their success when she was crowned in 2005.

Sports and business

Two Icelanders have taken the title "World's Strongest Man" four times each: Magnús Ver Magnússon and Jón Páll Sigmarsson, who died in 1993 at the age of 33. A colourful character, Jón Páll had his status as national hero reinforced by the documentary film *Larger than Life*, which broke Icelandic box-office records on its 2006 release.

A few other Icelanders have made the transition into the international sphere, most notably footballers, such as Eiður Guðjohnsen – who had a distinguished career at Chelsea in the English Premiership before moving on to Barcelona, Monaco and in 2010 Tottenham Hotspur – and Ágúst Sigurvinnson who had a successful career in Germany. It was cause for public lament in the German press that Sigurvinnson refused to give up his Icelandic citizenship in order to become a naturalised German and play with the German national team. Iceland established an unlikely influence in the English game in 2006, with the £85-million takeover of West Ham United by Eggert Magnusson and Björgólfur Guðmundsson. Eggert left the club in 2007, while Icelandic billionaire and former Landsbanki chairman Björgólfur resigned in 2009 after being declared bankrupt. Earlier, in 1999, Stoke City was bought up by a consortium of Icelanders, spearheaded by fruit-and-vegetable distributor Gunnar Þór Gíslason.

A handful of Icelandic companies have not only excelled in the international business arena in the recent past, but continue to flourish in spite of the country's financial calamities. As well as deCODE Genetics *(see page 73)*, the brainchild of ex-Harvard professor Kári Stefánsson, there is Össur, which has been carving out a name for itself as a leading researcher and producer of prosthetics. Another is Marel, a top developer and producer of high-technology scales and software for the fishing industry.

Whenever an Icelander "makes it" on the international level, the entire Icelandic nation basks in his or her success. These people often achieve larger-than-life status in their home country; never mind that they may be queuing in front of you at the supermarket. President Ólafur Ragnar Grímsson, for instance, won office in 1996 partly on the strength of his previous experience in the international arena. Prior to his election he had done a great deal to open doors for Icelandic businesses in Asia and America and had been granted numerous international awards for his work. He was re-elected for another four-year term in 2008.

My people and your people

Icelanders often claim that theirs is a classless society. This claim has some basis in that there is certainly a lot of class mobility. But there exist, like everywhere else, disparities of income and status: some families are considered older and are more "aristocratic" than others. Generally speaking, Icelanders are obsessed with their genealogy and most can trace their ancestry back at least six or seven generations. Some even have family tables that go back beyond the age of Iceland's settlement into the realm of legend – perhaps with a Norse god or two sitting proudly at the top of the family tree. The common enquiry "who are his people?" is not just snobbery, however. It is a relevant question in a society where everyone is

LEFT: a still from the film *Children of Nature* (1991).
ABOVE RIGHT: Magnús Ver Magnússon, four times winner of the title "World's Strongest Man".

related to everyone else in the tenth generation.

The national inferiority complex also comes into play – and it has obviously been around for some considerable time. The author of the 12th-century *Landnámabók (Book of Settlements)*, which charted the progress of the first pioneers who came to Iceland, stated his purpose in writing as follows: "so we would better be able to answer foreigners who upbraid us for our descent from slaves or scoundrels if we knew our true origins for certain."

Small-scale society

Despite remnants of old snobberies, modern-day Iceland is on the whole an informal, egalitarian and

ICELANDIC NAMES

The continued widespread use of the patronymic system, whereby a surname is derived from the father's (or mother's) christian name, is an ancient Scandinavian custom. "Son" or "daughter" is tacked on; thus Björk Guðmundsdóttir is Björk, daughter of Guðmundur. Her brother would be Guðmundsson. Some families do have family names, but they are often of foreign origin: Zoega, Schram and Petersen. It used to be possible for family names to be bought for cash by up-and-coming parvenus who considered them smarter and more aristocratic; now it is not permitted to take a new family name. The tradition makes things a lot easier for anyone seeking to trace their family roots.

familiar society. Everyone from the President down is addressed by their first names. Jón the doorman greets Jón the eminent politician with a cheery hello – they come from the same fishing village and are probably second cousins. As you shower after an early-morning dip in the local swimming baths, there might be a famous pop-star getting changed in the cubicle next to you. But Icelanders do not identify easily with the idea of fame, with its paraphernalia of bodyguards and exclusiveness. They are used to everyone being accessible. The President grants interviews to any member of the public who wishes to see him and top sportsmen and pop-stars usually have to keep their day jobs, as few can afford to go professional.

And it is very easy to be famous yourself. Anyone with application and talent can stand for parliament, present a television programme, set up an art exhibition or play in a football team. Anyone can be a published author – and usually is. One in 10 Icelanders publishes something in the course of their life and writing a book is considered almost a form of National Service. If you fail to hit the headlines in your lifetime you will at least do so after your death. Even the most obscure person can be sure of at least one long obituary, with a photo, in the newspapers on the day of their funeral. Pillars of the community may run to several pages over many days.

The concept of being a participating member of society is very strong. As a Japanese academic who settled in the country noticed: "Everyone is equal, so everyone is important. Everyone is a participant in society, it isn't possible to opt out, to deny your responsibility." Just as being a member of the community is an honour, being excluded from it is the worst possible dishonour. In the Saga Age, criminals were not killed or imprisoned, but outlawed – made outcasts from their society.

Every individual matters and in return is obliged to participate. Iceland supports three daily newspapers, two major TV channels, a national theatre and opera plus dozens of orchestras, art galleries, theatre companies, radio stations and museums. None of these could hope to survive unless individuals visited the theatre at least once a year, took two newspapers, supported the arts, and so on.

Spending and debt

Surveys have shown that in many areas Icelanders are closer to the US in their attitudes than to Europe. Icelanders are believers in market forces.

In their personal tastes, they have a slight tendency towards ostentation, glamour and displays of wealth. But this materialism is partly a matter of economic survival. Importers and retailers would go out of business unless every household found it an absolute necessity to purchase the newest model laptop or flatscreen television, or whatever is the latest strange gimmick to seize, albeit briefly, the nation's collective imagination. As the late Nobel-prize winning author Halldór Laxness once declared, "it is, in general, expensive to be an Icelander."

The spend, spend, spend mentality was encouraged by an economy plagued through the years by soaring inflation. Icelanders tended to be compulsive in their spending habits and are renowned for scooping up the latest gadgets. "Keeping up with the Joneses" is a national pastime, and some Icelanders have appeared to continue with these spendthrift ways regardless of the country's financial crisis *(see page 157)* – old habits obviously die hard.

The nation has always been gripped by a collective compulsion to work all the hours that God sends. Icelanders are fierce devotees of the Protestant work ethic – no doubt a throwback to the days when a person's worth was measured in the number of hours of hard labour they could deliver per day. Moonlighting is extremely common, and many people managed to hold down two or even three jobs at the same time (at least before the crash). As a result, they are always doing things at the last minute and are late for everything: unpunctuality is one of the country's vices.

The pre-financial-crash "shopping trips" organised by Icelandair to Glasgow became legendary amongst the city's retailers: a determined army of 50,000 Icelandic tourists would spend £23 million (US$37 million) each year in Britain.

Working hard

It has often puzzled foreigners why Icelanders devote so much time, money and effort to building palatial houses equipped with state-of-the-art furnishings when they are always at work and therefore never at home to appreciate them. But work

LEFT: taking a snowmobile tour on a glacier.
RIGHT: cycling Iceland.

is not just a way of getting money: it is an end in itself, a means of gaining self-respect. Although the Icelandic welfare state is fairly comprehensive, it is seen as something of a shameful thing to claim money off the state. "The comprehensive ability to work is the hallmark of the Icelander, whether a desk-bound intellectual, a farmer or a fisherman," comments anthropologist Finnur Magnússon.

This devotion to the Protestant work ethic was demonstrated during the World War II. "British work" – employment that was offered by the English military forces occupying the country – was despised by the Icelanders as fit only for layabouts and degenerates. The reason seems to

have been because it was too easy and well-paid.

This extreme work ethic and pride in a job well done makes the recent financial crisis even more galling for Icelanders. For individuals to have worked so hard, and yet to be left with impossible debts, is desperately hard to swallow. Uncharacteristic amounts of wrath have been directed at the bankers and the government, and Icelanders have also ruefully examined their own behaviour. But Iceland has a history of weathering storms. Its people are gritty and resourceful, and no doubt hard work will be the key to pulling them through the turmoil.

At the same time Icelanders have always had a secret fascination for a more bohemian lifestyle. Hard-nosed businesspeople will occasionally take the time to hang out philosophising with the regulars in one of Reykjavík's innumerable coffee-bars, and even publish a book of poems on the quiet. In Iceland, poets and artists command begrudging respect and seem to have a special dispensation to lead a ramshackle, layabout lifestyle. As Laxness put it ironically, "since time immemorial, the Icelandic nation has had to battle with men who call themselves poets and refuse to work for a living."

However, it must be admitted that in most cases the old Protestant work ethic tends to win out. Back in the 1960s, Icelandic hippies, although they were quite adept at tuning in and turning on, never really got the hang of dropping

Most Icelanders are very quick to latch onto new trends, which sweep across the entire nation with lightning speed. Video recorders had only been in the country for a couple of months before there were film-rental shops on every street corner. When aerobics teacher Sóley Jóhannsdóttir opened up a studio in Reykjavík, the occasional class wasn't enough for her customers. She recounts: "Icelanders never do anything by halves – it's four times a week for most of my regulars with additional circuit-training lessons as well." Every household in Iceland has its sunbed, barbecue, footspa and set of new-age crystals, the detritus of crazes past; and at the time of writing,

out. The real diehards had to head over to Copenhagen if they wanted to bum around in style – back home in Reykjavík they would have been too embarrassed not to have a job.

Playing harder

Icelanders take their work seriously but are equally single-minded about their play. An inability to do anything in moderation is in fact one of the most characteristic national traits, as is demonstrated by a trip to downtown Reykjavík on a Friday or Saturday night (*see page 148*). This excess, however, is also partly explained by the high price of alcohol – it is too expensive to indulge in every day so many people prefer to save up for one almighty binge at the weekend.

in spite of the grim economic conditions, there were waiting lists for the next must-have items – flatscreen TVs and Rolex Submarine watches.

Non-violent society

The Icelanders are intrinsically a gentle people, and, despite having a fair share of the prevailing 21st-century social plagues – including drugs, porn, latch-key kids and so on – society is essentially non-violent, and Reykjavík is one of the safest capitals in the world. Even boxing was banned until as recently as 2002 – Icelanders prefer the far more elegant ancient sport of *glíma* (which resembles sumo wrestling).

The lack of serious crime means that society can be rather at a loss as to how to treat its more anti-social and violent elements. Even the most vicious of criminals rarely gets sentences of more than seven years, and the lenient sentencing in sexual abuse and incest cases – in which the perpetrator often escapes any sort of rehabilitation – has been criticised in recent years. Progressive and forward-looking as it may be, Iceland still seems to prefer to turn a blind eye to some of the more "sensitive" issues.

The other side of the coin is that, in general, Icelanders are broad-minded and tolerant about most things. In June 2010, for example, a bill was passed giving all couples the same marriage rights regardless of sexual preference, allowing

grannies and grandpas left to fend for themselves in high-rise blocks. A recent survey showed that Icelanders put family as their top priority, above friends, free time and even their beloved work.

Iceland's Valkyries

In recent times the Icelandic woman has become somewhat of an archetype, combining Nordic beauty with physical and spiritual strength. The popularity of this image undoubtedly received a boost through the three Miss World titles and the election, in 1980, of Vigdís Finnbogadóttir to the office of President. At the time of her election Vigdís was a single mother with an adopted

gay couples to get married in church. Single mothers are admired rather than frowned upon: everyone is happy to welcome children into the world whether they have two resident parents or one. Although a few moralists have predicted imminent destruction of the social fabric from such a lax set-up, marriage, which for many years was seen as irrelevant, is coming back into fashion – even though many bridal couples have their own offspring acting as bridesmaids and pageboys.

Above all, Icelanders also have a greater respect for family ties than many other societies. They take care of each other – there are few neglected

> There are fewer atheists than in any Western country except the US – 97 percent of Icelanders say they believe in God, although only a fraction attend church regularly.

daughter and, as such, represented a new era. She was also a survivor, having triumphed over breast cancer. In short, she combined femininity with strength, and common sense with strongly held personal views, albeit ones that she was not permitted to voice publicly by virtue of her office.

In fact, women have always played a forceful role in Icelandic society. The sagas and old tales are full of strong, matriarchal figures – from

LEFT: partying on the dancefloor at a Reykjavík club.
ABOVE: the Icelandic police force.

Aud the Deep-Minded, one of the greatest of the pioneers, to the irascible Bergþora, Njáll's wife (*see pages 94–5*). Ancient lawbooks indicate that the medieval Icelandic woman enjoyed a great deal more emancipation than the majority of her European counterparts. She had equal rights in marriage, could own property and could even hold a *goðorð*, or chieftainship.

Feminist advances

The women of Iceland are veterans of mould-breaking feminist activity. Iceland was one of the first countries in the world to introduce female suffrage: women were given the right to vote in

going on a one-day mass strike to remind their menfolk of the essential role they played in society. Secretaries downed note-pads, bank-clerks and teachers stayed at home, mothers handed babies over to bewildered fathers – and the country was brought to a standstill.

When the Women's Decade drew to a close in 1985, a second walk-out was staged. Then-President Vígdis joined the protest, causing a constitutional crisis by refusing to sign a decree that would force striking air stewardesses back to work. Male government ministers eventually forced her to sign, but her stand was much appreciated by her female compatriots.

The Woman of the Mountains is a quasi-supernatural persona who plays a similar role in the national psyche to Marianne in France and John Bull in England.

municipal elections in 1908 and general enfranchisement in 1915. Between 1908 and 1922 a number of women-only panels of candidates were put forward for municipal and parliamentary elections, with considerable success.

Icelandic women first hit the international headlines in 1975, when they marked the beginning of the United Nations Women's Decade by

In 1983, Iceland became the first country to elect a women-only party to parliament. The Women's Alliance (WA), a grass-roots radical movement with no leaders and an economic model based on the concept of "the thrifty housewife," had three of its members elected only a couple of months after the party was formed – and doubled its support at the following election. Support for the WA went down in the 1990s, however, mostly due to internal disagreements and the party formally disbanded before the 1999 elections.

Icelandic women today

In 2009 Iceland elected prime minister Jóhanna Sigurðardóttir, who is not just the country's first female prime minister but is also the world's first openly gay head of government. In the year of her election, Forbes listed her as one of the world's top 100 most powerful women. Five of Jóhanna's 11 cabinet ministers are women, a balance of the sexes that is reflected generally in highest-level politics, where 43 percent of MPs are women.

The new government was preoccupied with financial concerns, but still found time to ban strip clubs in March 2010. It is the first time that such a law has been passed in Europe for feminist rather than religious reasons – Jóhanna specifically stated that the intention of the law was

behind Norway, Finland and Sweden. So what has made this remote island in the North Atlantic such a hot-bed of feminist activity? Dr. Guðrún Agnarsdóttir says the low population is highly relevant. "A small community expects a lot from each individual, and each individual's contributions are also more likely to be noticed and appreciated." Supreme Court judge Guðrún Erlendsdóttir considers it very important that women in Iceland have always kept the old Norse tradition of retaining their natal surnames when they marry. But the factor that all eminent women in Iceland mention when asked about their emancipation is

that women would be treated "as equal citizens rather than commodities for sale".

Sixty-four percent of students in university education are women; it is perhaps significant that single mothers are given plenty of support – the University of Iceland, for example, has several on-campus crèches and kindergartens. Paternity leave is some of the most generous in the world, with fathers entitled to the same amouny of time off as mothers.

On the international gender gap index, Iceland is ranked fourth out of 130 countries,

the sea. "Icelandic women are strong because the wives of seafarers have to be," says former President Vigdís Finnbogadóttir.

Indeed, this tradition of holding the fort stretches right back to the Viking era, when women would be left in control of the farms while the men went pillaging and raiding. Today, women play a vital role in the economy. Almost 80 percent of women work in either full or part-time employment. One of their main grievances is that their salaries are still on average 35 percent lower than that of men, and that like women elsewhere in the world, they are still having to do most of the work in the home as well as outside it. ❏

LEFT: outdoor swimming. **ABOVE:** Iceland's women's rights record is exemplary.

ıllſu ē aðz lagðæ hueini þa ꝩ ſa
ız ꞇ ſkıpaðꝛæ ıbꝛaꞇ ꝩ lh heꝑꝛ
vıꝑ logu oꞇ kꝛ ħæꝛꝛaꞇꝛ ſuū

A ꝼꝛ LꝛOꞇꞇ uꝛꝛ

þꝛa heꝛgaꞇ lnuꝛd uꞇꝛ
lħꝛa ıſħu ꝛꝑı nıū hundꝛæꞇ
nıū agᷓ ꝛ ꝑꝛıſu æꝛ ē þæ
dlæꞇı ħꝛ ħꞇꞇc haꝛꝛꝑᷓ ꝛꝛoꝛ
ꝛꝛ æꝛ. en æ þꝛꞇꞇæ æꝛe þ
uꝛægıħaꞇ ħꝛ olæꝛſ ꝛ lı
þꝛꝛdæ aꞇꞇæ gudꝛꝛandꝛ
doꝛꝛ ſueꞇ bꝛꝛı þꝛꝛ eꝑꝛ
eꝛ huꝛꞇ ħaꝑdꝛ ū ħa læꝛꝛ
bollæꞇ. ꝓ uꝛꞇꝛ ꝩ ſunꞇꝛ ſæ
ſueꞇı utꝛ nepꝛꝛdꝛ olæꝛꝛ
eᷓ lħ uꝛꞇꝛ uꝛꞇꞇıc auſın ıſħu
ꝛꝛguliꝛꞇ ſuo oꞇ ħꝛ. ꝺꝛ oꝛ.

ICELANDIC LITERATURE

Iceland has a proud literary and linguistic heritage, most
famously captured in the medieval sagas which tell of the
early settlers, their lives, families and struggles

The rich literary tradition of Iceland, in tandem with the preservation of the purity of the language, is of great importance to the national identity. Above all, the Icelandic saga is one of the world's most astonishing literary achievements and an important contribution to European culture. The anonymous 13th-century saga authors, who lived in a desolate northerly island in the midst of a raging civil war, were the first Europeans to write prose in their own language rather than in Latin. Why the sagas were written, whether they are history or fiction, who composed them, no-one knows. But the greatest of them – the romantic *Laxdæla Saga*; the thrilling adventures of the two outlaws Gísli Súrsson and Grettir; the tale of the rogue warrior-poet Egill Skallagrímsson; and above all the magnificent epic *Njáls Saga (see pages 94–5)* – can hold up their heads proudly in the midst of any literary company from Homer to Shakespeare.

Classified under the term "saga" – which in Icelandic simply means "story" – are countless historical chronicles, romances, legends, and lives of kings and holy men. Best known are the family sagas – 40 or so chronicles about various Icelandic families in the years following the land's settlement. The events they describe therefore occur around 200 to 300 years before the sagas were written, but until the 20th century they were taken as undisputed historical fact, passed down the generations orally until being finally recorded on manuscript. More recent scholarship, however, holds that they are basically works of fiction. The identity of the

---

PRECEDING PAGES: detail of a vellum manuscript of one of the sagas. **LEFT:** reading matter for those long cold nights. **RIGHT:** an illustration of the blind Höðr killing Baldr, from an 18th-century manuscript.

authors remains a mystery, although the chieftain Snorri Sturluson *(see panel on page 42)*, author of *Heimskringla*, the history of the Norwegian kings, is generally acknowledged to have also written the saga of Egill Skallagrímsson.

Bloody chronicles

To summarise a saga story-line is almost impossible. They are great epic sprawls, which span many generations with dozens of characters and sub-plots. One 18th-century Icelandic scholar summed them up with the sardonic epigram "farmers at fisticuffs". He has a point – much of the action centres around blood-feuds, killings and conflict – but there is much more to them. They were written at a time of social chaos, when Iceland, North Europe's first republic, was being brought under the rule of foreign monarchs because of internal power struggles and conflicts. They contain a retrospective warning to the authors' contemporaries. As Njáll, the sage-prophet hero of *Njáls Saga*, says: "with laws we shall build our land, but with lawlessness it shall be laid waste." At the same time, there is a certain nostalgia for a heroic golden age where men fought for honour rather than power and politics.

Bearing in mind that Iceland was being subjugated to the Norwegian king, there is a rather wistful recurring theme of Icelanders being feted and honoured at foreign courts, and being showered with gifts by, or getting the better of, various European monarchs. In the short saga of Halldór Snorrason, for example, the eponymous hero actually forces the Norwegian king Harald Hardrada at swordpoint to hand over his rightful bounty.

Morality and fate

The saga narrators make few moral judgements, and the sagas themselves are not concerned with good and evil in the modern sense. Most of the characters are mixed, and unmitigated villains are rare – the cunning lawyer in *Njáls Saga*, Mörður Valgarðsson, is one of the few that spring to mind

A LIFE'S WORK

Árni Magnússon was an Icelandic scholar who devoted his life to tracking down, saving and collating the vast number of vellum saga manuscripts that were taken away to Denmark during the days of colonial rule. Educated in Denmark, Árni returned to Iceland in 1702 to conduct a census and spent the next decade obtaining every medieval document that could be bought and laboriously copying out the rest.

Árni's almost supernatural knack of sniffing out manuscripts has become legendary: on one occasion he discovered a vellum that had been made into a template from which to cut out waistcoats! Árni took back with him no fewer than 55 cases full of manuscripts. As one of the leading scholars in Scandinavia, he was able to continue the task from his post as Secretary of the Royal Archives in the University of Copenhagen, using his considerable influence to amass the world's best collection of Old Icelandic documents.

Tragically, fire swept through Copenhagen in 1728 and although Árni pulled most of his manuscripts from the flames, many were lost. Modern historians believe that the best parts of the collection were probably saved, but the trauma may have been too much for the ageing scholar, who died 15 months later. The research institute in Reykjavík named after him still keeps most of the manuscripts, but only a few are on public view; the Culture House in the city centre now has the largest display (see page 149).

(for more on characters, see pages 92–3). Despite being composed in a Christian society, the sagas portray the old pagan Viking morality. Oathbreaking, meanness and cowardice are the worst sins; open-handedness, courage and honour the greatest virtues. "Better to die honourably than to live on in shame," as *Flóamanna Saga* puts it.

Fate plays the strongest role in determining men's actions. Tragedy is usually the result of *ógæfa*, meaning more or less "ill luck".

The sagas are written in a highly distinctive terse and economic style. The dry, laconic viewpoint, both of the narrative and the characters, sometimes borders on parody. One dying Viking's words, as

As Iceland began to claim self-rule from Denmark in the late 1800s, it became a matter of intense national importance that the country's literary heritage should be returned after centuries of "exile" overseas. When the country became independent in 1944, ownership of the manuscripts was contested. After years of internal debate and two domestic legal cases, Denmark agreed in 1961 to return the bulk of the manuscripts, hanging onto those relating to other Scandinavian countries. A decade later the first two books – the precious *Codex Regius* (containing the Poetic Eddas) and *Flateyjarbók* (the most important collection of sagas) – crossed the Atlantic in a Danish naval

he has a spear thrust into his gut, were "I see the broad spears are now in fashion."

The long journey home

The sagas themselves play a key role in the national psyche – they are symbolic not only of the nation's heroic past and literary achievements, but also of its survival. Many of the original vellums were hunted down and removed to the University of Copenhagen in Denmark during the 17th and 18th centuries. The most famous and indefatigable collector was Árni Magnússon *(see opposite)*.

LEFT: the Saga Museum, Reykjavík. **ABOVE:** Stofnun Árna Magnússonar (the Arni Magnusson Foundation), Reykjavík.

frigate. On 21 April 1971, thousands of spectators flocked to Reykjavík harbour to watch the manuscripts' arrival, carried ashore by naval officers in a solemn ceremony.

Since that day, 1,807 manuscripts have been returned by successive Danish governments. The Icelandic Manuscript Institute, founded in 1961 to take on the responsibility of caring for the books, was renamed the Árni Magnússon Institute in 1972 after the great Icelandic researcher.

Sagas in modern Iceland

Numerous phrases from the old sagas spring readily to the lips of many modern Icelanders. For example, *"Fögur er hlíðin"* ("how fair the slopes are"), the first line of Gunnar of Hlíðarendi's lyrical speech, when he decides not to go into foreign exile but instead to stay in his beloved homeland and face his doom, has been a patriotic catchphrase since the 19th-century struggle for independence. One of Njáll's famous sayings, *"með lögum skal land byggja"* ("with laws shall we build our land") was a punning slogan of a leading Icelandic record company – *"lögum"* can also mean "tunes".

Heroes and villains of the sagas live on in the language. A large boulder is known as a *Grettistak* after the strongman's ability to lift such things, and a liar is known as a *lygamörður* after the villain of *Njáls Saga*, Mörður Valgarðsson.

Saga sites

Although the sagas are a complex mix of fact and fiction, their events can usually be pinpointed to actual places. There are usually no concrete remains at these saga sites, but it is still fascinating to visit valleys, hills and islands that resonate with the echoes of these ancient tales.

Reykjavík's 871 +/- 2 Settlement Exhibition *(see pages 146–7)* is the location of Iceland's best-preserved Viking longhouse; quite possibly the home of Ingólfur Arnarson, the First Settler, whose story is told in the *Landnámabók*. However, perhaps the most well-known saga site is Snorri's pool at Reykholt in the west of Iceland *(see page 209)*. Also in the west are the remains of Erik the Red's farmstead Eiríksstaðir, in Haukadalur valley. Excava-

tions from 1997–9 proved that ruins of a turf lodge there date from between 890 and 980 *(see page 213)*. Today a reconstruction of Erik's home has been built close to the archaeological remains.

In northern Iceland, the outlaw Grettir Ásmundarson, hero of *Grettir's Saga*, spent several years hiding out on the sheer-sided island of Drangey and once swam from Drangey to the the hot spring Grettislaug *(see page 234)* on the mainland.

The setting for *Hrafnkells Saga* is the farm Aðalból *(see page 287)* in the east of the country, where the current owner is creating a saga walking trail around the property, while in the southwest, the Rangárvallasýsla district provides the background for *Njáls Saga*. Visit the Saga Centre in Hvolsvöllur to discover local sites connected to the story *(see pages 94–5 and 179)*.

Keeping the sagas alive

Unlike most ancient literature elsewhere, which was composed and enjoyed by a small and privileged elite, the sagas have always been the property of the common people. Also uniquely, because the Icelandic language has remained so little changed since medieval times, they remain accessible to the ordinary people of Iceland in their original language. The sagas are still read and enjoyed: nearly every Icelander is familiar with the characters and plots of the major works.

Other Icelandic literature: poetry

The Icelandic literary tradition extends far beyond the hallowed sagas, however. The golden age of Icelandic literature, beginning around 1100 with the historical chronicle *Landnámabók* (*Book of Settlements*), was one of the richest and most diverse in medieval Europe. Even more invaluable for providing a feeling of the way of life, thoughts and priorities of these people, is the poetry they have left behind them. Icelanders were, from the start, poets. Between the 9th and 13th centuries there were 100 Icelandic poets working around the courts of Europe; after the end of the 10th century the position of court poet in Scandinavia was held only by Icelanders.

The poet or *skáld* had an elevated, even mystical status. He was entrusted with preserving the tribe's deeds in his poems, and raising morale with heroic verse. The Icelandic *skálds* have always been important members of society. Many, for example, took an active part in the independence struggle – and poetic talent has always been regarded as the sign of a noble personality.

The Eddic poems, like those by the *skálds*, were composed in accordance with strict rules of internal rhyme and alliteration, but are much more accessible. Dealing with heroic or mythological subjects, they were written down at the same time as the sagas, but most probably composed much earlier. Poems such as *Hávamál* give a vivid insight into the Viking mind, revealing a people preoccupied with honour who were sociable, generous but highly pragmatic: "Cattle die, kindred die, we ourselves also die," runs one oft-quoted line, "but the fair fame never dies, of him who well deserves it".

Iceland's loss of independence *(see page 45)* dampened creativity, although the old language

grímsson, born in 1807, reached the hearts of his people as no-one else has before or since. Known as "the nation's beloved son," he was the first Icelander to have a statue raised to his memory by his countrymen. A Romantic in the high tradition, he was at the forefront of the struggle for independence from Danish rule, and his poetry is full of love for his native land.

Jónas was a poetic radical; like Wordsworth, he wrote in the common tongue rather than highflown poetic simile. He was also a highly qualified botanist, and travelled round the highlands each summer, collecting material for a comprehensive account of Iceland's natural history – a

and literature remained treasured through hard years of poverty. Since medieval times, Icelanders have always been able to read and write – children could not be confirmed until they were literate – and learning has been held in high esteem. Foreign travellers wrote of being addressed in Latin and ancient Greek by filthy half-starved natives, and taken into huts to look at priceless manuscripts.

Poetry and politics

In the 19th century, with improving social conditions and a growing independence movement, the *skáld* came back into his own. The poet Jónas Hall-

LEFT: refreshments outside the Eymundsson bookshop, Reykjavík. **ABOVE:** reading away the winter.

> Although not of Nobel Prize-winning stature, Arnaldur Indriðason's crime fiction rarely leaves the top of Iceland's bestseller lists. In 2006, a creditable film version of his chilling murder-mystery Jar City achieved an international release.

huge task he was never to complete. From rural North Iceland, Jónas spent much of his adult life in Copenhagen where he wrote some of his best work, including *Ísland*, a testimony to former glories and a call for a better future that every Icelander knows by heart:

Iceland, happy homeland,
fortunate frost-white mother,

where is your ancient honour,
your freedom and deeds of renown...

He suffered much hardship and exposure during his explorations, and these, together with poverty and drink, took a heavy toll on his health. He put the seal on his reputation by dying a true poet's death – young, poverty-stricken and alone.

Contemporary voices

By far the most important modern literary figure is Halldór Kiljan Laxness, winner of the 1955 Nobel Prize for Literature, who died in 1998. Laxness broke away from the idealisation of peasant life prevalent in Icelandic writing, portraying the

Stubborn, infuriating, hamstrung by debt, but nevertheless "the most independent man in the country", Bjartur represented the archetypal Icelander. *World Light* is another epic dealing with a slippery mass of themes: human weakness, aspiration, and the poet's role in society. Laxness was a prolific writer and his creations evolved alongside his own complex psychological, spiritual and political development.

Pétur Gunnarsson, one of the first "urban novelists", innovated the use of colloquial, humorous first person narrative. Þór Vilhjálmsson makes use of fragmented language and cultural reference to come to terms with modern life, while Guðber-

dark underside of rural life, which caused resentment amongst those who felt he was presenting Iceland in a bad light. He also played around with language, changed spellings, used street language and made up or even borrowed words – also considered unpatriotic acts.

But, in his own way, Laxness was as fervent a patriot as any. His novel *Iceland's Bell*, set in the 18th century, contains references to the contemporary independence struggle. The postwar *Atom Station*, from the time of the NATO airbase controversy, contains pointed criticism of the politicians who were ready to sign away their country's independence out of greed. His best-known creation is Bjartur of Summerhouses, the peasant crofter hero of *Independent People*.

gur Bergsson criticises the American-worshipping culture of the postwar period through absurd humour. Among women writers Svava Jakobsdóttir has developed a unique brand of surreal feminism, while the lyrical narrative method of Vigdís Grímsdóttir is much admired.

There have also been great innovations in poetry. The *atomskálds* of the 1950s caused a storm when they broke all the old rules and began to write in free verse. But modern or traditional, the latter-day *skálds* of Iceland still take their responsibilities seriously. They are above all guardians of the holy trinity: language, land and nation. ❑

ABOVE LEFT: the 19th-century poet Jónas Hallgrímsson. **ABOVE RIGHT:** the late Halldór Laxness.

The Icelandic Language

Icelanders know in their heart of hearts that their language is, as the poet Einar Benediktsson said, "more noble than that of any other nation"

To the Icelander, the mother tongue is far more than just a method of communication: it is the essence of culture, and its nurture and preservation is inextricably tied up with the survival of national identity and pride.

Icelandic is one of the North Germanic family of languages, its nearest relatives still in use being Norwegian and Faroese. Thanks to centuries of comparative isolation, it is still very similar to old Norse, the language that was spoken by most of Northern Europe during the 7th to 11th centuries, and is the only language to still use the old runic symbols of ð (eth) and þ (thorn). Although no longer isolated, the language continues in its unaltered state – for Icelanders will fight to the death against any influences which might corrupt or change their beloved mother tongue.

Preserving an ancient language

What would be regarded in other countries as normal linguistic development is seen as national disasters in Iceland. There is, for example, "dative sickness" – a debilitating contagious disease which causes sufferers to put nouns which should be in the nominative or accusative case into the dative. Like most ancient languages, Icelandic is a complex minefield of case endings, subjunctives and inflections which can catch out many native speakers, let alone foreign students. Nevertheless, any grammatical slip-ups are considered social solecisms of the worst order, and if committed by a guardian of public linguistic morals, such as a radio-show host, a grave offence.

In the spirit of individuality typical of Iceland, foreign influences on the language are kept strictly in check, and great care is taken to prevent Icelandic becoming diluted. Icelanders have no truck with such international loan-words as "radio", "telephone" or "computer", which have infiltrated many other languages; instead academic committees are set up to find proper, Icelandic words for these various newfangled phenomena. Thus, the computer was chris-

RIGHT: mobile phones have prosaically been christened *farsími*, literally a travelling phone.

tened *tölva* – a mixture of the word *tala* ("number") and *völva* ("prophetess"). The telephone became *sími*, from an ancient word meaning "thread". A helicopter is a *þyrla* or "whirler"; a jet aircraft is a *þota* or "zoomer". The practice even extends to scientific language, which is kept as firmly non-Latin as possible. The general public joins in the fun of "word-building", and a raging debate almost always seems to ensue.

Some of these neologisms are wittily creative. Even such an eminently post-Freudian figure as the voyeur is cut down to size in Icelandic as a *gluggagægir*, the name of one of the 13 traditional harbingers of Christmas, who used to spy in through farm win-

dows. In the 1990s, the tiny "beepers" or breast-pocket pagers used to call busy businessmen to the nearest phone, were dubbed *Friðþjófur*, a man's name meaning literally "thief of the peace".

Another way in which tradition is preserved is in people's names: a surname is derived from the christian name of one's father or mother – hence Eiður Sigurðsson is the son of Sigurð, while Björk Guðmundsdóttir is the daughter of Guðmundur *(see also page 76).*

Icelandic is known as the Latin of the North not only because the language itself has remained unchanged – it has also preserved, in its literature, the ancient Norse culture. Because it is almost unchanged since the Middle Ages, it makes the medieval sagas readily understandable to the modern Icelandic reader. ❏

HEROES AND HEROINES OF THE SAGAS

The sagas are populated with memorable and vividly drawn characters that are very human in their desires, actions and frailties

One of the recurring themes of the Icelandic sagas is the difference between the fortunate "light" heroes and the unlucky "dark" heroes. The romantic Kjartan Ólafsson of *Laxdæla Saga* is an archetypal light hero – handsome, accomplished and brave. In a similar mould is Gunnar of Hlíðarendi in *Njáls Saga*: "He was a handsome man...extremely well-bred, fearless, generous and even-tempered... It has been said that there has never been his equal."

The conventional romantic hero pales against the enigmatic figure of the dark hero. Like the warrior-poet Egill Skallagrímsson (*above left*), they are often ugly, awkward, complicated men, at odds with society. Egill ("thick-necked and big-shouldered, hard-featured, and grim when angry") is a boastful bully, prone to rages, who commits his first killing at the age of six. At the end of a long and brutal life, his family prevent him from starting a fight – just for the fun of it – at the Alþing. The old man, now bald and blind, buries his silver in a fit of pique, along with the two servants who helped him to hide it.

The saga women were no less formidable than their male counterparts. *Njáls Saga* contains two bloodthirsty and ruthless women – Hildigunnur and Hallgerður Long-Legs. But queen of these indomitable women is Guðrún Ósvífursdóttir, heroine of *Laxdæla Saga*, who marries four times in the course of her stormy career, and ends her days as Iceland's first nun.

ABOVE: For centuries, the Alþingi, the national assembly of the Icelanders, took place on the plains at Þingvellir, the scene of many of the events recounted in the sagas.

RIGHT: one of the main "light" heroes, **Njáll the Wise** is the main protagonist of Njáls Saga (*see pages 94–5*), a sagacious man, a pacifist and a true friend.

LEFT: a Thor amulet. During the course of the sagas, the heroes converted their faith from the worship of Odin and Thor to Christianity – a cause of many disputes.

HISTORY AND FICTION

In the Middle Ages the Icelanders were the historians of the North. The surviving saga manuscripts by anonymous authors preserve most of our present knowledge of North European history and learning during this period. At the same time they sketch the outlines of Nordic identity. In a sense, they are frontier literature, in which the descendants of the settlers reflect on their origins, legends and back upon the settlement period as a golden age, with a well-functioning commonwealth of free chieftains.

The sagas were intended not only as a record of events but also as entertainment. Their authors therefore added a generous pinch of fiction to these tales of families and feuds. This mixture is probably what has given them their enduring appeal. Passed down through generations of Icelanders retelling saga tales on a winterís night, they are still a central part of the national consciousness.

ABOVE: **Grettir the Strong** is the "dark" hero of Grettis Saga: an outlaw, strong and courageous, but quarrelsome and extremely unfortunate.

LEFT: one of the most remarkable female saga characters, **Hallgerður Long-Legs** is beautiful… and wicked. When her husband Gunnar is fighting for his life, he asks for a lock of her long hair to mend his broken bow-string; but she reminds him of a slap he gave her years earlier – and declines.

In Pursuit of Njáll

The best place to start a saga tour is at Hlíðarendi, Gunnar's farm and the focus of the first part of Njáls Saga – considered the greatest of the sagas

The action of *Njáls Saga* – the most widely read saga today – takes place in a small stretch of the southwestern coastal plains between the Rangá and Markarfljót rivers. Written by an unknown scholar in the 13th century, *Njáls Saga* is the rip-roaring tale of a 50-year blood feud.

Njáls Saga is divided into three parts. The title character, Njáll Þorgeirsson, is the most skilled lawyer in Iceland, blessed with second sight and universally respected for his fairness and integrity. A farmer who never raises his sword in anger, he is bound by the strict codes of family loyalty and honour. Oddly, Njáll plays a small role in much of the saga, reacting to rather than shaping events.

The first part of the saga concerns Njáll's friendship with the greatest champion of the land, Gunnar. Gunnar's farm, Hlíðarendi, is set above the marshy Rangá plains on Route 261 (turning south from the Ring Road east of Hvolsvöllur; *see page 179*). It now consists of a few white buildings and a pretty church among some trees in a mellow, peaceful landscape.

Gunnar could fight so skilfully that "he seemed to be brandishing three swords at once". He was a fair-minded fellow, slow to anger and keen to avoid trouble. His problems began when he married the beautiful, manipulative Hallgerður Long-Legs, who had arranged the demise of two previous husbands for slapping her face.

Hallgerður started up a feud with Njáll's equally shrewish wife, Bergþóra. Each of the women ordered the murder of the other's slaves in an escalating feud that the friends Njáll and Gunnar refused to be drawn into. Relatives of the victims became involved, until Gunnar was prosecuted at the Alþingi for butchering some assailants in self-defence. Sentenced to outlawry for three years, he was riding away from Hlíðarendi when his horse stumbled and he looked back. "How lovely these slopes are," he said, "more lovely than they ever seemed to me before, golden cornfields and new-mown hay. I am going back home, and I will not go away."

Treacherous Hallgerður

The decision was fatal. Gunnar's enemies soon surrounded the farm, although he kept them at bay with his bow and arrow until his string broke. Gunnar asked his wife for two locks of her hair to plait a new bowstring, but the treacherous Hallgerður – who had

ABOVE: Skarphéðinn slides away on a frozen river after killing Þráinn Sigfússon. **RIGHT:** Stóra-Dímon across the plains of the Markarfljót River. **RIGHT TOP:** a 19th-century artist's impression of Vikings at sea.

once been slapped by Gunnar – refused. Gunnar's reply to this death-sentence is one of the sagas' most famous lines: "To each his own way of earning fame... You will not be asked again." Gunnar took many of his enemies with him, but was finally slaughtered.

The ambush of Þráinn Sigfússon

The bloodshed was far from over. Njáll's three sons – Helgi, Grímur and the eldest, Skarphéðinn – helped take vengeance on the killers of Gunnar. But they also wanted to kill Þráinn Sigfússon, a vain relative of Gunnar's who had been present at an earlier ambush. South of Hlíðarendi, half way between Gunnar's home and Njáll's on the rough but passable Route 250, is a rounded hill in the middle of the plain. Today called Stóra-Dímon, it was in Njáll's time known as Rauðaskriður, or "Red Skree", and is where the three Njálssons lay in wait one winter's morning in 995 for Þráinn Sigfússon and his friends.

The ambush was spotted, and it looked as if Þráinn would get away, but Skarphéðinn leapt onto the glassy ice of the Markarfljót, skidded downstream and sliced Þráinn over the head with his axe. The gymnastic Skarphéðinn had swooped off to safety before anyone knew what had happened.

Njáll was horrified when he heard of the killing. He organised a settlement at the Alþingi and even adopted Þráinn's orphaned son, the cherubic Höskuldur, to smooth things over. Höskuldur grew up to take over the farm Ossabær, which is now a ruined site on

Route 252 heading south, but the Njálssons grew jealous of him. One day the three sprung upon him without warning in a corn field and cut him down.

Putting the Njálssons up to this butchery was the diabolical Mörður Valgarðsson who loathed Gunnar and plotted to destroy Njáll's family. His chance came when arrangements for a money settlement over Höskuldur's murder fell through at the Alþingi. Höskuldur's kinsman, Flosi Þórðarson from the Skaftafell area, was about to accept a deal from Njáll when Skarphéðinn insulted him, suggesting that he was regularly sodomised by a troll.

Bergþórshvoll

Follow route 252 to the site of Njáll's farm, Bergþórshvoll. The modern farmhouse is uninspiring, but you can still see the three hills of the saga; on a clear day, the snow-covered peaks on the horizon make a spectacular sight. Having stuck by his bloodthirsty sons, Njáll spotted Flosi with 100 men bearing down on the farm. Instead of fighting, he ordered them all to retire to the house – effectively committing suicide, since Flosi promptly set the place on fire. Njáll and his wife refused an offer of mercy, preferring to die with their three sons. Only Kári Sólmundarson escaped.

Interestingly, archaeological digs undertaken at Bergþórshvoll in the 1920s and '50s have found evidence of a Saga Age burning (the accepted date is 1011), suggesting that the story may be true. ❑

LIVING WITH THE ENVIRONMENT

Iceland is a place of extremes, from long nights in winter and even longer days in summer, to heavy snow, to the threat of volcanic eruptions

The English traveller John Stanley, who visited Iceland in 1789, commented: "I pitied the poor Icelanders who could not like swallows gather themselves together for a flight to a climate less hostile to the comforts of human existence. What the Icelanders can enjoy deserving the name of happiness during the long winter I cannot imagine."

There is less reason to pity the poor Icelanders these days. Warm, centrally heated houses have taken the place of damp turf huts, electric light does much to compensate for long hours of darkness, and powerful snow-ploughs mean that only the most isolated settlements are cut off during the winter months.

In fact, during winter, the inhabited areas around Iceland's coast do not experience the bitter extremes of cold that the country's name would suggest. Unlike most other countries at this latitude, Iceland is washed by the warm waters of the Gulf Stream and moderate southwesterly Atlantic winds.

Although summers are definitely chilly by most people's standards, Icelandic winters are actually milder than in more southerly places such as New York or Moscow. It is unusual for temperatures to fall below -10°C (14°F) in Reykjavík.

The dreaded wind and rain

Even so, as any visitor to Iceland will quickly find out, living with the climate here is still no picnic.

PRECEDING PAGES: riding the stocky Icelandic horse. **LEFT:** soaking up some of those rare summer rays at Borgarfjorður-Eystri. **RIGHT:** rainy day in Reykjavík.

The same Gulf Stream and mild winds that bring moderate weather run up against the Icelandic mountains and the icy polar air to create some wretched weather of wind and rain. Although there are the occasional freak summers, Reykjavík normally enjoys only one completely clear day every July. In January, the average goes up to three.

The combination of gales and rain renders umbrellas completely useless, and locals joke that Iceland is the only place where rain falls from all directions – including a horizontal one. Even so, it is not uncommon to see Icelanders wandering around without any protection during heavy downpours. Ask them why and they might shrug: "It's rained here since I was a child. I don't even notice it any more."

The weather is worst around the southwest, improving markedly around Akureyri, the north and east. But the true norm for Icelandic weather is its sheer unpredictability, shifting rapidly from clear to miserably wet, then back again, several times in the course of a single day.

The polar night

Despite the blessing of the Gulf Stream, the Icelandic winter is still a cold, long and miserable affair. At this high latitude, it is also particularly dark. Iceland's mainland lies south of the Arctic Circle (only part of the northern island of

of migrating birds, particularly the golden plover (*lóa*) – the "harbinger of spring" – are reported extensively in the local press. By the middle of May the grass is turning green and wild flowers are appearing. When summer truly arrives in June, the long winter wait seems almost worth it. Although temperatures are hardly tropical, between 12–15°C (54–60°F), the sun shines almost all night.

Strictly speaking, it is only above the Arctic Circle that the true "midnight sun" occurs, whereby the sun never dips below the horizon. This can be seen on the island of Grímsey, from the mountains close to Ólafsfjörður or from the northeast coastline near Raufarhöfn (the

Grímsey is within its bounds), and so avoids the extreme months of darkness endured by northern Greenland and the Arctic icecap. Even so, things here are quite bad enough. During December and January there are no more than five hours of daylight a day anywhere in the country.

That's when Icelanders begin to suffer from *skammdegisþunglyndi*, "short day depression". As some sort of compensation, winter is the best time to see the ghostly aurora borealis (northern lights) – shimmering green and mauve waves of astral electricity flickering in the starry sky.

Waiting for the sunshine

Across the country, Icelanders wait impatiently each year for signs of spring. The first sightings

TO THE RESCUE...

Iceland's unpredictable weather can have dangerous consequences. Stranded trippers and mountaineers need not despair completely, however – as long as they notified the National Association of Rescue Groups of their journey before they set off. This fine body of volunteers will monitor travellers and organise search-parties if they do not return to base on schedule. They don't take kindly, however, to having to risk life and limb rescuing people who have got into trouble through sheer foolhardiness, so make sure that you take sensible precautions, such as not venturing onto a glacier alone, or attempting to climb unknown mountains or in unfamiliar areas except with an experienced guide.

northernmost point of the mainland, just 2.5km [1½ miles] south of the Arctic Circle). However, even without the true midnight sun, real night never falls during June and July. The sun only just skims below the horizon at midnight: an extended dusk is the only sign of the day's passing, and the stars cannot be seen until August.

Summer fever

Foreign visitors have often commented that Icelanders remind them of hibernating animals, sleeping in winter and letting rip in summer. June and July – and, to a lesser extent, August – are the times when Iceland's national parks are filled to

At any time of year, Iceland's unpolluted arctic air makes visibility almost supernaturally clear. Far away objects often seem deceptively close: on a fine day in Reykjavík, for example, the distant icecap of Snæfellsnes seems only a few miles away.

Treacherous seas, unstable land

The ocean is the source of Iceland's livelihood, but it can also be a killer. Despite enormous improvements in safety aboard fishing vessels, the life of the fisherman remains a dangerous one.

Nor is one safe on Icelandic dry land, either. Scientists at National Civil Defence monitor each tiny seismological tremor with concern. In the

overflowing on weekends and when the country's interior is criss-crossed with frantic drivers speeding around in their huge-wheeled vehicles. The *joie de vivre* is contagious and normal rules go by the board, with even very small children playing out in the street until midnight. Visitors often find these endless days difficult to cope with: it's not easy to sleep when the sun is glistening through the window. However, there are advantages: photographers will find the golden light of the early mornings and late nights in Iceland at this time of year particularly beautiful.

LEFT: lounging by a natural jacuzzi at Hveravellir.
ABOVE: keeping the roads open can prove a major challenge.

absence of an army, the NCD is also responsible for conducting rescue operations in the event of other natural disasters; storms, avalanches, floods and volcanic eruptions are all major threats.

On average, there is a volcanic eruption somewhere in Iceland every five years. During the 20th century there were more than 20 eruptions, many of which occurred unseen, deep beneath the mighty glacier Vatnajökull. No-one, however, failed to notice two of the most famous – the one off the south coast in 1963, which formed a completely new island, Surtsey; and 10 years later, the eruption on the Vestmannaeyjar (Westmann Islands). Suddenly, in the middle of the night, what was believed to be an extinct volcano on the inhabited island of

Heimaey began to erupt. Fortunately, the fishing fleet was moored in the harbour that night, and every one of the 5,300 inhabitants of the island was successfully evacuated to the mainland *(see panel on page 187)*.

A much more devastating eruption was that of Lakagígar in 1783, especially as the country's inhabitants could not then call upon modern technology to aid them. The lava flow, produced by some 100 craters in a volcanic fissure more than 25km (15 miles) long, was the greatest ever recorded in human world history, and it eventually covered an area of 565 sq km (218 sq miles). It was Iceland's most cataclysmic natural

naturally under the earth's crust. This water is also used to heat the 150,000 sq metres (37 acres) of greenhouse, used for growing fruit and vegetables, in the town of Hveragerði – the country's market-garden under glass *(see page 169)*.

Geothermal energy is also the reason that Icelanders can enjoy an open-air swim on the most bitterly cold and snowy morning – and soak afterwards in a 45°C (113°F) hot pool. Swimming in Iceland is not so much a hobby as a way of life, and the geothermal pools have a total attendance of around 1.6 million people a year. Icelanders have been used to regarding their geothermal water as a bottomless pit – one swimming

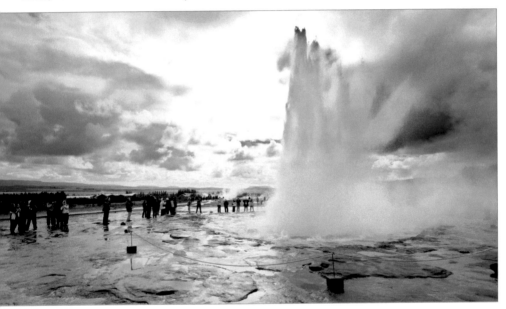

disaster, and the eruption, and the Haze Famine that came in its aftermath, caused the deaths of thousands of people *(see page 51)*.

Another old enemy is erosion. Iceland was once, according to the old chronicles, heavily forested, but now there is a startling absence of trees, and most natural vegetation is scrubby tundra. The lack of trees means there is little to bind the soil, which is bad news on a such a windswept island.

Exploiting the volcanic landscape

A natural force can occasionally be tamed and made to earn its keep. Iceland's homes have been provided with cheap and environmentally friendly hot water and heating for the past 70 years by geothermal energy – water heated

Swimming baths are one of the main focuses of social life in Iceland, and many of the country's most important decisions are made in lunch-time hot pool sessions.

pool, for example, uses up 1.3 million tons of water a day – but there are indications that the reserves in Reykjavík may be drying up because of overuse.

One natural resource that is in no current danger of overexploitation is hydroelectricity. With so much surplus energy, it seems logical to try to export some of it abroad. The practicalities of laying underwater cables to Scotland, Germany and even Canada have been discussed for over 20 years.

A growing worldwide demand for electricity coupled with the development of ultra-low resistance wires mean that the scheme will probably become a reality within the next decade.

Tourism is very much on the increase in Iceland, and is one of the island's most important industries, bringing in 13 percent of the total foreign currency earnings. However, the environment, seemingly so rugged and powerful, is actually extremely fragile – and the authorities are as a result not keen to see it grow out of control. "Iceland isn't open safari country," says Þóroddur Þóroddsson of the National Conservation Council. "We want tourists who are sensitive to the environment."

land travel is possible throughout the year, albeit a little difficult at times. If the road network seems, to the outsider, to be a series of primitive narrow roads, at times dispensing altogether with the need for tarmac, the outsider should bear in mind that it is a huge, and vastly expensive, transport network for such a small population in such a large country. The quality of the roads has advanced by leaps and bounds since the 1960s, and every year further stretches of unsurfaced track disappear under a layer of tarmacadam.

Policy laid down by the Ministry of Communications aims to keep all major roads passable,

Keeping the roads open

Although Iceland does not fully merit its chilly name, winters are prolonged and snow can be heavy, but this does not discourage the Icelanders from travelling as much as possible all year round. A few decades ago, the sea was the most important route for travel between Iceland's dispersed coastal communities. Roads hardly existed, and the coastal boats transported passengers and goods alike. Today, however, overland travel has become the norm.

A vastly improved road system means that

LEFT: Strokkur geyser – Iceland is blessed with bountiful supplies of geothermal energy.
ABOVE: dog-sledding in winter.

as far as possible, throughout the winter months: the first priority is given to keeping open routes between centres of population within each region. These are generally cleared every working day, and even more frequently in the event of unusually heavy snow. Roads out of Reykjavík, north to Borgarfjörður and east to Hvolsvöllur, for instance, are very rarely closed to traffic for more than a few hours at a time.

The second-highest priority is placed upon keeping clear roads linking one region to the next, such as the South to the East Fjords, or the route from Akureyri to Reykjavík. These roads are cleared two or three times weekly on average.

Minor roads, however, are cleared less frequently, if at all. Mountain tracks across the interior are normally closed by snow by the end of October. Although these roads are largely free of snow again by May, meltwater turns them into impassable seas of mud, and they are only reopened once they are dry enough to sustain traffic, usually in late June or early July, after assessment by the Public Roads Administration. This body closely monitors traffic on the highlands;

> Iceland has more than 13,000km (8,000 miles) of roads, and approximately 8,000km (5,000 miles) of them are classified as major roads.

unauthorised travel on the muddy roads in early spring can cause severe damage, and offenders are subject to heavy fines.

Although all efforts are made to keep the road network functioning, ordinary family cars will struggle with winter driving conditions. Icelanders have therefore taken enthusiastically to large four-wheel-drive vehicles and wintertime travel in the souped-up, giant-wheeled versions of these cars has become a popular hobby.

Alternative routes

Some major routes over highland passes – such as those into the mountainous West Fjords – are subject to such heavy snowfalls that they cannot necessarily be kept open through the winter, and they may be closed for weeks or months. Alternative routes at lower altitudes remain open, and in some regions the sea route provides the main winter link between communities. In the West Fjords in particular, travel by sea still remains almost as important as in the past.

Air travel is of unusual importance in Iceland, and even more so in winter. It takes about five hours to drive the 389km (243 miles) to Akureyri from Reykjavík, in good conditions. By air, you can get there in 45 minutes. In winter, with uncertain road conditions, the comparison becomes even more favourable. Flights are relatively rarely cancelled, although there can be delays, and Icelandic pilots attain great expertise in taking off, flying and landing in difficult, icy conditions.

The air route is also, of course, the emergency route into and out of most communities during the winter months. Scheduled flights operate frequently to major centres such as Akureyri, Ísafjörður and Egilsstaðir, and less often – although still regularly – to a host of small centres around the country, where there may be no more than a landing strip and a windsock to indicate the "airport".

Icy conditions

Snow is not the only hindrance to winter travel, though. Roads are often dangerously icy, mainly because of a tendency for Icelandic temperatures to hover around freezing point for much of the winter. The temperature may be 2–3°C (35–38°F) when snow falls, then warm up to reduce the snow to the consistency of a smooth mush. The thermometer might then plummet to -10°C (14°F), and the mush freezes, smooth as a skating rink.

Winter tyres are essential from November to April, even in towns, where all roads are cleared regularly in snow, and salted to reduce ice. Many Icelanders opt for studded tyres, which give a better grip on icy road surfaces, although braking remains a problem on slippery roads. Heavy-tread snow tyres offer better braking, but may not provide enough grip for driving up slippery slopes. If you want to learn how to handle a car in a skid, Iceland is the place. With roads this slippery, you learn fast. ❑

ABOVE LEFT: keeping your car from skidding on the icy roads is a concern.
RIGHT: the sheer drop of water at Skógafoss.

Environmental Protection

A land of some 100,000 sq km (38,610 sq miles), and only 318,000 people, with clean air and clean water, Iceland was relatively slow to see the need for conservation

In today's interdependent world, Iceland is facing a dilemma – how can its pristine environment and outstanding natural beauty be protected from the ravages of industrialisation and global warming? It's a problem that has vexed the Icelandic people and which has attracted attention from environmentalists the world over.

Increasing awareness has resulted in measures to reverse soil erosion, limit gravel mining in volcanic areas, and regulate the fishing that is essential to the economy. Other advances are stricter limits on off-road driving, and even cycling on mountain tracks.

The interior dam project

When, in 2003, the Icelandic government approved the building of a gigantic dam in an area of the uninhabited interior of the country known as Kárahnjúkur, the environmental movement gained a whole new *raison d'être*. The country's biggest ever construction project centred on a highland valley on the northeastern edge of the mighty Vatnajökull glacier, one of Europe's last areas of untouched wilderness and summer breeding grounds for the rare pink-footed goose.

This graceless complex of reservoirs, tunnels, shafts, canals, embankments, roads and five dams was constructed to harness the power of two rivers, the Jökulsá á Dal and the Jökulsá á Fljótsdal. The largest of the dams, fed by an artificial reservoir measuring 57 sq km (22 sq miles), is contained by a 193-metre (633-ft) wall which can be seen for miles around. The project has increased Iceland's production of hydroelectric power by 60 percent, but this power is only nominally for Iceland's benefit. It is channelled through a vast on-site power station to provide electricity to an American-owned aluminium smelter just outside Reyðarfjörður in the East Fjords.

Within this region, most people strongly support the project, as the aluminium smelter has generated badly needed new jobs. Elsewhere, however, particularly in the capital, people are less enamoured; in a high-profile protest even Björk's mother went on hunger strike to express her heartfelt opposition to the construction plans. In September 2006, the filling of the dam triggered one of the biggest demonstrations in Icelandic history, led by former president Vigdís Finnbogadóttir. Fifteen thousand people marched through the streets to gather outside the Icelandic parliament in protest. Opponents claimed the Kárahnjúkur project was the first of many planned for Iceland, and that the then-government was wilfully selling off the country's pristine nature for short-term profit.

In 2009, a new coalition government came into power. Inevitably, its focus has been on rebuilding the shattered economy, but its manifesto emphasised the importance of long-term environmental protection. Environment Minister Svandís Svavarsdóttir has recently rejected several controversial proposals, such as one for a new dam on the Þjórsá river. Her actions have caused anger amongst pro-industry supporters, but lent a modicum of hope to Iceland's environmentalist movement.

LEFT: Iceland's glaciers are under threat from rising temperatures. ABOVE: much of the countryside remains unspoiled. ABOVE RIGHT: the power station at Reyðarfjörður. RIGHT: grey seals in the West Fjords.

Wearing away the soil

Land erosion is a problem in many countries, but in Iceland it presents a major environmental challenge. Human occupation since the time of the Settlement has caused more damage to the natural environment than in any other country in Europe. Iceland has lost 50 percent of its original vegetation and 95 percent of its tree cover, with the result that two thirds of Iceland's terrain is now subject to erosion, ranging from slight to extremely severe.

The first settlers unwittingly began this gradual destruction when they introduced sheep to the land, which steadily grazed away entire areas of vegetation. Population growth put additional pres-

sure on the country's fragile ecosystem: trees, which once held the soil in place and sheltered smaller plants from the heavy sea sprays, were felled to provide fuel and building timber.

Today, serious efforts are underway to reverse the damage. The Soil Conservation Service of Iceland (SCS) and the Iceland Forest Service (IFS) were created as far back as 1907 to rescue the country from desertification. The IFS oversees the plantation of tough species such as larch, birch and spruce, whose roots keep the fine sandy soil from blowing away. The soil reclamation project known as Hekluskógar (Hekla Forests), currently underway around the Hekla volcano in the south of Iceland, is the biggest such programme in Europe. Its aim is to stop the spread of the ash desert around the volcano by planting 100,000 hectares (247,100 acres) of birch forest.

In June, visitors can't fail to notice the swathes of purple-blue lupins that bloom all over the country. The flower has been used extensively since the 1950s to cover vast barren areas, pinning down the fine soil and fixing it with nitrogen. However, the lupins' spread has been *too* successful in some places, where it has invaded delicate heathlands and displaced native vegetation. Today there are battles to eradicate the plant from sensitive spots such as Skaftafell, in Vatnajökull National Park.

The marine environment

Control and regulation of the seas and fish stocks off Iceland is at least as important to the country as on-land conservation. During the Cod Wars with the United Kingdom in the 1970s, the government set a 322-km (200-mile) limit for its territorial waters. The extended fishing zone was not just to prevent competition from foreign vessels; it was partly created so that the government could more easily control how much fish was caught.

After several years of bumper catches, with the cod take nearing 508,000 tonnes (460,000 US tons) in 1982, cod stocks became dangerously low. A complex quota system was introduced in 1984 to limit the catch. Every fishing vessel now receives an annual quota, specifying how many tons of each fish it is allowed to haul in. The system took some pressure off cod stocks by increasing the number of other species fished, and there are signs that cod numbers have recovered a little since their all-time historical low in 1993. However, many other commercially caught species are now being overfished themselves.

A new national park

Iceland has more than 80 protected nature reserves, and until recently had four national parks – Þingvellir, Snæfellsjökull, Skaftafell and Jökulsárgljúfur. In June 2008, the latter two were joined together to form the Vatnajökull National Park, Europe's biggest at 12,000 sq km (4,633 sq miles). The park covers over 11 percent of Iceland, including the whole of the Vatnajökull icecap. Its creation was largely a political move to draw attention to Iceland's fast-melting glaciers. ❑

HARVESTING THE SEA

Fishing has provided food, employment and wealth for
Iceland for centuries; the challenge now is to avoid
over-exploiting the limited resources of the sea

"Life is saltfish," wrote Iceland's Nobel Laureate,
the late Halldór Laxness, in the 1930s. At the
beginning of the 21st century, with the country's economy dependent on the sea more than
ever before, life is still saltfish, but it's also canned
fish, smoked salmon, frozen shrimps and caviar.

Fish has been an important export item from
Iceland ever since the stockfish trade to Britain
commenced in the Middle Ages. But fishing only
began to outpace agriculture in economic status
with the advent of motorised fishing vessels
around the start of the 20th century.

And while improvements in vessel technology soon made fisheries into Iceland's mainstay
national industry, at the same time they intensi-
fied the threat of overfishing by foreign deep-
sea fleets, which escalated until the famous Cod
Wars with Britain.

Fishing and fortune

The first 30 years of the 20th century were a time
of intense, fisheries-led economic growth. Iceland
was gradually escaping from Danish colonial
rule, and economic independence was an obvious prerequisite for true political independence.
Iceland's fishing industry has been coloured by
fierce nationalism ever since.

Salted whitefish – mainly cod, sold to Spain –
and iced whitefish and herring, sold to the UK and
northern Europe, were the mainstays of Icelandic
fisheries right up until World War II. Dependence
on those few markets had its limitations: for example, Spanish wine producers threatening to ban
imports of saltfish were able to "twist Iceland's

PRECEDING PAGES: river rafting. **LEFT:** crates of the
day's catch packed in ice for freshness. **RIGHT:** a
fisherman at Þórshöfn in 1908.

RICHES FROM THE SEA

Situated in the region of the North Atlantic Ocean
where warm Gulf Stream waters merge with the cold
currents travelling down from the Arctic, Iceland's relatively unpolluted fishing grounds offer near-perfect
conditions for an enormous variety of marine species.
These include demersal (bottom-feeding) fish, led by
cod, haddock, redfish (ocean perch), saithe (pollack),
ocean catfish and flatfish such as Greenland halibut
and plaice. There are also shellfish such as shrimp,
scallops and Norway lobster (nephrops or scampi
tails). Finally there are river-migrating fish, such as
wild salmon, trout and Arctic charr, as well as pelagic
(topwater) fish including herring and capelin.

arm" into lifting a six-year alcohol prohibition in 1921. Later, the collapse of the fish market in the Great Depression devastated Iceland's economy.

The fish boom begins

Unemployment ran high right up until World War II, when Iceland suddenly became the only large fish-producer in the whole of northern Europe. Icing their catches, Icelandic fishing vessels sailed directly to Britain, often suffering fatalities from U-boat attacks. Meanwhile, superior freezing technology was developed. This would become the key to the postwar fisheries boom, which targeted both the UK and American markets.

local population and absence of large-scale manufacturing industries keep "home-grown" pollution to a bare minimum. Iceland even exports the technology for catching and handling fish: in some specialist areas, such as the electronic weighing of fish at sea using scales that automatically compensate for the roll of the boat, Iceland is a world leader.

Surviving in a high-risk industry

Seafood is, however, a notoriously shaky business – size of catches can never be taken for granted and prices fluctuate far more than in land-based food processing. Unstable as its economy has

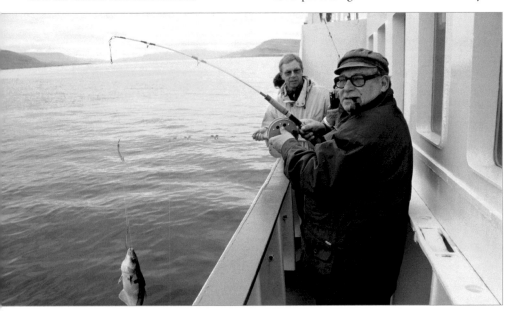

Iceland made good money during the war and allocated funds for the modernisation of the trawler fleet, and an era of larger catches and more diverse markets began. Frozen block and fillets went to both sides of the Atlantic. During the Cold War, Iceland kept good trading relations with Eastern Europe, and the Soviet Union became a major buyer of products such as salted herring. Meanwhile, the diversification which remains the key to Iceland's survival as a specialist fish-producing nation began.

Of increasing importance in this environmentally conscious age is the cleanness of Iceland's fish. The fishing grounds are far enough from the industrial centres of Europe and North America to remain very pure, while the small

been, Iceland buffered itself against heavy market shocks by shrewdly spreading its coverage and its product range.

The US was Iceland's main buyer of frozen fish from the 1970s to the mid-1980s, until a sliding dollar made Europe a more attractive proposition. Today, Iceland's biggest European customer is the UK, followed by Norway, Spain and the Netherlands. The most important sales to the UK are of fresh and frozen cod; Norway buys quantities of fish oil, Spain favours halibut, and the Netherlands are partial to haddock.

Nigeria has shot up the market table recently, and is Iceland's biggest buyer outside Europe. Japan, the world's largest seafood market, became important for Iceland in the 1980s, yet

Although only around 4 percent of the Icelandic population is employed in the fishing industry, fish make up some 41 percent of Iceland's total exports.

hardly competed with established lines sold elsewhere. The oriental taste is for flatfish, whole-frozen redfish (Europeans and Americans prefer fillets), shell-on shrimp (the British and Danes prefer peeled), and previously unexploited delicacies such as capelin roe, whole-frozen female herring, cod milt (sperm) and sea urchins.

population is employed on fishing vessels and 1.7 percent in land-based processing plants.

The Cod Wars

The big problem since the start of the 1990s has been supply. Major stocks are at or beyond the maximum level of safe harvesting, and with a fleet powerful enough to vacuum-clean the ocean floor in a couple of weeks, the industry is being forced to scale down its operations. This is not a new problem. Overfishing by foreign fleets was a strong fear in Iceland in the early postwar period. The traditional 3-mile (5-km) exclusive fishing zone around Iceland's coast was extended

In terms of demand, the future looks promising. Awareness of the healthiness of a protein-rich, low-cholesterol seafood diet, backed by the clean image of the waters where Iceland catches its fish, look set to keep demand buoyant well into the 21st century.

Fisheries contribute 41 percent of Iceland's exports, and a seafood-led boom in 1987–8 saw the country's economy clock up one of the highest annual growth rates in Gross Domestic Product in European history, at over 8 percent. All this, although only 2.4 percent of Iceland's

LEFT: sea angling for pleasure. **ABOVE:** *harðfiskur*, or hard, wind-dried fish, is a popular snack and great for taking on trips thanks to its lightness.

to 4 miles (6.5km) in 1952, and even though this seems like a drop in the ocean now, it sparked massive protests and a temporary ban on fish imports from Iceland in the UK. The first real "Cod War" began in 1959 when Iceland upped its territorial waters to 12 miles (20km) and Royal Navy frigates were sent in to protect, unsuccessfully, British trawlers from being evicted or arrested by Iceland's tiny coastguard force.

Eventually the dispute was resolved, only to be followed by successive extensions to 50 miles (80 km) in 1972 and 200 miles (330km) in 1975. This renewed more ferocious clashes, although no fatalities ever occurred. While the British gunboats rammed coastguard vessels and fired shots over their bows, the ultimate deterrent in the Icelandic arsenal was the dreaded "clippers" – rather like garden shears – which were used to cut trawls from British vessels, removing both their nets and their catches. Some of these clippers are now proudly, if rather mock-heroically, on display in the National Museum in Reykjavík.

On one occasion, the world's press almost outnumbered the naval ratings when a British frigate and Icelandic gunboat had a confrontation on the high seas. Fortunately, the opposing captains had a keen sense of occasion and the ensuing exchange was not of shots but of Biblical quotations which were delivered broadside by loud-hailer. Initially taken aback, journalists

managed to salvage just enough Scripture knowledge to award the result to the Icelandic team.

More considered formal arguments gradually swung international opinion over to Iceland's point of view, and a "truce" was eventually agreed in 1976 – by which time the UK itself had announced its own 200-mile (330-km) limit.

Protecting the sea's bounty

Part of the philosophy behind extending the fishing zone was not just to prevent foreign fishing, but to be able to control how many fish were caught. After several years of bumper harvests, with the cod take nearing 508,000 tonnes (460,000 US tons) in 1982, the time came to put the brakes on Iceland's own fleet. Even as the Cod Wars were in full

swing, Iceland had learned that it could overfish all by itself: the "herring boom" in the Northeast collapsed in the late 1960s when the fish virtually disappeared from one season to the next.

When cod numbers plummeted in a disconcertingly similar manner, a complex quota system was introduced in 1984. Today, the Ministry of Fisheries and Agriculture keeps a close eye on fish stocks, checking to see that numbers look healthy. It then grants each fishing vessel a tonnage quota for individual species of fish. Boat owners are free to swap or trade their quotas among themselves to maximise efficiency – and to make money.

> The territorial waters limit that Iceland established in the 1970s has since become a standard for international marine legislation.

Many skippers claim they have been transformed overnight from heroic hunters into accountants. Unfortunately, years of poor spawning have forced the government to cut quotas regularly. Tradeable quotas have become a claim on a scarce resource, and the value of "paper fish" – the cod swimming unsuspectingly with a quota on its head – has grown at a rate that would draw looks of disbelief even from people who habitually play the money markets.

Future of the fishing industry

Following the 2008 financial crisis and collapse of the króna, Iceland applied for EU membership. Previously this would never have been seriously considered mainly because prohibitive EU quotas would have a detrimental effect on the country's all-important fishing industry. The application was due for consideration in 2010, and fishing rights are sure to be a knotty discussion point.

As the sea fishing industry struggles, so the fortunes of the farmed-fish market have also fluctuated, with the biggest blow occurring in 2007 when two of Iceland's biggest salmon farms went out of business. Iceland is the world's largest producer of Arctic char, although its export of 3,200 tonnes looks like small fry when set next to its cod catch of 150,000 tonnes in 2008. Icelandic aquaculturists are currently experimenting with breeding spotted wolf fish and blue mussels, and the Ministry of Fisheries and Agriculture is predicting cautious growth in the industry. ❑

Whaling

Most Icelanders regard the harvesting of the seas around their country as a virtual birthright and are strongly pro-whaling

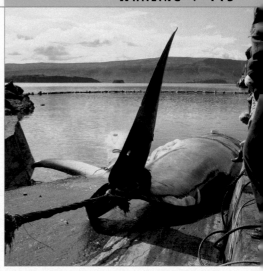

Whaling is a topic that arouses passionate feeling in Iceland today – a 2009 Gallup poll found that 77.4 percent of Icelanders support the commercial hunt.

When a 20-year global moratorium on whaling was introduced in 1986, Iceland continued whaling, exploiting a loophole in the legislation that enabled it to whale for "scientific" purposes. By 1989, when Iceland stopped all whaling amid a domestic political furore, 292 fin whales and 70 sei whales had been killed for "research".

The hunting continues

It was widely expected, though, that Iceland would resume whaling when the time was right. Indeed, just three years later, in 1992, the country pulled out of the International Whaling Commission (IWC), of which it had been a founding member. It cited growing frustration with a new protocol that would reintroduce commercial hunting under strict international limits. Iceland then set up a rival organisation with Norway, Greenland and the Faroe Islands in the hope of challenging the power of the IWC. However, after ten years, Iceland rejoined the IWC. When it did so, it registered a reservation to the commission's moratorium on whaling. Although IWC members are bound by the moratorium not to hunt commercially, Iceland has always insisted that because it registered its opposition, it does not have to abide by the moratorium.

Amid international outcry from conservation groups and anti-whaling nations, the Icelandic government announced in 2003 that it would catch 36 minke whales for "scientific research", later selling the meat commercially to the neighbouring Faroe Islands, whose government claimed it was exempt from a ban on importing whale meat (the Faroe Islands have self-rule under the Danish crown). Conservationists feared that this was a first step towards the full resumption of commercial whaling.

ABOVE RIGHT: Iceland's decision to resume commercial whaling in 2006 has been deplored by environmentalists. **ABOVE LEFT:** wafer-thin smoked salmon.

Sure enough, in late 2006, the government announced that Iceland would resume the commercial hunting of whales. The Icelandic fisheries ministry issued a statement claiming that it would keep catches within sustainable limits. Initially the quota was set at 30 minke whales and nine fin whales per year (the latter are internationally recognised as an endangered species). In 2008, ministry research recommended that up to 100 minke whales and 150 fin whales could be caught sustainably. Whale catches currently end up in domestic supermarkets and on restaurant menus, and Iceland would also like to open up export of whale meat to Japan, along with pro-hunt Norway.

To many outside observers, the 2006 decision to resume hunting might have appeared self-defeating. Iceland had been gaining a reputation abroad as one of Europe's premier whale-watching destinations, and tourist leaders were quick to point out to the government that butchering whales for the domestic food market was totally at odds with the nascent whale-watching industry. Iceland's fragile economy could ill afford any form of international boycott, be it from tourists choosing to take their holidays elsewhere, or from anti-whaling nations refusing to import Icelandic fish and fish products.

However, the worst fears of the tourist industry do not seem to have materialised. Tourist numbers have continued to rise since 2006, and the whale-watching industry has also grown, with around 100,000 visitors each year joining a tour. The new coalition government issued a press release in 2009, stating their belief that whale-watching and whale-hunting can exist side by side. ❑

LIFE ON THE LAND

With a short growing season and land of variable fertility, the Icelanders have come up with inventive and successful ways of farming

In the early 20th century, Iceland's farmers still lived much as their forebears had done for 1,000 years: they kept their sheep, grazed them in summer on the highlands, cut the hay in summer, rounded up the animals in autumn. After the autumn slaughter, some of the livestock were foddered on hay through the winter, while the meat was salted, smoked and otherwise preserved. During the winter, wool was knitted and woven into clothes for the household.

Around 100 years ago, with Home Rule granted by Denmark, things began to change rapidly: aided by the cooperative movement, farming developed from a subsistence activity into a business. The countryside was transformed. Some of the most marginal regions became totally depopulated. Young people left in droves to seek education and a better life (and mechanisation meant far less labour was needed anyway). Roads and telephones made isolation a thing of the past.

There are still some 3,000 working farms in Iceland, but farmers are plagued with problems, from desertification to over-production of lamb and milk. A quota system was introduced in the 1980s, although this has meant that over the last 30 years, many smaller farms have become economically unviable. Some survived by tapping into the tourism boom, with farm-stay holidays a potentially lucrative business (after all, there are no quotas on tourists).

The years ahead are likely to bring greater competition. Protectionist legislation and heavy government subsidies have hitherto helped farmers survive, but these are likely to be threatened in future by Iceland's participation in the European Economic Area formed by EFTA (European Free Trade Association) and membership application to the European Union.

ABOVE: ploughing the rich farming country near Akureyri – Route 8 offers panoramic views over the land.

ABOVE: the autumn sheep round-up, when sheep are herded down to the lowlands, takes place before the first snows fall on the uplands.

BELOW: The roofs of rural homes were traditionally turf-clad for insulation. The memory of a time when all Icelanders lived off the land still grips the national imagination, but in reality the rural life was often one of hardship and struggle against an unforgiving environment.

SUPPLEMENTING THE DIET

Iceland's dramatic sea-cliffs, clustered with millions of birds, were once known as "pantries", and Icelanders would often have gone hungry had they not had the nourishment of these natural food stores. In all the areas where sea-bird colonies are found, men would clamber down the near-vertical cliff-faces, gathering eggs from the nests. Today sea-birds' eggs are still gathered in some quantity. *Sprang*, the art of swinging nimbly down a cliff-face on a long rope, is still a much-practised skill in the Vestmannaeyjar *(see page 184)*.

Regarded as a great delicacy by many, sea-birds' eggs are commonly eaten in coastal villages in season, and are sold in supermarkets. The eggs of the guillemot are most often sold commercially. Other species were also hunted for food, and still are today, notably puffins and guillemots. Other than sea birds, the goose, wild duck and ptarmigan are practically the only birds hunted for human consumption.

ABOVE: Iceland is too far north to grow cereal crops comfortably, as the climate is too cool and the growing season too short. A number of farmers have started to grow hardier cereals, like rye and barley, with the help of fertilisers. These grains are used in animal fodder, replacing expensive imported cereals, and barley is also being grown for human consumption.

RIGHT: the fairytale hues of guillemot eggs, the type of sea-birds' eggs most frequently sold.

FOOD AND DRINK

A unique line in traditional delicacies provides variety from the ever-present, but high-quality, staples of fish and lamb. A plentiful supply of cosy restaurants makes eating out a pleasure

Icelandic food is based on fish and lamb, the two ingredients most readily available in the country. Throughout the centuries they have been boiled fresh, and smoked, salted, pickled or dried to store for the winter months.

The fish is likely to be among the most exquisite you have ever tasted. Indeed, many Icelanders simply refuse to eat fish when they go abroad because it just doesn't taste the same as it does back home. Fish generally arrives in the shops a matter of hours after it has been landed and is accordingly juicy, tender and fresh. Haddock and halibut are often boiled or grilled and served with a prawn sauce or simply with butter. Salmon and trout are served fresh or smoked – traditionally using dung. Thin slices of smoked fish are served with hot spring-baked rye bread. Try herring, smoked, pickled or the tinned variety in mustard or garlic sauce. Nothing is wasted and you will find

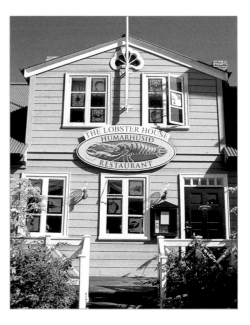

> Traditionally served with potatoes, white sauce and peas, hangikjöt *is a festive Christmas and New Year dish, but is eaten eagerly at any time of the year.*

cod's cheeks and roe alongside salmon and prawns on the fish counter.

When it comes to lamb, there's the tender smoked variety, often served in the home with pickled red cabbage and sugar-browned potatoes, as well as regular lamb chops or steaks. Another favourite is smoked mutton, *hangikjöt*, which means "hung meat". Traditionally served with potatoes, white sauce and peas, *hangikjöt* is a festive Christmas and New Year dish, but is eaten eagerly at any time of the year. In fact whatever form it comes in, Icelandic lamb, although rather expensive, is delicious since sheep are left to wander freely in the mountains all summer long, grazing on the herb-rich pastures.

Chicken and beef are also popular. In fact, chicken has become increasingly so in recent years with the rise in fast-food outlets and oriental restaurants; be that as it may, chicken remains one of the most expensive meats available in Iceland.

Traditional delicacies

Whilst in Iceland look out for any restaurant serving up more traditional fare. Whalemeat (*hval*), mostly from minke whales, is commonly found on menus, to the consternation of some tourists.

It is usually soaked first in milk to extract some of the oil, and then served as medallions or steaks. It tends to be an expensive meat product due to the high costs associated with whaling.

Seabirds, particularly puffin (*lundi*) and guillemot (*svartfugl*), which once saved destitute Icelanders from starvation (*see page 117*), are now considered something of a delicacy. A particular favourite is smoked puffin, accompanied by a delicate blueberry sauce. Seemingly Icelanders have no qualms about eating their national bird – after all, salted or smoked, puffins were one of the dietary staples of centuries past.

Many other traditional foods have survived to

strangest of dishes, washed down with generous amounts of beer or schnapps. Almost everything a sheep can provide ends up being eaten: don't be surprised to spot *svið*, a whole sheep's head, burned to remove the wool and then boiled, staring at you from your plate. This delicacy is served up at the þorrablót feast either in halves or off the bone and pressed into a kind of pâté. Accompanied by mashed turnips, it tastes better than it looks – even, surprisingly, the eyes. Pride of place goes to pickled rams' testicles, pressed into a nightmarish cake. Not a dish for the faint of heart, but oddly digestible in small quantities.

Guts, blood, fat and a dash of meat for form's

this day and are as popular as ever. Adventurous types in search of authentic food and blessed with a cast-iron stomach will relish the midwinter þorrablót feast (mid-January to mid-February, although many items are available all year). The feast is largely an act of homage to the old methods of preserving food. One of the best places to sample a þorrablót menu is at the Fjörukráin restaurant in Hafnarfjörður (*see page 160*), just outside Reykjavík. Here you really can pretend you're back in Viking times and sample the

LEFT: Reykjavík's Lobster House restaurant. **ABOVE LEFT:** the Þorrablót feast is a chance to sample medieval delicacies. **ABOVE RIGHT:** Reykavík's Baejarins Beztu hotdog stand, as once frequented by Bill Clinton.

sake, nattily sown up in sheep's stomachs, create another dish appropriately called *slátur* (slaughter). *Slátur* is not confined to the midwinter feast; it is eaten regularly in Icelandic homes. The dish comes in two varieties: *lifrarpylsa*, which means "liver sausage" but isn't, and the darker, fattier *blóðmör* or blood pudding, which is like Scottish haggis without the spice.

One of Iceland's most notorious food rituals is the ceremonious intake of rotten shark (*hákarl*) and schnapps. After being buried for three months or more, shark becomes acrid and ammoniac; rubbery and rotten, it is washed down in small cubes with ample quantities of the Icelandic spirit, *brennivín (see page 121)*. A few nips beforehand for courage's sake is not a bad idea either! Icelanders view eating *hákarl* rather like the dark midwinter itself. It strikes an emotional chord deep within the soul; and once over, the joy of having survived makes life seem instantly brighter again.

Dairy products

Cows in Iceland feed on fresh grass, free from pesticides, and are raised without the use of growth hormones and antibiotics. Well worth a try as a snack or dessert is *skyr*, a rich type of curd, high in calcium and low in calories, which resembles a thick, creamy yoghurt in consistency. Competition from flavoured yoghurt and ice cream has led dairy producers to create a number of varieties of

skyr such as blueberry, pear or vanilla. However, the genuine article is still sold unflavoured, ideally with cream stirred in and topped with wild crowberries.

Súrmjólk, soured milk, is eaten at breakfast with brown sugar. If you want normal fresh milk, choose the cartons marked *nýmjólk* (full-fat) or *léttmjólk* (semi-skimmed). *Mysingur* is a sweet spread made from whey which is popular with children. Those with a sweet tooth will also love rich Icelandic ice cream, which is sometimes made and sold directly from the farmhouse – look out for signs when you're driving in dairy country.

Icelandic cheeses are generally mild Gouda-type varieties, and are rarely matured. There is no tradition of cheese eating after dinner found in some European countries.

Breads and pastries

Although sandwiches are generally served on white or wholegrain sliced bread, rye is a popular ingredient in bread-making. Healthy, filling rye bread is often consumed at breakfast with toppings of ham, cheese, pâté or jam. Rye is also the key ingredient in *flatkökur*, which as the name suggests are flat, rounded, unsweetened pancakes with a somewhat smoky taste. These can be found in most corner shops and supermarkets and are a good source of fibre and excellent for picnics. Iceland's cakes and pastries have a heavy Danish influence, and are devoured with cream (and gusto) over cups of strong coffee. Popular varieties include a square-shaped Danish pastry with gooey vanilla filling, cinnamon buns *(snúður)*, layer cake *(lagkaka)*, and traditional twisted Icelandic doughnuts known as *kleinur*.

EATING OUT

Dining out in Iceland has undergone tremendous changes in the past 20 years. Many young Icelandic chefs have sought training abroad, then returned home to apply their new-found gourmet knowledge to traditional ingredients. The restaurant scene has been hit by a great wave of energy, enthusiasm and experimentation, and dining out in Reykjavík is consequently a real treat.

Iceland takes utmost pride in its fresh fish and lamb, but there is also a growing local-food movement with a strong emphasis on seasonal, organic ingredients. Langoustines from Höfn; reindeer and pink-footed geese from the eastern highlands; shrimp from the north; seabirds' eggs taken from cliffs around the country in spring; and crowberries,

blueberries and wild mushrooms picked in early autumn all feature on Iceland's menus and are worth savouring.

Prices are not low in Iceland's better restaurants – but you are paying for excellent meals made with high-quality ingredients. In Reykjavík, many restaurants also offer good-value fixed-price tourist menus or buffets in summer, which include a soup or starter followed by a fish or meat main course and coffee. Prices are lower at lunch. Children under six usually eat for free and 6–12 year olds pay half price. It is rare, though, to find these sorts of special offers outside the capital, where good-quality dining is anyway thinner on the ground (mainly because the countryside's tiny hamlets and villages can't support great numbers of restaurants).

Fruit and vegetables

Iceland proudly boasts of bananas that are grown in greenhouses in the south of the country, but most fruits and vegetables are still imported. Unfortunately, long transit times take their toll on the freshness of the produce on offer, particularly in smaller countryside supermarkets; onions, especially, can be rotten on the inside. The high cost of importing fruit and veg means that customers pay lofty prices for these unhappy-looking specimens.

Tomatoes and cucumbers are grown under glass in Iceland in places such as Hveragerði, and so tend to be less woeful than other produce. Rhubarb is one of the very few vegetables that thrives in Ice-

What to drink

Coffee is the national drink of Iceland, consumed from early morning to late at night, at home, at work or even walking down the street. Refills are usually included if you buy a cup of standard coffee in a café, and some petrol stations have a free jug on the counter for their petrol-buying customers. In recent years, there has been a veritable explosion in the coffee culture in Iceland and it's now possible to get expertly brewed espressos, cappuccinos and lattes.

Traditionally, drinking alcohol mid-week has not been part of Icelandic culture, although it is becoming more common to have a glass of wine

land's inhospitable climate. It is harvested in late spring, sometimes appearing on the dessert menus of Reykjavík's restaurants.

Vegetarianism, whilst not unknown, is not something Icelanders particularly adhere to. Vegetarians will be just fine in Reykjavík, where there are two dedicated vegetarian restaurants, a veggie café and several health-food outlets offering non-meat-based meals. Outside the capital, most restaurant menus have one vegetarian option – almost always a pasta/cheese/tomato dish, which can get tedious. Vegans will generally be limited to self-catering.

LEFT: Danish rye bread accompanies a platter of fish, smoked lamb and more. **ABOVE LEFT:** fishy appetiser.
ABOVE RIGHT: Brennivín, the local spirit.

or beer with a meal when dining out. A strong Protestant work ethic is usually cited as the cause… along with the inflated price of alcohol. The bottle that is expensive enough at the state liquor store will invariably be around three times higher in price at a restaurant. Even house wines generally cost around ISK600–1,000 per glass, and a decent bottle of wine in a good restaurant will cost upwards of ISK5,000. Beer, whilst not exactly inexpensive, is generally a more affordable ISK700 per half litre.

Iceland's local home-produced drink is *brennivín* ("burnt wine"), a caraway-seed-flavoured spirit, that is drunk icy cold. It is generally referred to as "Black Death", which gives an idea of its strength. You have been warned. ❏

A NATURALIST'S PARADISE

Iceland is home to, or a stopping-off point for, a wide variety of birdlife; and although it has only one indigenous land mammal, the arctic fox, there are a number of introduced species as well as seas rich in marine mammals

Any traveller to Iceland with even a vague interest in birdlife should bring along a pair of binoculars and a good ornithological guide. Around 70 species of birds breed annually in every corner of Iceland (including year-round residents and those which migrate to Iceland each spring), while more than 370 different species have been seen in the country at one time or another.

Some species regularly winter in Iceland before flying further north to breed in summer. For others, Iceland is merely a stopping off point on their migration journey. Many are accidentals – individual birds which have drifted across the ocean on prevailing winds. Those of North American origin are of great interest to European bird-watchers and mostly occur in the south in autumn.

Seventy breeding species is not a great deal, but the actual bird population is numerically large: some of the commonest species, like the puffin, are present in millions. The Icelandic environment is particularly favourable to sea

Even those who cannot tell a hawk from a handsaw may find themselves flicking through ornithological guides in search of identifying features: Iceland promises first-time and dedicated "twitchers" endless pleasure.

birds, which make up around 25 of the country's breeding species (*see also pages 226–7*), but is less welcoming to passerines (perching birds) whose principal food source – insects – is in short supply. While just over two-thirds of the world's

birds are passerines, they comprise only one seventh of Iceland's avian population.

Most of Iceland's birds are also found in Scandinavia and Northern Europe. Three species, however, are American: the Barrow's goldeneye; the great northern diver or common loon; and the harlequin duck, which breed practically nowhere else outside North America.

Heralds of spring

Both the arctic tern and the golden plover are migratory birds commonly regarded as harbingers of spring. The golden plover, which generally arrives in early April, is a particular favourite with Icelandic poets:

LEFT: bird-watching by the Jökulsárlón iceberg lagoon in Southeast Iceland. **RIGHT:** the great northern diver.

Lóan er komin að kveða burt snjóinn/kveða burt leiðindin, það getur hún./Hún hefur sagt mér að senn komi spóinn,/sólskin í heiði og blómstur í tún.
"The plover has come and she'll sing away winter / Drive off all sorrow as only she can / She says that the whimbrel soon will be coming / Sun on the valley and hayfields in bloom" – by Páll Olafsson (1827–1905).

The arctic tern, which usually appears in early May, is one of the wonders of the ornithological world. It migrates each spring from Antarctica, 17,000km (10,500 miles) away. The arctic tern is a graceful flyer, often seen hovering over water. It also makes unnerving "dive-bombing" attacks on

start flying ashore for the breeding season, after spending the winter out on the North Atlantic. Their main breeding grounds are on sea-cliffs (particularly in the Vestmannaeyjar/Westmann Islands and the West Fjords), and also on low-lying offshore islands such as Grímsey.

These unusual birds do not simply build a nest – they dig a burrow, up to 1.5 metres (5ft) deep, where a single egg is laid. On the sea cliff, puffins are usually found nesting at the top, where a little soil and vegetation provides the space to dig. Puffin pairs will return year after year to the same burrow. After the 1973 eruption on Heimaey island, many returned to find their bur-

The lake (Tjörn) in Reykjavík is a natural habitat for wild birds. As well as a variety of ducks, geese and swans, it also has a breeding colony of arctic terns and the occasional red-necked phalarope.

humans who enter its nesting colonies in June and July, screeching "*kría!*" (also the bird's name in Icelandic).

The puffin is Iceland's commonest bird, with a population of 8–10 million. The comically dignified stance of this decorative bird has earned it the nickname of *Prófastur* (The Dean). Around the third to fourth week of May each year, puffins

rows buried under a thick layer of lava. Rather than nest elsewhere, they tried to burrow to their old nesting places; some died in the attempt.

Rare birds

One of the most famous of the island's bird species is, sadly, extinct. The great auk (*Pinguinus impennis*) was a big, awkward, flightless sea bird, about 70cm (27ins) high, and very tasty, according to the fishermen who hunted it for food. The last breeding pair of great auks was killed on Eldey in 1844 (*see also pages 226–7*).

An endangered species still native to Iceland is the gyrfalcon, the largest of all falcons at 51–60cm (20–23ins) long. About 300 pairs are estimated to breed each year. The gyrfalcon has a colourful history as one of Iceland's most prestigious and valuable exports. Due to their skill and manoeuvrability in the air, gyrfalcons were prized as hunting birds and made gifts fit for kings and princes. In medieval times, up to 200 trained birds were exported each year, and in the 16th century the king of Denmark (who also ruled over Iceland) claimed a monopoly on the trade, which made a significant contribution to the royal coffers.

Although falconry largely died out in Europe by the 18th century, it continues in other parts of the world. Even today, an illicit trade in hunting falcons exists, and isolated attempts have been made to steal falcon eggs and chicks and

and the capercaillie – the ptarmigan adopts protective white colouring in winter. Humans share the falcon's taste for ptarmigan, which is part of the Icelanders' Christmas dinner and traditionally hunted on the heathland of Þingvellir National Park *(see page 171)*. Ptarmigan numbers fluctuate: hunting was banned in 2003 and 2004 when the bird appeared to be in decline.

Iceland's most numerous bird of prey is the merlin. Smaller than the gyrfalcon at 27–32cm (10–12ins) long, the Icelandic merlin is a unique subspecies, *Falco columbarius subaesalon*. It lives mostly on passerines such as redwings, wheatears and meadow pipits.

smuggle them out of the country. The smugglers (including, on one occasion, a German "tourist" with two chicks hidden in his luggage) have been apprehended and heavily fined. Iceland's gyrfalcons enjoy special protection: their nesting places are kept secret, and carefully monitored. No-one may approach the nests, or photograph them, except by permission of the Ministry of Culture.

The gyrfalcon lives in close community with its preferred prey, the ptarmigan (*Lagopus mutus*). Considerably smaller at 35cm (13ins) than its European relatives – the red and black grouse

LEFT: Atlantic puffins catching fish.
ABOVE: a gyrfalcon.

Lord of the skies

The largest of Iceland's birds of prey is the rare white-tailed eagle, up to 90cm (3ft) long, with a wingspan of up to 2.5 metres (8ft). This is a close relative of the bald eagle, the US national bird. During the early 19th century, there were 200–300 breeding pairs in Iceland. The bird was accused, however, of carrying off lambs, and it certainly disturbed eider colonies by taking both eggs and chicks. A bounty was offered for eagles, and they were shot and poisoned by farmers and eider breeders until, in 1920, only 10 pairs remained. Since 1913 the eagle has been fully protected by law, and is making a slow recovery. Today, breeding pairs number around 65, so prospects for the future seem promising.

By the sea

Iceland's coast and offshore islands provide marvellous opportunities to birdwatch at close quarters. The islands of Breiðafjörður, for instance, teem with shag and cormorant, along with the occasional white-tailed eagle. The grey phalarope – much rarer than its red-necked cousin – also breeds there. On sightseeing cruises from Stykkishólmur, birdwatchers can sail in close to the birds.

Bird-cliffs are found around the country, although the mixture of species nesting on the cliffs varies from region to region. The common guillemot, for instance, prefers the north, while the Brunnich's guillemot is found most often in the

south. The cliffs provide ledges and hollows not only for the ubiquitous puffin, but also for fulmars, kittiwakes, guillemots and razorbills.

Látrabjarg, at Iceland's westernmost point, is one of the world's great bird-cliffs. Sixteen km (10 miles) long, the cliffs soar 500 metres (1,600ft) up from the sea. The cliffs that fringe Hælavíkurbjarg and Hornbjarg, in the far northwest, are less accessible, but certainly no less

> In Þjórsárver, in the depths of the highlands, is one of Iceland's largest breeding sites of the pink-footed goose, with around 25,000 pairs.

spectacular. Other bird-cliffs can be seen on the Vestmannaeyjar (accessible by sightseeing cruises from the main island, Heimaey), plus Krísuvíkurbjarg on the southwestern peninsula, Reykjanes. The Snæfellsnes peninsula, in the west, is also an excellent area for viewing cliff birds and other seabird species.

Grímsey island, 40km (25 miles) off the north coast, was until recently the only Icelandic habitat of the very rare little auk, which was so well protected by law that you needed to obtain a permit simply to approach the nesting area. The bird has not bred here now for several summers, although it is still a winter visitor. About 16,000 pairs of gannets nest on Eldey island off the Reykjanes peninsula, the fourth-largest gannet colony in the world. Casual birdwatchers, however, are not welcome as Eldey is a closely protected bird sanctuary.

Bogs, marshes and wetlands also provide impor-

BIRDLIFE AT LAKE MÝVATN

Lake Mývatn *(see pages 261–7)*, in the north, is a unique natural phenomenon; a large lake, 37 sq km (14 sq miles) in area, yet with a depth of only 1–4 metres (3–13ft). It is also fed by underground hot streams from the adjacent active geothermal and volcanic area, which raise the temperature higher than one would expect both at this northerly latitude and at its altitude of 277 metres (908ft) above sea level. Even in severe winters, the lake never freezes completely, thanks to this input of warm water.

This benign environment means that Mývatn is a paradise for ducks, providing lavish feeding whether for divers or dabblers, and all of Iceland's duck species save the eider (which prefers life at sea) are found breeding

here. Most common is the tufted duck (with an estimated 3,000 pairs), then the scaup (1,700 pairs) and Barrow's goldeneye (700 pairs). Other common species include the common scoter, red-breasted merganser, long-tailed duck, gadwall and teal, while the mallard and pintail are less common. The goosander, shoveller and pochard are rare. The harlequin, which likes fast-flowing waters, is found on the adjacent Laxá river.

Many other bird species are also found in the unspoiled countryside around the lake. The Slavonian grebe nests at Mývatn, and the short-eared owl on nearby marshes, along with snipe and red-necked phalarope. Merlins and gyrfalcons nest in the nearby mountainous areas.

tant habitats for many species of birds, including the whooper swan, the greylag goose, and waders like the whimbrel and golden plover.

Accidentals

The southern coast of Iceland is a particular favourite with birdwatchers who are on the lookout for exotic "accidentals", lost birds that have flown from North America and mainland Europe. Breiðamerkursandur, a wasteland of glacial sand south of Vatnajökull glacier, is one of the world's main breeding areas for the great skua, a fascinating bird to observe as it makes its piratical attacks on other birds.

lands. Wholesale draining of marshland has slowly but surely been destroying the water rail's habitat, and it is also an easy prey for the fast-moving and bloodthirsty mink, so its call may not be heard in the marshes of Iceland for very much longer.

Mammals in the wild

Iceland was never connected to any ancient land mass, so it's hardly surprising that it has few native animals – although a variety of marine mammals have been established on its coasts for millennia. The only land-based Icelandic mammal to predate the human settlement of the country is the arctic fox *(Alopex lagopus)*, which is thought to

In the Skaftafell area of Vatnajökull National Park, another excellent location for birdwatching, the wren is particularly common. Though the smallest of all the Icelandic birds at 12–13cm (5ins), it is larger than wrens in nearby countries, and is defined as a special subspecies, *Troglodytes troglodytes islandicus*.

One Icelandic bird you cannot expect to see is the water rail. This extremely shy species is so wary and elusive that it has hardly ever been photographed, although its call may be heard in its typical habitat, reedbanks edging marshy low-

have walked to Iceland over the frozen sea during the Ice Age. Two variants exist: the "blue", relatively rare in other Arctic areas, comprises about two-thirds of Iceland's fox population; it is dark brown in summer, and turns a lighter brown in winter, with a bluish sheen. The "white" variety only lives up to its name when in winter camouflage; its summer coat is greyish-brown with a grey or white belly. Exceptionally well insulated, the arctic fox grows a thick and furry winter coat, including fur on the soles of its paws.

Icelandic farmers long blamed foxes for the deaths of lambs and eider ducks, and have trapped or shot them since the Settlement *(see page 33)*. Research has shown, however, that they pose little threat to livestock. The fox is

LEFT: a white-tailed eagle, one of the most spectacular species in Iceland, moves in for the kill.
ABOVE: a great skua on the lookout for prey.

hunted across the country to control numbers, apart from in Hornstrandir nature reserve in the Westfjords, where it enjoys protected status and has consequently become quite fearless. In some areas, red foxes from commercial fur farms have escaped to the wild and mated with native arctic foxes, producing hybrids.

Rodent residents

Iceland has several naturalised mammals introduced, deliberately or not, over the years. Four rodent species have settled here, arriving as stowaways on ships. These are the long-tailed field mouse or wood mouse (*Apodemus sylvaticus*),

ogists believe that the long-tailed mouse must, like the fox, pre-date human habitation, as 1,000 years would not account for the development of this sub-species' differences from its mainland cousins. The brown rat is believed to have arrived in 1840, and spread rapidly to every region. The black rat has been sighted from time to time since 1919, but is not firmly established.

Another addition to Icelandic fauna was accidentally introduced into the wild. The American mink (*Mustela vison*) was brought to Iceland in the 1930s for the first attempts at fur farming but, like the red fox, a number of animals escaped. Within 35 years, the species had spread all over the country

house mouse (*Mus musculus*), brown rat (*Rattus norvegicus*) and black rat (*Rattus rattus*). The house mouse, brown rat and black rat are only found in and around urban areas; of them only the brown rat is common.

The long-tailed field mouse (a uniquely Icelandic sub-species, *Apodemus sylvaticus grandiculus*) certainly merits its name, with a tail as long as its body (8–10cm/3–4ins). It is found both near human habitation and in remote areas; eats mostly plants, berries and fungi, as well as small insects; does not hibernate; and sometimes takes shelter in houses and outbuildings in cold weather.

Both the house mouse and long-tailed mouse are long-established residents in Iceland, probably dating back to the original settlement. Some zool-

except for the central highlands, a localised area of the southeast and some islands. These blood-thirsty predators cause havoc among nesting birds such as puffins, guillemots, ducks and eiders by taking eggs and chicks. They also feed on fish, small birds and mammals. They are hunted by farmers, although their numbers remain high.

Imports from Lapland

Another of Iceland's wild mammals is a reminder of a well-meaning but misguided attempt to alter the Icelandic way of life. Several dozen reindeer (*Rangifer tarandus*) were introduced from northern Scandinavia in 1771–87, when Icelanders lived in penury, on the verge of starvation. The beasts were imported so some Icelanders could adopt the existence of the nomadic Sami people (also known as Lapps). The experiment did not work and the reindeer reverted to the wild, adding an exotic touch to the uplands, and some meat to hunters' tables.

By 1817, reindeer were widely distributed in many areas, and their growing numbers gave rise to fears that they were overgrazing the upland pastures, traditionally sacrosanct to the sheep. A

Examples of Iceland's wild mammals, which are at times hard to spot in the wild, can be viewed at Reykjavík's zoo.

rarely be spotted in summer, but in the depths of winter they sometimes descend to lowland farms and villages in search of adequate grazing.

Attempts have been made to introduce the musk ox (*Ovibos moschatus*) and the mountain hare (*Lepus timidus*) into Iceland, but with no success.

Mammals of the sea

Iceland's rugged coast sustains a range of marine mammals. Seals are most likely to be spotted, with two species, the common or harbour seal and the grey seal, breeding in Iceland. The country boasts about half the world population of harbour seals, which can often be seen sunning themselves on

royal charter of 1817 permitted unlimited hunting of the animals, except for juveniles under a year old. Half a century of indiscriminate slaughter left the reindeer stocks in a poor state by 1882, when hunting was restricted.

Thanks to a total hunting ban from 1901 to 1940, the herds made an excellent recovery, and the population is now about 3,000. Herds are now found only in the mountains and valleys in the east of Iceland. They graze on mosses, fungi, lichens and grasses, but will also nibble shoots of shrubs and young trees. The shy creatures can

the black sands of remote fjords. Five other species breed on Greenland and the polar ice floes, and make occasional visits to northern Iceland: they include the ringed, bearded, harp and hooded seals, and the Atlantic walrus.

Medieval Iceland was famous for the whales off its coast, and today whale-watching tours do a booming business. Most typically spotted off Icelandic are minke whales and harbour porpoises; the latter are usually seen in pods of 3–10 animals, but sometimes congregate in their hundreds. Other commonly seen species include humpback (easy to distinguish as they raise their tail flukes vertically before diving), fin and killer whales; and, less frequently, blue, sperm and pilot whales. ❏

FAR LEFT: an arctic fox, Iceland's only indigenous land mammal, in its brown summer coat. **LEFT:** a baby grey seal. **ABOVE:** a successful whale-watching trip.

PLACES

A detailed guide to every region of Iceland,
with principal sites clearly cross-referenced
by number to the maps

Iceland is one of the world's most spectacular destinations, with vast empty landscapes illuminated by sparkling, clear sub-arctic air and cosy fishing villages sheltering from Atlantic storms beneath gargantuan cliffs. It's a paradise for anyone with a love of nature and the great outdoors, lent a surreal edge by the presence of the restless tectonic activity beneath.

Reykjavík is a pleasantly small, personable and lively capital city, the perfect base for exploring the so-called "Golden Circle", which includes some of Iceland's best-known natural spectacles such as the waterfall Gullfoss, the eponymous Geysir and Iceland's historical centre, Þingvellir. Also within easy reach is the amazing Blue Lagoon spa resort. Beyond the black sand beach at Vík, Iceland's southernmost point, lie Iceland's most accessible glaciers and Skaftafell, part of the immense Vatnajökull National Park and a favourite hiking spot among locals.

North of Reykjavík is the historic Snæfellsnes Peninsula, the setting for many an Icelandic saga, while further north lies the remote, windswept West Fjords region with some of the wildest (and wettest) landscapes in Iceland.

Akureyri, Iceland's only large town outside of the capital, is the jumping-off point for exploring the North. Nearby Lake Mývatn is Iceland's most popular

tourist spot outside the "Golden Circle", where dramatic volcanic activity can be seen at close range. In the Northeast is Jökulsárgljúfur, another awe-inspiring section of Vatnajökull National Park, whose series of canyons leads to Dettifoss, Europe's most powerful waterfall. The East Fjords region holds tiny fishing villages and rugged scenery that manages to retain its character despite the new Fjarðaál aluminium smelter.

Finally, there is the interior – an area quite different from the rest of Iceland. Almost all coastal roads are passable in two-wheel drive cars; but routes through the interior demand four-wheel drive or a specially designed touring bus. The coast has hundreds of villages and farms offering accommodation; in the interior, camping or bed-/floorspace in a basic mountain hut are the only options. Weather by the coast is relatively warm, if often wet; temperatures in the interior can plunge to dangerous levels without warning. ❑

PRECEDING PAGES: Reykjavík in winter; Jökulsárlón glacier lagoon; Ásmundur Sveinsson Sculpture Gallery. **LEFT:** sculpture at Arnarstapi. **ABOVE FROM TOP:** East Fjords scenery; seal on Húsey Farm, 60km (37 miles) north of Egilsstaðir.

Arctic Circle

Grímsey

Rauðinúpur
Hraunhafnartangi
Raufarhöfn
Þistilfjörður
Fontur

Langanes

ufjörður
Flatey
Kópasker
Öxarfjörður
Hölaheiði
Þórshöfn
Bakkaflói

Ólafsfjörður
Hrisey
Grenivík
Skjálfandi
Húsavík
Jökulsargljúfur
Ásbyrgi
Bakkafjörður

Dalvík

Ilskagi
kull

Eyjafjörður
Þjóðgarður Vatnajökull
(Vatnajökull National Park)
Vopnafjörður

85
Vopnafjörður
Héraðsflói

87
Dettifoss

Akureyri
Reykjahlíð
Dimmifjallgarður
Smjörfjöll
85
Borgarfjörður-
Eystri

Mývatn
94

821
88
Egilsstaðir
Seyðisfjörður

26
1
Þjóðgarður Vatnajökull
(Vatnajökull National Park)
Neskaupstaður

752
Eskifjörður

Sprengisandur
Skjálfandafljót
Ödáðahraun
Askja
Jökulsá á Fjöllum
Jökulsá á Dal
Fljótsdalheiði
Lögurinn
Reyðarfjörður
Reyðarfjörður

Hálslón
reservoir
Snæfell
1833
Stöðvarfjörður

sjökull
Tungnafells-
Jökull
Kverkfjöll
1860
Hraun
Djúpivogur
Papey

Þjórsá
Kvíslavatn
V a t n a j ö k u l l

Hámarinn
1573
Grímsvötn

26
Þjóðgarður Vatnajökull
(Vatnajökull National Park)
Snæfell
1383
1
Höfn

Þórisvatn
Tungnaá
Langisjór

Laki
812
Skaftafell
Snæfell

1
208
Kirkjubæjarklaustur
Skeiðarársandur
Ingólfshöfði

A T L A N T I C

O C E A N

N

Iceland

0		40 km
0		40 miles

REYKJAVÍK

The world's northernmost capital is a bright, colourful city. Rich in cultural attractions and with a vibrant nightlife, Reykjavík also has parks and wildlife areas surprisingly close to its centre

Reykjavik

Visitors are often unsure whether Reykjavík is a scaled-down city or scaled-up village. Probably it is both. Housing around one third of Iceland's population, it is the undisputed political, business, cultural and intellectual centre of the country. Yet it retains a certain slow pace and almost rustic charm that makes it unique amongst the world's capitals.

From the higher elevations the eye is drawn across the bay to the flat-topped mountain of Esja, often snowbound, its cold grey bulk a constant reminder of the sub-arctic location. It was here that the "official" settlement of Iceland began, after a few false starts, in the late 9th century AD. For centuries there was little to distinguish it from any other cluster of farms elsewhere in the country, although the strands of its noble fate had already been woven: while the practical details of settlement and development were entrusted to man, the site itself was originally chosen by the pagan gods. Ingólfur Arnarson, who has been given the title First Settler of Iceland, brought with him from Norway not only his family and cattle but also the high seat that was the symbol of the homestead. Following established Viking custom, Ingólfur dutifully tossed overboard the pillars on which the high seat was mounted – wherever they washed ashore, that was where the gods willed him to live.

It took over three years for Ingólfur's slaves to find the pillars, while the Viking himself stayed temporarily in the south, but eventually they turned up on the shores of what is now Iceland's capital. One of the slaves, less than impressed with the gods' choice, snapped that "to no avail we have crossed fine districts to live on this outlying wilderness", and ran off with one of Ingólfur's maidservants. But the other slave, Vífill, was given his freedom; he lived at Vífilsstaðir, now the site of a sanatorium, between Reykjavík

Main attractions
REYKJAVÍK 871±2 SETTLEMENT
    EXHIBITION
NIGHTLIFE
CULTURE HOUSE
NATIONAL MUSEUM
HALLGRÍMSKIRKJA CHURCH
SAGA MUSEUM

LEFT: the city in winter. **RIGHT:** geothermally heated pool at Laugardalur.

The first pipes bringing hot water to Rekyavík were laid in 1930. Today all the city's houses are heated from natural geothermal sources, removing the need for fossil fuels.

and neighbouring Garðabær, just to the south of the city. Ingólfur himself submitted to the gods' judgement and probably built his house in the old city centre, with a view of the duck-filled lake, Tjörnin.

In the shadow of steam

The First Settler, Ingólfur, named his new home Reykjavík (Smoky Bay), after clouds he saw rising from the ground, probably in what is now the Laugardalur area. The "smoke" was steam from geothermal springs – ironically, the same "smoke" that today makes Reykjavík an almost completely pollution-free city.

As for Ingólfur, he still has a presence in the shape of one of the statues so characteristic of the capital (by Einar Jónsson, 1874–1954). The First Settler is now perched atop **Arnarhóll hill**, at the virtual centre point of the Old Town, next to Government House, his back turned upon the Culture House (*see page 149*). The statue gazes across the harbour to where, on a clear day, the glacial cap of Snæfellsjökull glimmers mystically on the horizon, some 100km (60 miles) away to the north.

Reykjavík today

For a visitor, the old city centre is definitely the most charming part of the capital. Well-to-do residential streets, with their brightly coloured, corrugated-metal-clad houses and mossy lawns enclosed by picket fences, run alongside the shops, cafés and galleries of the main commercial thoroughfares. In contrast to the compact centre, Reykjavík's sprawling suburbs extend eastwards for mile after mile, all drab apartment blocks and busy roads.

The city as a whole has been undergoing a transformation in the past 10–15 years. Whereas visitors to Iceland once considered Reykjavík little more than a stopover en route to the country's undisputed main attraction – the landscape – the capital has now earned its stripes as a destination in its own right (a process encouraged by the availability of cheaper flights since the turn of the 21st-century). Its energetic and distinctive cultural scene is a constant source of fascination. After all, what other city with a population of just under 118,000 has an internationally acclaimed symphony orchestra, two

BELOW: fast food.
BELOW RIGHT: design favours clean lines with a dark edge.

major professional theatre companies, numerous independent theatre groups, an opera company, a national ballet and both a national and municipal art gallery? On top of this, dozens of smaller independent galleries and venues offer continuous exhibitions, recitals and performances throughout the year, and an annual arts festival attracts numerous renowned artists of international standing.

Reykjavík nightlife has also been discovered by visitors from around the world eager for something different and vibrant. The city's reputation as a "happening" place has largely grown out of the success of pop diva Björk since the early 1990s and the roster of international stars that have since taken to visiting the country.

Unlikely as it may sound, Reykjavík has also become increasingly popular as an attractive option for the cosmopolitan shopping enthusiast, particularly now that visitors benefit from more favourable exchange rates following the 2008 economic crisis. Icelandic design favours the clean lines and cool functionality of modernist Scandinavian products, but tends to use local materials and be infused by a darker spirit. Unusual and unmistakeable, Icelandic design is on the rise, and the city has a wide range of one-off shops selling homeware, clothing and jewellery, all within a relatively small geographical area.

Running the dog.

Exploring the old city

The old city centre is bordered roughly by Suðurgata to the west, Hafnarstræti to the north, Lækjargata and Fríkirkjuvegur to the east and Hringbraut to the south. Street names give some hint of the way Reykjavík looked in the 19th century and before. The traffic artery of Lækjargata ("brook street"), for example, followed a stream between the shore and the lake; eels were caught here once, but it is now buried beneath asphalt and flagstones. Today's main shopping street of Laugavegur ("pools road") points the way that women followed on foot or horseback to the Laugardalur hot springs to do their washing.

Austurstræti ❶ was once the city's

BELOW: one-off boutiques abound.

Houses clad in corrugated metal are a common sight in Reykjavík – a tradition dating back to when all houses were made of timber. Corrugated metal is a great shield against wind and rain, and allows the timber to breathe, so it is still used to cover timber houses today.

BELOW:
Austurvöllur Square.

most easterly point – the street's maidens were immortalised, like distant cousins of Heine's *Daughters of the Rhine*, by Tómas Guðmundsson (1901–83), Iceland's first urban poet. The town plaza **Austurvöllur** ❷ ("eastern field") is today a small park laid out around a statue of the nationalist hero Jón Sigurðsson. It is said that Ingólfur Arnarson actually grew his hay here.

Parallel to Austurstræti, Hafnarstræti ("harbour street") is no longer on the harbourfront – it was superseded by Tryggvagata, built during World War I on gravel and sand dumped to extend the waterfront, (then by the modern Geirsgata which is now on the harbourfront). Hafnarstræti houses the customs office, tax office and a couple of pubs, but the houses on the southern side of Hafnarstræti date back to the 19th century. At Tryggvagata 17 is **Hafnarhús** ❸ (open daily 10am–5pm; free; www.listasafnreykjavikur.is), one of three galleries belonging to the Reykjavík Art Museum, situated in the stylishly renovated former warehouse of the Port. **Kolaportið Flea Market** ❹ (open Sat and Sun 11am–5pm), situated on

Geirsgata, across from the harbour, is a cheerful occasion selling clothes, books and other assorted odds and ends. The food section is a must for anyone who is curious about traditional Icelandic fare; here are featured the tasty *harðfiskur* (dried fish), *hákarl* (cured shark), *síld* (pickled herring) and *hrútspungar*, the infamous pickled rams' testicles, as well as a wide range of other culinary novelties and delights.

Aðalstræti

Reykjavík's oldest buildings are on **Aðalstræti** ❺ ("main street"). In the 18th century, Aðalstræti was earmarked by High Sheriff Skúli Magnússon (nicknamed "the Father of Reykjavík") for a crafts and trades development project. An unusual effort to catch up with the outside world, it was a scheme for creating cottage industries – wool-dyeing, knitting, weaving, etc. Although it folded, the project left not only inspiration, ambition and skills, but also the capital's earliest surviving architecture.

The most tangible signs of Iceland's Viking settlement can be seen at the **Reykjavík 871±2 Settlement Exhibition**

The Rise of Reykjavík

For centuries after settlement, Reykjavík remained little more than a few farmhouses. In a census taken in 1801 its population was a mere 301 souls, mainly spread between the lake and the Old Harbour where the shops and offices of the old city centre now lie. The population was presumably even less in 1786, when Reykjavík was first granted a municipal charter as an official trading post. In 1901, Reykjavík still only had 5,000 inhabitants. The sudden leap to today's 118,000 has occurred mostly since World War II, as tens of thousands of provincial Icelanders moved to the capital in search of better job prospects and a more cosmopolitan way of life. However, Reykjavík's gain has been the countryside's loss: many areas are suffering decline as a result.

(Landnámssýningin; open daily 10am–5pm; charge; www.reykjavik871.is) at Aðalstræti 16. Here you'll find the remains of an oval-shaped Viking-age farmhouse just below the current street level, along with one of the country's most impressive and imaginative exhibitions. The layer of volcanic ash which lies just beneath the ruins has enabled archaeologists to date the structure to *c.*871 AD. With a hearth as its central point, the farmhouse covers around 85 sq metres (915 sq ft) and is thought to have been occupied until around 1000 AD.

Sandwiched between the museum and the **tourist office**, Aðalstræti 10 is the oldest surviving building in the city, built in 1764 to replace a 1752 weaver's shop that had burnt down. Its history is dotted with larger-than-life characters, including one-time owner Bishop Geir Vídalín (1761–1823). A cleric famed for his hospitality, Bishop Vídalín left an immortal dedication to the city's nightlife: "There are two places where the fires never die down – Hell and my house." Burning a hole through his wallet in the process, Vídalín won the dubious honour of becoming the only bishop in ecclesiastical history to be declared bankrupt. The building now contains a small exhibition about the city, and a large design shop showing off the best of Iceland's talent. On show across the road, beneath a thick layer of clear plastic, is one of the old wells that used to provide Reykjavík's residents with drinking water. Relics dating back to the Settlement have been found to the right of the well, at the corner of Aðalstræti and Túngata.

A plethora of pubs and restaurants lends a boisterous atmosphere to downtown Reykjavík by night, creating a beehive of activity more in keeping with a city many times the size. Nightlife begins late and lasts until early morning. Bar prices are high and most nightlifers "warm up" with a few drinks at home before taking the plunge. The "in" spots tend to change regularly; what was hip today may be passé tomorrow. Queues are quick to form when the action gets underway.

Humble beginnings

Iceland's **Government House** ➏ (Stjórnarráðið) stands on a small grassy bank

The tourist office at Aðalstræti 2 is open daily 8.30am–7pm in summer (1 June–15 Sept). At other times of the year it is open 9am–6pm weekdays, 9am–4pm Saturday and 9am–2pm Sunday. See www.visitreykjavik.is, tel: 590 1550.

BELOW LEFT: a designer boutique.
BELOW: Government House.

Embracing the Night

On weekend nights, those out on the town gravitate from bar to bar, bumping into old friends – it's this largely good-natured intimacy that sets Reykjavík's nightlife apart

S omething curious happened to Reykjavík nightlife at some point in the early 1990s – it became very hip, especially for foreigners with money. One of these was a British pop star who was so taken with the scene that he returned again and again before finally purchasing a share in his favourite pub – and a flat nearby.

The initial rush of recognition may have subsided a little in the years since, but that isn't to say that the scene has diminished. Clearly, Reykjavík nightlife is still something to write home about and international media still send their people over to chronicle the festivities and wind up with colourful exposés. Quite a change from the old days when tourists wearing hiking boots and cameras around their necks barely awarded the capital a second glance.

And what is it that's so appealing? Perhaps it's the rip-roaring, spine-tingling Viking intensity with which the Icelanders approach their merriment: Icelanders tend to work hard yet drinking mid-week is seen as verging on the alcoholic – which means that there is a real feeling of letting off steam at the weekend. Or all those Beautiful People, packed like sardines into the small trendy cafés or lined up in queues outside the baking night spots, shivering in the latest fashions; never mind that it's s a mere 5°C outside – that slip dress and those strappy sandals will stay on!

Inside, bartenders have their work cut out. A steady stream of alcoholic beverages leaves the bar, cocktail waiters and waitresses moving with amazing agility through the crowd. The loudness of the music makes regular conversation impossible. Bodies bop up and down and should there be a shortage of space the tabletops will do just fine, thanks. Actors and actresses rub shoulders with upstart politicians who rub shoulders with inebriated bohemians who claim to have solved the riddle of life.

Lækjartorg Square

At closing time, typically 5, 6 or 7am (at weekends; clubs and bars generally close at around 1am on weekdays, if they open at all), the lights go on, but the action continues out in the street. Everyone heads down to Lækjartorg Square to gather together sociably for a natter and maybe a smoke; if it's summer and the weather is good there will most certainly be a 5,000-strong crowd there, on the lines of a big outdoor house party. The crowd will be only slightly smaller if it's winter with a blizzard blowing.

Navigate your way through the throng and behold anything from ecstasy to wretched misery. For all this celebration comes at a price: a dark side does exist, in the form of drunken minors passed out in doorways or whacked out on illicit substances. Although the city's police are doing a commendable job, Reykjavík nightlife is neither as simple nor as benign as it once was. Now, for instance, more acts of random violence are perpetrated. And while one of the main hazards used to be traffic – the motorised kind – now there is trafficking of the highly organised kind.

For the most part however, capital revellers can enjoy the absence of serious crimes and misdemeanours: Reykjavík is still a relatively safe place to embrace the night. And that, too, might be something to write home about. ❏

LEFT: revellers congregating late at night.

overlooking Lækjartorg square, a stone's throw downhill from the First Settler, Ingólfur's statue on Arnarhóll. Built between 1765 and 1770, which makes it one of Reykjavík's oldest buildings, this unassuming whitewashed structure now houses the offices of the Prime Minister, yet it began its days less gloriously, as a prison workhouse. This building also housed the offices of the President of the Republic until 1996, when they were moved to premises at Sóleyjargata 1.

Behind the National Theatre on Hverfisgata is the **Culture House** ❼ (Þjóðmenningarhúsið; open daily 11am–5pm; charge; www.thjodmenning.is). This excellent museum contains a well-conceived exhibition of Iceland's ancient sagas and other medieval manuscripts and artefacts, displayed in sealed glass cabinets and dimly lit to aid their preservation. A visit here is a trip into a different world: swirling, flamboyant characters seemingly leap from every page telling the tale of life in the North Atlantic during the stirring Viking age. Upstairs, regularly changing exhibitions focus on different aspects of the country's heritage: past themes have included everything from the explosive creation of the island of Surtsey (see pages 20, 190–91), to drawings of sub-arctic flora, to the emigration of Icelandic Mormons to North America.

Further along Lækjargata, on the same side as Government House, stands a row of houses built in the mid-19th century. These narrowly escaped demolition some years ago and have been renovated; they now house two restaurants and the tourist information centre known as the **Icelandic Travel Market** (the government Tourist Information office is on Aðalstræti, see margin page 147). Further still, shortly before Tjörnin lake, the stately **Reykjavík Grammar School** (Menntaskólinn í Reykjavík) presides over the streetscape. This was the first school of its kind in the country and among its alumni are two Nobel Laureates: Halldór Laxness (literature, 1955) and Níels Finsen (medicine, 1903).

The **National Gallery** ❽ (Listasafn Íslands; open Tues–Sun 11am–5pm; free; www.listasafn.is), overlooking the lake at Fríkirkjuvegur 7 and next door to the grey and green Fríkirkjan (Free Church), is yet another historical building which has had its ups and downs.

Viking relics at the Culture House.

BELOW: waterfowl on the Tjörnin Lake in front of the City Hall.

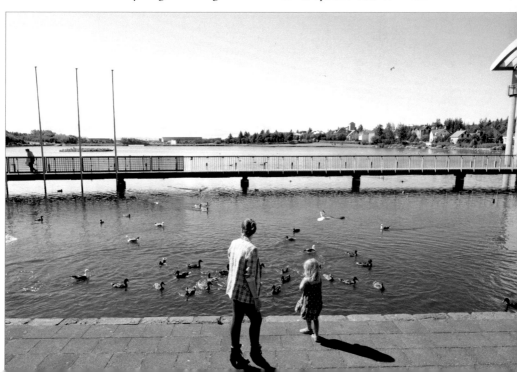

TIP

The Reykjavík Welcome
Card – available for 24,
48 or 72 hours – is
good value if you plan to
visit several museums
and galleries, and
unwind in one or more
of the city's seven
thermal pools. Bus travel
is included in the price.
For more information
see page 317.

It was originally built as a cold store in which to keep ice cut from the lake which was then used for preserving fish. Later it served as a fish-freezing plant and a hot dance spot – so hot, in fact, that it once caught fire. Now renovated, the small gallery has a fine permanent collection of work by Icelandic artists, including the country's first professional painter Ásgrímur Jónsson (1876–1958), supplemented by changing exhibitions. There is a café on the first floor with internet access.

The grey basalt **Parliament Building** (Alþingishúsið) ❾ on Austurvöllur square was custom-built in 1880–81 to house the ancient assembly. After more or less continuous operation in nearby Þingvellir *(see pages 171–5)* since the year 930 (albeit mostly as a court, because Iceland lost its independence in 1262), the Alþingi moved to Reykjavík in 1798. The building visible today was built to house it during the upswell of the 19th-century nationalist awakening.

Around Tjörnin lake

BELOW: the map inside City Hall.

On a clear day, it is worth taking some time to stroll around **Tjörnin lake** ❿, which regularly attracts over 40 species of birds – most noticeably ducks. There are seats and a pleasant walkway along its eastern side (below Fríkirkjuvegur), giving views of a splendid row of houses on the opposite bank.

The **City Hall** ⓫ (Ráðhús Reykjavíkur) was built on the edge of the lake in the 1980s – an impressive post-modern edifice in its own right, but disliked by many Reykjavík residents for clashing with its serene environs. There is a huge relief map of Iceland just beyond the entrance hall which is well worth a look, and at times this is the venue for free concerts and exhibitions. There is also a pleasant coffee shop with internet access and a lovely view of the lake.

On the north bank of Tjörnin, at the end of the City Hall walking bridge, is a corrugated-metal clad structure, which is fondly known as **Iðnó**. It was originally constructed to house a craftsmen's guild but is best-known for being the home of the Reykjavík City Theatre Company from 1897 to 1987. Iðnó reopened in 1999 after painstaking renovation transformed it back into one of Reykjavík's historical gems; it now serves as an occasional venue for music, dance and theatrical performances.

South of Tjörnin lake

A bridge across Tjörnin leads to some grassy park areas with a series of public sculptures, followed by the **University of Iceland** ⑫ (Háskóli Íslands), which was founded in 1911 – although its ponderous Third Reich-style main building dates from the 1930s.

Situated just east of the university is the **Nordic House** (Norræna Húsið), designed by the highly respected Finnish architect Alvar Aalto (Sturlugata; exhibition space open Tues–Sun noon–5pm; www.nordichouse.is). Its purpose is to cultivate and strengthen ties between the Nordic countries. To that end, it has a coffee shop complete with current Scandinavian newspapers, the restaurant Dill whose "New Nordic" menu gives Scandinavian staples a contemporary spin, a library and an ongoing programme of Scandinavian cultural events – many of which are free of charge.

On the edge of the university campus at Suðurgata 41 is the **National Museum** ⑬ (Þjóðminjasafn Íslands; open May–mid-Sept daily 10am–5pm, mid-Sept–April Tues–Sun 11am–5pm; charge; www.natmus.is), which is essential viewing for anyone interested in Icelandic history and contemporary society. The museum's main exhibition, *The Making of a Nation*, is gripping stuff, tracing Iceland's history from the Settlement down to the present day. The section on the use of DNA testing is particularly interesting, detailing research work on the teeth of the first settlers in order to determine their origins. Contemporary sections relate key periods in the country's development, such as the restrictive trade monopoly and the founding of the republic. Most of the archaeological finds around Iceland over the past few hundred years have ended up in the National Museum – including the impressive medieval wooden church door from Valþjófsstaður, carved in the 13th century with the story of a knight who slays a dragon.

Across from the National Museum, on the other side of Suðurgata, is the **National and University Library** ⑭ (Þjóðarbókhlaðan), housed in an airy, modern structure which opened in 1994 after a prolonged construction operation that lasted almost two decades (Arngrímsgata 3; open mid-May–Aug Mon–Fri 9am–5pm, Sat 10am–2pm; Sept–mid-May Mon–Thur 8.15am–10pm, Fri 8.15am–7pm, Sat 10am–5pm, Sun 11am–5pm). The library houses a manuscript collection and there are excellent research facilities for scholars, students and the general public.

Hallgrímskirkja

East from the lake, the roads slope uphill towards the imposing **Hallgrímskirkja church** ⑮ (open daily 9am–5pm; free), a modern concrete structure, built in nationalistic style to resemble volcanic basalt columns. Many visitors find it profoundly ugly, but climb the tower – or take the lift – and you are rewarded with the best views of Reykjavík and the deceptively close Snæfellsnes peninsula. On a clear day, as they say, you can see forever.

Completed in 1974, Hallgrímskirkja is designed to resemble columns of Iceland's basaltic lava. The tower, at 74.5 metres (244ft), is the second-tallest building in Iceland, after the Smáratorg office block in Kópavogur.

BELOW: an appreciative audience.

Hop on a harbour tour.

BELOW: exhibit at the National Museum.
BELOW RIGHT: Saga Museum mannequins.

In front of the church is a huge and impressive statue of Leifur Eiríksson, "Discoverer of America", a gift from the US on the 1,000th anniversary of the founding of the Alþingi in 1930.

Next to Hallgrímskirkja is the studio home of Einar Jónsson, now the **Einar Jónsson Museum** ⑯ (Safn Einars Jónssonar), which houses a collection of works by one of Iceland's great sculptors (Njarðargata; open June–mid-Sept Tues–Sun 2–5pm, mid-Sept–May Sat–Sun 2–5pm (closed Dec–Jan); charge; www.skulptur.is). Jónsson was a master of symbolism and epic, and many of his works combine a classical human form with symbols drawn from Norse, Greek and Oriental mythology.

If you head north from Hallgrímskirkja, you will come to the **Living Art Museum** ⑰ (Nýlistasafnið), another must-see for art connoisseurs (Skúlagata 28; open Tues–Sat noon–5pm; free; www.nylo.is). It was originally founded as a cooperative in the 1970s by a group of artists who opposed what they saw as the National Gallery's shunning of experimental art. The museum stages ongoing exhibitions by both Icelandic and foreign artists and has become a permanent fixture on the artistic landscape.

Southeast from the Icelandic Institute of Natural History is **Kjarvalsstaðir** ⑱ (Flókagata; open daily 10am–5pm; free) another part of the Reykjavík Art Museum. Situated in Miklatún park, this gallery is dedicated to Iceland's most famous modern artist, Jóhannes Kjarval (1885–1972). Kjarval worked on a fishing trawler until his artistically minded fellow workers ran a lottery to raise money for him to study in Copenhagen. The collection of his landscapes here is well worth seeing.

Landmark buildings

The literally outstanding feature of the Reykjavík skyline these days is the glass-domed **"Pearl"** ⑲ (Perlan) – a revolving restaurant that sits on top of the glistening silver hot-water tanks on **Öskjuhlíð** hill, offering a breathtaking view of the city on clear days from its panoramic viewing deck and café. The tanks can take 24 million litres (more than 5 million gallons) of hot water and cater for almost half of Reykjavík's water consumption. An impressive man-made **geyser** has been constructed outside the "Pearl", and Öskjuhlíð itself is a pleasantly leafy area thanks to tree-planting schemes and the creation of walking and cycling paths.

The "Pearl" is also the location of Reykjavík's **Saga Museum** ⓴ (Sögusafnið; open daily Apr–Sept 10am–6pm, Oct–Mar noon–5pm; charge; www.saga museum.is), an absorbing collection of lifelike silicon models of characters from Iceland's medieval literature. If you're keen to get to grips with the sagas, and have children in tow, the dramatic tableaux here are a much better option than the manuscripts inside the Culture House (however be warned that young children might be quite frightened by the pore-and-hair realism of the Viking models!). Beyond the Pearl, Reykjavík's purpose-built geothermal beach, **Nauthólsvík**, is a good place to catch the rays and bathe in a sublime seawater lagoon.

Located back down near the shoreline is what is probably Reykjavík's best-known building internationally, the **Höfði House** ㉑. This is the municipal reception hall behind whose clapboard exterior former presidents Ronald Reagan and Mikhail Gorbachev met in October 1986 to take their first bows before the *pas-de-deux* towards global disarmament. Now it is used for official city social functions, but is closed to the general public. At the time of its completion in 1909 to house the French consulate, Höfði was on the outskirts of the capital. It was sold to the poet and businessman Einar Benediktsson (1864–1940), who brought to the house not only his family but also a ghost. Reportedly, the ghost stayed on rent-free when the poet's family sold it to the British consulate, which grew in turn so tired of being haunted that the building was eventually sold to the city. An electrical fault, rather than the troublesome spectre, was blamed for the fire that damaged the building on its 100th birthday, on 25th September 2009.

The Höfði House, location of the 1986 summit between Reagan and Gorbachev.

Nature and high art

For all Reykjavík's modern expansion, the city's natural treasures remain as precious as ever. The **Laugardalur** area, a green belt situated northeast

BELOW: the exterior of the Perlan revolving restaurant.

WHALE MENU
STARTER
Lobster soup with Cognac
MAIN COURSE
Whale peppersteak served with fried vegetables, potato and pepper sauce
DESSERT
Icelandic Skyr Herefordstyle
Price kr. 5.900

PUFFIN MENU
STARTER
Smoked Puffin with fresh salad and raspberry vinegar
MAIN COURSE
Grilled breast of Puffin served with fried vegetables, potato and malt sauce
DESSERT
Icelandic Skyr Herefordstyle
Price kr. 5.900

Menus to suit all tastes.

BELOW: a splash of colour in Reykjavík's Botanical Gardens.

of the old city centre, has been largely preserved from development. It serves as the capital's main sports area with a large open-air, geothermally heated swimming pool, soccer stadium, sports hall and ice-skating rink. There is also the Viking-themed mini-rides of the **Family Park** (Fjölskyldugaðurinn) and adjoining **Reykjavík Zoo** ❷ (Húsdyragarðurinn; both open daily mid-May–Aug 10am–6pm, Sept–mid-May 10am–5pm; charge; www.mu.is), which contains domestic farm animals, animals native to Iceland and a small coldwater aquarium, rather than lions and tigers. The nearby **Botanical Gardens** ❷ (Grasagarðurinn; open daily May–Sept 10am–10pm, Oct–Apr 10am– 3pm; free) have an impressive collection of 5,000 plants and nearly the entire Icelandic flora.

Over the road from the soccer stadium is the sculpture gallery **Ásmundarsafn** ❷ (Sigtún; open daily May–Sept 10am–4pm, Oct–Apr Sat–Sun 1–4pm; free), a third part of the Reykjavík Art Museum dedicated to the sculptor Ásmundur Sveinsson (1893–1982). His works, inspired by saga events, folklore and everyday life, are set in and around his bizarre dome and pyramid studio/ home. The outdoor sculpture garden is impressive, and open at all hours – many tourists pass it regularly, as several hotels, including the Grand Hotel Reykjavík and Park Inn Ísland, are situated nearby.

Not far away on the shoreline is the **Sigurjón Ólafsson Museum** ❷ (Safn Sigurjóns Ólafssonar, Laugarnestangi 70; open June–Aug Tues–Sun 2–5pm, Sept–May Sat–Sun 2–5pm, closed Dec–mid-Feb; www.lso.is), dedicated to an Icelandic painter who lived from 1908 to 1982. In addition to the art collection there is a small family-run café with a lovely sea view and weekly music recitals in the summer.

The New Reykjavík

Since World War II the capital has been expanding to the east, leaving its past behind. In the 1980s, as it approached a six-digit population, more modern and grandiose architecture appeared on its skyline. A new commercial and cultural centre was built entirely from scratch some 4km (2½ miles) east of the old centre, including not only the large

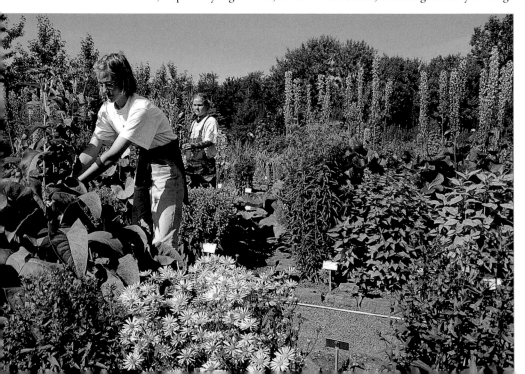

indoor shopping mall, **Kringlan**, but also a complex to house the Reykjavík City Theatre company.

As new residential suburbs sprang up – tasteless "concrete lava fields" such as Breiðholt and Árbær, each many times more populous than the largest of rural Icelandic towns – so this new part of Reykjavík has become the geographical as well as the business and commercial centre. This expansion is perhaps the most instantly visible result of Iceland's rapid shift from a traditional, rural country to a modern technological society.

Located on the edge of the Árbær suburb is the **Árbær Open-Air Museum** ㉖ (Árbæjarsafn; open daily June–Aug 10am–5pm; charge; www.arbaejarsafn. is), a living history museum that in the summer offers a schedule of events at weekends. A number of historical houses have been moved here from various locations in Reykjavík and around Iceland, and the past is re-created as accurately as possible. Household items and furnishings used throughout the centuries are on permanent display, and there is also an old turf church which is

a popular spot for wedding services. The atmosphere is compromised by the busy road that runs next to it, however.

Between the suburbs of Breiðholt and Árbær, and well within the city limits, runs the idyllic **Elliðaár** river, which pays handsome tribute to the lack of pollution in Reykjavík as one of the best salmon rivers in Iceland, with annual catches of around 1,600 fish. By tradition the city's mayor opens the fishing season on 1 May every year. Angling permits, being carefully shared out, are difficult for visitors to come by, but there is no problem in buying permits during the summer season for nearby **Lake Elliðavatn**, where there is good local trout in wonderfully calm and picturesque surroundings.

Elliðavatn borders the capital's **Heiðmörk** nature reserve to the south of the city, a popular spot for picnics and strolls, where wild patches merge harmoniously with areas reclaimed from wind erosion by the planting of trees.

Boat excursions

The island of **Viðey** ㉗ was given to the Reykjavík authorities as a birthday

BELOW: a capital city on a very human scale.

Whale-watching tours depart from the Old Harbour (Höfn) in the city centre from April to October.

BELOW: the Sólfar sun craft sculpture.

present in 1987 when the capital celebrated the 200th anniversary of its municipal charter. Today the island provides a haven for Reykjavík's inhabitants to "get away from it all". A small motorboat makes the five-minute trip from Sundahöfn harbour, 4km (2½ miles) east of the main Reykjavík harbour (daily from mid-May–August at hourly intervals 11.15am–5.15pm). One boat also leaves Reykjavík harbour at noon, returning at 3.30pm. Outside the summer season, there is a more limited weekend-only timetable.

High Sheriff Skúli Magnússon moved to Viðey in 1751 and had a fine residence – Iceland's first stone building – constructed there. After falling into disrepair, Skúli's former home was restored in 1988 and now houses a summer café and a top-drawer restaurant serving unusual, historically themed food. The church on the island dates from 1774 and is also one of the oldest in the country; before the Reformation, Viðey housed the richest monastery in Iceland, which

owned a good part of Reykjavík and the land beyond, until it was torn down by Lutheran zealots. An ambitious scheme for a fisheries operation was launched in the early 20th century but eventually went bankrupt; remains of the "ghost town" can be visited on a pleasant walk around the eastern part of the island, which takes about an hour.

Departing from the main harbour in Reykjavík, three companies, Elding, Hvalalíf (Life of Whales) and Sjósigling offer daily **whale-watching tours** ❷⁸ (Apr–Sept 9am and 1pm, June–Aug 9am 1pm and 5pm, Oct 1pm only) in Faxaflói, the bay which lies between the capital and the Snæfellsnes peninsula. Minke and humpback whales are the most common species spotted on the tours, though there's also the chance of seeing killer whales, dolphins, sei and blue whales. In puffin-breeding season (mid-May–mid-August), the boats sail past the rocky islands of Lundey or Akurey which are home to up to 30,000 puffins, giving you a chance to see these comical birds at close quarters.

Greater Reykjavík

Reykjavík and the towns surrounding it grew so fast during the late 20th- and early 21st-century boom years that they now form an almost continuous conurbation, known as the **Greater Reykjavík Area**. The recent economic crisis has caused a rise in emigration, but the area is still home to some 165,000 people – over half of Iceland's total population. The urban area extends some 11km (7 miles) to the east of the old city centre. Most of these towns are new and quite colourless, including Kópavogur, which has swollen in recent years to accommodate 30,000 people and is thus the second-largest community in Iceland. One of Kópavogur's claims to fame is that it is home to the country's biggest shopping mall, Smáralind, opened in October 2001. Sightseeing tours from Reykjavík take in some of the more interesting and historic places, such as Hafnarfjörður and Bessastaðir (*see pages 160 and 162*). ❑

Why is Iceland so Broke?

In 2008, the boom years were erased by a crash that brought Iceland's economy to its knees and caused the prime minister to resign

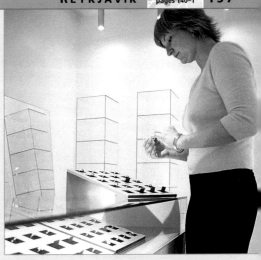

Iceland was in buoyant mood. The tiny country had spent a decade being feted by foreigners, tourism was booming, house prices soared, cranes covered the horizon in a country-wide construction boom. Icelandic businessmen bought up foreign businesses like children choosing sweets, and Icesave, a subsidiary of Iceland's national bank Landsbanki, was offering incredible interest rates to overseas savers.

In October 2008, this rampant spending came to an abrupt halt when the first wave of the worldwide financial crisis swept away Iceland's entire economy. The króna lost one-third of its value overnight, the Icelandic stock market suspended trading, all three of the country's national banks went into receivership, and the country teetered on the edge of bankruptcy, saved only by huge loans from its Scandinavian neighbours and the IMF. For months, protestors rioted in Reykjavík, eventually forcing the prime minister Geir Haarde to resign in February 2009.

Iceland's wealth had been illusory, a glittering crust lying over a deep black pit of debt. Oddly, Iceland's very geography was a contributory factor. Its physical isolation and harsh climate means that it is virtually 100 percent dependent on expensive imports, and a small population means that the burden of high prices cannot be spread. Many Icelanders were holding down several jobs and working up to 80-hour weeks to pay off mortgage, car and appliance loans, a situation compounded by Icelanders' expensive tastes.

The burden of debt

Excessive debt levels were not limited to individuals. The government had borrowed abroad since the 1960s, partly to maintain the country's first-class living standards. Pre-crash Iceland had one of the world's highest levels of foreign debt per capita: its banks' deficits had grown to around 17 percent of its annual GDP. The banking sector was out of all proportion to the country's economy, and had few

ABOVE RIGHT: pre-crash Iceland maintained a veneer of wealth.

real assets to back it up. When the subprime-related "credit crunch" affected world markets, the Icelandic bubble was the first to burst.

Two years after the crash, everyday life is still affected by high inflation, wage cuts, redundancies, cuts in services and currency restrictions. Unemployment stands at 7.6 percent (up from 2.3 percent in 2007), and an average of around 80 businesses per month are going bankrupt.

Before the crash, 300,000 British and 118,000 Dutch customers deposited their savings in Icesave. When the money vanished, the UK and Dutch governments reimbursed savers to the tune of £4.5 billion and €1.53 billion respectively. Iceland is legally bound to pay a significant chunk – €20,000 per saver – of this money back to the two governments. Icelanders also suffered financially when Landsbanki went bankrupt, and are aggrieved at paying twice over for what they see as individual bankers' mismanagement. They want Icelandic billionaire Björgólfur Thor Björgólfsson, who with his father and business partner owned 45 percent of Landsbanki, to bear some of the responsibility. Björgólfur Thor, however, holds Iceland's financial regulator, government policy, and the director and board members of Landsbanki accountable for the mess.

One of the first acts of the new government in 2009 was to apply for EU membership, intending to adopt the euro in 2011. The application could be hindered if Iceland does not repay the Icesave money; but if it increases its debt, it may not fulfil the criteria for joining the euro. However, the Icesave wrangle and Greece's financial problems, which call the future of the euro into question, have caused a swing in public opinion: a recent poll now suggests that 60 percent of Icelanders do not want to join the EU. ❏

RESTAURANTS, CAFÉS AND BARS

Restaurants

The price guide is for the average price of dinner per person, without wine:
$$$ Over ISK4,500
$$ ISK2,500–4,500
$ Under ISK2,500

Á Næstu Grösum (First Vegetarian)
Laugavegur 20B
Tel: 552 8410
Delicious, wholesome vegetarian food, an airy, relaxed atmosphere and good value for money make this a very popular place, particularly at lunch time. Indian theme on Fridays; lunch not served on Sunday. The entrance is on Klapparstigúr. $

Argentína Steak House
Barónsstígur 11
Tel: 551 9555
Top-quality steaks, lamb and reindeer are served at this justifiably popular restaurant which is open daily from 6pm. The atmosphere is warm and inviting but enjoying a bottle of good wine with your steak adds hugely to the cost. $$$

Austur-Indíafélagið
Hverfisgata 56
Tel: 552 1630
Unlike most other countries, Indian food in Iceland is expense-account stuff. However, at Austur-Indíafélagið, at least, the quality of the fare is excellent and the service is among the best in Reykjavík: friendly, professional and tactful.

Open daily from 6pm.
$$$

Austurlandahraðlestin
Hverfisgata 64A
Tel: 578 3838
Despite a tongue-twisting name, this Indian takeaway is a real find. All your favourite spicy Indian treats to take with you or, alternatively, there are a handful of tables inside. $

Dill
Nordic House, Sturlugata 5
Tel: 552 1522
A gourmet's delight, this elegant new Scandinavian restaurant specialises in local, organic ingredients cooked in contemporary "Nordic Kitchen" style. Prepare yourself for mouthwatering dishes such as smoked haddock with blue mussels, reindeer with blueberry sauce, and almond cake with cinnamon ice-cream. $$$

Fiskfélagið (Fish Company)
Vesturgata 2a, Grófartorg
Tel: 552 5300
Just opposite the main tourist office, this atmospheric new fusion restaurant gives traditional Icelandic ingredients an international makeover. If you have the stomach space, the seasonal "Around Iceland" menu provides four courses of the freshest local food prepared with great skill and imagination. $$$

Gallery Restaurant
Hótel Holt, Bergstaðastræti 37
Tel: 552 5700
Dining at this leading restaurant inside Hótel Holt is sure to impress. The magical combination of top-notch gourmet French cuisine and exquisite artwork decorating the walls is unparalleled anywhere in the city. Menus change

frequently, but be sure to ask if smoked puffin breast in blueberry sauce is available. $$$

Hornið
Hafnarstræti 15
Tel: 551 3340
This was the first Italian restaurant to open in Iceland and it has been popular ever since. The atmosphere is relaxed and the pizzas and pasta dishes are excellent. There's also a range of Mediterranean-influenced fish dishes. It is almost always packed in the evening so a reservation is recommended. $$

Icelandic Fish & Chips
Tryggvagata 8
Tel: 511 1118
The fish-and-chips here are given a healthy spin, made with organic potatoes and the freshest quality fish. No wheat or

BELOW: Hornið, an Italian with a cosy atmosphere.

sugar is used in the fish batter, the chips are roasted rather than deep-fried, and the unusual selection of dressings is made using low-fat, yoghurt-like *skyr*. It does a roaring trade in take-aways, too. **$$**

Jómfrúin
Lækjargata 4
Tel: 551 0100
An excellent choice for lunch, when the restaurant is full with homesick Danes. A seemingly endless choice of filling Danish-style open sandwiches. Choose carefully and lunch need not cost more than ISK1,700. **$**

Lækjarbrekka
Bankastræti 2
Tel: 551 4430
In an atmospheric timber building dating from 1834, this cosy restaurant with period furniture, chandeliers and heavy drapes is known for its gourmet set menus featuring lobster, puffin or lamb. It's an excellent choice for a special occasion. Finish off with a drink in the snug lounge upstairs. **$$$**

Rosso Pomodoro
Laugavegur 40
Tel: 561 0500
A good choice for Italian food whilst out shopping on Reykjavík's main thoroughfare. Excellent pizzas, pastas, salads and fish dishes in a pleasantly modern atmosphere. Look out for special lunch offers. **$$**

Þrír Frakkar
Baldursgata 14
Tel: 552 3939
They've been serving whale steaks at this cosy neighbourhood French-style bistro for years and it's still the best place in town to sample the meat, should your conscience

allow. Otherwise, an accomplished menu of fish dishes, including the traditional *plokkfiskur*, a kind of fish and potato mash, is on offer. **$$$**

Vegamót
Vegamótastígur 4
Tel: 511 3040
An extremely popular bistro in the centre of town serving a varied menu of good-value food: everything from fresh fish to TexMex dishes. Plentiful brunch options are available until 4pm on Saturday and Sunday. It's also a relatively cheap place for a beer. **$$**

Við Tjörnina
Templarasund 3
Tel: 551 8666
Undoubtedly one of the city's finest fish restaurants located close to Tjörnin lake, as the Icelandic name suggests. A unique menu with creatively prepared fish which never fails to tantalise the tastebuds. **$$$**

Cafés

b5
Bankastræti 5
One of Reykjavík's newest bistro-bars, sleek b5 actively encourages its customers to linger over their coffee and light Scandinavian-style meals by lending out books, newspapers and laptops.

Café Paris
Austurstræti 14
Tel: 551 1020
A Reykjavík institution that's been here as long as anyone can remember. Its central location overlooking Austurvöllur square and the parliament buildings is unsurpassed and it's a good choice for decent coffee and light snacks. In summer there's outdoor seating.

Grái Kötturinn
Hverfisgata 16A
A basement café renowned across the city for its excellent hearty breakfasts and bagels. Small, arty and intimate place to stop for a cup of coffee or a bite to eat.

Kaffi Hljómalind
Laugavegur 23
The decor is eccentric and service can be erratic, but this community-run café deserves your support. The coffee is fair-trade, food is organic and locally sourced, and all profits go to charity.

Kaffi Sólon
Bankastræti 7A
Half bistro, half bar, this airy, contemporary place overlooking the main street is a good bet for a tasty lunch. Stylish interior, a wide selection of coffees and some tantalising cakes.

Kaffivagninn
Grandagarður 10
Tel: 551 5932
Unpretentious harbourside place where local fishermen come for coffee and wholesome home-cooked fare.

Mokka
Skólavörðustígur 3A
The oldest coffee house in Iceland, which has been plying the masses with the dark stuff since 1958. There's never any music here – it's a place to come with friends for a chat over a cup of coffee.

Bars

101 Bar
Hverfisgata 10
Attached to the stylish 101 Hotel, this super-cool bar is a place for an early evening cocktail or two before heading downtown. Just soak up the chic surroundings and

indulge in some celebrity-spotting.

Dubliner
Hafnarstræti 4
Long-established Irish pub in the heart of town, with Guinness and a decent array of whisky.

Hverfisbarinn
Hverfisgata 20
Another winner, this inordinately popular bar/nightclub has been a Reykjavík favourite with younger drinkers for several years now.

Istofan
Vegamótastígur 4
This long-standing favourite is a practical pub, popular with an older artistic, intellectual crowd who want good conversation with their beer.

Kaffibarinn
Bergstaðarstræti 1
Often packed to capacity, this tiny Bohemian bar has one of the coolest reputations in Reykjavík and attracts a mixed and lively crowd. With DJs from Wednesday to Sunday.

Oliver
Laugavegur 20A
Bar, nightclub and restaurant (in the daytime) all rolled into one, this eclectic place is a good choice for a drink and a dance. It's one of the city's "places to be seen", so be prepared for weekend queueing.

Thorvaldsen Bar
Austurstræti 8
A restaurant by day, Thorvaldsen transforms itself into a very fashionable bar/nightclub when evening arrives, that is popular with a 30+ throng. Dress smartly.

THE REYKJANES PENINSULA

Reykjavík

Situated just south of the capital, the Reykjanes peninsula is a compact area to visit. The undisputed highlight is the stunning Blue Lagoon, but there are also excellent bird-watching sites and nature reserves

Main attractions
HAFNARFJÖRÐUR
BLUE LAGOON
REYKJAVEGUR TRAIL
KRÍSUVÍKURBJARG CLIFFS

The Reykjanes peninsula is easy to ignore – a smallish promontory southwest of **Reykjavík ❶**, it is undeniably overshadowed by the capital's greater pulling power. Yet most people's first glimpse of Iceland is actually of Reykjanes – Keflavík international airport is situated right in its heart.

Almost all arriving tourists simply jump aboard a bus or hire a car, and head for the mountains or the city without a backward glance. But one really should give the region a little time:

the principal sights can be seen on a day tour, but hikers, whale-watchers, birdwatchers and devotees of the Blue Lagoon may find it harder to tear themselves away.

Lashed by the Atlantic

Situated in Iceland's far southwest, the peninsula bears the full force of the violent storms that regularly pile in from the Atlantic. Small, nondescript fishing villages dot the coastline, while much of the inland area consists of lava fields, some of which flowed as recently as the 14th century. In fact the peninsula is a continuation of the Mid-Atlantic Ridge which pushes apart two immense plates of the earth's crust at the rate of around 2cm (¾ inch) each year. Pillow lava and tufa formations from Ice-Age eruptions give some indication of what the submarine ridge looks like. While the broad expanses of volcanic rock may seem grey and barren at first glance, in fact they have donned a coat of Iceland's typical grey-green moss, soft and springy underfoot. The tenacious moss has paved the way for higher plants, which thrive in the more sheltered areas. Two hundred species of grasses, mosses and flowering plants have been identified, with the occasional birch or other tree.

Hafnarfjörður

The gateway to Reykjanes, only 15 minutes by bus south of central Reykjavík,

LEFT: the Blue Lagoon.

is the old town of **Hafnarfjörður ❷**. This was one of Iceland's most important ports long before Reykjavík had even grown into a village: in the 15th century it was run by English traders and in the 16th century by Germans, before the Danes imposed their trade monopoly of 1602.

Situated within the craggy Búrfell lava field which covers most of the peninsula, Hafnarfjörður has a population of 26,000. It is a part of the Greater Reykjavík area but is by no means a satellite town of the capital, with its own thriving port and fishing industry, and a broadly based local economy. The cool, white **Hafnarborg Arts Centre** (open Wed–Mon noon–5pm; charge) by the harbour-side is a genuine highlight of the town, offering art shows and musical events, as well as a peaceful coffee shop. A pleasant public park, **Hellisgerði**, is situated in the middle of the town, in among the lava. **Hafnarfjörður Museum** is based in three separate buildings: at Vesturgata 8, **Pakkhúsið** contains an interesting canter through the town's history and a little toy museum; next door is **Sívertens-Hús**,

once the home of local bigwig, Bjarni Sívertsen, dating from 1803 and the oldest building in town (both open June–Aug daily 11am–5pm (Pakkhúsið also opens Sept–May Sat–Sun 11am–5pm); charge); at the opposite end of the social scale is **Siggubær**, a tiny house belonging to a former fisherman (open June–Aug Sat–Sun 11am–5pm; charge).

Hafnarfjörður is also well known for its "hidden population". For as long as can be remembered, people have believed that elves, dwarfs and other harmless urchins live in its lava cliffs in peaceful coexistence with other town residents. There is even a map available at the local tourist information centre, showing hidden sites where these mysterious beings live (*see pages 248–9*).

In addition, Hafnarfjörður has become the "Viking centre" of Iceland. The nation's only Viking restaurant, Fjörukráin, is located at the harbour, where traditional food is served with lively song and celebration. During the ancient Viking month of Þorri (late Jan–late Feb), this is one of the best places to sample the pickled, smoked, dried and salted foods, such as rams'

Hafnarborg Arts Centre, a highlight of Hafnarfjörður.

BELOW: much of the peninsula is made up of moss-covered lava fields.

Pakkhúsið (part of Hafnarfjörður Museum), housed in a renovated 19th-century warehouse, recounts the history of the town, providing an insight into a close-knit Icelandic community. There is also an exhibition of children's toys.

testicles, cured sharkmeat and blood pudding, that once sustained people through the long winter months. In summer, over two weekends in late June, fighting displays and feasting are staples of the town's annual Viking Festival.

Bessastaðir

Bessastaðir ❸, north of Hafnarfjörður and just across the Skerjafjörður inlet from Reykjavík, has been the presidential residence since 1941, but the site has a much older history. Bessastaðir is first mentioned in the *Íslendinga Saga (Saga of the Icelanders)* by Sturla Þórðarson, and archaeological excavations have yielded a range of artefacts dating back to the Middle Ages, when the place belonged to the famous Edda-author Snorri Sturluson *(see page 42)*. After Snorri's death, the farm was confiscated by the king of Norway and remained a royal estate right up until the late 18th century (the present-

day building and the adjacent church date from this period). From 1805 Bessastaðir was the site of the highest educational institution in Iceland, the Lærði skólinn, for some 40 years.

Unless you are a foreign VIP being given a formal presidential reception at Bessastaðir, the interior of the house is off limits. However, visitors can take a peek inside the church, which was consecrated in 1796. Considerable repairs were carried out in 1946–8: the original stone floor disappeared under concrete, but can still be seen in the vestibule and tower. The windows illustrate themes from Icelandic ecclesiastical history. The altarpiece, by the Icelandic artist Muggur, is a triptych, painted in 1921.

Along the peninsula

Route 41 along the north coast of Reykjanes leads to the twin towns of **Njarðvík** and **Keflavík** ❹ (combined population 14,000), both trading centres since the Middle Ages. The two towns have virtually joined together in recent years, with a shared economy based on fishing and other commercial enterprises. In 2006, the speedy and contro-

Reykjanes Peninsula

0 — 5 km
0 — 5 miles

versial closure of the American air base at Keflavík, where around one in 17 of the local population was employed, had an unsettling effect on the area, although it is slowly regenerating. In Njarðvík, the new **Viking World** (Víkingaheimar; open daily 11am–6pm; charge) exhibition investigates Viking life and New World exploration, and is based around a reconstructed Viking ship.

Beyond Keflavík is the outcrop known as **Miðnes ⑤**, whose biggest settlements are the tiny fishing outposts of **Garður** and **Sandgerði**. Garðskagi, the headland just northwest of Garður, makes an interestingly windswept place for bird- and whale-spotting, while just south of Sandgerði is the small **Hvalsnes** church, built in 1887. The church's most treasured possession is a gravestone handcut by the poet Reverend Hallgrímur Pétursson in 1649. The stone came to light during excavations in 1964. The ruins of the village **Bátsendar** are nearby, destroyed by a freak tide at the end of the 18th century.

The dirt road Route 425 follows the coast to the peninsula's southwestern tip, passing bleak lava fields, a low-key bubbling-mud geothermal area, and a hands-on energy exhibition based inside the **Reykjanesvirkjun power plant** (open May–mid-Sept daily noon–4pm; charge). Nearby is Iceland's oldest lighthouse, Reykjanesviti.

Grindavík ⑥, now a typical fishing community of about 2,800 people, can look back on a long and eventful history. It was a major trading centre during the Middle Ages, and in 1532 a business rivalry between English and Hanseatic merchants led to the murder of an Englishman, John "the Broad". Barbary pirates raided Grindavík in 1627, capturing a number of Danes and Icelanders, plus two merchant ships. Today Grindavík is a quiet and unassuming town, with a statue to the families of local fishermen lost at sea and the **Icelandic Saltfish Museum** (Saltfisksetur Íslands; Hafnargata 12a; open daily 11am–6pm; charge) dedicated to the keystone of Iceland's survival.

Surreal spa

Iceland's most famous tourist attraction is located just outside Grindavík, only 15km (10 miles) from the airport. The **Blue Lagoon ⑦** (Bláa Loníð; open daily June–Aug 9am–9pm; Sept–May 10am–8pm; charge; www.bluelagoon.com) is a dreamy, steamy spa complex that epitomises the country's faintly unearthly reputation. Little wooden bridges crisscross the lagoon's blue-white waters and hot-pots; a cave-like sauna is carved into the lava; and a thundering waterfall delivers a pounding massage. The complex also contains a spa treatment area, restaurant, snack bar, shop, conference facilities, and, should you care to spend the night, there is a guesthouse just over the lava field. All summer long (June–August), however, the changing rooms get crowded and it may be worth getting up early to beat the crowds. Also note that the mineral-rich water has adverse effects on your hair, so bring plenty of hair conditioner. If you're impressed by the Blue Lagoon's healing properties, a range of eponymous skin and bathing products are on sale across the island (*see panel below*).

*The **Reykjavegur** trail extends over 130km (80 miles) from the southwestern tip of the peninsula to the Nesjavellir power plant east of Reykjavík. You can reach most of the trail's stage points by car, and walk from one to the next in a day (there are seven stages). This region is one of the few places on earth where you can observe continental drift from marked out and accessible areas – a route booklet is available from tourist information centres.*

BELOW: enjoying the benefits of bathing at the Blue Lagoon.

The creeping thistle (Cirsium arvense), otherwise rare in Iceland, grows in Grindavík. Local tradition claims that it grew up on the spot where both Christian and heathen blood was spilt.

In spite of its evocative name, the lagoon is not a natural phenomenon but a fortuitous by-product of Iceland's geothermal energy usage. The nearby Svartsengi power plant pumps mineral-laden water from up to 2km (1¼ miles) beneath the earth's surface, at a temperature of 240°C (470°F). The superheated water passes through a dual process, on the one hand to generate electricity, and on the other to heat fresh water. This run-off water, rich in silica, salt and other elements, once flowed out into a pool a few hundred metres from the present lagoon's site. Psoriasis and eczema sufferers noticed that bathing in the water seemed to ease their symptoms. Once the word was out, the lagoon was moved to its current location, and state-of-the-art facilities, carefully designed to complement the surrounding landscape, were built around it.

Hot spot

Geothermal power in a more natural setting can be seen east of Grindavík at **Krísuvík ❽**, within the Reykjanes-fólkvangur nature reserve. Here *solfa-taras* and boiling mud springs surround

BELOW: soaking away those cares in the Blue Lagoon.

the world's largest blowing steam vent. While the intention has always been to harness the geothermal energy at Krísuvík for heating purposes, nothing has yet come of this. The whole area seethes with subterranean heat, so tread carefully and keep to the paths to avoid being scalded.

Near Krísuvík is the dramatic and somewhat spooky **Lake Kleifarvatn**, reputed to be the home of an aquatic monster. If you are not put off by this, you can also fish for trout here. Permits are available in Reykjavík, Hafnarfjörður and Keflavík. On the coast beyond Krísuvík is **Krísuvíkurbjarg ❾**, one of Iceland's best-known bird-cliffs: the most numerous inhabitants are kittiwakes, while fulmar, razorbill, common guillemot and Brunnich's guillemot are also plentiful. Puffin, shag, herring gull and black guillemot, though less common, can be observed at Krísuvíkurbjarg, and seals can often be seen basking on the shore. Further offshore, one may occasionally glimpse groups of whales.

About 14km (9 miles) off the Reykjanes shore lies the island of **Eldey ❿**, a high rocky pillar towering 77 metres (250ft) out of the sea. Eldey is home to

Spa Benefits

There is an array of unusual health-giving salts, sprays and lotions on sale at the Blue Lagoon. Products contain a blend of minerals, silica mud and algae found naturally in the lagoon's geothermal seawater. A range of face care products is available to smooth and moisturise the skin, as well as cleansing products such as silica purifying shampoo, algae and mineral body scrub designed to cleanse and purify. The active ingredients have been proven to revitalise, nourish and protect human skin. They are particularly effective in treating certain conditions such as psoriasis. Various skin treatments are also on offer, such as a thirty-minute salt glow whereby the skin is polished with a mix of mineral salts to remove dead cells and stimulate blood circulation.

one of the North Atlantic's largest gannet colonies – around 16,000 birds nest on the island each year. The island is a nature reserve, and a permit is needed to visit. On a less positive note, the island is also the place where the last of the great auks was clubbed to death in 1844 (see page 227).

Church of miracles

The little **Strandarkirkja** ⓫ church on the south coast between Krísuvík and Þorlákshöfn has a bizarre history. Tradition says that a ship on its way to Iceland ran into a storm; the crew prayed for deliverance, and promised to build a church if they were saved. An angel appeared on the shore and guided them to safety; they landed at the spot where Strandarkirkja stands today. A tradition arose that the church could work miracles: through the centuries seamen in peril have prayed and promised donations to Strandarkirkja, and they still do t, this little church, which no longer has any parish to serve, is reputed to be one of the wealthiest in Iceland.

Near Strandarkirkja, at the small lake Hlíðarvatn, is the farm **Vogsósar**.

Formerly a parsonage, the farm was the home of the Reverend Eiríkur (1638–1716), who added a dash of magic to his pastoral duties. A famous folktale tells how one wintry day, travellers passing by the farm helped themselves to hay from Eiríkur's haystack without asking. After feeding their horses on the stolen fodder, they continued down to the river; but when they got there, the horses began to drink and drink, and couldn't be made to walk on. Eventually Reverend Eiríkur himself appeared at the ford, and after observing the scene, he remarked "The hay of Vogsós is thirsty hay. You shouldn't give it to your horses again."

A little further to the west is the abandoned farm **Herdísarvík**. Above the farm is a big crag from which impressive lava streams have flowed. This was the home of the great Icelandic poet Einar Benediktsson, who died here in 1940. Herdísarvík bay may have inspired some of Benediktsson's lines from *Surf*: "I hear in thy short-lived waves wearingly rolled / The footfall of time that e'er onward must hold / And my blood surges on with the bruit of the main....." ❑

At the Innri-Stapi cliff near Lake Kleifarvatn, there is a bronze plate beside the road that commemorates an Icelandic guide who was so fond of the area that his ashes were scattered over the lake at his request.

RESTAURANTS, CAFÉS AND BARS

Café Duus
Duusgata 10, Keflavík
Tel: 421 7080
This bright, cheerful café/restaurant/bar is located right next to Keflavík's picturesque small-boat harbour. Fittingly, its menu features several pages of fresh fish and seafood dishes. **$$**

Fjörukráin
Strandgata 55, Hafnarfjörður
Tel: 565 1213
If you're looking for traditional Viking fare, this is the place to come: shark, dried haddock and lamb shank are generally on the menu. During þorri (late Jan–late Feb), there's a Viking banquet featuring

delicacies such as singed sheep's head and pickled rams' testicles, as well. **$$–$$$**

Lukku Láki
Hafnargata 6, Grindavík
Tel: 426 9999
This jolly little pub, twinkling with fairylights, makes a great place for a beer. It also does tasty, no-nonsense bar meals which are worth sampling. **$–$$**

Ráin
Hafnargata 19A, Keflavík
A long-established restaurant with tasty fish dishes, pizzas and salads and fine sea views. It's also a popular place for a beer in the evening. **$$$**

Salthúsið
Stamphólsvegur 2, Grindavík
Tel: 426 9700
The town of Grindavík is the largest producer of saltfish in Iceland, so it makes sense to try some while you're here! If bacalao doesn't beguile, this saltfish restaurant also offers several beef, lamb and chicken mains. **$$**

Veitingahúsið Vitinn
Vitatorg 3, Sandgerði
Tel: 423 7755
In the tiny fishing village of Sandgerði, this unexpected bistro makes a good stop for a lunchtime sandwich or a slice of cake. It metamorphoses into a pleasant

little fish restaurant at night. **$$**

Vocal Restaurant
Flughótel
Hafnargata 57, Keflavík
Tel: 421 5222
A first-class restaurant is available inside Icelandair's Flughótel, 10 minutes' drive away from the international airport. A wide variety of expertly prepared dishes, in particular lamb and fish, is always on the menu. **$$$**

The price guide is for the average price of dinner per person, without wine:
$$$ Over ISK4,500
$$ ISK2,500–4,500
$ Under ISK2,500

THE SOUTHWEST

This area is full of historical sites from the time of the sagas, plus a wealth of natural wonders, all within comparatively easy reach of the capital and the Ring Road

The rich farming land of southwest Iceland has made it one of the most densely populated parts of the country since the Saga Age. Today it is also the most heavily visited: some of Iceland's most famous attractions are within striking distance of Reykjavík, tied together under the label of "the Golden Circle".

Every day, hundreds of travellers are bussed from one natural marvel to another, with scarcely enough time to draw breath between snapshots. This may be fine for anyone on a short stopover in Iceland and is probably an unfortunate necessity for those without their own transport. But others will prefer to take a more leisurely pace around the region, stopping in the more obscure valleys and farmhouses to appreciate Iceland's mellow rural atmosphere.

East of Reykjavík

The Ring Road east of Reykjavík quickly ascends to a volcanically scarred mountain pass. The moss-covered scoria lava field here, known as **Kristnitökuhraun**, was spewed up from the earth around AD 1000. The **Hellisheiði** area is a good walking destination en route from Reykjavík, with a well signposted trail network and detailed maps available.

There are panoramic views as the road descends towards the southwestern plain, with steaming crevasses and yellow sulphur markings on the slopes above **Hveragerði ❶**, a town of 2,300 people that has made a living from harnessing geothermal activity. It has the highest concentration of greenhouses in Iceland, and provides the country with much of its home-grown produce, including tropical fruits like bananas. A small geothermal area sits in the centre of town, while the Naturopathic Health Association of Iceland operates a clinic here for spa and mud cures. Lying just to the

Main attractions
STOKKSEYRI AND EYRARBAKKI
ÞINGVELLIR
GEYSIR
GULLFOSS
STÖNG VIKING LONGHOUSE AND
   ÞJÓÐVELDISBÆR
ÞÓRSMÖRK
SKÓGAR FOLK MUSEUM
VÍK

PRECEDING PAGES: Reykjanes Peninsula boat. **LEFT:** Strokkur geyser. **RIGHT:** at Þjóðveldisbær, a re-creation of times past.

Eyrarbakki's oldest building, dating from 1765, houses the Folk Museum.

north of town are the hot springs of **Grýla**, named after a hungry local she-troll with a penchant for devouring small children. Hveragerði's neat little modern-art gallery **Listasafn Árnesinga** (Austurmörk 21; open May–Sept daily noon–6pm, Oct–Apr Thur–Sun noon–6pm; free), provides a non-geothermal treat.

While Hveragerði itself is unlikely to hold travellers' attention for more than a couple of hours, it can be a base for hikes into the surrounding countryside – the nearby mountain **Selfjall** to the north of the town and the lava tube **Raufarhólshellir** to the southwest are popular destinations.

The next town along the Ring Road is **Selfoss ❷** (population 6,500), the centre of Iceland's thriving dairy industry and a major road intersection. On the highway just before town, **Hjarðarból** (tel: 567 4203 or 864 4203) offers farmhouse accommodation.

Stokkseyri and Eyrarbakki

To the south of Selfoss lie two tiny fishing villages which between them hold several unusual visitor attractions

and three highly rated restaurants (see page 181). In **Stokkseyri ❸**, the **Ghost Centre** (Draugasétrið; June–Aug daily 1–8pm, Sept–May Sat–Sun 1–6pm, (closed Jan–Feb); charge) sets out to spook its customers with a dark audio-guided walk through Iceland's supernatural stories. In similar vein, **Icelandic Wonders** (same opening hours) next door explores local superstitions about trolls, elves and the Northern Lights (see page 203).

More serious-minded is the village of **Eyrarbakki ❹**, set by the shores of a driftwood-strewn black sand beach. This was one of Iceland's main fishing ports from the 12th to the 19th centuries, and has several 18th-century buildings still intact. The oldest, simply called "Húsið" ("The House"), contains an interesting little **Folk Museum** (tel: 483 1504; open June–Aug daily 10am–6pm, Apr–May and Sept–Oct Sat–Sun 2–5pm; charge; www.husid.com). The **Maritime Museum** (same opening hours) is in an adjacent building. East of the villages lies the wide Ölfusá estuary and the Fuglafrið-land reserve, a prime location for bird-watching.

Þingvellir

Route 35 turns off north of Selfoss at the hillock of **Ingólfsfjall**, where the First Settler, Ingólfur Arnarson, is said to be buried. Among a group of smaller craters is the 55-metre (180ft) -deep Kerið, blasted out 6,500 years ago and now containing a lake. Continuing north it is possible to reach **Þingvellir National Park** ❺ (also accessible directly from Reykjavík), the historical heartland of Iceland, which became a Unesco World Heritage Site in 2004.

When Iceland's unruly early settlers decided to form a commonwealth in AD 930, the site they chose for their new national assembly, the Alþingi, was the natural amphitheatre of Þingvellir ("parliament plains"). It was a grand experiment in republicanism at a time when the rest of Europe wallowed in rigid feudal monarchies, and it lasted, despite the odd lapses into chaos, for over three centuries.

Today Þingvellir is still regarded with reverence by Icelanders, its historical weight reinforced by a serene natural beauty. Declared part of a national park in 1928, the historical section is set along the north of Þingvallavatn – at 84 sq km (30 sq miles), Iceland's largest lake – and by the banks of the **River Öxará** ("axe river"). On the horizon in every direction lie low mountains, snowcapped for much of the year: to the north lies the volcano of Skjaldbreiður ("broad-shield") – whose lavas created Þingvellir – flanked by the mountains Botnssúlur, Hrafnabjörg and Ármannsfell. The latter is home, it's said, to Ármann, a spirit who is the guardian of Þingvellir. To the south lies the geothermally active Hengill.

The lava plain of Þingvellir itself is covered with wildflowers in summer and sumptuous shades of red in the autumn. This is also a spot where the two halves of Iceland – the Eurasian and North American tectonic plates – are tearing apart. Aerial photographs show that the great crack of **Almannagjá** ("everyman's chasm"), on whose flanks the Alþingi was held, is just one fissure in a huge series running northeast like an ancient wound through the plains. Occasional earthquakes have reshaped the site: a quake in 1789 caused the plain to drop about 1 metre (3ft). The

The Ghost Centre at Stokkseyri.

A Key Place in History

Almost every important moment in Icelandic history has taken place at Þingvellir. When the Alþingi was first held here, this was the fringe of the farm Reykjavík, which was owned by the descendents of the First Settler, Ingólfur Arnarson. Here the decision was made for Iceland to convert to Christianity in AD 1000. This was the place for legal cases to be argued and voted on, although they were often finally resolved by the Viking recourse to arms and the field of Þingvellir would be soaked in blood. In time, this violence would grow out of control, and it was at Þingvellir in 1271 that Icelanders voted away their independence.

The Alþingi at Þingvellir kept operating as a court until the 1760s, although with less and less relevance as first Norway and then Denmark asserted colonial control. Even so, Icelanders kept a special affection for Þingvellir, as a place where, no matter how imperfectly, the country had managed its own affairs. When Iceland finally did declare its nationhood again in 1944, the field of Þingvellir was the obvious place for the ceremony.

Laying Down the Law

By their own admission, Icelanders have always been rather quarrelsome – aptly, the law of the land covers every possible contingency

Much of Icelandic history does seem to concern aggrieved characters making a choice between taking up the sword or going to court. The annual Alþingi set up in AD 930 offered the best of both worlds: legal proceedings with an adjournment while the litigants fought pitched battles. They could then apologise to the court, sit down and allow the proceedings to continue.

"Icelanders", wrote an 18th-century English commentator, "have surpassed all other nations in legal chicanery. Jurisprudence was the favourite study of the rich. A wealthy Icelander was always ambitious to plead a cause before the Alþingi, and the greater skill he showed in the art of prolonging... the greater was his celebrity. A man gained as much reputation for defeating his adversary in a lawsuit as for killing him in a duel."

Law covered every contingency imaginable. Thus: "If a man holds his weapons in a peaceable manner, as a person ordinarily does when he is not going to use them, and when they are in this position another man runs against them and wounds himself, he who held the weapons is liable to the punishment of banishment if competent witnesses can prove that he held them in this apparently quiet manner, in order that the other might run against them and be wounded thereby."

Categorising the crime

This law – and a hundred like it – reflected the fine calculation that made the punishment fit the crime. The case of a man who seduced a girl and was then wounded by the girl's father was considered all square. Punishment, when required, fell into three categories: death and two types of "banishment" exile or house arrest. The last normally carried the option of a fine; just as well because it was almost impossible not to break laws and most people would have spent much of their life indoors.

The crimes of witchcraft and theft commonly carried the death penalty, but those of murder or manslaughter rarely so. Thieves were beheaded; those convicted of witchcraft, usually men, were burnt or drowned to reduce the risk of trouble with their ghosts. Killing was shameful only if it was done in an underhand manner, like killing someone asleep. In other circumstances, which drew no distinction between self-defence and mindless butchery, it could be sorted out by the payment of a fixed penalty determined by the victim's social status.

In retaliation for effrontery or insult, killing was absolutely honourable, merely requiring a public announcement of the deed, which had to be made on the same day. After the event, care had to be taken not to conceal the body beyond a covering to protect it from scavengers. If insults were not immediately dealt with by the offended party, offenders were liable to exile. Indictable insults included throwing sand at someone, a punch, and attempting to throw a man into a mire "though he may actually not fall therein". Exile lasted 20 years and in practice was not far short of the death penalty. An exile had a price on his head and could be killed with impunity

In today's Iceland the rule of law and order is no less important. In line with the other Nordic countries, renowned for their no-nonsense approach to alcohol, Iceland operates one of the toughest drink-driving laws in Europe and alcohol limits for drivers are far stricter than in the UK, for example. Meanwhile, the possession of even small quantities of soft drugs can lead to heavy fines and possible imprisonment. ❑

LEFT: Vikings in discussion.

plates are drifting apart at a rate of around 2cm (¾in) each year.

Journey into the past

The **visitor centre** is located on the eastern side of the Öxará River, to the north of the historic sites. From here a track heads south to the church and farmhouse, while a path veers off southwest to the Lögberg, viewpoint and educational centre on the other side of the river. The point where the latter crosses the Öxará is **Drekkingarhylur**, the famed "drowning pool" that came into use in the 16th century. Men condemned to death were beheaded, but women who committed adultery, infanticide or perjury were tied up in a sack and flung into the pool, which was then deeper and more turbulent than it is today. A short distance upstream is the Öxarárfoss waterfall.

The path continues to what was the focal point of every Viking Alþingi: **Lögberg** , the "Law Rock", today marked by a stone and a flapping Icelandic flag, right by the Almannagjá fissure. On the smoother ground below, the Lögrétta (Legislature)

took place, attended by the 36 (later increased to 39) *goðar* or chieftains who would debate new laws. All free men were welcome to listen or comment, but only the *goðar* could vote. It was also the site of the Quarter Courts, one for each section of the country. The proceedings were considered so important that farmer-warriors rode in from every corner of Iceland, some taking as long as 17 days to arrive from the East Fjords.

The whole business was run by the Law-speaker, who was elected from among the chieftains. His was a difficult job: apart from keeping the proceedings orderly, he had to recite from memory all of the Icelandic laws, one third every year, from the Lögberg. The acoustics here are still excellent.

Scattered amongst the grass and lava on either side of the Lögberg are the few remains of various **búðir** ⓑ, or booths. Every chieftain set up his own personal booth for the two weeks that the Alþingi lasted (usually from the Thursday after 18 June each year), a canvas-covered place to sleep, eat, drink and meet. The stones that can be seen today all prob-

Relaxing outside Fjöruborðið restaurant, Stokkseyri

BELOW:
Þingvellir National Park.

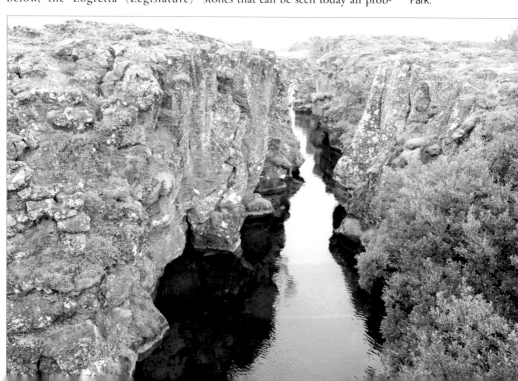

ably belong to booths from the 18th century. The remains of Hotel Valhöll, which burned to the ground in July 2009, are on the site of Snorri Sturluson's booth, **Valhöll** ⊙.

The path continues up to the **Interpretive Centre** and lookout point at the top of the Almannagjá fissure, with great views across to the church and the Þingvellir plains.

Religious centre

On the east bank of the river is the glistening white **Þingvallabær farmhouse** ⊙ and **Þingvallakirkja church** ⊙. The older part of the farmhouse, built in 1930, is today occupied by the park warden; the newer section, dating from 1974, is the summer residence of the Prime Minister.

A church at Þingvellir was the first in Iceland to be consecrated, probably soon after the conversion of 1000, although not at this location. The present version dates from 1859. Inside, there is a pulpit from 1683 and a treasured altarpiece, painted by Ófeigur Jónsson of Heiðarbær in 1834, that had been taken from Iceland and wound up in a church on the Isle of Wight in southern England. It was rediscovered only in 1974, and returned to Iceland in time for the 1,100th anniversary of the Settlement, which was celebrated at Þingvellir. There are three bells in the church steeple: one dating from the Middle Ages, one from 1698, and the third called Íslandsklukkan ("Iceland's bell") that was cast to ring out for Iceland's independence in 1944.

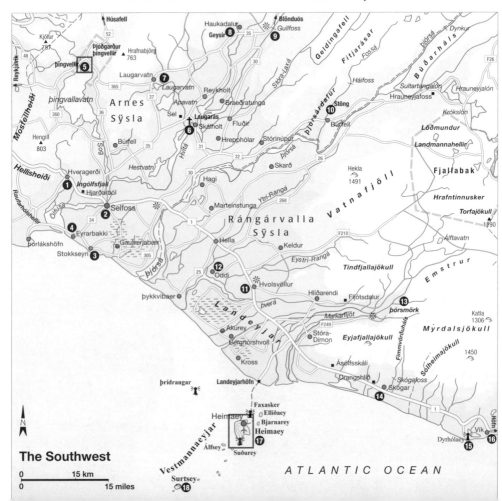

The Southwest

0   15 km

0   15 miles

There are two cemeteries at the church, the higher one a circular plot of ground with only two graves in it: both of poets, the illustrious nationalists Jónas Hallgrímsson (1807–45) and Einar Benediktsson (1864–1940). Just to the north of the church is **Biskupabúð**, the "Bishops' booth", which is the largest ruined booth in Þingvellir and one that dates back to its earliest Viking times.

Walk back to the visitor centre from here, with a short detour to a strip of land, **Spöngin G**, caught between two fissures. Some historians believe that the Lögrétta was initially held on the flat land near here, but had to be moved closer to the Lögberg when the Öxará was diverted. On the opposite side of the bridge is **Peningagjá G** ("coin rift"), a fissure whose bottom glitters with shining silver: the Danish king Frederick VIII instigated the coin-throwing tradition on a visit here in 1907.

Around Þingvellir

It is possible to take day hikes into the surrounding countryside. Almost all paths lead to the old sheep farm of **Skógarkot**, abandoned in 1936, to the west of Þingvellir. About one kilometre south is **Skógarkotshellir**, a long cave that has never been fully explored. The less energetic can enjoy a drive on the narrow dirt roads around Lake Þingvallavatn, lined with luxurious summer houses for Reykjavík inhabitants.

From Þingvallavatn, roads cut off in every direction – west to Reykjavík, north to the deserts, east to Geysir and south to Selfoss – following the ancient routes that were once ridden by Viking farmers, every June, to their unique, quixotic assembly. The road (52) north is the **Kaldidalur** route between Þingvellir and Húsafell. This rocky track usually opens during July when the snows melt around the Langjökull icecap, and will give a small taste of the interior. Shield volcanoes dominate the skyline, the most impressive being the evenly shaped Skjaldbreiður (1,060 metres/3,500ft), while, on the ground, colourful tundra flowers stud ancient

lava flows. River crossings are straightforward and the track runs very close to the hanging glaciers of the icecap.

Skálholt

Returning to Route 35, heading northwards, the road now enters an area that is known as Biskupstungur, between the Brúará and Hvítá rivers. The main attraction is **Skálholt G**, Iceland's first Christian bishopric and for over 700 years its theological powerhouse. Skálholt's power was built by an influential dynasty of chieftain-priests. First it was the farm of Gissur the White, the browbeating holy man who had led the pro-Christian faction at the AD 1000 Alþingi. His talented son, Ísleifur, was educated in Germany to become the first properly trained Icelandic priest and, in 1056, Iceland's first bishop. Finally, Ísleifur's eldest son, Gissur, took up where his father had left off, making Skálholt the undisputed Church centre of Iceland, its many schools financed by the first tithe to be imposed in northern Europe.

Skálholt maintained its position of power even through the violence of

A 17th-century grave at Þingvellir cemetery.

BELOW: a bishop is consecrated in 14th-century Iceland.

Visiting Gullfoss waterfall is a dramatic experience, with the huge volume of water producing a deafening roar audible from miles away.

BELOW: the hot spring at Vígðalaug.

the Reformation, but in 1797 the holy see was moved to Reykjavík and Skálholt all but disappeared. In 1953 – precisely 900 years after the ordination of Bishop Ísleifur – the foundations were laid for the new church that now stands on the site. In the process, archaeologists discovered the remains of one of Skálholt's many cathedrals that had burned down in 1309. At 50 metres (165ft) in length, it is thought to be the largest wooden church in Iceland at the time of its construction.

Even more unexpectedly, excavators found the carved stone coffin of Páll Jónsson, another of the learned, tough early bishops. According to *Páls Saga*, the bishop's death in 1211 was greeted by an earth tremor and deluge. When excavators opened the coffin in 1953 – revealing the skeleton and walrus-bone bishop's crook – there was one of the biggest downpours that Skálholt had seen in years. Today Páll's coffin is in the church's crypt. The best exit from the crypt is out of the wooden door, through an underground passage that was part of the medieval cathedral.

Within sight of Skálholt, 3km (2 miles) away, the idyllic working farm of **Sel** (meaning "summer farm") offers accommodation among sheep-filled fields. Just further on is the village of **Reykholt**, which has a geyser that erupts several times an hour and a pleasant, thermally heated swimming pool. Lying south of Skálholt is **Laugarás**, a verdant, geothermally active area with a camping ground. The paved Route 37 turns off directly north of Route 35 to the spa village of **Laugarvatn ❼** by the shores of the lake of the same name. Summer brings hundreds from Reykjavík to enjoy its pleasures, including the hot spring **Vígðalaug**, used as an all-weather baptism spot by the first bishops of Skálholt.

The land of boiling waters

Both Routes 35 and 37 finally lead to **Geysir ❽**, which has given its name to all such water spouts around the world. Sadly, the Great Geysir, which started erupting in 1294 and used to reach heights of around 60 metres (200ft), hasn't performed well for decades. In the 20th century, eager tourists tipped gravel and bits of rubbish into its mouth in an effort to force an explosion, and soap powder was used to break the surface tension on special occasions such as Independence Day; but the geyser continued its slump into a state of near-dormancy. Many people were therefore stunned when Geysir suddenly erupted in June 2001, seemingly quite out of the blue. Water spouted up to 40 metres (130ft) into the air, and the activity continued periodically over several weeks. However, this extraordinary occurrence had a perfectly rational explanation: earthquakes in Southern Iceland caused subterranean pressure that gave the great Geysir renewed vitality. Since those turbulent times, Geysir has calmed down again; it still erupts a couple of times a day, but generally only to a height of around 10 metres (33ft).

For the rest of the time, visitors will have to be content with the smaller but more reliable geyser, **Strokkur** ("the churn"), which spits up its column of water every five minutes or so to a height of around 20 metres (66ft). Meanwhile, the whole Geysir area is geothermically active, with walking trails marked out among steaming vents and glistening, multi-coloured mud formations. Don't stand downwind of Strokkur unless you want to get soaked; keep behind the roped-off areas; and definitely refrain from putting your hands in water pools to test their temperatures – it may sound silly, but an average of seven tourists are scalded every week in summer by doing just that.

The greatest waterfall

Nine kilometres (6 miles) further along Route 35 is the big attraction of the Golden Circle tour and perhaps Iceland's best-known natural wonder: the waterfall **Gullfoss** ❾ ("golden falls"). A path from the main upper parking area leads down to the deafening double falls, where the River Hvítá tumbles 32 metres (105ft) into a 2.5km (1½-mile) ravine. Trails climb past the waterfall's northern face, allowing you to get within an arm's length of the awe-

some flow. Wear a waterproof, or the clouds of spray that create photogenic rainbows on sunny days will douse you from head to foot.

By the café, a small exhibition space adorned with a plaque remembers Sigríður Tómasdóttir, a farmer's daughter who lived on the nearby farm Brattholt. In the 1920s, private plans had been drawn up to dam the Hvítá river at Gullfoss for a hydroelectric project, but Sigríður walked to Reykjavík to protest to the government and even announced that she would fling herself into the waterfalls if construction went ahead. The government instead bought the falls and made them a national monument.

From Gullfoss, the road stretches ahead into the uninhabited deserts of central Iceland, and on a clear day you can see the icecap **Langjökull** ("long glacier") in the distance.

Viking relics

For anyone even vaguely interested in Saga Age history, it is worth making the dusty, bumpy trip to the excavated Viking longhouse of **Stöng** ❿, and to its re-created twin, **Þjóðveldisbær** ("the

The English poet W.H. Auden noted in the 1930s that Icelanders were already using liquid Sunlight soap to encourage Geysir to explode. The soap had to be imported, since the thinner local type did not work.

BELOW:
archaeological remains at Stöng.

Kitted out for safe sailing on Laugarvatn lake.

BELOW: Háifoss, Iceland's second highest waterfall.

Commonwealth farm"), which lies close to Búrfell hydroelectricity station.

Both are situated in **Pjórsárdalur** ("bull river valley"), off Route 32, formed 8,000 years ago by the biggest lava outpouring since the Ice Age. The valley is overshadowed by the snow-capped form of **Mount Hekla**. Instead of a classic volcano cone, Hekla is part of a rather squat series of ridges, becoming progressively squatter with each eruption; however, even this is usually hidden behind the thick bank of clouds that earned Hekla its menacing name, which means "hooded." The seafaring Irish monk St Brendan might have been the first to see Hekla's volcanic pyrotechnics as he sailed past Iceland in the 6th century, and soon after settlement Hekla showed that it was a presence to be feared. The volcano's notoriety grew such that, in medieval Europe, Hekla was widely known to be one of the twin mouths of hell. It has remained active, with the last eruption in February 2000.

Stöng was the farm of the warrior-farmer Gaukur Trándilsson, whose saga, sadly, has been lost. He moved there at the end of the 11th century, but in 1104 Mount Hekla erupted without warning, soon covering the once-lush valley with a thick layer of white ash. Stöng and 20 other nearby farms had to be abandoned, and Pjórsárdalur was never resettled. In 1939, archaeologists uncovered Gaukur's house: it was in the form of two long rooms built end to end, with two annexes for the dairy and lavatory. As Iceland's best example of an early medieval home, it became the model for the nearby reconstruction of Þjóðveldisbær, begun in 1974 to mark the 1,100th anniversary of Iceland's settlement.

It's worth visiting the turf-covered reconstruction first, designed by architect Hörður Ágústsson using the Stöng floorplan and built by traditional methods (note the irregular-shaped planks of wood for the roof, fitted together so as not to waste an inch of the precious building material, and the marks of axes used to plane them).

The original Stöng is hidden away several kilometres further along a very poor dirt road. A large wooden shed has been built over the ruins to protect them from the elements, but it is never locked. Although only the stone foundations remain, this damp, slightly over-grown set of stones is the best place in Iceland to get the historical imagination working. On a fine day, those with spare time might want to take the two-hour walk beyond Stöng to Iceland's second-highest waterfall, **Háifoss**.

Following the south coast

Back on the Ring Road, the unassuming towns of **Hella** and **Hvolsvöllur** ⓫, both with around 800 inhabitants, mark the beginning of the countryside where perhaps the most famous of the Icelandic Sagas, *Njáls Saga*, took place. The **Saga Centre** (open June–Aug daily 9am–6pm; www.njala.is) in Hvolsvöllur has a simple exhibition that tells the story of *Njáls Saga (see pages 94–5)* in an easy yet comprehensive way. The centre is signposted from the main road. However, if you're interested in Iceland's rich literary history, make sure to visit the Culture House (where the ornately written sagas themselves are on display) and the National Museum before leaving Reykjavík *(see pages 149 and 151)*, as these two museums provide the visitor with the clearest understand-ing of Viking life in Medieval Iceland.

Between the two towns, Route 266 heads south to **Oddi** ⓬ which has been home to some of Iceland's most crafty inhabitants, including the lawyer and saga writer, Snorri Sturluson; and Oddi's first inhabitant, Sæmundur the Learned. Sæmundur was well known to be a wizard: the man had no shadow, since it had been stolen by the devil while he was studying at the "Black School" for satanists in Paris. Sæmundur offered his soul if Satan could take him back to Iceland without getting him wet. In the shape of a giant seal, the devil swam the North Atlantic with Sæmundur on his back, but as soon as they got near the coast, Sæmundur whacked him on the head with a prayer book. The wily wizard swam the rest of the way and, since he was soaked, kept his soul.

The church at Oddi today was built in the 1920s, but has a number of curious artefacts on display, including a silver chalice dating from the 14th century.

Thunder god's forest

East of the Ring Road along Route F249 is the valley of **Þórsmörk** ⓭ – literally,

Ruins of the turf houses by Drangshlíð farm near Skogar.

BELOW: a glacier burrows into Þórsmörk.

The arch at Dyrhólaey.

"Thor's forest" – one of Iceland's most spectacular but inaccessible wilderness areas. Sealed off by three glaciers, two deep rivers and a string of mountains, Þórsmörk has received added protection since 1929, when it became a nature reserve. The single dirt road into the park is impassable to everything but the specially designed high-carriage mountain buses – and some of the "Super Jeep" oversized Icelandic four-wheel drives, which can make it in when the glacial rivers are low, usually in the early morning. In 2010, glacial flows (*jökulhlaups*) from the Eyjafjallajökull eruption washed away part of the road (now repaired), and visitors to Þórsmörk were recommended to bring sunglasses, closed shoes and plenty of water as a precaution against suffering from the effects of volcanic dust.

Despite the difficulties, Þórsmörk often attracts well over 1,000 Icelandic campers every summer weekend and a growing number of foreigners on day trips (there are no hotels or guesthouses here, but there are three mountain huts and a clutch of summerhouses, all overseen by Hostelling International Iceland). Visitors are rewarded with spectacular glacier views, fields of wildflowers, pure glacial streams and forests of birch and willow full of birds – particularly blackbirds, ravens and wagtails.

The Ring Road continues south along a narrow plain of farmland between the black sand coast and rugged cliffs that lead to the icecap **Eyjafjallajökull**. This placid-looking glacier was brought to the world's attention in the spring of 2010 when its underlying volcano erupted, throwing a black ash plume up to 11km (7 miles) into the atmosphere, and closing down European airspace for six consecutive days. Farms and settlements south of the glacier such as Skógar and Vík were evacuated during the eruption, but life quickly returned to normal once it was over.

Ruins of indeterminate age crop up at intervals along this section of the Ring Road, giving the area considerable atmosphere. Beside the driveway to the farm **Drangshlíð** are some collapsed turf houses built into caves. Three kilometres (2 miles) further east, **Skógar** ⓮ is home to a meticulously managed

Folk Museum (open daily June–Aug 9am–6pm, May and Sept 10am–5pm, Oct–Apr 11am–4pm; charge), the most visited of its kind in Iceland, and run since 1949 by a local character, Þórður Tómasson. Apart from a 6,000-piece collection, the museum has examples of different types of Icelandic housing through the ages. There is the summer-only Edda Hotel at Skógar, as well as the splendid waterfall **Skógafoss**, whose sheer fall offers one of south Iceland's best photo opportunities.

The trek from Skógar to Þórsmörk, passing between the icecaps of Eyjafjallajökull and Mýrdalsjökull over the **Fimmvörðuháls** pass, is very popular with the hardy between June and September, and the trail can become quite crowded in July. The 2010 eruptions began at Fimmvörðuháls, disrupting a section of the trail; a new path has now been marked out that skirts the fresh lava flow.

Six kilometres (4 miles) east of Skógar, **Fúlilækur** ("foul river") announces itself with the overpowering rotten-egg stench of sulphur. The river emerges from beneath the **Sólheimajökull** glacier, which can be seen from the road,

and originates near the volcano Katla, whose subterranean activities beneath the Mýrdalsjökull icecap have often sent glacial tides to devastate this area – and may again, as eruptions of Eyjafjallajökull have often been a precursor to Katla's outbursts.

Further on, Route 218 cuts south to **Dyrhólaey** ⓯, a protected nature area with a steep cliff and a much-photographed natural rock arch out to sea; this is one of the best places to photograph puffins in south Iceland. Saga hero Njáll's son-in-law Kári had his farm here.

Vík ⓰ (sometimes referred to as Vík í Mýrdal to distinguish it from other Víks) is a small town of around 300 people set along a dramatic stretch of coastline: here the North Atlantic swell hits the land, its waves crashing dramatically on a long beach of black sand. At the end of the beach are the **Reynisdrangur**, towering fingers of black rock standing out to sea and inhabited by colonies of arctic terns. The relentless, battering wind adds to the Gothic scene – helping to make this the only non-tropical beach to be rated by *Islands*, a US magazine, as one of the world's top 10 beaches. ❏

RESTAURANTS AND CAFÉS

Eldstó Café
Austurvegur 2, Hvolsvöllur
Good homemade soup, sandwiches and cakes are available at this little café in Hvolsvöllur. **$**

Fjöruborðið
Eyrarbraut 3, Stokkseyri
Tel: 483 1550
A renowned and highly popular lobster restaurant by the sea, well worth the drive down from Reykjavík. **$$$**

Geysir Restaurant,
Hótel Geysir, Geysir
Tel: 480 6800
Uses local organic produce whenever possible, in everything from wholesome soups to top-notch lamb dishes. **$$–$$$**

Hafið Bláa
Ölfusá Estuary, tel: 483 1000
West of Eyrarbakki, this fabulous fish restaurant has 360-degree views of the sea and estuary. Go for seafood soup, grilled lobster or the catch of the day. **$$$**

Halldórskaffi
Víkurbraut, Vík
Occupying a former 19th-century store, near the beach, this cheerful café-restaurant gets frenetic in summer. **$$**

Kaffi Klettur
Reykholt
Tel: 486 1310
A pleasant choice in sunny weather, this wooden lodge has outdoor tables in a

large green garden. Weekends only Sept-May. **$$**

Kaffi Krús
Austurvegur 7, Selfoss
Tel: 482 1672
A crowded café-bar but a good lunch stop, with bagels, burgers and pasta dishes served up in an atmospheric wooden house. **$–$$**

Lindin Restaurant
Lindarbraut 2, Laugarvatn
Tel: 486 1262
Specialising in wild game and fresh trout, caught daily from the lake on the restaurant's doorstep. **$$–$$$**

Menam
Eyravegur, Selfoss
Tel: 482 4099

A real find in provincial Iceland: a genuine Thai restaurant serving up tasty green curries and superb noodle dishes. **$–$$**

Rauða húsið
Búðarstígur 4, Eyrarbakki
Tel: 483 3330
Eyrarbakki and Stokkseyri boast three of the best restaurants on the south coast, and this is one of the trio: the grilled seafood is particularly impressive. **$$**

The price guide is for the average price of dinner per person, without wine:
$$$ Over ISK4,500
$$ ISK2,500–4,500
$ Under ISK2,500

VESTMANNAEYJAR (THE WESTMAN ISLANDS)

The comparatively recent volcanic origins of this small and scattered group of islands off the southwest coast are clearly visible in their rugged appearance

Main attractions
HEIMAEY
FOLK MUSEUM
ELDFELL
SKANSINN
CLIFFTOP WALK FROM
  HERJÓLFSDALUR

In the earliest years of Iceland's settlement, five Irish slaves ambushed and butchered their master Hjörleifur Hróðmarsson, blood-brother of the first successful settler, Ingólfur Arnarson. Dragging along a handful of slave women, they commandeered a rowing boat and – according to the ancient *Landnámabók (Book of Settlements)* – escaped from their farm near Vík to one of the small green islands visible from the country's south coast.

Not surprisingly, the slaves' newfound freedom was short-lived. Two weeks later, the other Viking settlers tracked them down, stormed their camp and mercilessly put the escapees to death. The whole archipelago is named after this incident: the Vestmannaeyjar (in English, the Westman Islands) is literally translated as "islands of the western men".

Today the Vestmannaeyjar (pronounced, roughly, *vestman-air*) have become one of Iceland's most popular destinations. Comprising 16 small islands and some 30 rocks or skerries, they combine a seductive serenity with raw natural beauty: the archipelago is among the world's newest volcanic creations, and one of its islands, Surtsey, only emerged from the ocean in 1963.

Even Heimaey – the largest of the group and the only one with a permanent human population – is scarred black with fresh volcanic flow from the 1973 eruption that nearly caused it to be permanently abandoned (*see panel on page 187*). The eruption changed the shape of the island forever, adding 15 percent to its area and introducing a new volcanic peak, Eldfell, which now dominates the main town. Sections of Eldfell's slopes still steam and are warm to the touch, and one can easily imagine that this is how the earth looked at the time of its formation.

PRECEDING PAGES: a rocky outcrop on the edge of Heimaey, home to sea-birds.
LEFT: Heimaey beneath the ever-threatening Eldfell volcano.

Violent birth

Although this area off Iceland's southern coast had been the scene of underwater volcanic activity for hundreds of thousands of years, scientists estimate that the first land did not emerge from the sea here until 10,000 years ago, and most islands were not formed until 5,000 years ago – the blink of an eye, in geological terms.

As a result, most of the islands are tiny, rugged and inhospitable. Each is ringed by sheer cliffs, topped with lush vegetation and crowded with sea birds: more species gather here than anywhere else in Iceland. These jagged outcrops are visited only by the islanders, who make treacherous sailings to collect birds' eggs and hunt puffins in spring and summer (most of the puffins caught for food in Iceland are from the Vestmannaeyjar). Their seasonal huts can be seen on the clifftops.

Visitors stay on/in **Heimaey** ⑰ (pronounced "*hay-may*"), the name of both the largest island and its township. Heimaey can be reached by a 25-minute flight from Reykjavík or a 40-minute ferry trip from Bakki south of Hvolsvöl-

lur, which is a two-hour drive from Reykjavík *(see margin, page 189)*.

Heimaey's 4,100 inhabitants are a hardy and independent breed, steeled by generations of isolation, brutal living conditions and an extensive history of disasters. After the Irish slaves' abortive attempt to hide out here, the island was first occupied by a certain Herjólfur Barðursson, a reclusive farmer who had become tired of the constant strife on the mainland. Life was relatively peaceful – if not particularly easy – on the island for several centuries, until it became a target for pirate raids.

As if to repay the islanders for the depredations of their Viking ancestors, a series of cut-throats descended on the Vestmannaeyjar: British pirates ruled the islands for almost a century, and then, in 1627, Barbary corsairs (erroneously identified as 'Turks' by the beleaguered Icelanders) arrived from north Africa. Well into the 20th century, island children were terrified by the tale of the bloodthirsty heathens who put 36 men and women to the sword and carried off more than 200 as slaves. Those who tried to hide in

Signpost with a puffin theme.

BELOW LEFT: the memorial to lost fishermen stands near to Heimaey church (**BELOW**).

*House graveyard –
markers in Heimaey
town indicate the
location and the
history of the
buildings entombed
deep beneath the lava
flow of 1973.*

BELOW:
Heimaey harbour.

the cliffs were shot down like birds.

Epidemics wracked Heimaey for the next couple of centuries, while the 1783 eruption of Laki on the mainland killed off the fish around the islands, reducing its inhabitants to living on sea birds and an edible root called *hvönn* (with plenty falling to their deaths from cliffs in pursuit of both).

Later, fishing accidents would take a dreadful toll: twice, when the island's population was less than 350, storms sent more than 50 men to the bottom of the sea on a single day. In the 19th century, some 100 fishermen from Heimaey drowned, a fact of life which may have accounted for the population's famous sangfroid in the face of the 1973 volcanic eruption.

Fishing capital

Today Heimaey is one of the most important fishing centres in the whole of Iceland, with the efforts of just 1 percent of the country's population producing some 12 percent of its exports. After Reykjavík and Grindavík, Heimaey is the home port of more fishing vessels than any other town in Iceland. A large part of the catch is processed on the island, giving locals a healthy slice of the country's prosperity.

Heimaey town Ⓐ is spread out around the harbour, where over 100 colourful trawlers can dock in the natural windbreak of the lava wall created by the 1973 eruption. The setting is spectacular, with rugged brown bluffs on one side and the two volcanic peaks, Eldfell and Helgafell, on the other. Keep an eye out for the colourful mural painted by school children on the side of a building near the harbour, depicting the fateful morning of the eruption.

East of the harbour, the street Kirkjuvegur runs along the edge of the **1973 lava flow**. Buried beneath this dry, dusky-red mass are 400 of Heimaey's homes and buildings – around one-third of the town was swallowed in the eruption. Steps and pathways have been built onto the convoluted lava fields, here covered with a thin film of green moss, through which the wind whistles eerily. At the edge of the lava, the rather curious **Pompei of the North** project has excavated the ruins of one house, formerly Suðurvegur

25, and aims to dig out another seven as a reminder of the destruction.

With few cars in Heimaey, the streets are empty and peaceful – in fact, their utter desolation on Sundays gives them the haunting feel of a Bergman film. Points of interest include the picturesque white **church**, with a statue commemorating the island's fishermen lost at sea, and the **Folk Museum** (open mid-May–mid-Sept daily 11am–5pm; charge) above the library, which has a well-organised set of relics, model ships and photographs of the 1973 eruption. To see live Icelandic fish (and sometimes puffin chicks in season), visit the **Aquarium and Natural History Museum** (open mid-May–mid-Sept daily 11am–5pm, mid-Sept–mid-May Sun 3–5pm). Particularly odd are the Icelandic cod, which appear to be made of white plastic, and the horrifying Icelandic catfish, a fish that boasts piranha teeth and a bad-tempered, strangely human expression.

Exploring the island

Unless you have brought a car over by ferry from the mainland, or have the time and energy to walk, the easiest way to visit Heimaey's attractions is on one of the bus tours run by Viking Tours (tel: 488 4884).

A rough dirt road has been cut to **Eldfell ❸**, the 221-metre (725ft) -high peak formed during the 1973 eruption. The spectacular view from the base clearly shows how one sixth of the island is now fresh lava flow. The vista stretches across brightly painted corrugated iron roofs to the harbour and, on a clear day, to the mainland. A short walk leads up the barren, steaming tephra slopes. If the ground seems warm to the touch, carefully dig a few inches down – it's hot enough to bake bread, a quirk sometimes demonstrated by Heimaey's tour guides. Roads have also been cut into **Kirkjubæjarhraun ❸**, the 3 sq km (7½-acre) lava field spat up in 1973, but little else disturbs the dark lava's contorted expanse besides geothermal units, heating the town's water and houses.

On the very northwestern edge of the lava flow is Heimaey's most picturesque area **Skansinn**, where a 15th-century fortress once defended the harbour. Next to nothing remains of the structure, but the view is pretty, looking down onto **Landlyst**, once the island's

Stafkirkjan, the stave church.

BELOW LEFT: evacuating the island in 1973.

Crisis on Heimaey

Early on 23 January 1973, a mile-long fissure cracked open without warning on the eastern side of Heimaey, and a wall of molten lava poured out towards the town. Islanders were told to abandon their houses immediately. By great good fortune, the entire Heimaey fishing fleet was in dock that night: some 5,300 people left the island on trawlers and not one life was lost.

Over the next five months, some 33 million tons of lava spewed from the fissure, threatening to devastate the island. Hundreds of tonnes of tephra (volcanic debris) hailed down on the town, smashing windows and igniting houses. By early February the greatest danger was from the 165-metre (500ft) wall of lava moving towards the harbour – the lifeline of the local community. In an attempt to avert disaster, two commercial dredging ships equipped with water cannons pumped over 43 million litres (11½ million gallons) of water a day to cool the lava. Heimaey was covered in a blanket of steam, and the lava flow was stopped before it blocked the harbour entrance. More pumps worked around the clock for the next three months to help cool over 5 million cubic metres (176½ million cubic ft) of lava. Scientists pronounced the eruption over in July, and the residents were able to begin returning home.

The close-knit community on Heimaey – the only one of the Vestmannaeyjar archipelago's 16 islands (plus a further 30 tiny islets) to be permanently inhabited.

BELOW: the three-day Þjóðhátíð party in early August.

maternity hospital; and **Stafkirkjan**, a stave church presented to Heimaey in 2000 by the Norwegian government to celebrate 1000 years of Christianity.

On the other side of town, a road leads past a surreal monument in the shape of giant football, to the lush natural amphitheatre of **Herjólfsdalur D**. This grassy crater was once thought to be the home of the island's first settler, Herjólfur Barðursson, but archaeologists recently unearthed the foundations of Herjólfur's house next to the golf club. These days, Herjólfsdalur is famous as the camping ground where thousands of Icelanders gather around a giant bonfire for three days to celebrate the Þjóðhátíð festival in early August. Pro-

digious feats of drinking make this long weekend a must for many Icelanders, but most foreigners find it a good time to avoid the island.

Puffin cliffs

There are splendid views of several block-shaped islands, including **Hæna**, **Kafhellir** and **Hani**, from the path across the nearby golf course. The cliffs here house the island's most accessible puffin colony. Although the islanders hunt puffins (*see panel on page 190*), their attitude towards these ungainly birds is not entirely mercenary. Late in August every year, tens of thousands of baby puffins leave their nests as darkness falls. Instead of being guided out to sea by the moon, however, some of the fledglings become disorientated by the town's lights and accidentally waddle into the township of Heimaey. To save the pufflings from cats, dogs and cars, Heimaey's children collect them in cardboard boxes and, come daylight, ritualistically fling the birds out to sea – and, hopefully, a successful puffin career. At least they will not end up on island dinner tables until they reach adulthood, since an unwritten law holds that the young puffins should not be eaten.

From Herjólfsdalur, precarious trails requiring mountain equipment lead along the cliffs to the northern promontory of **Ystiklettur**, above the harbour. An easier cliff-side walking path runs parallel to the road south to **Stórhöfði** Ⓔ, where a lighthouse looks out over the exposed coastline. This is officially the windiest place in Iceland: gales of 250kph (150mph) and waves of 23 metres (75ft) have been recorded here during storms.

Boat cruises

A visit to Heimaey would not be complete without an excursion on the waves. A small boat leaves twice-daily from the harbour, bouncing its way around the whole island and finishing with a saxophone solo from the captain inside the echoing Klettshellur sea cave. The trip gives views of Heimaey's steep cliffs crowded with sea birds (gannets, shearwaters, storm petrels, and five species of auk including guillemots and puffins) and usually several sure-footed sheep perched on what appear to be almost vertical green fields. If you're lucky, orcas (killer whales) can be spotted among the smaller islands, their glistening black and white flanks clearly visible as they leap from the waves.

Klettsvík Bay Ⓕ was briefly the home of Keikó, the world-famous killer whale, star of the film *Free Willy*. Captured off the coast of Iceland in 1979, Keikó spent three years in an Icelandic aquarium before being airlifted to Marineland in Niagara Falls, Ontario, where he was trained to perform. After spending seven years as an amusement-park attraction in Mexico, Keikó made his film appearance, which drew public attention to the poor conditions in which he was being kept. Once he had been nursed back to health, in September 1998 the 6.5-metre (21ft) -long animal, weighing about 4,500kg (10,000lb), was airlifted to a special pen in Klettsvík bay, the next stage of releasing him back into the wild. Keikó did manage to swim to Norway in 2002, but sadly died the following year.

The final draw in Heimaey is the **Volcano Show** (mid-May–mid-Sept, two or four shows daily) at the local cinema. This is a documentary film about the volcanic eruption that has become emblematic of the islanders' constant battle with Nature.

Half man, half seal

One night in March 1984, a fishing vessel capsized 5km (3 miles) off Heimaey's coast. All of the crew quickly perished in the freezing winter seas, except for a fisherman named Guðlaugur Friðþórsson. He staved off the confusion of hypothermia by talking to hovering sea birds, and set off swimming for shore. It took him six hours – about five hours longer than anyone else has ever survived in water that temperature.

As if that weren't enough, Guðlaugur swam ashore onto some of the sharpest lava on the island, cutting his feet and losing blood as he stumbled to the town. Doctors could not find his pulse, but the fisherman survived. Later, when the London Hospital Medical College performed tests, Guðlaugur's body fat proved to closely resemble that of a seal. It's a story

TIP

A new harbour, Landeyjarhöfn, near Bakki, has been built 30km southeast of Hvolsvöllur, shortening the distance between the mainland and Heimaey from 40 nautical miles to 7. From Landeyjarhöfn, there are a minimum of four ferries daily in each direction, taking around 40minutes (for details, see page 316).

BELOW: on the ferry deck.

TIP

Since Surtsey is off-limits to all but a small number of research scientists, the only way to get close to the island, though not set foot on it, is on a boat trip organised by Viking Tours (tel: 488 4884). Departures are on request and require a minimum number of passengers. There's a good chance you'll spot whales on the journey, too.

BELOW RIGHT: a puffin hunter with his catch.

that islanders recount fondly, as if to steel themselves for the next skirmish with the sea, the winds or the volcanic peaks that threaten them every day.

The birth of an island

The youngest island, **Surtsey ⑱**, burst from the North Atlantic in a dramatic eruption in 1963. Captured on film by airborne camera crews, highlights of its fiery, four-year-long birth were seen around the world, providing a unique glimpse of how volcanic islands are formed. It is still giving scientists unique and invaluable data on how virgin habitats are colonised by plant and animal life.

The eruption began below the waves in the Mid-Atlantic Ridge, the submarine mountain chain that runs into the south coast of Iceland. Island fishermen were the first to notice smoke rising from the sea in November 1963. Molten lava spewing onto the sea floor was cooling on contact with the icy waters, but soon a pile of volcanic debris had risen the 130 metres (430ft) to the surface to create a burning mass above sea level. A pillar of black ash,

intertwined with a stream of steam, was sent 10km (6 miles) into the air – looking menacing from nearby Heimaey and visible from as far away as Reykjavík. The first flights over the site confirmed that a 16th member of the Vestmannaeyjar was forming: fluid lava was piling up over the mound of tephra and solidifying, turning it from a giant volcanic refuse heap into a permanent presence.

A scientific laboratory

The new island was named after the fiery Norse giant Surtur, who sets the world alight at Ragnarök, the end of the world. For the next four years, until June 1967, Surtsey provided the world's scientific community with the spectacle of its ongoing formation, before finally settling down to an area of 1.57 sq km (½ sq mile) and 155 metres (510ft) in height. During the same period, two smaller islands emerged from the eruption but have since eroded away and disappeared below the waves. Indeed, other islands in the archipelago, which formed in the same way as Surtsey several thousand years ago, have been

Hunting for Puffins

The appealing, stubby-winged puffin is regarded as a particularly mouthwatering delicacy in Iceland, especially in the Vestmannaeyjar. The islanders' affection for the puffin as Iceland's national emblem does not discourage them from seeing it as a source of food – and one which has helped them to survive hard times. Today's puffin-catchers swing nets with 3-metre (10ft) -long handles to catch the birds on the wing – puffins are slightly clumsy in the air. On Heimaey the puffin-catchers can most frequently be seen at work on windy days on top of the cliffs by the golf course in the west of the island. Some 16,000 puffins are caught on the island every summer, destined for the dinner table.

The catchers are careful to avoid catching immature birds so that the colony's numbers are not endangered. The record for a single puffin-catcher is 1,202 birds in one day. Puffin and guillemot, usually under the generic name of *svartifugl* (the Alcidae family of birds), appear on the menus of some of the more adventurous restaurants in Reykjavík. The dark, gamey meat, with a slightly fishy taste, is sometimes served fried or boiled, often with a distinctly exotic curry sauce, or alternatively it may be smoked. It is a great favourite with Icelandic gourmets.

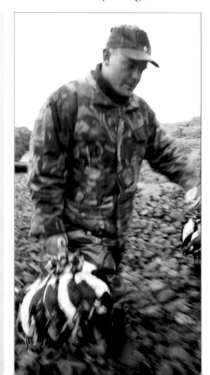

substantially eroded by the heavy seas and the wind since their creation. Surtsey too has been reduced in size by half since its formation, but will probably continue to exist for several centuries before it loses the war against wind and waves and vanishes for good.

Fascinating as Surtsey's formation had been, its greatest scientific value started after the eruption had ended. Its 1,000°C (1,830°F) surface temperatures during the eruption had left it completely free of any living organism: the island became a sort of natural laboratory approximating how Iceland itself must have been when its first segments emerged from the sea some 20 million years ago. In line with its unique scientific status, in 2008 Surtsey was added to the Unesco World Heritage List as an example of a pristine volcanic island and its newly evolving ecosystem.

Seeds arrived on the island in its first summer, carried by the wind, sea and passing sea birds. The first sprouting plants were noticed during the following year, 1965, even before the island's eruption had completely finished. By the end of 1967, no less than four species of plants had established themselves around the coastline.

Midges and flies were the first animals to settle the island, with seals making an appearance after the surrounding seas became restocked with fish. In 1970, black-backed gulls became the first birds to nest on Surtsey. Since that time, scientists have observed 60 bird species on the island – some are just stopping off on their migration to other shores, while others are making this their new home.

Surtsey is still a scientific station and remains off-limits to casual visitors. Any uncontrolled intrusion might upset the island's natural development, either by damaging fragile plant life or accidentally bringing in new presences (a seed caught on a visitor's shoe, for example, might sprout into a plant). Fly-overs in light aircraft, taking about two hours, however, can be organised in Reykjavík (contact tourist office for details, page 341). ❑

BELOW LEFT: Surtsey erupts from the waves during the island's dramatic birth in the 1960s.

RESTAURANTS

Café María
Skólavegur 1, Heimaey
Tel: 481 3160
The most cosmopolitan place to eat in Heimaey with excellent puffin on the menu as well as an array of fish, lamb, pizzas and crêpes. **$$**

Fjólan Restaurant
Vestmannabraut 28, Heimaey
Tel: 481 3663
Next door to Hótel Þórshamar, this high-ceilinged restaurant isn't the cosiest, but service is friendly and there's a good à la carte selection of seafood, fish and meat mains. **$$**

Kökuhús
Bárastígur 7, Heimaey
Great cakes, buns, sandwiches and coffee at this handy bakery in the centre of town. **$**

The price guide is for the average price of dinner per person, without wine:
$$$ Over ISK4,500
$$ ISK2,500–4,500
$ Under ISK2,500

THE SOUTHEAST

In this region overshadowed by the vast Vatnajökull icecap and precariously situated on expanses of glacial debris, the highlight is the rugged and popular Skaftafell area of the Vatnajökull National Park

Icelanders often say that their country was unfairly named, since it is, after all, strikingly green for much of the year – and it is an undeniably odd fact that Iceland and Greenland were christened the wrong way round. But anyone paying a visit to the southeast of the country will have ice on their minds, no matter what the season. The whole area is dominated by Europe's largest icecap, Vatnajökull, whose enormous glaciers creep down through every crack in the coastal mountains like oozing blue putty. Indeed, such is the size of Vatnajökull – as large as the entire English county of North Yorkshire – that driving along its southern flank can take several hours and is one of the most memorable trips this part of the country has to offer. Snout after snout of chiselled ice and snow edges its way down from the icecap tentatively towards the Atlantic, treating visitors to some truly jaw-dropping scenery.

Volcanoes regularly erupt beneath it, devastating farmland with sudden explosive flows of melted ice and debris (known as *jökulhlaups*) as large in volume as the Amazon River. Little wonder then if the Viking explorers – including the First Settler, Ingólfur Arnarson, who spent three years in the southeast – thought the name "Iceland" appropriate.

The damage caused by Vatnajökull's glacial flows made much of the coast next to impassable for centuries. Until the Ring Road was finally driven through in 1974, parts of the southeast were among the remotest in Iceland. To reach Skaftafell or Höfn by land, for example, one had to drive the entire 1,100km (680 miles) around the north of the country.

Today the highway from Reykjavík to the southeast is fully paved, and the glacier-riddled Skaftafell area of the Vatnajökull National Park has become

Main attractions
LAKI AND LAKAGÍGAR CRATERS
SKAFTAFELL
VATNAJÖKULL ICECAP
JÖKULSÁRLÓN GLACIAL LAGOON
GLACIER EXHIBITION, HÖFN

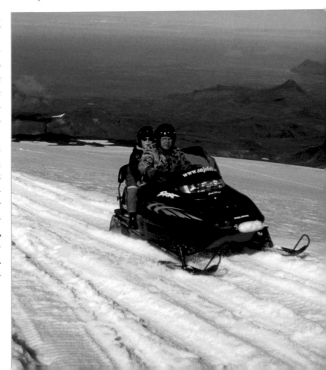

PRECEDING PAGES: Jökulsárlón glacial lagoon. **LEFT:** Skaftafellsjökull reflected in a lake in Skaftafell, part of Vatnajökull National Park. **RIGHT:** skidooing.

the most popular wilderness area in the country. (In fact, on June and July weekends, it becomes so crowded that it is probably best avoided by travellers.) Meanwhile, the drive along the coast passes a luxuriant, haunting landscape dotted with tiny farms and historic settlements.

Systrakaffi, the place for a bite in Kirkjuæjarklaustur.

Curse of the Irish monks

The gateway to the southeast is the town of **Kirkjubæjarklaustur** ❶ (call it "cloister" and you will be understood). This is a green oasis in the volcanic desert formed by the eruptions of the Laki craters in 1783 – an event that devastated Iceland and is still considered to be one of the worst natural disasters in recorded history.

Kirkjubæjarklaustur was first settled by Irish monks, who fled the Vikings but left a curse that no pagan would ever live here. A Christian Norseman named Ketill the Foolish (so named by his peers for converting from the worship of Thor) lived on the site quite happily for many years. But when another Viking,

Hildir Eysteinsson, decided to move in, he no sooner clapped eyes on his future farm than he dropped down dead. Perhaps, reasoned the Norsemen, Ketill had not been so foolish after all.

Religion plays a big part in the rest of Kirkjubæjarklaustur's history. In 1186, Benedictine nuns set up a convent here (*klaustur* means cloister), which was closed in the 16th-century Reformation. It can't have been a model institution, since two of the nuns were burned at the stake: one for sleeping with the devil, the other for maligning the Pope.

Contemporaneous with the nuns' convent at Kirkjubær, was the monastery at Þykkvibær, a short distance away. It is said that the abbot and the monks of Þykkvibær often went up to Kirkjubær to see the mother superior and the sisters. On one such occasion both the abbot and some of the monks spent the night at Kirkjubær. The story goes that in the middle of the night the mother superior went with a light to check on the propriety of the sisters' conduct. In one cell, she came upon a monk and a nun sleeping together. The mother superior was about to reprimand the nun when the

The Southeast

latter noticed her superior's headgear and said: "What is that you have on your head, dear mother?" Then the mother superior realised that she had taken the abbot's underpants by mistake and put them on her head instead of her bonnet. As a result, she softened her voice, saying as she retreated: "We are all sinners, sister".

During the 1783 Laki eruptions, a wall of lava looked like wiping out the settlement when the local curate, Jón Steingrímsson, herded everyone into the wooden church. There he delivered the ultimate fire-and-brimstone sermon whose effect, with great chunks of ash smashing down just outside the window, can only be imagined. When the sermon had finished, the congregation stumbled outside to find that the lava had been diverted and the church saved. The modern **Steingrímsson memorial chapel** has been built on the old church's site to commemorate this neat piece of divine intervention.

Today Kirkjubæjarklaustur is a pretty but somnolent outpost of 117 people, with the waterfall **Systrafoss** spraying down from steep cliffs as its backdrop.

The 1783 lava fields, dotted with pseudo-craters, can still be seen just south of town, en route to the curious **Kirkjugólf** – the name means "church floor", since Viking settlers assumed it was part of a stone floor built by the curse-happy Irish monks. It is, however, a natural formation, with the tops of hexagonal basalt columns fitting together as perfectly as tiles.

Most people stay in Kirkjubæjarklaustur as a jumping-off point to the infamous **Laki volcano** ❷ and its 2.5km- (1½-mile) -long crater row **Lakagígar**, responsible for the 1783 eruptions. Over a period of 10 months, 30 billion tons of lava and three times as much sulphuric acid belched forth from the so-called "Skaftá fires". Not only were whole communities wiped out by the flow, but Laki sent up a cloud of noxious gas that began the "Haze Famine" and killed a fifth of Iceland's already much-diminished population and half its livestock – a toll so dramatic that plans were made to evacuate the island completely. Today Laki is extinct, but the craters at its base are still steaming. There are some fantastic views to be had from the peak.

TIP

Laki can be reached only by four-wheel-drive vehicles. Tours run there daily in summer from Kirkjubæjarklaustur.

BELOW: Svartifoss.

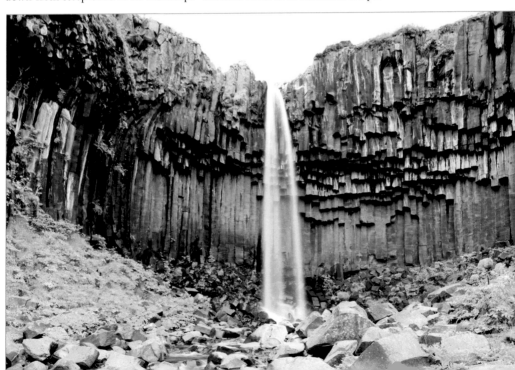

The mountain and its unearthly craters, a surprisingly fragile environment in spite of their devastating history, nestle within the protective boundaries of Vatnajökull National Park.

The Ring Road east of Kirkjubæjarklaustur runs to the attractive farm of **Foss**, named for the thin waterfall flowing from the cliffs on the property, followed by the basalt columns of **Dverghamrar**. A sunken plain of moss-covered lava – once again created by Laki – must be crossed before finding the farm of **Núpsstaður** ❸, at the base of the imposing 770-metre (2,500ft) cliff called **Lómagnúpur** ("loon peak"). Núpsstaður has one of Iceland's most charming 17th-century churches and a still-working antique harmonium.

At this point begins **Skeiðarársandur** ❹, the biggest of the southern *sandurs* – great wastelands of black sand and glacial debris carried out by volcanic eruptions from underneath Vatnajökull. Before the Ring Road was built, the only way across here was on horseback, accompanied by one of the farmers from Núpsstaður who had spent their lives learning to navigate the treacherous terrain. Today, cyclists dread this stretch of road most in Iceland: it is completely monotonous, and regular sandstorms make any open-air activity a misery.

Long bridges and flood barriers have been built to counteract any further glacial flows created by eruptions of **Grímsvötn**; although located under Vatnajökull, it is the most active and potentially lethal of Iceland's many volcanic craters. The last eruption under the ice began at the end of September 1996. More than two months later, on the morning of November 5th, the long-awaited glacial burst began. Large parts of Skeiðarársandur disappeared under black and muddy floodwater, electric cables across the sands were destroyed, as was the main road itself. The bridges over the Sæluhúsakvísl and Gígja rivers were swept away, and the 906-metre (2,980ft) -long bridge over the River Skeiðará was badly damaged. South of the road the flood carried immense amounts of sediment to the sea and the beach stretched 800 metres (2,600ft) further out into the ocean than it had before the flood. Two days later, when the burst came to an end, a million tons of ice had broken

BELOW: snapping the view at Vatnajökull glacier.

away from the margin of Skeiðarárjökull glacier, which dominates the view on the north side of the road. Since the glacial burst, the bridges and road have been renewed and restored.

Skaftafell

Approached from the west, **Skaftafell** ❺, the most popular area of Vatnajökull National Park, is announced by views over its rugged peaks and the three glaciers that have worked their way between them: from the left, **Morsárjökull**, **Skaftafellsjökull** and **Svínafellsjökull**. The twin glaciers of **Kvíárjökull** and **Fjallsjökull** can be seen further on. These are all dwarfed by **Öræfajökull**, a glacier whose peak, **Hvannadalshnúkur**, is the highest in Iceland at 2,110 metres (6,700ft). All are fingers of the icecap **Vatnajökull** which, like other icecaps in Iceland, is believed to have been formed not during the Ice Age but in another cold period just 2,500 years ago.

Skaftafell National Park was established in 1967 and expanded in 1984 to take up some 1,600 sq km (580 sq miles). In June 2008, this protected area became part of the newly created Vatnajökull National Park – at a mighty 8,300 sq km (3,200 sq miles), covering 12 percent of Iceland's total area, Vatnajökull is now Europe's largest national park.

Settlers first came to Skaftafell in the Saga Age, and there are still two farms here, one of which now operates as a simple bunkbed-and-washbasin guesthouse. The park service operates an **Information Centre** ❶ and café next to a parking area and large camping ground. On summer weekends, this becomes a cross between a particularly raucous Reykjavík pub and a refugee camp, so anyone interested in communing with nature should come on a weekday.

All walks into the park depart from this point. The easiest is to the snout of the glacier **Skaftafellsjökull** ❸, less than half an hour away. Covered in volcanic refuse, the ice is actually a shiny grey, like graphite. You can climb onto the edge of the glacier, but be careful. It's slippery – and a fall would dunk you straight into a near-freezing meltwater stream that soon disappears underground. If you want to get up onto the glaciers, it's best to book a guided walk: in summer, two companies operate staffed huts in Skaftafell car park that offer guided walks with crampons and ice axes.

The most photographed attraction in Skaftafell is **Svartifoss** ❸, a short walk into the park. The waterfall is surrounded on both sides by black basalt columns, giving it a grand organ-pipe effect and its name ("Black Waterfall"). The path continues on to the peak of **Sjónarsker** ❹ and then further into the mountains: the more energetic can make a day-trip to include views of Morsárjökull and Skaftafellsjökull, which look like twin seas of ice.

In the **Morsárdalur** valley, surrounded by high mountains and huge icecaps, you will also find one of the most impressive woods of the country, with birches reaching a height of 10 metres (33ft). It's in this area, too, that you'll find one of Iceland's many natural hot pools: across the Morsá River and a short hike up the hillside behind, a trail leads to a sublime geothermal source

Exploring glaciers calls for special equipment.

Vatnajökull Icecap

Vatnajökull, 1,000 metres (3,300ft) thick in parts, is the largest icecap in the world outside of those countries which are designated as polar regions.

At first sight Vatnajökull displays a general resemblance to the main polar ice sheets, but its nature is quite different. This is a so-called temperate glacier. Its temperature is at melting point, or very close to it, at any given depth. The exception is in the top layers, where frost may remain until far into the summer, although the timing for that is subject to variations.

During the first centuries after settlement the glaciers of Vatnajökull were smaller than they are now, but towards the end of the 12th century the climate began to cool and the ice started to expand. Vatnajökull's glaciers reached their greatest extent during the 18th and 19th centuries. Since 1890 however, they have withdrawn and thinned, especially during the period from 1920–60. Between 1960 and into the 1990s, Vatnajökull thickened and the recession of its glaciers slowed, although global warming is now starting to reverse this trend at alarming speed – a recent report by Iceland's climate change committee forecasts that all of Iceland's glaciers will have vanished by 2150.

which has been dammed to create a small round pond where weary hikers can cast off their clothes and steam to their heart's content while enjoying an unsurpassed view of the unsullied expanses of the national park – a quintessentially Icelandic experience.

The Information Centre can give instructions for other day trips into the park. Nature lovers can spot over 200 species of plants around Skaftafell as well as Iceland's usual plethora of birds. The surrounding Skeiðarársandur wasteland is also one of the most important breeding areas for great skuas in the northern hemisphere.

The lake of ice

East of Skaftafell along the Ring Road is the farm **Svínafell**, which was the home of Flosi Þórðarson, the murderer of Njáll and his family in *Njáls Saga*, followed by **Hof ❻**, which offers picturesque farmhouse accommodation and has a small turf church. It is near here that the First Settler, Ingólfur Arnarson, lived before moving to Reykjavík – the promontory of **Ingólfshöfði** marks the site. It was here that Ingólfur spent his first winter

in Iceland before setting off in search of his high seat pillars, which he had tossed in the water as he approached the Icelandic coast. (The posts, an important symbol of power, were later discovered where Reykjavík is located today.) In clear weather, this flat headland is the first glimpse of Iceland that most visitors get since the promontory is where Iceland-bound planes usually touch down. The headland is now a **nature reserve**, perfect for birdwatchers, and is accessed by the most unusual method – by guided haycart tour across the blacksand estuary. Bird-watching is at its best during the breeding season in May and June, although trips depart from the farm **Hofsnes** until August.

Immediately after a suspension bridge over the Jökulsá River is one of Iceland's most photographed sights: the iceberg-filled lake of **Jökulsárlón ❼**. The ice has calved from the glacier Breiðamerkurjökull, which runs into the lake, burying its snout underwater. The lake was formed only when the passage to the sea was blocked by land movements in the 20th century: geologists suggest it could come unblocked in the near future,

BELOW: boat trips on Jökulsárlón can be booked at the lagoon, or beforehand through Vatnajökull Travel (tel: 894 1616) who will also provide bus transportation to and from the nearby town of Höfn. There are departures several times daily in summer.

draining the lake and making the Ring Road impassable. Boat cruises operate around Jökulsárlón several times daily in summer, weaving among the glistening ice formations. Sometimes the guide on the boat fishes out of the water a small piece of the astonishingly dense, clear ice so that you can have a closer look.

James Bond fans may get a sense of déjà vu at Jökulsárlón – the opening scenes of the film *A View to a Kill* were shot here.

Excursions on the icecap

East of Jökulsárlón, a turn-off to the left advertises trips to **Jöklaferðir** at the top of Vatnajökull. The road itself is passable only by four-wheel-drive vehicles, but those without such transport can meet the bus from Höfn at the car park here, every morning at 9.30am from June to August for the ride up. A small chalet has been built at the edge of the icecap, and hire of snowcats can be arranged. It's not entirely environmentally sound – so much noise and the first touches of air pollution on the pristine icecap. On a clear day, you can see for miles across the white sea of Vatnajökull, and trips usually include a stop at a ravine.

The river valleys along this part of the Ring Road are beautiful but thinly populated, and the flatlands of **Mýrar** ⑧ are excellent for birdwatching. On one farm here, **Bjarnanes**, a troll woman named Ketillaug is said to have been seen taking a kettle of gold up into the multi-coloured alluvial mountain **Ketillaugarfjall**. There is one day of the year when humans can try and take the kettle from her, but those that attempt it are subject to hallucinations – typically of the farm below catching fire – and always run back to give the alarm.

Höfn

The southeast's administrative centre, with a population of about 1,600, is **Höfn** ⑨. The name means "harbour" and indeed it has one of the few in the southeast. The town's fortunes improved rapidly with the completion of the Ring Road in the 1970s, turning it from a one-horse town to its present, ungainly concrete self. But what it lacks in aesthetic appeal is made up for by its beautiful setting on **Hornafjörður** fjord, which is almost completely cut off from the sea by spits to form a tranquil lake. The spits can be further explored by organised boat and quad-bike tours from town.

There is a **Folk Museum** (open mid-May–mid-Sept daily 1–5pm; free) with a mixture of exhibits from around the region, but much more interesting is the **Glacier Exhibition** (Hafnarbraut 30; June–Aug daily 10am–6pm, May and Sept daily 1–6pm, Oct–Apr Mon–Fri 1–4pm; charge), which has an amazing film of the 1996 eruption under Vatnajökull and the ensuing flood which washed away part of the Ring Road. Upstairs you'll be able to watch a couple of short video clips from the James Bond films, *A View to a Kill*, and *Die Another Day*, which were filmed around the nearby glacial lagoon, Jökulsárlón. From Höfn it's also possible to arrange a "glacier tour" of Vatnajökull which includes snowcatting and a visit to the glacial lagoon in a single, easy trip. ❏

RESTAURANTS

Fosshótel Skaftafell
Freysnes, Skaftafell
Tel: 478 1945
Fairly-priced meat and fish dishes are served every evening inside the hotel restaurant. $$

Hótel Klaustur
Klausturvegur 6,
Kirkjubæjarklaustur
Tel: 487 4900
Fine dining inside the Icelandair-run hotel. $$$

Humarhöfnin
Hafnarbraut 4, Höfn
Tel: 478 1200
Höfn is famous for its langoustines,

which are the speciality of this cosy restaurant in the town's old co-operative building. $$$

Kaffi Hornið
Hafnabraut 42, Höfn
Tel: 478 2600
The cosiest choice in Höfn, this log cabin by the main road serves large, flavoursome portions of pasta, burgers and fresh fish. $$

Ósinn
Víkurbraut 20 Höfn
Tel: 478 2200
This pleasant restaurant inside Hótel Höfn has good value

buffet dinners. $$

Systrakaffi
Klausturvegur 13,
Kirkjubæjarklaustur.
Tasty homemade cakes and buns at the village's one and only cafe-cum-restaurant. Also serves more expensive dinners. $–$$

The price guide is for the average price of dinner per person, without wine:

$$$ Over ISK4,500
$$ ISK2,500–4,500
$ Under ISK2,500

AN EVER-CHANGING LANDSCAPE

From volcanoes to glaciers, Iceland is home to a concentration of nature's wonders, both hot and cold, greater than in any other place on earth

In 1963, the island of Surtsey exploded out of the sea off Iceland in a great arch of flame and lava. It was only the latest natural wonder in Iceland's long, turbulent life. The Mid-Atlantic Ridge, which runs through the middle of the country from southwest to northeast, is the cause of the geothermal activity that has shaped much of Iceland's geology and unique landscape. Equally responsible are the thousands of years of glaciation, and the glacial meltwater, which together have modified the land.

The area close to the Mid-Atlantic Ridge has the greatest number of volcanoes: all around smoke and steam rise constantly. Here can be found spouting geysers, hot springs and craters – both active, like those near Mývatn, and inactive, solidified into fantastic lava shapes or filled with calm lakes. In some areas the ground is still very warm, and Icelanders may even use a small covered pit as an oven to bake a delicious speciality – lava bread.

At the other end of the scale are glaciers, many of which pour like frozen torrents from the icecap Vatnajökull. One of these glaciers, Breiðamerkurjökull, creates a particularly photogenic scene: when it calves (when a mass of ice breaks off), it fills the nearby Jökulsárlón lake with icebergs. The glaciers are bleak and dramatic moonscapes of peaks, crevasses and a surprising range of colours from dirty black to pure icy blue. Meltwater feeds many of the powerful waterfalls that are also a feature of this dramatic land.

ABOVE: visitors are fascinated by the burst of water and steam that spouts to a height of around 20 metres (66ft) from the Strokkur geyser, roughly every 10 minutes.

ABOVE: the pseudo-craters of Mývatn – one of the most volcanically active regions on earth – come in hugely varying sizes, formed when lava flowed over wetlands.

BELOW: Dettifoss is Europe's most powerful waterfall, dropping 44 thunderous metres (145ft) into a canyon in Jökulsárgjufur, part of the northeastern section of Vatnajökull National Park.

THE NORTHERN LIGHTS

The bewitching aurora borealis, commonly known as the Northern Lights, flashes, flickers and pulses across the winter sky like silent fireworks. This eerie green lightshow, sometimes tinged with purples, pinks and reds, has been the source of many a high-latitude superstition: the Vikings, for example, believed it was the Valkyries riding across the sky. The scientific explanation is no less astonishing. The lights are actually caused by streams of charged particles – "solar wind" – that flare into space from our sun. When the wind comes into contact with the Earth's magnetic field, it is drawn towards the Poles where its electrical charge agitates particles of oxygen and nitrogen in the atmosphere, making them glow.

Solar activity follows an 11-year cycle, which is due to reach its peak again from 2011 to 2012. In Iceland, the lights are best seen between November and April…but as with all natural phenomena, sightings are not guaranteed. Choose a cold, clear moonless night, and a place with minimal light pollution; then look heavenwards and hope.

BELOW: viewed from afar, some of Iceland's icecaps appear smooth and white. Up close, areas are pushed into peaks or pitted with streams, and are often streaked with old volcanic ash or scrapings of grey-black rock.

BELOW: Skútustaðagígar, the pseudo-craters on the southern shore of Lake Mývatn, come in hugely varying sizes, formed when lava flowed over the wetlands.

SNÆFELLSNES AND THE WEST

This large area between Reykjavík and the West Fjords is easy to explore and has a variety of places to visit, from sites associated with the sagas to remote fishing villages

Reykjavík

Icelanders, in their more lyrical moments, are apt to dub their homeland the Saga Isle. This description is particularly appropriate for the Snæfellsnes peninsula and the West, where some of the most dramatic events of the sagas took place. Names of farms, villages and towns conjure up the presence of historical characters such as the warrior-poet Egill Skallagrímsson and the chieftain and scholar Snorri Sturluson. Along these shores, constantly swept by the wind and the rain, occurred the terrifying hauntings of *Eyrbyggja Saga* and the tragic romance of *Laxdæla Saga*.

The West echoes with historic and literary associations, but the jewel in its crown is the work of nature alone: the Snæfellsjökull icecap, at the western end of the Snæfellsnes peninsula. At 1,446 metres (4,743ft), the glacier dominates the surrounding countryside. From as far away as Reykjavík, 100km (60 miles) to the south across Faxaflói bay, Snæfellsjökull can be seen when the weather is clear, shimmering on the northern horizon.

North from Reykjavík

The glacier-bound traveller setting out from the capital can choose from two routes for the first leg of the journey to the north: either to follow the scenic coast road as it stretches 20km (12 miles) east and then the same distance west

again along the sides of Hvalfjörður fjord; or to take the shortcut through the 6km (3¾-mile) toll tunnel under Hvalfjörður.

Taking Route 1, the Ring Road north out of Reykjavík, a detour east on Route 36 leads to two famous farms: **Laxness** where the writer Halldór Laxness was born; and **Mosfell**, where saga figure Egill Skallagrímsson died – supposedly after ordering his slaves to bury his treasure, and then slaughtering them to ensure secrecy. The Ring Road leads along the roots of **Mount Esja**, 918 metres (3,011ft) high, before turning into **Hvalfjörður**. In

Main attractions
SETTLEMENT CENTRE OF ICELAND
REYKHOLT
HÚSAFELL
SURTSHELLIR
SNÆFELLSJÖKULL
STYKKISHÓLMUR
FLATEY

PRECEDING PAGES: the coast at Arnarstapi.
LEFT: the church at Búðir. **RIGHT:** sightseeing at Breiðafjörður bay.

The view looking east along the Snæfellsnes peninsula from Arnarstapi.

the mountains at the head of the fjord, about an hour's walk above the road, is Iceland's highest waterfall, **Glymur ❶**, at 198 metres (650ft). The modern church at **Saurbær ❷** on the northern coast of Hvalfjörður is dedicated to the memory of Iceland's greatest devotional poet, Reverend Hallgrímur Pétursson, who served this parish in the 1600s.

On the peninsula at the northern side of the fjord lies the town of **Akranes ❸** (population 6,500), offering hotels, guesthouse accommodation and restaurants. About one kilometre to the east in **Garðar** is an interesting **Folk Museum** (daily June–Aug 10am–5pm, Sept–May 1–5pm; charge), with the emphasis on maritime history and a good collection of boats. In the ancient **cemetery** is a stone given to Iceland by the Irish government in 1974, to commemorate 1,100 years of settlement: an inscription in Icelandic and Gaelic remembers the role of Irish monks in the island's discovery.

Continuing north, the town of **Borgarnes ❹**, near the mouth of **Borgarfjörður** fjord, has grown up close to the very spot, **Borg**, where Egill Skallagrímsson lived in the 10th century. The son of one of the first Norse settlers, Egill was a paradoxical figure: a fierce and often cruel Viking warrior, he was also a great poet in the *skaldic* tradition of intricate word-play and metaphor. A striking new multimedia exhibition at Borgarnes, the **Settlement Centre of Iceland** (daily June–Aug 10am–7pm, Sept–May 11am–5pm; charge), uses the sagas to explore Iceland's early history. Half of the centre is dedicated to Egill, and uses rough-hewn sculptures and dra-

Snæfellsnes and the West

0   20 km
0   20 miles

matic sound and lighting to depict key moments in his violent life.

These vignettes are taken, of course, from one of the country's best-loved sagas, *Egils Saga*, which preserves the warrior's poetry for posterity, and was probably written by one of his descendants, Snorri Sturluson *(see panel on page 42)*. In 1241, Snorri was ambushed and murdered by his enemies on the orders of the King of Norway at his home at **Reykholt** ❺ – today a tiny hamlet some 36km (22 miles) east of Borgarnes on Route 30.

Snorri's farmstead is long gone, but a hot pool remains where the scholar and chieftain once bathed *(see page 88)*. A tunnel (now partly restored) led from the pool to the farmhouse. A modern statue commemorates Snorri's masterly *Heimskringla (History of the Norwegian Kings)*, which saved centuries of Norwegian history from oblivion, and a research centre in the village gives a detailed insight into Snorri's life and turbulent times.

Lava caves and waterfalls

The green, rolling country of Borgarfjörður is at its most beautiful up beyond Reykholt. **Hraunfossar** is a multitude of tiny cascades tumbling into the Hvítá river along a 1km (½-mile) stretch. A footbridge crosses the river at the churning **Barnafoss** waterfall, where the Hvítá flows through a rugged chasm. At nearby **Húsafell** ❻, summerhouses cluster in one of Iceland's largest woods. Húsafell farm is first mentioned in *Laxdæla Saga*. Its most famous occupant was Snorri Björnsson, who lived here at the end of the 18th century. Besides being a well-known sorcerer he was said to have tried his strength on the 180-kg (400-lb) boulder **Kvíahella**, which still can be seen close to the pens that he built.

The area is full of geothermal water. In Húsafell alone you will find two swimming pools, three hot pools, a water slide and a steam bath. Near the farmhouse is an open-air exhibition of the sculptures of Páll Guðmundsson, who lives and works in Húsafell, using stones collected from river gorges in the nearby mountains.

Hidden beneath **Hallmundarhraun**

lava field lies Iceland's largest lava cave, **Surtshellir**, 1.5km (1 mile) in length. Signposted from the road, the cave is found by following a marked trail. Good shoes and torches are essential for exploring. Surtshellir was already known in the Saga Age, when a band of outlaws lived in the cave. It took some time for the farmers to overcome them, and place names refer to this time in history – for example Vopnalág ("weapons hollow") and Eiríksgnípa ("Erik's pike"). Ancient traces of human habitation can still be seen today. Close to Surtshellir is another cave, **Stefánshellir**, which also makes an interesting tour. A third cave in the area, called **Víðgelmir**, was closed to visitors at the time of writing.

West to the peninsula

To the west along paved Route 54 from Borgarnes lies the Snæfellsnes peninsula and its mysterious glacier. The first landmark is **Eldborg** ❼, a perfectly symmetrical scoria crater 112 metres (367ft) high, formed in a volcanic eruption 5–8,000 years ago. The crater, which commands magnificent views, is about 40 minutes' walk from the main road.

Bringing Iceland's early history to life at the Settlement Centre of Iceland, in Borgarnes.

BELOW: early exploration of the Surtshellir lava cave, *c.*1860.

BELOW RIGHT: the start of the descent at Snæfellsjökull in Jules Verne's *Journey to the Centre of the Earth*.

The **Kerlingarskarð** pass along Route 55, which reaches 311 metres (1,020ft) above sea level, was once a hazardous trail which claimed many lives in bad weather. Tales of ghostly apparitions have long been attributed to it, and even today stories are told of travellers who sense the presence of an "extra passenger" in the car as they cross the pass.

A peculiarity of the Snæfellsnes peninsula is its mineral springs, producing naturally fizzy water – a rarity elsewhere in the country. Probably the most famous is on **Ölkelda** farm (literally "ale spring", the Icelandic name for a mineral spring) near **Staðarstaður** ❽ on the south side of the peninsula. Staðarstaður is believed to have been the residence of Ari the Learned (1068–1148), author of the *Book of Icelanders*, one of the most important sources on the nation's early history.

At the horse farm **Lýsuhóll**, mineral water is found in a geothermal area: it produces hot, bubbly water, which is used to heat a swimming pool. **Búðir** ❾, once an important fishing centre, became better known for the hotel of the same name, now rebuilt having been destroyed by fire in 2001. **Arnarstapi** ❿ and **Hellnar** ⓫,

small fishing villages beneath the Snæfellsjökull glacier, are famed for their strange rock formations and their birdlife. Close to Hellnar is a sea cave, **Baðstofa** ("farmhouse loft"), where bizarre effects of light and colour are seen. Opposite the cave, on the beach, a small coffee-shop is run in the summer by the locals. Adjacent to Hellnar is the now-deserted farm of Laugarbakki, birthplace of Guðríður Þorbjarnardóttir, one of the heroines of the Norse discovery of Greenland around AD 1000. She emigrated to Greenland as a young girl, then later settled with her husband, Karlsefni, in Vínland, the Norse colony in North America, where she gave birth to her son Snorri, the first white child to be born in North America. Natural wonders at Arnarstapi include **Sönghellir** ("song cave"), with remarkable acoustics, and a huge stone arch. Sea birds nest on the cliffs in their thousands.

The focus of the peninsula, the **Snæfellsjökull glacier** ⓬, can be approached from Arnarstapi to the south or Ólafsvík to the north, although the former is easiest. The summit is four to five hours' walk; or you could drive part way along the F570 (if you have your own car: hire

Journey to the Centre of the Earth

During the late 19th century, the book *Journey to the Centre of the Earth* by French writer and pioneer of science fiction, Jules Verne, became essential reading. Published in 1864, it tells the story of the German geologist, Professor Lidenbrock of Hamburg, and his nephew Axel (called Harry in some English translations), who discover a coded message about a path into the centre of the earth which descends from the Snæfellsjökull in Iceland. With their Danish-speaking guide (Iceland was part of Denmark at this time), the three intrepid explorers descend into the bowels of the earth and embark on a remarkable adventure. Their subterranean world is filled by an immense ocean and after encounters with unsavoury monsters, a prehistoric human and a powerful maelstrom, the book's heroes are finally swept upwards to the earth's surface, emerging on the volcanic island of Stromboli off southern Italy.

Snæfellsjökull is an active volcano, with its last eruption (a major one) taking place around 1,800 years ago. The mountain's explosive past has riddled its surface with lava formations, craters and a large number of caves – the likely inspiration for it as Verne's choice as the portal into the earth's interior. The distinctive shape, and impressive bulk, of the mountain has also imbued it with a natural mystique bound to stimulate a novelist's imagination.

cars are not usually insured for F-roads) and then walk; or join a snowmobile tour run by the Arnarstapi-based company Snjófell (www.snjofell.is). The rutted stretch of road from Ólafsvík really requires a 4WD vehicle. The walk up to the glacier itself is fairly easy, but in summer a guided walk is recommended for the glacier itself, as crevasses start to open up in the ice; global warming means that increasingly glacier walks only run until late July. The highest of the three mountain peaks is difficult to scale without special climbing gear. A ski lift goes partway up the mountain in winter.

Test your strength

Further down the coast from Hellnar, by **Malarrif**, stand two lofty pillars of rock, **Lóndrangar**. The taller, 75 metres (248ft) high, is called "Christian pillar", and the lower is "heathen pillar". While fishing remains the livelihood of the peninsula, some communities have now disappeared, leaving only traces of the centuries of fishing seasons: 60 boats used to row out from **Dritvík** ⓭, for example, where today there is nothing left but spectacular wilderness – including the great rock

formation called **Tröllakirkja** ("church of the trolls").

Those who wish to try out their muscle-power in true Icelandic tradition should stroll along the shore from Dritvík to Djúpalón where four boulders present an age-old test of strength. The aim is to lift them up onto a ledge of rock at about hip height. The largest, *Fullsterkur* ("full strength") is 155kg (341lbs), the second, *Hálfsterkur* ("strong enough"), 140kg (308lbs), the third, *Hálfdraettingur* ("half strength"), 49kg (108lbs) and the last, *Amlóði* ("weakling") 23kg (50lbs). *Amlóði*, unfortunately, is now broken. Lifting at least *Hálfsterkur* was a requirement for joining the crew of a boat from Dritvík.

Ólafsvík and Stykkishólmur

Now a deserted farm and church just inland from Rif, **Ingjaldshóll** was once a major manor and regional centre. Just to the east, **Ólafsvík** ⓮ is one of the larger communities on the peninsula with a population of 1,005. It is also Iceland's first established trading town, granted its charter in 1687. Ólafsvík offers a hotel,

Snæfellsjökull looms large over the western end of the peninsula.

BELOW: natural arch at Arnarstapi.

TIP

Breiðafjörður bay, off the north coast of the Snæfellsnes peninsula, is one of the best places in Iceland for seeing rare white-tailed sea eagles and other birdlife. Boat trips run from Stykkishólmur from mid-May to mid-September. Book through Seatours, tel: 433 2254.

guesthouse, golf course and swimming pool. An old merchant's storehouse from 1844 has been restored and houses the local tourist office and **museum** (open daily June–Aug 11am–5pm; charge).

Stykkishólmur ⑮ is the principal town on the Snæfellsnes peninsula and the starting point for those who are going to the West Fjords by ferry. Nearby is **Helgafell ⑯** ("holy mountain"), a 73-metre (240ft) hill. According to local folklore, those who climb Helgafell for the first time will have three wishes come true, provided a few conditions are observed: you must not look back or speak on the way; you must make your wishes facing east; you must not tell anyone what they are; and only benevolent wishes are allowed. Even if your wishes are not fulfilled, Helgafell is worth climbing for the spectacular views of **Breiðafjörður** bay.

Helgafell has, in fact, always been considered supernaturally charged. The first settler here, Þórólfur Mostraskegg, built a wooden temple to Thor at its summit. His son, the curiously named Þorstein Cod-Biter, claimed that on Helgafell he was able to see Valhalla, where dead Norse warriors drank with the gods.

In the 10th century, Helgafell became a Christian holy mountain with its own church built by Snorri the Priest. According to the *Eyrbyggja Saga*, a long blood-feud was sparked off when a certain family group, unmindful of Helgafell's religious significance, used it as a toilet. Helgafell is supposedly also where Guðrún Ósvífursdóttir, heroine of *Laxdæla Saga*, lived out her last years as a hermit.

Stykkishólmur offers two hotels, guest-houses and youth-hostel accommodation. Bird-watching or sea-angling trips out onto the fjord from Stykkishólmur harbour are a highlight of a visit here. The local **Folk Museum** (open June–Aug daily 11am–5pm; charge) is housed in a beautifully restored timber house dating from 1828. Known simply as the **Norwegian House**, it was imported in kit form from Norway. Stykkishólmur's new church overlooks the town. Newer still is the **Volcano Museum** (Eldfjallasafn; open daily mid-May–mid-Sept 11am–5pm; charge), set up in 2010 by a local volcanologist to give visitors an insight into Iceland's explosive character.

Sub-arctic archipelago

The car/passenger ferry *Baldur* plies Breiðafjörður between Stykkishólmur and Brjánslækur in the West Fjords, calling at the island of **Flatey ⑰** *(see page 316 for details)*. Breiðafjörður is dotted with about 2,700 islands, which once supported a large population thanks to the abundant fisheries. Flatey was the site of a 12th-century monastery and a major cultural centre until the 1800s. One of the greatest treasures of Icelandic literature, *Flateyjarbók* (the Flatey Book), was preserved here for centuries before being presented to the Danish king in the 16th century. In 1971 it returned to Iceland.

The islanders gradually deserted their remote homes during the early part of the 20th century, and few remain. Flatey, though, is a delight, a perfectly preserved example of what an Icelandic village used to be. While the island is all but uninhabited in winter, many families spend their summers there renovating the lovely old timber houses of their ancestors. A

BELOW: the Volcano Museum in Stykkishólmur.

triumph of painstaking restoration is Iceland's oldest, and smallest, library (4.75 metres by 3.43 metres, or 15ft 6in by 11ft 3in), built in 1844 to house the collection of the Flatey Progress Society.

Viking romance

North of the Snæfellsnes peninsula is **Hvammsfjörður** fjord, with the village of **Búðardalur** at its head. Route 59 runs along **Laxárdalur** (Salmon River Valley). This is saga country, and almost every place name strikes a chord for Icelanders. In the **Haukadalur** valley (Route 586) is the site of the farm **Eiríksstaðir**, the home of Erik the Red, dicoverer of Greenland, and birthplace of his son Leifur Eiríksson. A replica **longhouse** (open daily June–Aug 9am–6pm; charge) at the site – a turf lodge built using traditional tools and materials, with central fireplace and a seating ledge set into the 1.5-metres (5-ft) thick walls – gives visitors a sense of how this adventurous Viking family lived. Erik's son Leifur, who later travelled to America some time around AD 1000, is thought to have been born here. Just east of Stykkishólmur, the uninhabited island of **Oxney** also

A display in the Norwegian House in Stykkishólmur.

once played home to Erik and Leifur.

The farm **Hjarðarholt**, just outside Búðardalur, is the birthplace of Kjartan Ólafsson, whose ill-starred love for Guðrún Ósvífursdóttir from **Sælingsdalur**, 30km (18 miles) to the north, is the central theme of *Laxdæla Saga*. Geothermal springs made Sælingsdalur an important centre in Guðrún's day, when there was a hot bathing pool, of which traces can still be seen, at the farm of **Laugar** ⓘ. A modern swimming pool now uses the natural hot water, while a summer hotel and a small **Folk Museum** (open summer daily 1–5pm; charge) operate in the school.   ❏

RESTAURANTS AND CAFÉS

Búðarklettur
Brákarbraut 13-15, Borgarnes
Tel: 437 1600
The Settlement Centre's restaurant serves hearty pasta, fish and meat mains. Many have a traditional slant – think smoked lamb and herring on rye bread. **$$**

Fimm Fiskar
Frúarstígur 1, Stykkishólmur
Tel: 436 1600
The simpler of Stykkishólmur's two main restaurants – a fish-lover's paradise. **$$**

Fosshótel Reykholt
Reykholt. Tel: 435 1260
The only place to eat in Reykholt, the hotel restaurant serves an array of fish and meat dishes. **$$**

Hótel Búðir
Búðir, Snæfellsnes Peninsula.
Tel: 435 6700
Reopened after a devastating fire, this is one of Iceland's finest hotels. Seafood and game are the specialities served in its oceanside restaurant. **$$$**

Hótel Flatey
Flatey island. Tel: 555 7788
The island's guesthouse contains a cosy café, with mouthwatering cakes and classic Icelandic seafood dishes (fish stew, fish balls, grilled salmon etc.). **$–$$**

Hótel Hamar
Golfvöllurinn, Borgarnes
Tel: 433 6600
Superb local food is served

at this Icelandair hotel at Borgarnes golf course, with vegetables grown on the premises and schnapps from the distillery over the road. Evening meals only. **$$$**

Krákan
Sæból 13, Grundarfjörður
Tel: 438 6999
A village institution which has been operating for years, "The Crow" has had a white, bright makeover following a recent fire. Excellent fish suppers. **$$**

Narfeyrarstofa
Aðalgata 3, Stykkishólmur
Tel: 438 1119
Top-notch fare in this intimate café-restaurant spe-

cialising in tasty scallops and a good choice of fish dishes with a Mediterranean flavour. There's also a selection of burgers on the menu. **$$**

Snjófell
Arnarstapi. Tel: 435 6783
A cosy diner in a building constructed in traditional turf-roofed style, Snjófell offers fish straight from the nearby harbour, plus burgers, pizzas and a summertime cake buffet. **$–$$**

> The price guide is for the average price of dinner per person, without wine:
> **$$$** Over ISK4,500
> **$$** ISK2,500–4,500
> **$** Under ISK2,500

THE WEST FJORDS

This remote, inaccessible region has whole areas
that are deserted, creating natural reserves of a
beauty and fertility unknown elsewhere in Iceland

Shaped like an outstretched paw, the West Fjords region appears at first sight to be one of the least hospitable parts of Iceland. The absence of fertile lowlands has, since the days of settlement, forced the inhabitants to look to the sea rather than to the land for their livelihood. Land travel has always been difficult – sometimes even dangerous – in this area, which is characterised by rough and steep mountain slopes, shores that every now and then are cut off by the tides, and tiny communities under constant threat from snow avalanches or earth slides.

Since the days of settlement the inhabitants of the West Fjords have lived their lives on isolated farms, without any regular contact with the outside world, and here, at the westernmost point of Iceland, an independent, and in many ways strange, local culture has developed. Under the rough and rocky mountains, the belief in monsters, ghosts and evil spirits has become more deeply rooted than in any other part of the country.

The mechanisation of the fishing industry in the 20th century made life here somewhat more comfortable, but government-imposed fishing quotas in recent years have resulted in a steady stream of emigrants from the West Fjords to Reykjavík. Meanwhile, many small farms in the area have been abandoned as unprofitable – with more and more farmers giving up as the years go by.

Travellers in the West Fjords face a string of serious obstacles, including some of the worst roads in the country. Yet the region offers Iceland's most dramatic fjords and some of its best hiking, while soaring cliffs host literally millions of breeding sea birds. And, once the proverbial ice is broken, its self-reliant people prove to be among the most hospitable in the land. *(See also box page 222.)*

Main attractions
ÍSAFJÖRÐUR
HORNSTRANDIR NATURE RESERVE
ÖNUNDARFJÖRÐUR BEACH
DYNJANDI WATERFALL
LÁTRABJARG BIRD-CLIFFS
MUSEUM OF WITCHCRAFT AND
  SORCERY (HÓLMAVÍK)

PRECEDING PAGES: an aerial view of the West Fjords landscape. **LEFT:** an elderly couple. **RIGHT:** Hrafnseyri, and the chapel dedicated to Jón Sigurðsson.

TIP

Routes 60 and 61 converge at Ísafjörður, forming a circular route around the West Fjords that can be driven in two to three days. However, if you include a few detours it is easy to spend a full week.

A base for exploring

Most visitors make **Ísafjörður** ❶, the focal point of the region, their base. With a population of 2,700, it is the only town of any size, with a choice of accommodation and some good restaurants. The site of a 9th-century farmstead, **Eyri** is the oldest part of town, with one of Iceland's best natural harbours. On a fine summer evening, a stroll through the Old Town is an unforgettable walk through the past. The oldest buildings at the end of the sandspit are four restored timber buildings dating from the 18th century. More by accident than design, these ancient (by Icelandic standards) houses were left standing as fish factories and warehouses sprang up around them.

Oldest of the four is **Tjöruhús**, built in 1733–42, followed by the adjoining **Krambúð**, dating from 1761 and originally a shop. The meticulously restored **Turnhús** (Tower House) was built in 1744. It once housed a salt-fish plant and now contains the **West Fjords Heritage Museum** (open July–Aug Mon–Fri 10am–6pm, Sat–Sun 10am–5pm; June Mon–Fri 10am–5pm, Sat–Sun 1–5pm; charge). Exhibits trace the development of the town and its fishing industry, with all sorts of unusual nautical paraphernalia. Ísafjörður has excellent skiing facilities in the **Seljalandsdalur** valley above town.

Around Ísafjörður

The broad fjord of Ísafjarðardjúp, on which Ísafjörður sits, almost severs the West Fjords in two. Near its mouth to the northwest of Ísafjörður is **Bolun-**

West Fjords

garvík ❷, the second largest town in the region. Between here and **Hnífsdalur** is the steep mountainside Óshlíð, where avalanches and landslides have often occurred. In Bolungarvík is Ósvör, an old fishing hut from rowboat times, which has been restored and turned into an interesting **Maritime Museum** (open June–mid-Aug daily 10am–5pm; charge). There is also a **Natural History Museum** (open June–mid-Aug Mon–Fri 9am–noon, 1–5pm, Sat–Sun 1–5pm). A jeep track continues to **Skálavík** where those seeking solitude will find plenty at a remote, uninhabited bay facing the Greenland Sea.

Route 61, which hugs the southern shore of Ísafjarðardjúp, southeast from Ísafjörður, was completed in 1975. Súðavík is the only village in these parts, developing from a Norwegian whaling-station *c*.1900. Of the 70 houses in Súðavík 23 were completely destroyed by the 1995 avalanche; the village was afterwards rebuilt in a safer area. Its newly opened, community-run **Arctic Fox Center** (open daily 9am–5pm; charge) contains a permanent exhibition on one of Iceland's few mammals, the elusive

Arctic fox. Once hunted for its fur, the creature is still culled around the country to protect livestock, but is a protected species in the West Fjords region.

Further along, close to the tip of the Ögurnes peninsula is **Ögur**, an impressive farmstead; built in the 19th century, it was at the time one of the largest in Iceland. At Mjóifjörður is the Djúpmannabúð roadside cafeteria, and the only petrol station along this stretch of coast. Another ancient farm site is at **Vatnsfjörður**, in its heyday a wealthy estate that produced several pastors of note. The village of **Reykjanes** ❸, at the head of Ísafjarðardjúp, is one of several places in the West Fjords with geothermal water. There are a summer hotel, swimming pool and greenhouses here.

The road continues as Route 635 along Ísafjarðardjúp's northern shore to **Kaldalón** ❹, a sheltered beauty spot. A small glacier here tumbles down from Drangajökull, the only large ice-field in the north of Iceland. At the head of the valley there are some grassy islets, then moraine brought by the descending glacier tongue.

With an intensely convoluted coastline, road journeys in the region are long and winding.

BELOW: Ísafjörður.

Stuffed exhibits at the Arctic Fox Center, Súðavík.

BELOW RIGHT: cheery bollard.

Beyond Kaldalón, the road comes to an abrupt halt at Unaðsdalur valley, where the uninviting Snæfjallaströnd ("snow mountain coast") begins. The snow line is lower here than anywhere else in the country – even in mid-summer, some snow lies at sea level.

Islands and wilderness

Two of Ísafjarðardjúp's islands are inhabited (although barely: each has just one tenanted farm!): **Vigur** and **Æðey** ("eider island"). There are regular boat tours from Ísafjörður in the summer. A walk around Vigur gives the visitor an opportunity to enjoy the rich birdlife in its natural environment. Thousands of eider ducks, arctic terns, puffins and other sea birds can be found on the island. There is also a small and homely coffee-shop in the mid-19th century farmer's house, as well as a mini post office, where guests can mail their cards and letters. Æðey is the biggest island in Ísafjarðardjúp and, as its name suggests, also has an impressive bird population.

Ísafjörður is also the jumping-off point for trips to the uninhabited nature reserve of **Hornstrandir** ❺ to the north. The Reserve includes the whole area north of Skorarheiði from the end of Hrafnfjörður to the end of Furufjörður. Abandoned by its farming community during the first decades of the 20th century and free from the destructive grazing of sheep, plants and wildlife alike thrive on a scale unknown elsewhere in the country. Here you can wade knee-deep in meadows of wildflowers, fertilised by the guano of countless breeding sea birds, and listen at sundown for the haunting bark of the arctic fox, unpersecuted and tamer here than anywhere else in Iceland. The Nature Reserve is off limits to all motor traffic, making the only way to explore it by boat or on foot. There is no accommodation and little evidence of the once-flourishing farming community. Traces of bridle paths crisscross the mountain passes, linking the fjords and inlets.

The Emptying Land

Rural depopulation is known throughout Iceland. However, in the West Fjords it has been a particularly serious problem for decades, threatening the continued existence of many remote communities and totally claiming the lives of others. Human settlement of the Hornstrandir peninsula of the West Fjords, for instance, was always marginal at best: winters came earlier, snow lasted longer and temperatures were always lower than elsewhere in the region. Surprisingly life here, although tough, was prosperous, at least for a while. At Hesteyri in Hornstrandir, abandoned houses and a church suggest a once flourishing settlement. A trading place since 1881, Hesteyri was the base for a Norwegian whaling station until 1912, ruins of which are still clear to see. In the 1920s a herring processing factory was built in the village where about 80 people lived. This closed in 1940 and in 1952 the last inhabitants moved away. Not only was the harsh climate of Hornstrandir an added challenge but the only source of geothermal water in the peninsula is Reykjafjörður, several days' hike away. Elsewhere in the region, poor communications have been to blame for rural depopulation. Even today, travel around the region can be exasperating due to the highly indented nature of the coastline and the fjord system at its heart. Stony, mountain plateaux between the fjords only add to the difficulties.

In summer, a ferry operated by Sjóferðir sails daily from Ísafjörður to a number of destinations in Hornstrandir bringing day-trippers, hikers and descendants of the original landowners who now use the remaining old farmsteads as summer cottages. Another ferry also sails south from Hornvík along the Strandir coast to Norðurfjörður *(see page 225)*, making it possible to travel south from Hornstrandir without first backtracking to Ísafjörður in order to continue your journey. All ferry times are available from the tourist office in Ísafjörður.

Scheduled stops include Aðalvík and Hesteyri in the northwest, Hornvík in the north, Hrafnfjörður in the southwest and Veiðileysufjörður in the west. The return voyage itself is an adventure as a day trip, but most people choose to disembark at either Aðalvík or Hesteyri and hike east across to Hornvík. Another option is to take the ferry to Hrafnfjörður and then hike north to Hornvík. Check the times and sailing schedule of the ferry carefully before setting out because these destinations are not served on a daily basis and Hornstrandir is a pretty remote location – it's not somewhere to get stranded.

Sea birds and driftwood

Not far from the Hornbjargsviti lighthouse rise the majestic bird-cliffs at **Hornbjarg ⑥**, the nesting ground for tens of thousands of pairs of noisy guillemots, Brunnich's guillemots, razorbills, puffins, kittiwakes and fulmars. Not for the fainthearted, **Kálfatindur** peak, the highest point along the cliffs, is a 534-metre (1,760ft) vertical drop to the Greenland Sea. From its lofty summit, the noise is deafening and the view simply breathtaking – some claim to have seen the distant Greenland icecap from here.

In view of Kálfatindur is attractive **Hornvík Bay ⑦**. It has a long sandy beach, some impressive waterfalls, a plentiful supply of driftwood and is a pleasant camping spot. In a rare bout of clear weather (for some reason, more likely in late summer), the place is nothing short of idyllic and makes an ideal base from which to explore the area. Across the bay is **Hælavíkurbjarg**, another impressive bird-cliff. Spring still

TIP

Given the circuitous nature of many roads in the West Fjords, one of the best ways to get to and around the region is by air. Indeed, there are no fewer than three airports in the area, a sure sign of the difficult terrain: Ísafjörður, Bíldudalur and Gjögur on the Strandir coast. The aerial views of the West Fjords' flat-topped mountains can be breathtaking.

BELOW: a female eider duck on its nest, surrounded by saxifrage.

Icelanders go to great lengths to take guillemot eggs from their precarious cliffside nests.

BELOW: expect the unexpected on Iceland's roads.

draws daring Icelanders to lower themselves on ropes down the cliff-face and collect the prized guillemots' eggs.

Besides seal-hunting, coastal farmers of the West Fjords have always harvested something else from the sea: driftwood. These benefits are unevenly distributed as some farms have better driftwood-beaches than others. There has always been a lot of driftwood on Hornstrandir and it was extensively used in the past, as little timber was imported. Dealing in wood was profitable for local inhabitants, and many of them were also known as skilled craftsmen, making useful items out of driftwood, such as tubs and barrels, and selling them in the West Fjords and other parts of the country. Driftwood is still collected in Hornstrandir, now mainly used for fenceposts, which are sold all over Iceland.

South of Ísafjörður

Route 60 winds over several high passes to link the fjords south of Ísafjörður. A tunnel has been made through the basalt rocks of Breiðadalsheiði, which at 610 metres (2,013ft) is the highest pass in the area; it was often blocked in the past, cutting off villages for days, sometimes weeks, at a time.

The village of **Suðureyri** ❽, 17km (10 miles) off the main road, is buried in the shadow of the extremely steep **Súgandafjörður** fjord. The village's main claim to fame is that it lives without direct sunlight throughout the four winter months, longer than any other village in Iceland. The sun's rays first peek over the high mountains and strike the village on 22 February each year, an occasion celebrated, as everywhere else in the West Fjords, with "sunshine coffee".

Önundarfjörður ❾, a fjord between the Barði and Sauðanes headlands, is unmistakable because of its sandy beach which almost straddles the fjord in a golden arc. On rare sunny days the shallow waters heat up and locals from nearby **Flateyri** throng to bathe in the Greenland Sea. The headland, on which the 250 inhabitants of Flateyri live, was probably left there when a large part of a mountain cleaved into the sea. In 1792 Flateyri became an authorised trading place, and fish and fish-processing are still the main industries. There is said to have been a pagan temple on the hill Goðahóll above the village. Flateyri suffered an avalanche in 1995 that killed 20 people, after which a 20-m (66ft) -high avalanche dam was built to protect the settlement from further such catastrophes.

Across the fjord, the historical parsonage of **Holt** ⑩ was the birthplace of the 17th-century bishop, Brynjólfur Sveinsson. The attractive timber church here dates from 1869 and contains artefacts from the time of Bishop Brynjólfur.

Dýrafjörður, the next fjord south, ranks among the most scenic in Iceland – sheer mountains seem to rise straight from the shore, leaving little or no lowland for farming. The inhabitants have made do with other resources and the village of **Mýrar** ⑪ has Iceland's largest eider duck colony of 7,000 pairs. The first settler at the nearby farm Alviðra was none other than a son of King Harald Fairhair of Norway. Today it offers accommodation to travellers.

National saints and sinners

Across the fjord, **Þingeyri** ⑫ (population 260) was the first trading post in the West Fjords. It takes its name from an ancient assembly whose sacred site was said to be enclosed by walls at either end of the mountain **Sandfell**, rising above the village. The old residents still remember the walls and in the town there are ruins of an ancient booth, used by visitors to the assembly, which are a historical monument.

From the top of Sandfell (accessible by 4WD or on a gentle one-hour walk from Þingeyri), there is a beautiful view of the mountains separating Dýrafjörður from Arnarfjörður. This mountain ridge is often called the "West Fjord Alps". In the 19th century the French wanted to establish a colony in Þingeyri to support their fishing fleet, but were turned down. In nearby **Haukadalur** valley there is a French seamen's cemetery. This valley is also the setting for the tragic events of the saga of Gísli Súrsson. Outlawed for a suspected vengeance killing,

Gísli spent a gruelling 13 years on the run, but was eventually tracked down and slain. Saga-Age ruins in the valley are thought to be Gísli's farm Hóll and his brother-in-law's neighbouring farm Sæból (8km/5 miles along the fjord from Þingeyri).

The village of **Hrafnseyri** ⑬, in Arnarfjörður fjord, was the birthplace of nationalist Jón Sigurðsson (*see panel on page 56*). There is a small **museum** (open June–early Aug 10am–8pm; charge) and a **chapel** to his memory.

Further along the fjord, an indistinct route leads up Fossdalur valley to **Mount Kaldbakur** ⑭, the highest peak in the region. It is officially 998 metres (3,273ft) high, but locals have added a cairn to credit the region with its only 1,000-metre peak. In clear weather the full-day hike is well worth the effort, with views as far away as the Snæfellsnes icecap.

Dynjandi waterfall ⑮ is a collection of cascades located at the head of the northern arm of Arnarfjörður. Fjallfoss ("mountain falls"), the main cascade, literally drops 100 metres (328ft) off the edge of the mountain, fanning

Traditionally the difficulty of a high pass was measured by the number of fish-skin shoes that were worn through to cross it. In the passes south of Ísafjörður a nine-skin pass was not unusual. Nowadays these routes are more of a test of the nerves of the driver and the suspension of the car.

BELOW: the picturesque cascades of Dynjandi waterfall.

out to a width of 60 metres (197ft) at its base. Dynjandi continues falling in a series of individually-named cascades: Hundafoss, Strokkur, Göngumannafoss, Hrísvaðsfoss and Sjóarfoss.

The most westerly point in Europe

Some kilometres beyond here the road splits. If you head west, Route 63 passes the fishing villages of **Bíldudalur** and **Tálknafjörður** (5km/3 miles off the main road). From Bíldudalur, the difficult but impressive Route 619 passes the opening of several valleys, before it ends at the **Selárdalur** farm, where the pastor Páll Björnsson (1621–1706) lived, well known for his wisdom and his persecution of witches. He was said to have been an excellent speaker and an unusually good linguist. According to a legend, a black-sailed schooner was once seen off Selárdalur. People feared that pirates were on board. The pastor went out to the vessel, spoke to them in an eastern language and told them the area was full of witches. As a result the pirates exchanged gifts with him and sailed away.

Also on Route 63 is the larger town of **Patreksfjörður**, which has a small guesthouse and an exhibition about pirates, although little else of real interest to the visitor. Across the fjord, **Hnjótur** 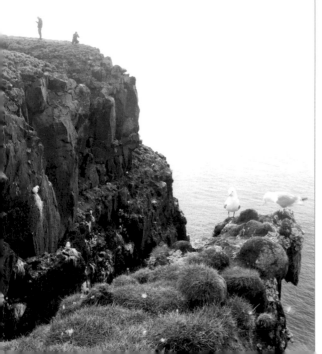 ⑯ has the **Egill Ólafsson Museum** (open late May–mid-Sept daily 10am–6pm; charge), featuring diverse objects relating to fishing, farming, aviation, rescue missions and local West Fjords characters. Exhibits are neatly presented and original drawings show how the old tools and equipment were used.

The real lure of the area is the bird-cliffs at **Látrabjarg** ⑰, at the westernmost point of Iceland – and thus Europe. Extending for 14km (9 miles) and rising to 444 metres (1,465ft) at their highest point, the cliffs are home to one of Iceland's greatest concentrations of sea birds. The thousands of puffins here often allow visitors to approach to within a few feet of them as they stand above their cliff-top burrows. On Monday, Wednesday and Saturday in high season, a bus service stops at the cliffs on the journey between Ísafjörður and the Breiðafjörður ferry, allowing around two hours' exploration time. The bird-cliffs have also been the scene of human dramas. When the British trawler *Dhoon* ran aground below the cliffs in the winter of 1947, a remarkable rescue operation by the local farmers saved all 12 crew members. Lowering themselves by ropes as if they were collecting eggs, they hauled the exhausted men up the 200-metre (650ft) cliff-face to safety. Southeast of Látrabjarg is Iceland's most magnificent stretch of golden sand, **Rauðasandur**.

Another first settler

At the head of Patreksfjörður fjord, Route 62 crosses over to the southern coast of the West Fjords – **Barðaströnd** – a region that gets more than its share of foul weather. This entire stretch of coast has little over 500 inhabitants – the unforgiving elements might have something to do with it. This was where the Viking Hrafna-Flóki made one of the first settlements in Iceland, long before Ingólfur Arnarson

BELOW: Látrabjarg, marking Europe's western boundary.

arrived. The *Landnámabók (Book of Settlements)* relates that the fishing was so good that Flóki neglected to make hay for his livestock, and they perished over the winter. In spring he climbed a high mountain and, looking north, saw ice-filled fjords. It was this drift ice, and not the glaciers, that prompted him to name the land "Iceland" on his eventual return to Norway. However, it is said that he came back some years later and spent the rest of his life in Iceland.

Brjánslækur, at the entrance to Vatnsfjörður, is the terminal for the Breiðafjörður ferry, which connects twice daily (no Saturday service outside high season) with Stykkishólmur on the Snæfellsnes peninsula.

Route 60 continues south around the fjords, a long and winding drive. There is a chance of spotting the rare white-tailed sea eagle here, though only around 50 pairs of this now protected species remain after centuries of hunting. The main settlement here is **Bjarkalundur** ⓲, the unofficial gateway to the West Fjords, with a hotel and camping facilities within sight of the twin peaks of Vaðalfjöll.

The Strandir coast

The rugged eastern flank of the West Fjords is one of the least visited parts of Iceland. The population of the area has been steadily declining, and now the only town of any size is **Hólmavík**, which has basic facilities. It draws in visitors with its unusual **Museum of Icelandic Sorcery and Witchcraft** (open daily June–mid-Sept 10am–6pm; charge). Farming in the region is hard and good harbours few: **Djúpavík**, for example, a once-bustling herring station, is now virtually abandoned, but has a wonderfully situated hotel.

The village of **Norðurfjörður** is the end of the road. Beyond here, a hiking trail follows the coast to Hornstrandir. Allow between 10 and 14 days, expect all kinds of weather, take double the normal rations – and don't count on meeting another soul.

From Norðurfjörður, there's also a summer ferry connection to Hornvík in Hornstrandir which sails twice a week from late June to mid–August. ❏

Fish for sale sign – and it doesn't get much fresher than this.

RESTAURANTS, CAFÉS AND BARS

Café Riis
Hafnarbraut 39, Hólmavík
Tel: 451 3567
A tasteful café/bar/restaurant with pizzas, burgers, freshly caught fish, and Icelandic dishes such as puffin breast with blueberries or smoked lumpfish. **$$**

Edinborg
Aðalstræti 7, Ísafjörður
Tel: 456 8060
Popular for coffee or more substantial meals. Summer saltfish feasts give visitors a chance to sample traditional West Fjords cuisine. **$$**

Hópið
Tálknafjörður
A straightforward selection of sandwiches, burgers, pizzas and fish dishes at this café-bar in Tálknafjörður. **$**

Hótel Djúpavík
Djúpavík village. Tel: 451 4037
Enjoy the freshest fish at this friendly hotel and restaurant, one hour's drive from the nearest "town" on the isolated Strandir coast. **$$**

Hótel Flókalundur
Flókalundur. Tel: 456 2011
Trout, roast lamb and garlic lobster are some of the evening meals served. Also a popular coffee stop. Open late May–mid-Sept. **$$–$$$**

Hótel Núpur
Dýrafjörður, Þingeyri district
Tel: 456 8235
A small-but-select evening

menu is served in summer. Fish takes pride of place, along with the restaurant's speciality, goat meat. **$$–$$$**

Talisman
Skipagata 3, Suðureyri
Tel: 450 9000
Modern restaurant in a tiny village, focusing on locally-sourced, organic produce. **$$**

Thai Koon
Hafnarstræti 9, Ísafjörður
Tel: 456 0123
Authentic Thai food at this simple spot at the town's main shopping mall. **$**

Vagninn
Hafnarstræti 19, Flateyri
Tel: 456 7751
Freshly caught fish is always

on the menu here. **$**

Við Pollinn
Hótel Ísafjörður, Silfurtorg 2, Ísafjörður. Tel: 456 3360
The most upmarket place in town to eat, with excellent fish dishes and superb views of the fjord. **$$–$$$**

Þorpið
Aðalstræti 73, Patreksfjörður Tel: 456 1295
A selection of salads, fish dishes and lamb, plus great views over the fjord. **$$**

> The price guide is for the average price of dinner per person, without wine:
> **$$$** Over ISK4,500
> **$$** ISK2,500–4,500
> **$** Under ISK2,500

OBSERVING ICELAND'S SEA BIRDS

One of the most unforgettable sights in Iceland is that of a huge, cliff-side sea bird colony – a common and noisy occurrence in breeding season

Sea birds can be seen and heard everywhere in Iceland – circling overhead or offshore but, most often, stacked in vast, raucous colonies on steep cliffs and island coastlines. They live here in their millions, and many more birds arrive in late spring to breed – some 25 species in all, plus a few more on passage north or south. No wonder the great aim for many human visitors to Iceland is to watch these birds, sometimes by walking and climbing long distances to see the colonies. Watching sea birds is easiest by boat or from a nearby cliff, where the gap in between gives the birds a sense of security.

The northernmost island of Grímsey, on the Arctic Circle, is home to about 90 shepherds and fisherfolk. But great breeding colonies of birds outnumber them by their thousands – fulmars, including the rare blue fulmar, guillemots, including the Brunnich's sub-species, gannets and many others.

Even Reykjavík, with 118,000 inhabitants, also has its own colonies of auks, gulls such as kittiwake – easily distinguished by the cry that gives it its name – eiders and many other ducks. Near the golf course, a colony of Arctic terns use the golfers for diving practice.

In Iceland's great peninsulas, the West Fjords, Snæfellsnes and islands such as the Vestmannaeyjar, pointing the binoculars at the ever-changing sea or the steadfast cliffs, you do not have to be an expert to feel the thrill of finding a species that, to you at least, is new.

ABOVE: thousands of sea birds sit calmly as the waves pound against the great sea cliffs on the west of the Snæfellsnes peninsula to the north of Reykjavík.

BELOW: the razorbill's chunky beak, with its vertical white stripe, can be part of the mating ritual – a bird attracts a mate by using its beak to make a castanet-like rattle.

BELOW: a vivid red beak, short red legs and unmistakeably noisy cry make the arctic tern easy to spot.

THE LAST OF THE GREAT AUKS

The great auk was once the king of the auk species – black and white seabirds with short, stubby necks, including guillemots, razorbills, little auks and puffins. At one time, there were great auk colonies in Iceland, North America, Greenland and the Faroes.

But the great auk had one major disadvantage. It was flightless. Sitting stolidly on a rock, the great auk was easy prey for hunters in remote areas. The colonies grew smaller until, by the start of the 19th century, few remained except on St Kilda and on Iceland's islands. Still, they were hunted. In 1844, two hunters visiting Eldey island, southwest of the Reykjanes peninsula, strangled the last pair of great auks, and stamped on the egg that the two birds were tending.

RIGHT: large, strong-flying gannets, which make spectacular steep dives for fish, come to Iceland's cliffs during the breeding season.

ABOVE: the modestly sized puffin, with its distinctive curved red, blue and yellow beak in summer, is everyone's favourite. Pairs of puffins breed and raise their young in burrows on clifftops.

HÚNAFLÓI AND SKAGAFJÖRÐUR

This rugged region of mountains, waterfalls, cliffs
and islands has been largely bypassed by tourism
– few turn off the Ring Road to find the coast's
more remote attractions

Reykjavik

utting into the icy Arctic Ocean, the Skagi peninsula divides the northern coast of Iceland into the Húnaflói bight and Skagafjörður fjord. It is well worth taking time to follow the narrow dirt roads into a windswept wilderness of basalt cliffs, nesting sea birds, black volcanic sand spits and beaches frequented only by seals.

Rural backwater

The Ring Road runs through some rich agricultural land here, its alluvial soil weathered from some of Iceland's oldest rocks. The entry point to the area is **Brú ❶** ("bridge") – a tiny hamlet which is really little more than a petrol station. It is dominated by the huge bulk of **Tröllakirkja**, a hill that stands over 1,000 metres (3,300ft) from the flat surrounding farmland. Brú is at the head of narrow **Hrútafjörður** fjord, formed by the extensive glacial moraines (deposits) which dominate the area. The land in this region is rich in minerals and this, coupled with high rainfall, encourages many rare alpine and arctic plants, particularly gentians.

The farmstead/youth hostel of **Ósar** lies 18km (12 miles) north along Route 711 on the **Vatnsnes** promontory, from where there are superb views across the **Húnafjörður bay** to Blönduós. In the foreground is the moraine-dammed inlet of **Sigríðarstaðavatn**, with the

Hóp lagoon beyond. Grey seals bask on sand spits at low tide while eider duck and terns nest among the lyme grass. A short distance along the shore is the distinctive basalt sea-stack, **Hvítserkur**, with three holes through its base and white guano flecking its ledges like icing. According to folklore this 15-metre (49ft) -high stack was a troll turned to stone by the sun.

Hóp ❷ is the largest saltwater lagoon in Iceland, virtually cut in half by a narrow sand spit and almost isolated from the sea by **Þingeyrasandur**, a low-lying,

Main attractions
SKAGASTRÖND
KRÓKSBJARG AND BAKKAR CLIFFS
WHITE-WATER RAFTING
(VARMAHLÍÐ)
HÓLAR CHURCH
HERRING ERA MUSEUM
(SIGLUFJÖRÐUR)

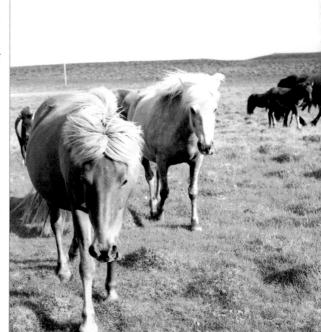

PRECEDING PAGES: the cathedral at Hólar.
LEFT: Hvítserkur arch. **RIGHT:** local horses.

North Central Iceland

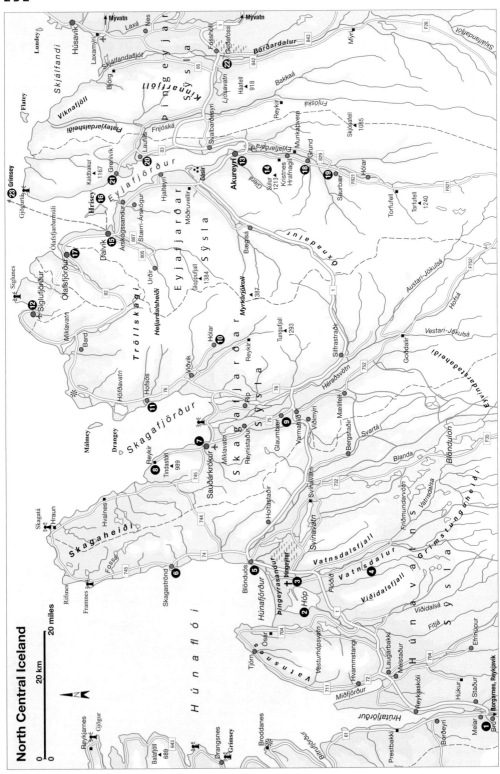

black sand dune with great swards of lyme grass on its seaward side. This was used in the past as a seed crop to mill for flour. Over the centuries, the dune has expanded seaward as more sand has been deposited by the ocean. Tundra plants have colonised the older dunes to provide great flashes of colour: purple thyme, yellow lady's bedstraw, white northern orchid, deep blue gentians, and parnassus grass and silverweed. Overhead, arctic skuas wheel about attacking arctic terns; below, running free across the sands, are Icelandic horses, which are particularly common in this area.

Medieval centre of learning

On the way to the dunes, the dirt track (Route 721) passes one of Iceland's greatest historical sites, **Þingeyrar ❸**, whose name reflects the site's original function as a þing (district assembly). The local bishop Jón Ögmundarson built one of Iceland's first Benedictine monasteries here in 1133. It quickly became a literary hot-spot, with monks working full-time transcribing the Bible and the sagas. Today nothing remains of these two early sites. The estate is a horse farm, guarded by a solitary and rather splendid basalt church, completed in 1877, which is open to visitors in the summer months.

Near to where Route 721 meets the Ring Road is **Þrístapar**, the hilly site of Iceland's last execution which occurred on 12 January 1830, when the murderers Agnes and Friðrik were beheaded. Across the road is the **Vatnsdalur valley ❹**, a geologist's dream dotted with steep mounds of ground moraine. Just as striking is evidence of Iceland's largest known landslip, which occurred here in October 1720. The side of the huge ridge, **Vatnsdalsfjall** (800 metres/2,624ft high), collapsed and dammed the river below to create a new lake – **Flóðið**.

The town of **Blönduós ❺**, with just over 800 inhabitants, is the best base for exploring this region. Situated where the River Blanda enters the Húnaflói, it is an important fishing community. The

town's bright houses contrast with the local green fields and grey screes.

The Ring Road crosses a bridge that spans the **River Blanda** (where a salmon fishing permit can cost a small fortune) and there is a turn-off to the heart of Blönduós, with its two small museums, brand-new swimming pool, hotel, hospital and garage.

In the middle of the river, to the east of Blönduós, is the island of **Hrútey**, reached via a small footbridge from the north bank. There is a circular path through the tundra scrubland and it is a good place for birdwatching. The river torrent slows as it passes into the tidal stretches of Blönduós, where rare ducks and divers congregate. From Blönduós, the Ring Road runs directly to Akureyri, passing eventually through the **Öxnadalur** valley, considered the finest scenery on the highway from Reykjavík. Alternatively, Akureyri can be reached following the rougher roads along the wild northern coast.

Remote wilderness

The **Skagi** peninsula lies northeast of Blönduós. The dirt highway that hugs

The bishopric of Hólar (see page 235) was once north Iceland's religious centre.

BELOW:
the stone church at Þingeyrar.

Basalt rocks near Vogurviti, formed in a series of extensive hexagonal lava steps. An unmanned lighthouse looks over the small lakes, sand spits and rocky shores, the habitat for countless birds.

BELOW: guesthouse in Sauðárkrókur.
BELOW RIGHT: most small settlements in Iceland do have a café and/or bar.

its western edge passes through a narrow band of agricultural land overshadowed by the mountains behind. **Skagaströnd ❻**, with a population of barely 500, was an important trading port in the 16th century, but today it is a quiet fishing centre built on a rocky outcrop. It is most famous today for its eccentric inhabitant Hallbjörn Hjartarson, a country-and-western fanatic who set up his own C&W bar (Kántrýbær) and radio station in town. Brightly coloured wooden houses edge a sweeping bay with the snow-splashed mountain peaks of **Spákonufell** as the towering backdrop.

North of Skagaströnd, sand dunes and shingle bays give way to cliffs. The ever-deteriorating road climbs upwards and across the top of the **Króksbjarg** and **Bakkar** cliffs – home to a large number of sea birds. Rows of sandstone outcrops contrast with the black basalt lava, usually hexagonal in section. Thousands of kittiwakes vie for nesting space on ledges whilst fulmars nest on the tops of the columns. Near to where the River Fossá cascades over the cliff is a small grassy headland undermined by

the sea – a great place from which to observe the sea birds. North is **Vogurviti**, an unusual outcrop of basalt rock (*see margin, left*).

Sauðárkrókur

Within the Skagafjörður fjord lie several small islands rich in birdlife. The most famous is **Drangey**, once a hideout for outlaws, including saga hero Grettir the Strong. The island can be reached from **Sauðárkrókur ❼**, the region's administrative centre at the head of the fjord. First settled by Scotsmen from the Hebrides, today Sauðárkrókur has a population of over 2,600, making it second in size to Akureyri on Iceland's north coast. Its many amenities include a swimming pool, cinema and even a gliding club. Thermal springs supply the town's hot water and a natural hot pool, Grettislaug, can be visited just to the north at **Reykir ❽**.

In Glerhallavík Bay, near the pool, thousands upon thousands of exquisitely beautiful quartz stones, polished by the pounding surf, have been washed up on the beach (though you should note it is forbidden to remove any of them). Access is only possible at low tide on foot from Reykir.

Another mountain track (Route 744) with superb views of the area runs over **Þverárfjall** into moorlands of cottongrass. South of Sauðárkrókur, at **Glaumbær ⑨**, is a finely maintained turf farmhouse **museum** (open June–early Sept daily 9am–6pm; charge), whose wood-fronted buildings have thick turf walls and roofs. **Áshús**, a house built in the 19th-century style that supplanted the turf house, contains a coffee-shop which also serves Icelandic pancakes.

South of Glaumbær, **Varmahlíð** is a small service town with a bank, hotel, tourist office and swimming pool. The rivers south of town are Iceland's best for white-water rafting. **Hestasport–Activity Tours** (www.activitytours.is), based at the town crossroads, run rafting trips on the beautiful glacial rivers Jökulsá Vestari and Jökulsá Austari.

East of Skagafjörður

The eastern flank of Skagafjörður is lined with steep mountains. The 1,300-m (4,265ft) -high interior beyond can only be penetrated by backpackers willing to brave the remnants of an ancient icecap. Accessible by car, however, is the ancient bishopric of **Hólar ⑩**, founded in 1106 and for over 600 years the religious centre of the North. The high-towered "cathedral", dating from 1763, is charming. The early 16th-century altarpiece, believed to be Dutch, was donated by Jón Arason, the last Catholic bishop of the area who was executed during the Reformation. A difficult hike, from Hólar to the Urðir valley and Dalvík, crosses the snow fields of Heljardalsheiði through some of north Iceland's finest scenery.

Further north is the little fishing village of **Hofsós ⑪**, containing the **Icelandic Emigration Centre** (open June–Aug daily 11am–6pm; charge). The centre, on the sea-front by the harbour, houses four exhibitions tracing the history of the 16,000–20,000 Icelanders who emigrated to America between 1850 and 1914; there is also an information service, library and souvenir shop. The centre's creation has gone hand-in-hand with restoration work on the village's most important historical buildings, including one of the oldest warehouses in Iceland, built in 1777 in the style of a log cabin.

Visitors driving north around Skagafjörður towards Siglufjörður will find their eyes drawn to the island of **Málmey** offshore. This concave-shaped outcrop of lava is 4km (2½ miles) long and rises at either end into high cliffs. **Siglufjörður ⑫** once sat in splendid isolation at the end of its own road, but a new tunnel (due to open in late 2010) will link it to neighbouring Ólafsfjörður. Set amidst a range of glaciated mountains, the town's current population of 1,200 is its lowest in recent history, but a generation ago this was the centre of the herring industry and home, at least seasonally, to 10,000 workers. The award-winning **Herring Era Museum** (open daily mid-June–mid-Aug 10am–6pm, early June and mid-Aug–mid-Sept 1–5pm; charge) traces the town's glory days in three historical buildings by the harbour. ❑

The English poet W.H. Auden visited Sauðárkrókur during his travels in 1936. He was unimpressed, noting that the town "might have been built by Seventh Day Adventists who expected to go to heaven in a few months, so why bother anyway?"

RESTAURANTS AND CAFÉS

Bíó Café
Aðalgata 30,
Siglufjörður
Expect reasonably-priced pizzas, burgers and succulent lamb chops in this simple but pleasant café-bar on the main street. **$$**

Kaffi Krókur
Aðalgata 16,
Sauðárkrókur
Tel: 453 6299
This is a very popular café and restaurant which serves delicious baked salmon as well as the usual selection of pizzas and burgers. **$$**

Lónkot
565 Hofsós,
Skagafjörður
Tel: 453 7432
For something special, try this gourmet restaurant 12km (7 miles) north of Hofsós, which prepares "fish from the fjord and birds from the cliffs". Open summer only. **$$$**

Ólafshús
Aðalgata 15,
Sauðárkrókur
Tel: 453 6454
This is another good choice in town – prices are a bit lower than at Kaffi Krókur though the range of

dishes is similar and equally tasty. **$$**

Við Árbakkann
Húnabraut 2, Blönduós
Tel: 452 4678
A basic cafe down by the waterfront with some salads, soups, sandwiches and cakes. Only open June–Sept. **$**

The price guide is for the average price of dinner per person, without wine:
$$$ Over ISK4,500
$$ ISK2,500–4,500
$ Under ISK2,500

AKUREYRI AND SURROUNDINGS

Akureyri is Iceland's second city, and makes an
ideal base for trips to the nearby fjords and some
of the country's most photographed attractions

By Icelandic standards, Akureyri
is a thriving metropolis: with
a population of only 17,000, it
is the country's largest town outside
of the Greater Reykjavík area. Sitting
squarely on the Ring Road, a hub for
bus and air transport, it has grown in
recent years into the undisputed centre
of the North.

Despite being only 100km (60 miles)
from the Arctic Circle, it enjoys some of
the warmest weather in the country in
summer, when it is not unusual to see
day after day of 20°C (68°F) temperatures and clear skies, bringing flowers
into the streets and turning Akureyri
into Iceland's version of the tropics.

The setting is spectacular: at the base
of Eyjafjörður fjord, Akureyri has a backdrop of sheer granite mountains tipped
with snow all year (in winter, an even
layer of snow usually makes this Iceland's premier skiing spot). And, while
Akureyri's modern architecture leaves a
lot to be desired, there are enough older
wooden buildings around town to give
it some provincial charm.

Gateway to the north

The first settler to claim the Eyjafjörður
region was the Norwegian Helgi the
Lean (named after a stint on the Orkney
Islands as a child, when he was poorly
fed by foster parents). Helgi had indis-

criminate religious habits: in traditional
pagan fashion, he tossed the high-seat
pillars from his longship into the sea,
allowing the god Thor to choose the site
of his new home. But when they washed
up 7km (4 miles) south of modern-day
Akureyri, Helgi named his farm Kristnes
(Christ's Peninsula), just in case.

The Viking farmers who ended up
around Eyjafjörður were relatively
peaceful, to judge from their low pro-
files in the sagas. A notable exception
was Víga-Glúmur. A morose and gan-
gly youth regarded as a buffoon by his

Main attractions
AKUREYRARKIRKJA
NONNAHÚS
AKUREYRI MUSEUM
GOÐAFOSS WATERFALL

PRECEDING PAGES: mighty Goðafoss.
LEFT: Akureyri from Eyjafjörður.
RIGHT: fishing at Dalvík.

Today Akureyri has one of the most active fishing fleets in Iceland. It also accounts for some 30 percent of Iceland's manufacturing output.

BELOW:
Akureyrarkirkja, reached after a steep climb.

peers, Víga-Glúmur surprised everyone on a journey to Norway by slaughtering a berserk warrior in combat. He became a worshipper of Odin and returned to Iceland to make the lives of his former tormentors a misery, becoming chieftain of the Eyjafjörður region by trickery and intimidation. However, he offended the goddess Freyja by butchering one of his in-laws in the goddess's sacred cornfield. After 40 years, Freyja had her revenge – in old age, Víga-Glúmur lost Odin's protection and had to abandon his estates. He died blind and alone.

The profit motive

The town of **Akureyri ⓭** grew from humble beginnings in the 16th century when Danish merchants built a couple of storehouses here. In the 1770s, the first permanent house was built, and the settlement became an authorised trading post in 1786, when it had a grand total of 12 inhabitants. The town failed to prosper, however, and lost its precious trading licence a mere 50 years later, before finally regaining it in 1862. An excellent harbour soon made this the centre of the new co-operative movement

among Icelandic farmers *(see page 116)*.

By the early 20th century, grandiose wooden mansions had filled the southern part of Akureyri. The spit at the northern part of town, **Oddeyri**, became the port and warehouse area, and it remains so to this day (the name Akureyri is a blend of *Akur*, meaning field, and *eyri*, spit, after the land that projects into the fjord). Akureyri has a university and a modest local flourishing of the arts, with several theatre groups, plus a number of nightspots and cinemas.

The residents have a mixed reputation in the rest of Iceland. The town is seen as the bastion of middle-class values and, despite the good weather it enjoys, its people are considered closed, traditional and even somewhat dour. Icelanders say that you can't get to know the people of Akureyri unless you are born and raised there – being conceived in the town while your parents were on holiday doesn't count. Even being raised there may not be good enough: tales are told of Akureyri neighbours who accidentally meet in Reykjavík and have long, friendly con-

Akureyri

0   300 m
0   300 yds

versations, only to act like virtual strangers once they return home. Whatever the truth of this, Icelanders have no qualms about flocking to Akureyri, especially at weekends, when flights from Reykjavík are packed, and people from every corner of the North drive in to their figurative "big smoke" for a taste of the action.

Exploring the town

Akureyri is compact enough to explore on foot, and the most logical place to start is the partly pedestrianised main shopping street **Hafnarstræti.** This is where the hustle and bustle (such as it is) of this small town's life takes place. An Akureyri institution, the **Bautinn restaurant** Ⓐ (tel: 462 1818) at no.92 sits on a crossroads and is a good place to watch the world go by. Ask to eat in the glassed-in pergola, which is lovely and bright on the numerous sunny days.

The fjord **waterfront** is only a short hop downhill from the restaurant, usually with a few picturesque trawlers sitting in port. Uphill, the basalt **Akureyrarkirkja** Ⓑ has dominated the town since its construction in 1940.

Designed by the architect Guðjón Samúelsson, the church can look distressingly unattractive in some lights. Even so, it is Akureyri's pride and joy, and worth the five-minute walk up Kaupvangsstræti for a visit. Inside, the stained-glass windows show scenes from Icelandic history and the life of Christ in a style that can only be described as cartoon-book. There is an organ with 3,200 pipes, while the centre window in the chancel was donated by England's Coventry Cathedral – it was one of the only parts that survived the bombing during World War II. Most curious is the model ship hanging from the ceiling, a tradition in Iceland, Greenland and the Faroe Islands to protect the parish's fishermen at sea.

A short climb up **Eyrarlandsvegur** leads to the **Botanical Garden** Ⓒ (Lystigarðurinn; open June–Sept Mon–Fri 8am–10pm, Sat–Sun 9am–10pm; free), famed for its 7,000 species of local and foreign flowers blooming outside in Akureyri's warm microclimate. The park was set up by a local women's association in 1912, then taken over by the town in the 1950s; two of the voluntary

BELOW: Akureyri's
Botanical Garden.

TIP

On the way back into town from the Botanical Garden on Eyrarlandsvegur, keep an eye out for Einar Jónsson's sculpture *The Outlaw*, depicting Fjalla-Eyvindur ("Mountain-Eyvind") and his wife Halla, who spent 20 years as outlaws, mainly in the interior of the country.

managers are commemorated by statues. With benches and well-kept lawns, the gardens are a perfect place to relax on a sunny afternoon.

Historical tour

From the main shopping street, walk to the foot of the church and follow the footpath up to Eyrarlandsvegur 3, to the building known as Sigurhæðir. Built in 1903, this was the home of one of Iceland's most revered poets and dramatists, Mattías Jochumsson. Jochumsson penned the lyrics for Iceland's national anthem, *Iceland's 1,000 Years*, in 1874.

Back downhill, head into Akureyri's old business district by taking a stroll south along Hafnarstræti, which leads you past the **bus terminal** and the near-defunct **tourist office** (due to relocate to harbourside premises in the new Hof Cultural Centre, at Strandgata 12, in winter 2010). The area still has many fine mansions in the so-called Icelandic frame-house tradition – to the uninitiated, they look like Swiss chalets. The last one was built in 1911, when other styles came into vogue, including the

use of metal sidings pressed into a brick pattern and painted over to look like stone and mortar. Near the intersection with Lækjargata is Akureyri's oldest house, **Laxdalshús ①**. Built in 1795, this tiny restored wooden building was occupied until 1978, when it was mostly as home to some 30 people from three or four families.

South along the waterfront following Aðalstræti is **Nonnahús ②** (open June–Aug daily 10am–5pm; charge). This is the restored home of Reverend Jón Sveinsson, nicknamed Nonni, author of the Nonni series of children's books that are still well loved in Iceland and continental Europe. The house, where Nonni spent some years of his childhood, was built in 1850 and has been maintained in its original form – even the kitchen still has its old implements – making this the most interesting of Akureyri's old homes.

The **Akureyri Museum ③** (Minjasafn; open June–mid-Sept daily 10am–5pm, mid-Sept–May Sat 2–4pm; charge) has an exhaustive collection of local memorabilia, from old farming tools to milk cartons, as well as some excellent 19th-century photographs. Outside, a small church, which was moved from Svalbarð across the fjord, sits beside Iceland's first nursery.

At the end of this picturesque street is a small museum, detailing Akureyri's 20th-century industrial heritage; and a drab kilometre walk down road 821, by the airport, is the newly revamped **Aviation Museum** (open June–Aug daily 11am–5pm; charge), with its large hangar full of antique aircraft.

Anyone still not sated by museums can head back into town to the **Akureyri Art Museum ④** (Listasafn Akureyrar; open Tue–Sun noon–6pm; charge), which offers visitors one of the best insights into the town's present-day cultural life.

At the northern edge of central Akureyri, on a rock between Glerárgata and Þórunnarstraeti, is a statue of **Helgi the Lean ⑤** (*see page 239*), with an impressive view over Eyjafjörður.

KEA

The people of Akureyri joke that virtually everything in their town is owned by KEA. Whilst this wry comment may not reduce the average visitor to fits of laughter, it is certainly true that KEA (incidently, nothing to do with well-known Swedish furniture store, IKEA) is omnipresent in this small town of 17,000 people. KEA, or the Kaupfélag Eyfirðinga, was founded in June 1886 by a group of farmers from around Eyjafjörður, to strengthen their hand in the negotiation of export prices for their sheep being sent to England. Ten years later KEA opened its first store – one of the first co-operative shops in Iceland – and a slaughterhouse for cows soon followed. Throughout the twentieth century things really boomed for the co-operative, which grew in size and became involved in numerous ventures. Indeed, a short stroll around Akureyri today reveals the KEA logo emblazoned on everything from fishing boats to hotels. KEA, proud of its northern roots, concentrated its business in and around the Akureyri region, although there were attempts to enter the Reykjavík market by building a shopping centre at the BSÍ bus station. In recent years, KEA has narrowed its portfolio (selling off its hotel chain, for one); and like every Icelandic business, it was hit hard by the 2008 crash. But its membership continues to grow, with almost half of Akureyri's loyal inhabitants belonging to the cooperative.

Short excursions

Pleasant as strolling around Akureyri can be, the real attraction is the surrounding area. A few short trips are very close to town. Only an hour on foot or 10 minutes' drive south is **Kjarnaskógar forest**, one of Iceland's few wooded areas, and a popular picnic place. Hikers can head for the symmetrical, Fuji-like **Mount Súlur** ⓮, visible on clear days from Akureyri. Drive west on Súluvegur (past the rubbish dump) to the small creek – look out for a wooden ladder over the barbed wire, then follow the yellow markers. You should allow several hours of hard (and not very inspiring) walking to reach the 1,213-metre (3,980ft) summit looking out over the **Glerá** valley. In winter, skiing fans head for the Skidastadir Lodge at **Hlíðarfjall**, offering the best slopes in the area only a 10-minute drive from town. Many non-skiers also head there for the view of the **Vindheimajökull** glacier.

Exploring the fjord

Perhaps the most popular day trip from Akureyri – and one that can be driven alone or organised through the tourist office – is along the western flank of Eyjafjörður fjord. The well-paved Route 82 offers sweeping views over the rich farming land of the area, with glacier-scoured mountains to the west (their peaks are often buried behind a steady line of grey cloud) and steely blue waters to the east. The district here is known as **Árskógsströnd**. As in the rest of the North, the fields are dotted in summer with hundreds of gigantic white plastic rolls containing hay for the winter – a high-tech innovation that has quickly replaced the more poetic but inefficient methods of traditional hay-gathering. Cows, sheep and geese wander at will, and it is not unusual for traffic to be stopped while a farmer leads a line of cattle over the road to pasture.

Although Route 82 can be followed directly north, a turn-off at Route 816 leads to a ruined medieval port area, called **Gásir**; for many centuries it was the biggest port in northern Iceland. Its overgrown ruins can still be made out in the grass. Another short side road (Route 813) leads to the farm **Möðruvellir**, birthplace of the children's writer Jón Sveinsson (better known as Nonni).

The Akureyri Museum is located in Villa Kirkjuhvoll.

BELOW LEFT: a statue of much-loved children's author Jón Sveinsson, and his one-time home, Nonnahús **(BELOW)**.

*Skiers enjoying the
snow around
Akureyri.*

There is a much-photographed farm-house at **Stærri-Árskógur**, flush against a steep mountain backdrop.

Dalvík 🅟 (population 1,400) is the dominant town on this side of the fjord. A prosperous fishing village today, Dalvík's claim to fame in Iceland is the 1934 earthquake measuring 6.3 on the Richter scale that brought rocks crashing down from the nearby mountain-side and destroyed about half of the town's homes. Its unusual little museum **Byggðasafnið Hvoll** (open June–Aug daily 11am–6pm; charge) has a room dedicated to local personality Jóhann Pétursson (1913–84), Iceland's tallest man. The ferry over to Grímsey island (*see page 253*) departs from Dalvík.

Hrísey Island

Hrísey island 🅟 is the second larg-est island off Iceland's coast, giving Eyjafjörður ("island fjord") its name. On a fine day, the 15-minute trip from Árskógssandur (just south of Dalvík) is well worthwhile – on weekends, there are usually some well-dressed folk from Akureyri making the excursion solely to dine on the island's special-ity, Galloway beef, as served up at the **Brekka restaurant**.

Hrísey is the only place in the coun-try where Galloway cattle are raised, and it is prohibited by law to remove them to the mainland. It is also the location of Iceland's quarantine centre: when it opened in 1974, all animals on the island had to be killed to minimise the risk of cross-infection. The result has been that Hrísey now supports some of the lushest vegetation in the entire country.

There is a small village here with a church for the 200 or so inhabitants, which during World War II was the billet for five British servicemen whose job it was to check up on all trawlers entering the fjord, with only a broken machine gun to back them up. Much of Hrísey is a nature reserve and so off-limits to hikers, but there are still plenty of trails across the flat moor-lands, covered in purple heather and full of birdlife.

North from Dalvík

A popular side trip from Dalvík is into **Svarfaðardalur** valley, a wetland nature reserve popular with birdwatchers, entering on Route 805 and returning along Route 807. From the end of Route 805, hikers and horseriders can head into the wilderness of **Heljardalsheiði** for camping trips in some of the finest mountain country in Iceland.

North of Dalvík, a nerve-wracking and treacherous gravel road winding along the steep coastline was made more bearable by the opening in 1991 of a 3.5km (2-mile) tunnel. This one-lane passage through the mountainside has become something of a tourist attraction in itself, although claustrophobes might prefer to risk the old road around the headland of **Olafsfjarðarmúli** – which, incidentally, is a good place to see the midnight sun in July, with views on a clear day to Grímsey island, on the Arctic Circle.

Ólafsfjörður ⑰ is a fishing village of 850 people nestled amongst a ring of snow-capped, 1,200-metre (3,900ft) -high peaks. Despite the setting, it has little more of interest than fishing boats and factories.

Points south

Heading south from Akureyri, Route 821 runs along the Eyjafjarðará river valley. The pretty farm **Kristnes**, built on the site where Helgi the Lean first settled, is 7km (4 miles) along on a hill with a strategic view of the fjord. A few minutes further south is another farm, **Grund** ⑱, which has one of the most unusual churches in Iceland; with its several Romanesque spires, it looks as if it has been transplanted from St Petersburg. The farmer Magnús Sigurðsson built it to his own design in 1906 to serve the whole river valley. The church broke a nearly millennium-old tradition by being built on a north-south axis instead of east-west.

A good example of a more traditional church, made of turf and stone, is at the farm of **Saurbær** ⑲, which is situated 27km (17 miles) south of Akureyri on Route 821. The quaint interior is open to visitors. At this point, the road continues to the farm of **Torfufell**, or across the river valley to return to Akureyri on Route 829. En route is the historic farm of **Munkaþverá**. Originally known as Þverá, this was the birthplace in the 10th century of the notorious Odinworshipping Viking Víga-Glúmur. In

Boarding the ferry to Hrísey island. Ferries operate from Árskógssandur every two hours for the 15-minute journey (for more details see page 316).

Horse-riding expeditions into the remote Fjörður peninsula are offered by Polar Horses (tel: 463 3179; www. polarhestar.is) at Grytubakki II farm 4km (2½ miles) outside Grenivík.

BELOW: Goðafoss.

the 12th century, a Benedictine monastery was built on the site, although none of it remains. Finally, at **Ytri-Hóll**, look out for a classic turf house that is still in use: the tiny chimney poking out from the grassy roof only makes it look even more like a hobbit's hole.

Eyjafjördur's eastern shore

The Ring Road runs east of Akureyri – giving some of the best views of the town – before running north and heading into the **Grýtubakkahreppur** district. Turn off at Route 83 for **Laufás ⑳**, a beautifully situated farm looking out over Eyjafjörður with a small white church and 19th-century turf farmhouse **museum** (open mid-May–mid-Sept daily 9am–6pm; charge). Built in the 1860s, the dirt-floored building was a vicarage and upper-crust home, and is now crowded with antiques. A famous touch is the carved woman's face and duck placed over the middle segment of the farmhouse. Just 22km (14 miles) from the Ring Road turn-off is the picturesque but somnolent fishing town of **Grenivík ㉑** (population 249). Only founded in 1910, Grenivík

is at the edge of the rugged Fjörður peninsula, which has been uninhabited since World War II.

The Ring Road continues east towards Lake Mývatn, but first passes the small lake **Ljósavatn** ("lightwater") and a turn-off to the farm of the same name. This was the Saga Age farm of the chieftain Þorgeir Þorkelsson, Law-speaker in the Alþingi in AD 1000, who was forced to decide whether Iceland should be pagan or Christian. As the *Kristni Saga* tells it, Þorgeir spent 24 hours under his cloak before deciding for the Christians. Riding back from Þingvellir to his home at Ljósavatn, he passed a giant waterfall and decided to toss all his carved images of pagan gods into its waters. This powerful waterfall, **Goðafoss ㉒** ("fall of the gods"), is virtually beneath the Ring Road a few kilometres further on, and is the easiest of Iceland's major falls to visit. Most cars and buses en route to Mývatn stop here at the small petrol station/store at **Fosshóll**.

The surrounding area of the **Bárðardalur** valley is a 7,000-year-old lava flow, through which the Skjálfandafljót river has cut a path to form Goðafoss. ❏

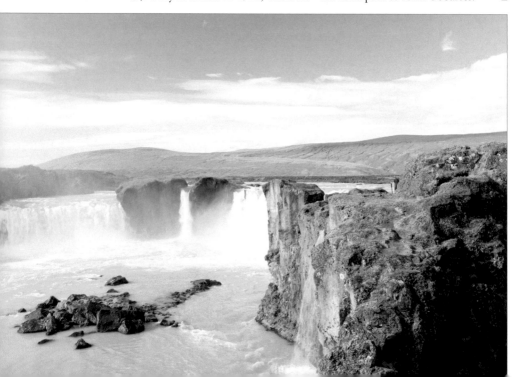

RESTAURANTS, CAFÉS AND BARS

Restaurants

The price guide is for the average price of dinner per person, without wine:
$$$ Over ISK4,500
$$ ISK2,500–4,500
$ Under ISK2,500

Akureyri

Bautinn
Hafnarstræti 92, Akureyri
Tel: 462 1818
An Akureyri institution which is always busy with locals and visitors alike. A good central location for burger and fries as well as a couple of more substantial meat dishes. **$$**

Café Paris
Hafnarstræti 96, Akureyri
Particularly popular at lunchtime for its good-value specials, this cheerful café on the main shopping street has a pleasant wooden interior and mellow ambience. **$**

Friðrik V
Kaupvangsstræti 6, Akureyri
Tel: 461 5775
Undoubtedly the finest place to dine in Akureyri. Owner and chef, Friðrik, trained at London's River Café and also worked in Reykjavík's Hótel Holt before opening this elegant first-floor restaurant serving creatively prepared fish dishes blending the freshest Icelandic ingredients with a subtle hint of the Mediterranean. **$$$**

Greifinn
Glerárgata 20, Akureyri
Tel: 460 1600

The most popular family restaurant in Akureyri with a huge choice of international dishes – BBQ ribs, Tex-Mex, pasta, pizzas, fish mains, even lamb vindaloo. Book a table on busy nights. **$$**

La Vita è Bella
Hafnarstræti 92, Akureyri
Tel: 461 5858
A good choice for well prepared Italian fare in the centre of Akureyri. Although the pasta and pizzas are good value, the meat dishes on the menu are expensive. **$$–$$$**

RUB 23
Kaupvangsstræti 23, Akureyri
Tel: 462 2223
A slightly gimmicky concept restaurant (you select a "rub" from a choice of spice mixtures to flavour your food), this is nevertheless an elegant seafood place with a menu that leans towards Japan. **$$$**

Strikið Brasserie
Skipagata 14, Akureyri
Tel: 462 7100
There are great views of the fjord from this pleasant brasserie which has tasty lamb and fish mains. Worth seeking out at midday for their special-offer lunches. **$$–$$$**

Out of town

Brekka
Hrísey island Tel: 466 1751
There are superb views from this hillside restaurant. Specialities are Galloway steaks (the cattle are raised on the island)

and blue mussels from the fjord. Open June–Aug. **$$–$$$**

Brimnes Hótel
Bylgjubyggð 2, Ólafsfjörður
Tel: 466 2400
Eating places in Ólafsfjörður are limited. This pleasant hotel restaurant, with fresh seafood dishes, pasta and pizzas, is your best bet. **$$**

Við Höfnina
Hafnarbraut 5, Dalvík
In summer, this working-man's caff by the harbour offers more elaborate evening meals with a seafood focus, including an Eyrarfjörður speciality, blue mussels cooked in stout. **$–$$**

Bars

Akureyri

Brynja
Aðalstræti 3, Akureyri
Those with a sweet tooth should visit this icecream shop, south of the centre.

It's a local institution, and the first port of call for most Icelandic visitors. **$**

Café Amour
Ráðhústorg 7
A great spot for an early evening drink right on the main square.

Græni Hatturinn
Hafnarstræti 96
This basement pub is the closest thing Akureyri has to a British pub. It's located beneath a café.

Sjallinn
Geislagata 14
The place to come for the cheapest beer in Akureyri, this pub is attached to the town's main club.

Vélsmiðjan
Strandgata 49
A good live music venue located down by the water's edge, this club opens Friday and Saturday from 10pm for drinks and dancing.

RIGHT: an Icelandic buffet lunch.

Icelandic Hauntings

One in every 500 inhabitants of Iceland is a ghost according to *Vættatal*, the spiritual *Who's Who* of Iceland by folklore historian Árni Björnsson

According to *Vættatal*, more than 500 ghouls, trolls and paranormal beings haunt Iceland, making a substantial – or perhaps insubstantial – addition to its quarter of a million human population. This high ghost quotient is not entirely unexpected, as the island is the perfect home for any spook, what with long periods of darkness in winter and an abundance of grotesque rock and lava formations providing perfect camouflage for monsters and ogres.

Flesh-and-blood Icelanders, it seems, enjoy excellent relations with their other-wordly neighbours. In a survey on the supernatural in Western Europe, Icelanders topped the league for ghostly experiences, with 41 percent claiming contact with the dead, compared to the European average of 20 percent.

Zombies, spirits and trolls

Traditionally, however, ghosts were not harmless visitations from the dear departed. They usually took

the form of an *afturganga*, a dead man turned zombie, and were capable of killing people or (worse) taking them to hell. Only the spiritual powers of a priest or the physical prowess of a strongman could exorcise such a nightmarish spook.

A very uncomfortable characteristic of the *afturganga* is his tendency to walk again before anyone knows he has died. One such was the Deacon of Dark River, who in the eighteenth century drowned on his way to his girlfriend's to take her to a dance. He nonetheless turned up, a little late, and the unsuspecting girl got on the back of his horse. As they rode through the night, she overheard him muttering:

The moon hides, as death rides,
Do you not see the white mark
On my brow, Garun, Garun.

Fortunately, this ditty held two clues to his true nature: firstly, ghosts always repeat things, and secondly they cannot say "God". The girl's name was Guðrún, and Guð is "God" in Icelandic. The terrified Guðrún managed to jump off seconds before the ghostly rider and horse vanished into an open grave leading straight to hell. She was never the same again, and some say she lost her mind completely.

Other forms of ghost are the *fylgja* or familiar spirit, and its close relations the *móri* and the *skotta*. These are shadowy, malevolent spirits, and when they are ill-wished onto a man, it is said that they will follow him and his descendants unto the ninth generation.

Then there are the trolls – elemental beings who, fortunately, turn into stone if they are caught outside in daylight. All of Iceland is dotted with trolls who stayed out just that little bit too long – including the great stone troll-cow, Hvítserkur, caught having a drink of sea-water just off the northwest coast.

The hidden people

All things considered, Icelanders probably prefer their more attractive neighbours from the other world, the elves. Like Hollywood filmstars, they look like humans – but are richer, more glamorous and usually completely amoral. According to one legend, the elves were the children that Eve hadn't finished washing when God came to visit; they were not fit to be seen, so she had to hide them. Thus, they are also known as the Hidden People, and with good reason: only 5 percent of Icelanders have actually met one. Nevertheless, elves are held in the highest regard, with 53 percent of the population either believing in, or not denying, their existence.

In legend, those who visit the elves and survive the experience return to the human world laden with riches but often strangely changed. In nearly all

Grundarfjördur, a rock stands between the houses numbered 82 and 86 – the elves live at number 84.

Despite these superstitious gestures, Dr Árni Björnsson says that true believers in elves and ghosts comprise only a very small minority in Iceland. "Most of us do not actively believe in these things, but on the other hand we are reluctant to deny their existence," he says. "It is really a form of scepticism. We live in a land which is highly unpredictable – what is grass and meadow today could be lava and ash tomorrow. So we have learnt not to rely too much on the factual evidence of our senses."

And, of course, the existence of elves in our modern world is such a nice idea. "People think it would be fun if they did exist, so they pretend to believe in them. Unlike other nations, we aren't in the least ashamed of it. In fact, we are rather proud of our elves." He adds: "Iceland is a big country for such a small population. We've plenty of room for neighbours of all kinds."

Indeed, this laissez-faire attitude is ensconced in folk tradition and the sagas. The medieval bishop, Guðmundur the Good, once set off to consecrate Drangey, to drive away the multitude of ghouls, fiends and devils that haunted this island. As he went about his holy work, a voice rang out from the rocks. "Consecrate no more, Guðmundur," it cried. "The wicked need some place to be." The bishop sensibly took the point and quickly returned to shore.   ❏

cases, the elves decide when and where they will be seen by humans. Usually, this is when they need assistance. Human women, it is said, are sometimes fetched by distraught elfen husbands to act as midwives to elf-mothers having difficulties in childbirth.

One 20th-century figure to have had an encounter with the Hidden People was trade-union leader Tryggvi Emilsson, who, as a young man, was saved from death by an elf-maiden after he had fallen down a gully. Her beauty, he said, haunted him for the rest of his life. Elf-women have been known to have even more intimate physical relations with human men, and are obviously more liberated than their human counterparts, often leaving their lovers holding the baby, as it were.

It is of some consolation that these semi-supernatural offspring are usually highly talented and handsome. Elf-men, on the other hand, make conscientious and kind lovers, according to the tales told by the few women who have been lucky enough to have tried one out.

The elves of Iceland are treated with great respect. The rocks and hills in which they make their homes are diligently preserved, for great harm traditionally comes to those that tamper with these elusive neighbours. Roads skirt round well-known elf-hills. One such is the road that runs from Reykjavík to the suburb of Kópavogur, which is actually called Álfhólsvegur, or Elf-Hill Road. On the main street of the town of

LEFT: an elf-maiden rising from her grotto. **ABOVE:** Christmas trolls. **RIGHT:** two rowdy trolls.

GRÍMSEY

Situated on the Arctic Circle, the island of
Grímsey is a remote outpost, home to huge
colonies of sea birds and just under 90 islanders

The folk on the remote, weather-beaten island of **Grímsey** ❷ tell the tale of a local minister who discovered that the Arctic Circle ran right through his house. He decided that it not only bisected his bedroom, it bisected his bed: the minister slept on one side of the Arctic Circle, his wife on the other, and rarely did either cross the great divide.

The apocryphal story is told and retold in various forms (sometimes it's a minister, sometimes an old magistrate), but it sums up the tongue-in-cheek attitude the Grímsey islanders have to the Arctic Circle – an imaginary line which, to the outside world, puts Grímsey on the map. They can only regard with some bemusement anyone who makes the pilgrimage all the way to their remote polar outpost just to say that they've walked across a geographical abstraction. "How did it feel?" someone might ask with good-natured concern. "Have your feet turned blue yet?"

But, although its location on latitude 66°30' N may still be Grímsey's claim to fame, a steady stream of travellers are finding out that the island has more concrete attractions to offer. The sheer isolation of this tiny piece of land, with a population of fewer than 100 souls, has its own peculiarly Icelandic appeal: the scenery is wild and beautiful, the

birdlife extraordinary, while the people remain beguilingly eccentric. And Grímsey has one of the strangest histories in Iceland, settled by chess-playing Vikings and supported by a 19th-century American millionaire. (And, frankly, it is quite fun to know that you're standing on the Arctic Circle.)

Island of chess players

Grímsey was first settled in the 10th century by a Viking named Grímur (hence the name Grím's island), whose descendants took the Icelandic obses-

Main attractions
SANDVÍK
CLIFFTOP WALKS
STANDING IN THE ARCTIC CIRCLE

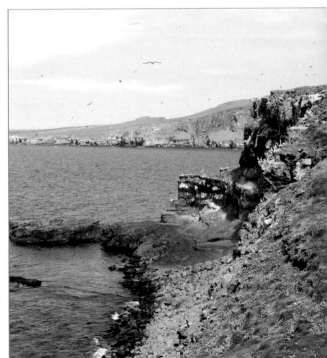

PRECEDING PAGES: puffins on Grímsey. **LEFT:**
a lighthouse in the midst of the isolation.
RIGHT: the coastline of wild Grímsey.

Scheduled services from the mainland sail from Dalvík, north of Akureyri, to Grímsey three times per week. The trip takes three hours. See page 316 for details.

BELOW RIGHT: a place of worship.

sion with chess to new extremes. Tradition has it that long summers and longer winters were spent devoted to the game, with some players spending weeks confined to their beds devising new stratagems. Chess was more important than life itself: it was not unknown for a player to fling himself into the sea rather than bear the shame of defeat.

Perhaps not surprisingly, Grímsey did not prosper as a fishing port. On one occasion in the 18th century, the entire male population except for the minister was lost in a single fishing accident (perhaps they were exhausted from playing chess). According to folklore, the minister took responsibility for repopulating the island himself.

Then, in the late 19th century, the island's eccentric reputation was brought to the attention of a wealthy North American named Daniel Willard Fiske – prominent journalist, Old Icelandic scholar, friend of both the Icelandic independence hero Jón Sigurðsson and the writer Mark Twain,

and, in 1857, chess champion of the US. Although Willard Fiske only glimpsed the shores of Grímsey as he passed it in a steamship, the island fired his vivid imagination and he decided to take its local population under his wing.

First Fiske sent the essentials: a gift of marble chess sets to each of the farms on the island. These were followed by masses of firewood and a bequest to finance the island's first school and library. Finally, on his death in 1904, Fiske left the inhabitants of Grímsey $12,000 – at that time the most money anyone had ever given to Iceland. Today, Fiske is still revered on Grímsey as a sort of secular saint. His birthday on 11 November is celebrated with a meeting and coffee in the community hall. Fiske's portrait still watches over the islanders from the library wall, but unfortunately, Grímsey hasn't kept up the love of chess. Hardly anybody plays it – these days, the favourite game is surfing the internet.

Last stop before the Pole

Until the 1930s, the only way to reach Grímsey was on the mail ship that left

A Nation of Chess Players

Probably introduced by the first settlers in the 9th century, chess was a common pastime in Iceland through the Middle Ages, as shown by numerous old expressions from the game which have been preserved in everyday speech. When Willard Fiske visited in 1879, he found eager players all over the country. Fiske published Iceland's first chess magazine, providing a theoretical training ground that guided the game into the realms of organised sport. In 1958, Friðrik Ólafsson became the nation's first grandmaster. The next generation was inspired by the "Match of the Century", which took place in Reykjavík in 1972, when Bobby Fischer wrested the world championship from Boris Spassky. Among the enthusiasts were Helgi Ólafsson and Margeir Pétursson, then in their teens and now both international grandmasters. In their wake came a further eight Icelandic grandmasters, bringing the country's total to 11.

Bobby Fischer became a fugitive from the US in 1992, after breaking sanctions by playing chess in the former Yugoslavia. In 2005, Iceland controversially gave Fischer Icelandic citizenship so that he could avoid facing criminal charges in the US. And so one of the greatest chess-players of all time lived out his last three years in a Reykjavík suburb, and was buried in Icelandic soil in a quiet country cemetery just outside Selfoss.

Akureyri once every six months (you could return six months later, provided bad weather didn't prevent the ship from running).

Today, there is a year-round ship service three days each week, taking about three hours each way from Dalvík. Light aircraft flights from Akureyri (daily in summer, less frequently the rest of the year) take only 25 minutes to cover the 41km (25 miles). Arriving by plane in Grímsey is a truly memorable experience since, more often than not, the plane flies low over the runway before attempting to land, in an effort to chase away the hundreds of birds which gather here to feed (*see page 256*).

Both the plane and the ferry allow same day return trips – which, until 1991 when a new guesthouse opened, was just as well, since the only accommodation was on the floor of the community centre. (Camping is permitted if you site your tent discreetly.)

Getting acquainted with the island is not difficult. There are 10 old farms on the island, but most of the inhabitants live in the "village" of **Sandvík** – the

name for the 15 houses lined up along the harbour.

After World War II, Grímsey still didn't have electricity, there was little fresh water and the occasional case of scurvy was reported among the islanders. Modern fishing techniques have brought affluence here – the township may have a rather scruffy look, but the houses are modern, there are satellite dishes to pick up television, greenhouses to grow vegetables and a large indoor swimming pool. Although there is only one road on Grímsey – 3km (2 miles) long – the island boasts a handful of private cars and several tractors.

The Grímsey **community centre** can be identified by the mural on its walls. Built on the site of the old school financed by Fiske, it still contains the library, original photographs of the benefactor and the only one of the 11 marble chess sets still in existence. Nobody seems to know where the rest have gone.

A short walk west of the village is the whitewashed, late-19th-century wooden **church**. Above the altar is a replica of Leonardo da Vinci's *Last*

TIP

The island is only 4km (2½ miles) by 2km (1¼ miles) in size, and can be circumambulated in about 5 hours. A hiking trail begins from the airport and strikes out across some especially tussocky grass towards the island's west coast and a several sheer bird-cliffs. Winding its way along the clifftops, the path gradually descends towards the harbour where it joins the main road. It's now a straightforward stroll past the church and the village store back towards the airstrip.

BELOW: the last propeller plane in the run-up to Christmas arrives.

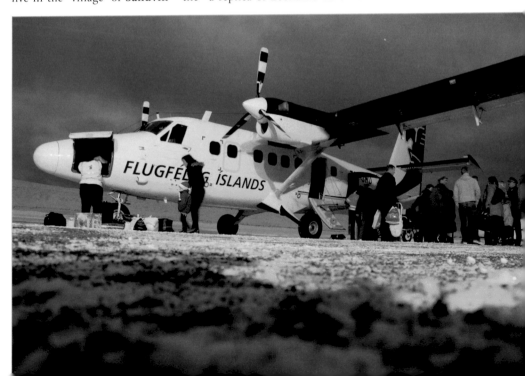

Supper, painted by a mainland artist, Arngrímur Gíslason. The nearby **parsonage**, which was built in 1909, is now maintained by a layman – Grímsey pays for a minister to come every three months from Akureyri (if he wants to come more often, he has to pay for the journey himself). It's long been rumoured on the island that the Arctic Circle runs right through the middle of the priest's bed, putting an icy division between him and his wife. However, in reality, this is extremely unlikely since the Arctic Circle is not constant but is currently creeping northwards, due to the earth's uneven orbit, at a rate of 15 metres (50ft) or so every year. It won't be for another 10,000–20,000 years that the northward movement will stop, by which time the Circle will have reached 68 degrees north, well to the north of Grímsey's geographical position, and will then start moving slowly south again.

Along the coast are the traditional fish-drying racks. There are four fish processing plants on the island, concentrating on salted fish and dried cod-heads (which are sold to Nigeria).

BELOW: arctic terns in flight.

Dive-bombers of the Arctic Circle

Heading back to the eastern end of the island, the road runs straight into the bitumen runway of the airport (where the Básar guesthouse, one of two places for formal accommodation, is also to be found). The runway is carpeted by resting sea birds – before some landings or take-offs, a car or tractor is driven up and down in an attempt to shoo away these potential hazards to aircraft. (On departure from Grímsey, it's not uncommon for birds to strike the aircraft's wings as they and it take off at the same time).

Usually that's the end of the matter. Should you be visiting in June or July, however, the scene is more like something from Alfred Hitchcock's *The Birds*. That's when the arctic terns are nesting all over the island, and anyone coming near a bird's young is fair game for a divebomb attack. The screeching call *kría! kría! kría!* (which is actually the bird's name in Icelandic) is the prelude to a possible peck on the back of the head – which is why, in this season, everyone wears a thick hat (a leather glove under a beany or beret is recommended) and carries a big stick (the Básar Guesthouse will lend out plastic rods to guests for self-defence).

On the northern side of the runway is the Grímsey road sign, theoretically marking the location of the Arctic Circle. Arrows point to various major world cities (including New York: 4,445km/2,763 miles; Sydney: 16,317km/10,027 miles; London: 1,949km/1,225 miles).

A path leads away from the airport towards 100-metre (330ft) cliff faces, which can be followed completely around the island. Soon the trail disappears beneath a bed of thick, matted grass, which seems to glow green against the blue of the sea. The polka-dot of yellow weeds finishes off the colourful effect (there are a total of some 100 species of flowering plant on Grímsey).

The cliffs on the north and east sides of the island are also where the most spectacular birdlife can be found, creating a din that is little short of cacophonous. Thirty-six species of bird nest on the island, including 11 different types of sea bird. There is a large puffin community, and it is quite possible to come within a few metres of these birds (but don't walk too close to the edge of the cliffs, since underground puffin nests can be accidentally crushed). There are fulmars, kittiwakes, gulls and arctic terns, and Grímsey was one of the last places in Iceland where the little auk, which usually nests closer to the Pole, came to breed (although they haven't been seen for the last few years).

Although it is located on the Arctic Circle, Grímsey's summers and winters are never as extreme as one would imagine: the June midnight is bright but never blinding, and there are about four hours of vague light in December (provided the weather isn't very cloudy, that is, in which case it stays dark).

Even so, life on the island is still tough, and it says something for the islanders' spirit that they have kept their numbers at around 100 while other tiny Icelandic islands have lost their wealth and population. Schoolchildren, who spend their last three years studying on the mainland, almost always return to Grímsey. Even though not many play chess here now, the island still shows the eccentric, indomitable spirit that inspired the old benefactor Daniel Willard Fiske. ❏

BELOW: midwinter aurora.

LAKE MÝVATN

This outstandingly beautiful area has the twin attractions of the serene lake at Mývatn, one of Iceland's major breeding grounds for birds, and spectacular volcanic activity

Reykjavik

Sitting just to the west of the Mid-Atlantic Ridge that is slowly tearing Iceland apart, the Lake Mývatn district is one of the most volcanically active regions on earth. Created by a powerful basaltic lava eruption 2,300 years ago, the lake and its surrounding landscapes are dominated by curiously shaped volcanic landforms such as pillars of lava. The surrounding wetlands are a favourite breeding and feeding spot for many varieties of waterfowl, especially ducks, attracted here by a plentiful supply of food in the form of the countless insects which congregate here in the summer months. In this respect, Mývatn is unusual: Iceland's relatively low summer temperatures and strong winds do not provide a ready habitat for insects.

In the mid-1970s, earthquakes centred here were felt in the entire north of the country, with lava erupting from nearby Mount Krafla over several years to spectacular effect. Activity continued through the early 1980s and today there are almost daily subterranean rumblings (although they are mostly too small to be noticed except by scientific instruments). Nowhere else in Iceland can you see the same combination of craters, fresh lava fields, hot springs, geysers and bubbling mud pools.

PRECEDING PAGES: Route 87 from Húsavík to Mývatn – volcanic activity can make for rough and tortuous roads. **LEFT:** Mývatn in autumn. **RIGHT:** the Námafjall geothermal field.

Meanwhile, the lake's natural beauty and role as a wildlife breeding ground led to it being set aside as a national conservation area in 1974 – a status that actually gives it more protection than a National Park. The lake is a veritable oasis on the fringes of Iceland's bleak northern deserts, supporting, among other things, the world's largest population of breeding ducks. As a result, Mývatn has established itself as Iceland's number one tourist attraction outside of the "Golden Circle" and a place that has been known to keep nature lovers

Main attractions
BIRDWATCHING AND SIGURGEIR BIRD MUSEUM
SKÚTUSTAÐAGÍGAR PSEUDO-CRATERS
HÖFÐI
HVERFELL
MÝVATN NATURE BATHS (JARÐBÖÐIN)
HVERIR GEOTHERMAL FIELD
LEIRHNJÚKUR CRATER

Whilst in the Lake Mývatn area be sure to sample some locally produced geothermal bread, *hverabrauð* (lava bread). Making use of the plentiful supply of free heat and power, the sticky, sweet loaves are baked in an underground oven heated by geothermal steam rising from deep underground. A less appetising local dish is fermented duck eggs; these tend to be foul-smelling and only for the more adventurous.

BELOW: Leihrnjúkur.

occupied for weeks. And while offering plenty to explore in its own right, it also makes a good base for trips to the Northeast and to Askja in the interior.

In search of sulphur

Although the winters are long and cold, covering the lake with ice for seven months of the year, Mývatn enjoys more sunshine and receives less rain than almost anywhere else in the country. As a result, it has been popular with settlers from the Saga Age onwards: in 1908, archaeologists dug up a Norse longhouse whose wall was over 40 metres (130ft) in length, and may have contained a temple of Thor.

Dating their ancestry back to those days are the Reykjahlíð family, whose farm covers the whole surrounding area – at some 6,000 sq km (2,300 sq miles) in size, it is the biggest farm in Iceland and more than twice the size of Luxembourg. The family's days of glory were in the 14th century, when sulphur was mined from Námaskarð on their land and sent to Europe to be made into gunpowder. This remote corner of Iceland helped keep the world's wars rolling until the 19th century, when other sulphur sources were found.

Farming in the area also prospered despite the devastating eruption of the Leirhnjúkur crater (10km/6 miles northeast of Reykjahlíð). The "Mývatn-fires" lasted for five years, from 1724 to 1729, wiped out three farms and wrecked Reykjahlíð's buildings – but created some of the bizarre lava formations which now make the area so fascinating.

Today the farm is still working, although the owners have invested in the tourist business and allow visitors access to almost every part of the property. Travellers started arriving in numbers to see Mývatn and its surroundings in the early 20th century, and the family built the first hotel, the **Hotel Reykjahlíð**, in the 1940s – it has since housed everyone from Prince Harald of Norway to a steady stream of backpackers. In 1968, a diatomite plant was opened at Bjarnarflag near Mývatn, and a small village, also known as **Reykjahlíð ❶**, sprang up around the hotel northeast of the lake to become the service centre of the area.

With hotels, camping grounds, super-

Lake Mývatn

markets and snack bars, Reykjahlíð is a functional base for travellers. It does have a **church**; although it was rebuilt in 1972, it is on the site of the original church that was in the path of the lava flow in 1729 and seemed certain to be destroyed. Miraculously, the lava parted literally at the church door and flowed on either side of the wooden building, an event that the devout ascribed to divine intervention.

Next to the Samkaup supermarket and petrol station, the **visitors' centre**, run by the Icelandic Nature Conservation Agency, has information on routes around the area and its natural history, with some excellent lava exhibits.

Circuit around the lake

A narrow road circles Lake Mývatn, connecting the various points of interest. The lake itself is 37 sq km (14 sq miles) in area, making it the fourth-largest in Iceland, but unusually shallow – the average depth is only 2 metres (7ft), with the deepest point only 4.5 metres (15ft). This shallowness allows the sun's rays to reach the bottom so creating a thriving growth of algae and plankton, including rare marimo balls – globes of green algae (*Aegagropila linnaei*) that occur in only four places in the world. The lake contains 50 islets.

The name Mývatn actually means "midge lake" and, for long stretches of the summer, clouds of these tiny flying insects can make any visit a misery. Billions usually emerge in June and August to dive into eyes, noses and ears with relentless energy. They are often joined by biting blackflies, so make sure you bring some insect repellent. (Head nets are, not surprisingly, sold in most shops.) It is cold comfort to learn that the midges are crucial to the lake's ecosystem: their corpses fertilise the lakeside and the larvae are a staple for birds and fish.

The surfeit of midges as fodder has also made the River Laxá, which flows through Mývatn, the source of Iceland's biggest salmon (they spawn in the lower part of the lake). Mývatn also offers the best trout fishing in the country.

The fields of fire

Heading north from Reykjahlíð, Route 87 crosses the lava flow from the 1720s

TIP

A great way to get to grips with the land-scapes around the lake is to take a sightseeing flight from the airstrip at Reykjahlíð with the Mýflug airline. Flights operate during the summer and require a minimum of two passengers. Tours vary in duration from twenty minutes to two hours, with the longer flights also taking in Krafla, Dettifoss, Ásbyrgi and the Jökulsárgljúfur canyon. There are full details of the options available at www.myflug.is where prices range from €60–230.

BELOW: there are easy walking routes in the area.

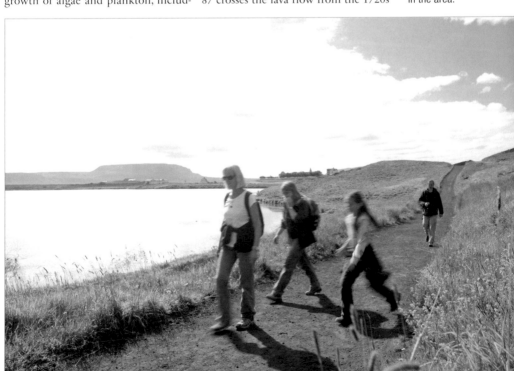

BELOW: lava formations at Dimmuborgir.
BELOW RIGHT: bird-watching devotees swear that the bridge on the Ring Road over the Laxá River is Iceland's premier location for spotting birds.

that dominates the topography of the village and the northern landscape of the lake. Called **Eldhraun** ("fire lava"), this barren landscape gives a glimpse of the desert that Route 87 runs into – so devoid of life that NASA sent its Apollo 11 crew for training missions here in the late 1960s. Keep an eye out on the left-hand side for a giant bubble of dried lava, where the surface layer has been cracked like a huge egg.

Turning left onto Route 848, the landscape becomes much greener and quickly reaches the marshes of the **conservation area**. This is the main breeding ground for the lake's birds, and during the nesting season (15 May–20 July) its shoreline is off-limits. Fifteen species of duck have been recorded on the lake, and up to 100,000 birds can be gathered here at once. Most of the birds are summer migrants, arriving from late April onwards. The tufted duck and the greater scaup are the most prolific species, but the beautiful Barrow's goldeneye, red-breasted merganser and the teal are also common. The Barrow's goldeneye is one of the few birds to spend the winter at Mývatn,

carefully choosing ice-free areas of the lake which are kept open by warm currents. Virtually the entire European population of the species breeds here. In addition to ducks, the unusual red-necked phalarope, Slavonian grebe and whooper swan are common visitors, as are the great northern diver and red-throated diver. Incidentally, there is a long tradition in the Mývatn area of collecting birds' eggs for private consumption. However, local people are sure to follow the age-old tradition of always leaving at least four eggs in the nest for incubation. For more information, ornithologists should head for the **Sigurgeir Bird Museum** (open daily mid-May–Aug 11am–7pm, Sept noon–5pm, Oct 1–5pm (reduced hours rest of year); charge) on the **Neslandatangi peninsula ❷**, which almost cuts the lake in two. The low-lying museum houses the private collection of avid bird- and egg-collector Sigurgeir, and also acts as his memorial: he died in 1999 at the age of 37. The museum contains an example of every species of Icelandic bird, except for the grey phalarope. There's a calm café with huge windows overlooking the lake – particularly serene at dusk – and bird hides nearby.

South of the conservation area, the 529-metre (1,735ft) peak of **Vindbelg-jarfjall** ❸, seen to the right, can be climbed in a couple of hours for views of the lake. Beyond that, another smaller lake, **Sandvatn**, is probably the best place in the area to see gyrfalcons.

South of here, the road now runs into the Ring Road. On the southern shore of the lake is Mývatn's secondary service centre of **Skútustaðir** ❹, with a petrol station, hotel, church and café-restaurant.

From here, there is an easy hour-long path around the **Skútustaðagígar pseudo-craters**. These were formed when water was trapped beneath flowing lava, boiled and burst up through the surface, creating what looks like volcanic cones. Some were formed so recently that their sides are still charred.

Picnic promontory

One of the most sheltered and relaxing spots on the lakeside is **Höfði** ❺, a forested promontory that has been turned into a reserve, with a small admission fee. There is a vaguely fairy-tale atmos-phere to the place, with paths running through flower-covered lava outcrops and forests of birch trees. Large rocks by the lakeside rocks also provide ideal picnic hide-aways.

A turn-off to the right leads to **Dim-muborgir** ❻ ("black castles"), a vast, 2,000-year-old field of contorted volcanic pillars, some extending as high as 20 metres (65ft). There is a helpful visitor centre and café (open June–Aug daily 9am–10pm, reduced hours Apr, May and Sept) here, offering guided walks in the area. A viewing platform looks out over the expanse, and visitors can wander about among the haunting arches, caves and natural tunnels. The most famous formation is **Kirkjan** (the Church), a cave that looks like the interior of a Gothic cathedral, and a 3-metre (16ft) hole that provides an amusing photo opportunity.

Further along the same road is the looming 1,000-metre (3,280ft) -wide crater of **Hverfell** ❼, formed in an eruption 2,500 years ago and these days likened to a giant football stadium. A steep path runs up the side of the crater, which is made entirely of loose volcanic rubble, or tephra. Hverfell's rim pro-

A common scoter, a species of diving duck common to Lake Mývatn but rare elsewhere in Iceland. Bird-spotters can see numerous other species of waterfowl, including the Barrow's goldeneye, one of the few North American species that breed in Iceland, as well as birds of prey including short-eared owls and gyrfalcons.

BELOW: Hverfell, one kilometre across.

The way down to Grjótagjá, an underground hot spring.

BELOW: the Mývatn Nature Baths.

vides one of the most sweeping views of the Mývatn area.

En route back to Reykjahlíð, a track to the right leads to **Grjótagjá** N, an underground hot spring made by a buckle in the earth, about 1km (½ mile) from the main road. The green waters may feel tepid to the touch, but below the surface they can be scalding, so swimming is forbidden.

A popular tourist attraction, the unique **Cowshed Café** (Vogafjós; open June–Aug daily 7.30am–11pm) backs onto a milking shed, so you can watch the working life of the farm while you sample Icelandic ice-cream.

Volcanologists' paradise

The Ring Road running east of Reykjahlíð immediately leads to a completely different landscape, a desolate, sandy plain of mixed orange and brown hues known as **Bjarnarflag** N. Further on is the site of Mývatn's former diatomite plant – which once processed the microscopic fossils called diatoms that were taken from the lake floor – a porous material used in filtering systems and as a filler, amongst other applications;

on the right is a brick factory, putting the local excess of tephra to good use. However, of more interest to visitors, the **Mývatn Nature Baths** (Jarðböðin við Mývatn; open daily June–Aug 9am–midnight, Sept–May noon–10pm; charge) are the north's answer to the Blue Lagoon. This sublime open-air geothermal pool lies just off the Ring Road and is an altogether more agreeable experience than its more famous cousin on the Reykjanes peninsula. There are far fewer bathers here, giving you the opportunity to loll undisturbed in the aquamarine waters as long as you like. The water comes from a local geothermal source and is cooled to around 38–40°C (100–104°F) to make it pleasant for bathing. In addition to the main pool, there are three steam saunas and (of course) hot-pots.

An overwhelming stench of sulphur greets travellers as the road climbs over the ridge of **Námafjall**, whose series of cracks – the largest appeared as recently as 1975 – betray its location plumb on the Mid-Atlantic Ridge. The Námafjall geothermal field has been drilled, revealing temperatures over 290°C (554°F) at a depth of 1.75km (1 mile). Steam and mud craters formed in this field during the Mývatn-fires of 1724, and new fissures spread south into the area in April 1728. At the pass is a parking area with views over the lake, and, stretching out on the other side is the famous geothermal field of **Hverir ⑩** – perhaps one of Iceland's most infernal and fascinating sights. Walkways run across the multi-coloured clay of the area, through dozens of bubbling mud pits and steaming vents. The surface here is particularly thin, and at some places likely to crumble, so to avoid being boiled alive in a mud pot, keep well within the marked paths.

Man-made disaster

A rough dirt road leads 7km (4 miles) north to the **Krafla area ⑪**, named after one of the mountains at the centre of the region. Pipes from the Krafla geothermal power plant form a metal doorway to the area, which is strangely appropriate: the construction of the plant in 1973, with its many bore holes into the earth's crust, is considered by some scientists to be responsible for triggering the eruptions that began here in 1975 – the first since the 1700s. Between 3–8km (2–5 miles) beneath the Krafla field lies a magma reservoir which is the source of local volcanic activity in the area. Magma builds up in the reservoir, causing the earth to rise, until it is released as rock intrusions or volcanic eruptions, resulting in the earth's surface sinking again.

The activity in the early 1970s, known as the "Krafla-fires" began with a dramatic spurt of molten lava that lit up Reykjahlíð by night. Some 15 eruptions followed in the next decade, but luckily the lava all flowed away from the small village and no major damage was done. However, volcanologists are expecting Krafla to blow again any time.

A stern warning sign (volcanic hazard zone – do not enter) at the first parking area here was put up during the 1984 eruptions to keep tourists away, but had the opposite effect: hundreds gathered here to watch the fireworks. The warning sign has now been removed, and during the summer there is still a stream

of visitors who go out to the black, partly warm lava field of the Krafla caldera that was spat up from the earth during the 1970s and 1980s, and the colourful crater of **Leirhnjúkur** (formed during the explosions of the 1720s). If you can forget the disconcerting possibility of being blown to kingdom come, this whole lifeless, primeval area gives as good a glimpse of the freshly formed earth as anyone is likely to get.

Further on, a second parking area sits at the base of **Víti** ("hell"), a dingey-brown explosion crater – now thought to be inactive. Its 320-metre (1,050ft)-wide bowl contains a pool of cold blue-green water (not to be confused with the other Víti crater further south, whose turquoise waters are warm and full of bathers – *see page 309*). Like the Blue Lagoon, the pool is a by-product of the cooling water from power plants, and its startling blue caused by the algae in the water. It is close to Mount Krafla itself, which, far from being a classic volcanic cone, is the rim of a larger caldera that has been worn and exploded almost beyond recognition. A walking trail leads around the crater rim. Víti was the initial source of the 1724 volcanic eruptions which blighted crop production for years afterwards. ❑

Cowshed Café

RESTAURANTS

Cowshed Café (Vogafjós)
Vogar, 2km outside Reykjahlíð village
Tel: 464 4303
Mozzarella and feta cheese from the herd of cows outside, trout and lamb smoked on the farm, and geyser bread baked in Mývatn's burning earth – the food at this quirky café couldn't get any fresher. **$$**

Gamli Bærinn
Reykjahlíð village

Tel: 464 4170
A dependable choice for soups and filling lunches as well as more substantial dinner dishes of fish and lamb. A pleasant, cosy interior makes this the premier choice for eating at Lake Mývatn. **$$**

Hótel Reynihlíð
Reykjahlíð village
Tel: 464 4170
Fine dining in the hotel restaurant beside the lake

which serves up expertly prepared fresh fish and meat dishes, making it a good choice for a special occasion in this part of the country. **$$$**

The price guide is for the average price of dinner per person, without wine:
$$$ Over ISK4,500
$$ ISK2,500–4,500
$ Under ISK2,500

THE GREAT OUTDOORS

The vast open spaces and wild landscapes of Iceland offer a wealth of opportunities for all who love the great outdoors

Iceland is an adventure holiday destination *par excellence*. Mountains, glaciers, lakes and thundering waterfalls are all here in abundance, and with its expansive wilderness areas and clear air, ever increasing numbers of visitors want to get out and experience all that wild nature for themselves. And there is a great deal on offer, from gentle hikes and horse-riding excursions to more demanding pursuits such as ice-climbing, white-water rafting and enough wilderness adventures to satisfy the most demanding free spirit.

One of the advantages of a rugged, sparsely populated country (about three people per sq km) is that you can *really* get away from it all. If you want peace and solitude, this is where you can be sure of finding it. Trekking holidays – usually undertaken as an organised group through a specialist agency – are the classic way to experience remote and roadless regions. Iceland's glaciers and icecaps are another major draw for those in search of a different kind of experience, be it skidooing, ice-climbing, cross-country skiing or simply walking in the pristine environment.

A great way to reach places where no vehicle (even a 4x4) can easily take you is on horseback. Riding all day among deserted valleys and mountains, fording rivers, leading your second mount which carries supplies and bedroll, you will gain real insight into the way Icelanders used to live.

For more details on what's available and a list of tour operators, see Travel Tips pages 332–5 and 341–2.

ABOVE: cycling can be hard going in Iceland, with rough roads and often poor weather. All the better for the intrepid enthusiast…

BELOW: the Icelandic horse is ideal for inexperienced riders. Farms all over the country offer horse-riding, from one-hour excursions to trips lasting several days.

GETTING INTO HOT WATER

ABOVE: idling away summer on the Lake Lögurinn shore.

RIGHT: white-water rafting on the Jökulsá Vestari River, in the Skagafjörður region.

BELOW: camp out under the stars before striking out on the endless trekking possibilities Iceland has to offer – Skaftafell National Park is one of the most popular areas.

Thanks to Iceland's lively geology, the country has an abundance of naturally heated geothermal water... and Icelanders take every opportunity to channel this water into their beloved swimming pools. Legally, every child must be taught how to swim, and students cannot graduate unless they have mastered this basic skill.

There are around 200 (mostly outdoor) bathing places, each with its own character and quirks. Places range from naturally occurring hot rivers and mountain pools known only to the initiated, to the modern municipal swimming baths found in every town, to mineral-rich seawater spas, such as the Blue Lagoon, whose waters are the by-product of a geothermal power plant.

A particularly Icelandic curiosity and one found in most municipal baths is the "hot pot", a small circular pool whose water steams at a deliciously high temperature (between 37°C and 42°C). These are the buzzing social centres of Icelandic life, where people gather for conversation, gossip and even business meetings. As Icelandic pools are filled with constantly flowing water, chemical cleaners are rarely used. In order to keep the water as clean as possible, all swimmers must take a shower in the nude before entering – which can come as something of a shock to the more bashful tourist.

RIGHT: ice climbing in the south of Iceland.

THE NORTHEAST

In this remote and little-visited region you can see sea birds and whales in their natural, unspoilt environment, and visit the unexpectedly lush Jökulsárgljúfur area, the northern section of Vatnajökull National Park

Main attractions
HÚSAVÍK WHALE-WATCHING TOURS
JÖKULSÁRGLJÚFUR NATIONAL PARK
ÁSBYRGI CANYON
DETTIFOSS
ÞÓRSHÖFN
VOPNAFJÖRÐUR

Bypassed by the Ring Road and its stream of regular traffic, the Northeast is one of Iceland's most isolated areas. Only two places usually attract significant numbers of travellers: the town of Húsavík, Iceland's "whale-watching capital"; and the Jökulsárgljúfur section of Vatnajökull National Park, whose canyons and waterfalls feature on a thousand postcards. Very few people continue on to explore the rugged coastline – largely because of poor transport services, bad roads and few good hotels.

However, if you're looking to explore off-the-beaten-track Iceland, this is one of the best places in the entire country. True, tourist attractions as such are few and far between, but the real draw of this corner of Iceland is to experience nature in the raw and to see a side of Icelandic life which is rarely glimpsed in some of the more cosmopolitan centres of the country. Here, life goes on much as it has for decades with little thought for tourism. You're guaranteed a rare insight into what it's like to live on the very edge of the Arctic, in a part of Iceland as obscure to most Reykjavíkers as it is to foreigners.

Yet the coastal route has a number of attractions for those with their own transport and an interest in finding out what lies off the beaten track. Dozens of atmospheric fishing villages cling precariously to this shore just south of the Arctic Circle. Exploring these quiet, conservative outposts and the craggy cliffs and wilderness areas around them reveals the harsh seafaring world that is in many ways Iceland's backbone.

Gateway to the northeast

The transport artery of the region, following the whole coastline, is Route 85. Approaching from Akureyri or Lake Mývatn, this road runs through the Aðaldalur valley right down to

PRECEDING PAGES: the torrent at Dettifoss, Europe's largest waterfall.
LEFT: Húsavík Church.

the shoreline of Skjálfandi ("shivering fjord"), an expanse of sand dotted by small lakes with an impressive wall of mountains as a backdrop.

Rows of picturesque fish-drying racks by the roadside fittingly announce the main town in the region, **Húsavík ❶** (population 2,200). The name "house bay" was given by the Swedish Viking Garðar Svavarsson, who journeyed to Iceland in the late 860s after his mother had seen it in a dream.

Long before the official First Settler, Ingólfur Arnarson, set foot on the island, Garðar spent a winter at Húsavík – and when he left, an unfortunate fellow named Náttafari was left behind with two slaves. The trio settled down permanently across the bay from Húsavík (the site can be seen from town), but have been disqualified from being considered Iceland's first settlers because their presence was involuntary.

Húsavík today is a tidy and agreeable town set above the first-rate harbour that provides for its existence: fishing and fish-processing are still major industries. The view of the colourful trawlers, murky black waters and snow-spattered granite mountains across the bay is particularly impressive. However, it is another harbour-reliant activity that draws busloads of tourists to this trim little town: Húsavík is Iceland's "whale-watching capital" thanks to its location on Skjálfandi Bay, a plankton- and fish-rich feeding ground. The two local companies who operate **whale-watching tours** *(see margin tip)* claim a 98-percent success rate for sightings. There are a huge variety of cetaceans off the coast, with the most commonly-sighted species being minke, humpback, white-beaked dolphins and harbour porpoises; luckier travellers might glimpse sei whales, northern bottlenose whales, fin whales, killer whales, pilot whales or even blue whales.

Before your whale-watching trip, it's well worth a visit to the excellent harbourside **Húsavík Whale Museum** (open daily June–Aug 9am–7pm, May and Sept 10am–5pm; charge; www.whale museum.is), which has exhibits on the history of whales and whaling in Iceland, and on whale species and biology; plus there's a gallery of whale skeletons.

Dominating the town is an unusual

TIP

Whale-watching tours, operated by two different companies, run from Húsavík up to nine times daily during the summer months. Trips can be booked with Gentle Giants (tel: 464 1500) and North Sailing (tel: 464 7272) at their ticket offices by the harbour. Should you fail to see whales (this includes dolphins and porpoises), the companies offer a free second trip.

BELOW: Husavík's Whale Museum.

The docks at tiny Flatley island.

cross-shaped **church**, with a 26-metre (85ft) spire and modern sculptures in the garden. The church, built in 1907, was designed by the Icelandic architect Rögnvaldur Ólafsson and made from Norwegian timber. It is among Iceland's most attractive churches and seats about 450 people. When it was built there were only 500 people living in the parish. The impressive altarpiece, depicting Lazarus raised from the dead, was painted in 1931 by Sveinn Þórarinsson from the neighbouring county of Kelduhverfi.

Along the road from the church, the **Icelandic Phallological Museum** (open late May–early Sept daily noon–6pm; charge) is the country's most offbeat museum. Inside, there are examples of the penises of every mammal found in Iceland or its offshore waters – except for Homo sapiens. However, it's just a matter of time before a human penis joins the collection: four donors have bequeathed their members to the museum.

Húsavík's other museum, **Safnahúsið** (open June–Aug daily 10am–6pm, Sept–May Mon–Fri 9am–4pm; charge) is the best in the northeast: prize exhibits include a replica of the 1584 Guðbrandur's Bible (the first translation of the Old and New Testaments into Icelandic, still considered the most ambitious publishing project ever undertaken in Iceland); and the polar bear that floated from Greenland to Grímsey island in 1973, only to be greeted by a bullet in the skull.

Arctic vista

For a panoramic view over the whole Húsavík area, drive one kilometre north of town to the unmarked yellow gate on the right, then continue as far as your car can take you (only a four-wheel drive should attempt the full distance on this dangerously slippery road). There is a viewfinder at the top, from which you can spot two small islands in the bay: **Flatey** had over 100 inhabitants 50 years ago but has now been abandoned, while **Lundey** is crowded only with puffins. Both can be visited in summer through the two Húsavík whale-watching companies.

The Northeast

From this point, the roads become dustier and road signs fewer. Lying north along Route 85 is the squat peninsula of **Tjörnes ❷**, whose 60-metre (200ft) cliff faces are renowned among geologists for their ancient fossils and easily visible geological strata (note that it is strictly forbidden to remove any fossils from this area). Non-geologists can get an idea of what is going on at a well-known but difficult-to-find site by the seashore, turning left onto a dirt road at the **Ytri-Tunga** farmhouse; the farm is unmarked but the road is before the **Hallbjarnarstaðir** farm, and crosses an electric fence. At Hallbjarnarstaðir there is a small **Mineral-and-Fossil Museum** (open June–Aug daily 10am–6pm; charge; tel: 464 1968). This was once the home of farmer Kári Sigurjónsson, who helped scientists to research shells. The exhibition tells the story of the prehistoric fossils from the Tjörnes layers in the cliffs below.

The road reaches the coast, then steeply descends the alarming cliff face at **Hallbjarnarstaðakambur Crest**, a dip on either side of the river where the layers of geological deposits are obvious

Rubbery slices of preserved shark – hákarl.

to the naked eye and fossils of molluscs lie scattered across the ground. At the shore, look out for a large greenish slab of rock, not native to Iceland, thought to have arrived from Greenland on sea-ice.

East of Tjörnes, the plain of **Kelduhverfi** is made up of sandy glacial wash (similar to the larger *sandur* in the south – *see page 198*), and is at the northern point where the two halves of Iceland are splitting apart. Volcanic activity in the 1970s was related to the eruptions at Krafla near Lake Mývatn. The whole area is at the mouth of the **Öxarfjörður** fjord. To the north of the highway is **Lake Víkingavatn ❸**, an important nesting site for Slavonian grebes. The nearby farm of the same name has been occupied by descendants of the same family since the 1600s.

Giant hoof print

The great attraction of the Northeast is **Jökulsárgljúfur ❹**, the country's longest river canyon at 25km (16 miles). Its full name, meaning "glacial river can-

BELOW: trekking to the Jökulsá canyon.

TIP

If you are planning to camp in the National Park, stock up at the Ásbyrgi petrol station and supermarket at the Ásbyrgi farm outside the park. This is the only place selling supplies within about 25 km (15 miles).

yon", is difficult for non-Icelanders to pronounce but can be referred to as Jökulsá Canyon – pronounced *yer-kool-sar*. Once private property within the huge Ás estate, the ravine and 150 sq km (58 sq miles) of the surrounding wilderness became the Jökulsárgljúfur National Park in 1973. In 2008, Jökulsárgljúfur became a part of the newly formed Vatnajökull National Park, which covers approximately 12,000 sq km of the country.

One of the area's gems is the great horseshoe-shaped canyon of **Ásbyrgi**, located almost immediately at the turn-off from Route 85. It's not hard to see why the first Viking settlers decided that the canyon had been formed by Sleipnir, the god Odin's flying horse, crashing a giant hoof into the earth. A 100-metre (330ft) cliff-face makes a smooth, 1km- (½-mile) wide ring around a profuse carpet of greenery, while a smaller outcropping of cliffs (suitably called Eyjan or "island") rises in the middle.

Geologists believe that the canyon was formed relatively recently by a gigantic *hlaup* or glacial flow from an eruption under the faraway icecap of Vatnajökull. The best view is from the furthest part of the canyon, which can be reached by walking 100 metres (330ft) west from the parking area. Turning east from the car park leads to a natural spring for drinking water, while taking the trail straight ahead ends up at a small lake full of ducks – their quacks echo around the natural amphitheatre.

Camping is permitted near the canyon's entrance, where an **information office** sells brochures detailing the park's main hiking routes. From here, a path leads to the top of the cliffs, climbing the canyon at its easiest point (although a rope is provided to help in the ascent). Once up, walkers can follow the cliffs, with excellent views over the whole canyon, or even take the trail as far south as Dettifoss – two days' walk away.

No matter whether you walk for an hour or a day, this is one of the most pleasant hikes in Iceland, and if you get tired, just lie on the heather and eat some of the wild bilberries that grow abundantly in the canyon's summery climate.

Towards Dettifoss

The rest of the park follows the powerful **Jökulsá á Fjöllum**, Iceland's second-longest river. Two roads run down the length of the park, one on either side of the river: the western road runs across some classic highland heather to **Vesturdalur** walking trails and the mysterious natural columns of **Hljóðaklettar ❺** ("echoing rocks"), which form a ghostly stone forest that can be explored for hours. Further on, the road heads to **Hólmatungur**, a lush stretch along the river canyon, before crossing a suddenly barren desert landscape to Dettifoss.

Unfortunately, the western road is deeply corrugated and, while two-wheel drives can make the journey, they need to crawl along at a gruelling 15kph (10 mph); and as this is an F-road, most hire cars will not be insured. The east-

BELOW:
Ásbyrgi canyon.

ern road is better, but after Dettifoss it becomes a jeep track.

Dettifoss ❻ is Europe's largest waterfall, and the effort needed to reach it only seems to add to the excitement. There is nothing contained or artificial here, no wooden boardwalks or viewing balconies installed to detract from Nature. Clouds of spray can first be seen several kilometres away; from the car parks, visitors scramble over square blocks of grey lava, hearing the thunderous drumming before getting a glimpse of the falls. Some 500 cubic metres (17,700 cubic ft) of water spill over its ledges every second: although it is just 44 metres (145ft) tall, the sheer hypnotic volume of the flow makes this arguably Iceland's most awesome sight.

For those who want to see more falls, **Hafragilsfoss** is 2km (1 mile) downstream, and **Selfoss** about the same distance upstream.

Cod coast

Heading north from Ásbyrgi leads to Iceland's least visited area. Tourist officials say that even the uninhabited centre of Iceland attracts more travellers than the Northeast coast.

The first village, **Kópasker ❼**, whose population of 126 almost all work in shrimp fishing, can seem like a ghost town on most days. Like the other villages of the area, Kópasker thrived on the herring boom until the late 1960s when herring migration patterns changed.

Beyond Kópasker is the flat, exposed peninsula of **Melrakkaslétta** ("fox plain"), where winds howl straight from the North Pole in winter and, on a bad day, summer can seem almost as dismal. The cliffs at **Rauðinúpur** are the only place in the world where it is possible to watch gannets nesting on land from below and the side rather than just from above. The northernmost part of mainland Iceland, **Hraunhafnartangi**, is marked by a lighthouse – the Arctic Circle lies just 2.5km (1½ miles) offshore.

Even so, the remoteness of the barren plain, which can support very little agriculture, is perversely appealing. The coastline is covered with driftwood from as far away as Siberia and supports a good deal of birdlife.

Although **Raufarhöfn ❽** made the transition from herring to cod fishing in the 1970s, it never recaptured the great days when thousands of seasonal workers came to its factories. Today there are many more buildings and jetties than the population of 220 can use, and Raufarhöfn is losing more young people to the cities. In an attempt to keep people in this economically important area, the Icelandic government built an airstrip, though it is no longer profitable to fly here (during long winters, the town had been completely cut off except by sea). Even so, the isolation of this town – which over long periods has not even had a local doctor – is extreme. In an attempt to attract tourists and boost the flagging economy, local hoteliers are building an Arctic version of Britain's famous Stonehenge on top of the hill which overlooks the village. The "Artichenge"

Drying fish the traditional way.

BELOW: Dettifoss waterfall swathed in spray.

Northeast teens.

BELOW RIGHT:
perenially popular,
Gamli Baukur
restaurant.

will be over 50 metres (160ft) in diameter and will act as a giant sundial, catching the long hours of sunshine during the summer months.

Southeast of Raufarhöfn is **Þórshöfn** ❾, a pretty fishing village with a regular air link to Akureyri where it's worth breaking your coastal journey. Although there's little in the way of specific sights, the busy harbour provides a focus to the village. One of the best hiking trails in the Northeast is now within easy reach.

From Þórshöfn, a dirt road heads north-east past the airstrip, into the windswept **Langanes** peninsula, whose marshy, cliff-bound expanses are the last word in Icelandic remoteness (it can only be visited by four-wheel drive or on foot). From the youth hostel and farm, **Ytra Lón**, the hike along the peninsula's edge passes a monument to some shipwrecked English sailors who managed to climb the 100-metre (330ft) cliffs only to die of exposure. There's a good chance you'll spot gyrfalcons on

the way to the peninsula's tip, Fontur, marked by a lighthouse.

Back on the main road heading south, Bakkafjörður is an uneventful and very small fishing village that is typical of the area, which most visitors bypass en route for the more rewarding **Vopnafjörður** ❿, set in a picturesque location at the head of its eponymous fjord. The snow-capped mountains behind the town trail downwards into the sea, complemented by the granite range across the fjord. Here the weather is better and the atmosphere more optimistic – the feeling is closer to the East Fjords than the Northeast. The village had its 15 minutes of fame in 1988, when local girl Linda Pétursdóttir became Miss World.

From Vopnafjörður, the highway runs away from the coast, passing **Burstarfell** ⓫, an excellent **Folk Museum** (open mid-June–mid-Sept daily 10am–6pm; charge) in a 19th-century farmhouse. The road now climbs into the northeastern desert, passing a viewing platform over **Lake Nykurvatn**, before rejoining the Ring Road in some of Iceland's most barren landscape. ❏

RESTAURANTS

Eyrin
Eyrarvegur 3, Þórshöfn
Tel: 468 1250
A standard small-town burger-and-pizza joint; the pool table draws in the locals. **$–$$**

Gamli Baukur
Hafnarstétt 9, Húsavík
Tel: 464 2442
A lively bar-restaurant, popular with both locals and visitors on whale-watching tours. The fish here is truly delicious and is served with creative sauces, including a tangy basil pesto. **$$**

Hótel Norðurljós
Aðalbraut 2, Raufarhöfn
Tel: 465 1233

Overlooking the pretty harbour and its fishing boats, this hotel restaurant with outdoor terrace has a superb location. The food here is some of the best in the Northeast – fresh and tasty and making full use of local ingredients. **$$**

Hótel Tangi
Hafnarbyggð 17, Vopnafjörður
Tel: 473 1840
Perfectly acceptable fare at this modern hotel on the main drag. **$$**

Kofinn Gourmet Hut
Harbour front, Húsavík
Just one dish per day is served from this unorthodox takeaway above the harbour, but that dish is

always something authentic from the region – reindeer burgers, freshly-caught cod, barbecued lamb. **$**

Salka
Garðarsbraut 6, Húsavík
Tel: 464 2551
This historic building, constructed in 1882, was the first cooperative shop in

Iceland. It now houses Salka restaurant, with a varied menu running the gamut from pizzas to sautéed lobster tails. **$$–$$$**

The price guide is for the average price of dinner per person, without wine:
$$$ Over ISK4,500
$$ ISK2,500–4,500
$ Under ISK2,500

The Most Useful Servant

One of the incidental advantages of Iceland's near total isolation over the centuries is that the Icelandic horse has survived almost unchanged for over 1,000 years

The Icelandic horse, the stocky breed introduced by the first Nordic settlers, is today protected by strict regulations which forbid the import of horses into Iceland, and which state that an Icelandic horse sent out of the country can never return to Iceland, for fear of importing diseases to which the local breed would have no immunity.

"Elegant" is not an adjective which springs to mind to describe the Icelandic horse. These chunky, thick-set, muscular animals bear little resemblance to their leggier European relatives, though they can put on a fine turn of speed. They have adapted to the cool climate by growing a thick, shaggy overcoat for winter, which is shed in the spring. In summer, their coats can be groomed to shining smoothness.

In spite of their relatively small stature (13 hands on average), Icelandic horses are famed for their strength and stamina. They have played a vital role in Iceland's history, for centuries a roadless, bridge-less land. Known affectionately as Þarfasti Þjónninn ("most useful servant"), the horse was the sole form of overland transport in Iceland until the arrival of the first car in 1904 (which was unsuccessful on Iceland's bad roads, and was returned to Denmark in 1908). Even today, the horse has a vital role during the autumn round-up, when sheep are herded from remote mountainsides.

Surefooted, intelligent, affectionate, home-loving and sometimes headstrong, the horse is also known for its five gaits. In addition to the conventional walk, trot and canter/gallop, it has two additional steps in its repertoire: the *tölt* or running walk, and the *skeið* or pace. Some can't manage the *skeið*; these are known as four-gaiters. The *tölt*, almost unknown in other breeds of horse, is a smooth run, which (unlike the trot) does not shake the rider about in the saddle and is understandably very popular for long-distance overland travel.

Horses for fun

However, horses are not just important as a working animal; horse-riding is now Iceland's number-one leisure activity. Riding clubs flourish all over the country, and various competitions, races, shows and meets are held throughout the summer months. Iceland's equine population numbers in the region of 80,000. Horse breeding and trading, up till now on a fairly modest scale, is becoming an important business.

Nineteen national organisations in Europe, North America and New Zealand are affiliated to the International Federation of Icelandic Horse Associations (FEIF), and international Iceland-horse championships are held annually. Iceland always sends a team of horses and riders to the world championships, and invariably carries off many of the prizes – although, frustratingly, the top local-bred Icelandic horses can never be sent to the international contests: since horses taken overseas are not re-admitted, no devoted rider would think of taking their best horse to compete in Europe only to leave it behind. ❏

ABOVE & LEFT: the shaggy-haired Icelandic horse.

THE EAST FJORDS

This region of Iceland, often overlooked by tourists, offers peace and tranquillity – from the long, thin lake Lögurinn, surrounded by forest, to remote farms and small fishing village

For travellers arriving from mainland Europe and the Faroe Islands by ferry, the jagged, snow-capped profile of the East Fjords provides the first glimpse of Iceland. It's a breathtaking sight as the boat edges into Seyðisfjörður fjord towards the town's ornate wooden buildings strung out along the seaboard. But not many stay to see what else this region has to offer. Iceland's eastern coast is thought of as a place to be passed through quickly en route to somewhere else.

This is a pity, and not just because the East enjoys some of the sunniest weather in the country. The rugged coastline and dry interior here are full of wilderness areas rarely visited by foreigners, although they are well known among Icelanders. And along the way are remote farms and fishing villages that, unusually for Iceland, have still hung on to a degree of old-world charm.

For the past decade, the region has been at the centre of the greatest environmental debate Iceland has ever known when it was chosen as the site for an immense dam and aluminium smelter. Construction on the smelter began in Reyðarfjörður in 2004, and was completed by 2008. It transformed the local economy and created scores of new jobs, yet its power is supplied by

the Kárahnjúkar Dam, which was built in an environmentally sensitive part of the interior.

Hub of the east

Whether arriving by ferry, car or bus, travellers use as an orientation point the East's most important urban crossroad, **Egilsstaðir** ➊ (population 2,300). The first houses were built here less than 50 years ago, and Egilsstaðir still has an unfortunate prefabricated feel. Egilsstaðir doesn't have a town centre to speak of and is instead composed

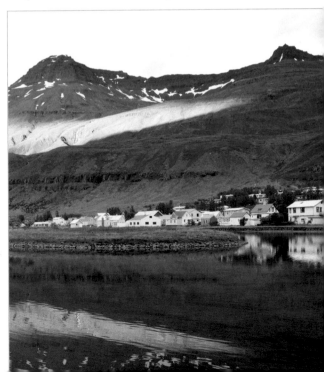

PRECEDING PAGES: turf house at Borgarfjörður-Eystri. **LEFT:** typical East Fjords scenery. **RIGHT:** Seyðisfjörður from the ferry.

Taking a dip in the North Atlantic.

of a small number of suburban streets, seemingly striking off in different directions from the Ring Road which slices through the settlement. As a result it's unlikely you'll want to linger and Egilsstaðir is best used as a staging post. Like many smaller towns in this part of Iceland, its social and economic life seems to hinge on the N1 petrol station. Flanking the station are the camping ground, tourist information office and a big supermarket.

Egilsstaðir also has some good-quality hotels which make a convenient base. Its sister-settlement, **Fellabær ❷** (population 400), lies across a long bridge – at 301 metres (990ft) this was the longest bridge in Iceland for many years – and enjoys a more picturesque setting. Try for lakeside accommodation in huts on

the Skipalækur farm; advance booking is advised.

The port of **Seyðisfjörður ❸**, where the ferry from mainland Europe docks, lies directly east along Route 93, and is surrounded by sheer mountains. The journey is worth making even for those not taking the boat: in complete contrast to Egilsstaðir, Seyðisfjörður is full of Scandinavian character, a town that approximates to one's mental image, so rarely fulfilled, of an Icelandic fishing town. Founded in the 1830s, it was soon one of the largest and wealthiest settlements in the East, full of elegant wooden homes that were shipped to Iceland from Norway in ready-made kit form. Today its huge harbour accommodates the *Norrøna* superferry owned by Smyril Line, which operates mid-

East Fjords

0   20 km

0   20 miles

April to the end of September and links Seyðisfjörður with the Faroe Islands and Denmark. The terminal building contains a café and tourist office.

Most of Seyðisfjörður's 700 inhabitants are involved in fishing in some way, and the arrival every autumn of herring schools in the shallow waters of the nearby fjords is still a cause for mass mobilisation at the fish factories. The ferry also brings Seyðisfjörður to life when it docks each week, on Thursdays in high summer and Tuesdays in the shoulder season. Classical music and light jazz concerts are held in Seyðisfjörður church every Wednesday evening from July to mid-August.

Nineteen kilometres (12 miles) out of town, at the tip of the southern headland, the remote nature reserve **Skálanes** offers basic accommodation to birdwatchers visiting its bird-cliffs; the reserve is accessible only by four-wheel drive.

There are fine views of the town and fjord from the highway, which winds up past small waterfalls into the **Fjarðarheiði** mountains. The best spot for taking photos is a columnar basalt

Woolly socks for keeping out the chill.

monument to the first postman of the region, who regularly made this journey on horseback when it was decidedly more dangerous than it is today.

Haunted highway

Another spectacular excursion from Egilsstaðir is to Borgarfjörður-Eystri, following Route 94 north. The highway passes the Edda Hotel at **Eiðar** before entering an expanse of marshland bordered to the north by the Jökulsá á Dal river. The whole area is crowded with birdlife.

Over a high pass, **Dyrfjöll**, one of Iceland's most dramatic mountain ranges, comes into view. Watch out on the left

BELOW: the looming hulk of Dyrfjöll.

Children can engage with the animals at Húsey farm.

BELOW:
sporting event in Borgarfjörður-Eystri.

for the bridge of a fishing trawler sitting in a field – it was dragged there on the back of a truck by a local, Fitzcarraldo, who wanted to piece together a boat in Borgarfjörður. He gave up half way, leaving a surreal vision for passers-by. This is an unnerving stretch of highway, with dramatic drops down into the sea and graphic evidence of recent landslides. Fatal accidents were so common here in the Middle Ages that they were attributed to a ghost named Naddi, supposed to live in a scree called Naddagil. In the early 1300s, a priest was brought out here to perform an exorcism, and just to make sure, locals erected a cross in 1306. The cross has been replaced innumerable times, but each bears the Latin inscription, *Effigiem Christi: qui transis pronus honora* – "You who are hurrying past should honour the image of Christ."

The town of **Borgarfjörður-Eystri** ❹ (East Borgarfjörður, to distinguish it from the bigger Borgarfjörður in western Iceland) is also known as **Bakkagerði**. It is ringed by dramatic mountains: the ochre range to the east, past the black sand beach, is made from an acidic form of lava called rhyolite. Along with pieces of jasper and agate, the rock is polished into everything from paperweights to gravestones at the **Álfasteinn café** (open June–Aug daily 11am–8pm), at the north end of the village.

The renowned artist Jóhannes Kjarval was born in Borgarfjörður and made the area famous in his paintings. He was said by one critic to have "taught the Icelanders to experience the beauty of their own landscape". A monument to the artist can be seen by the main road, just outside the village, and there is a small exhibition dedicated to him in the village community centre. However, a more fitting memorial can be found in the local **church**, which contains an altarpiece painted by Kjarval. It depicts a very Icelandic "Sermon on the Mount", with Jesus preaching in front of the Dyrfjöll mountains. Across the street from the church is a colourful turf house that is still inhabited and, towards the beach, a stone hillock called **Álfaborg** ("elf hill"), held to be inhabited by the hidden people (*see also* Icelandic Hauntings, *pages 248–9*).

Eastern isolation

A second road north of Egilsstaðir (Route 925, via the Ring Road) leads to **Húsey** ❺, a farm that has earned a measure of fame for its remoteness and serenity. Lying in the flatlands just south of the Jökulsá á Dal river, in the shadow of the Dyrfjöll mountains, Húsey's gaily painted corrugated-iron buildings date from the 1930s. The farm is still operational and until recently was one of the few in Iceland still to engage in the controversial practice of sealing. Walks can be made across the heather to the black sand beach nearby, where Iceland's two species of raptor – gyrfalcons and merlins – can often be seen hovering overhead; horse-riding trips can also be made into the surrounding wilderness. Húsey's utter peacefulness is seductive, and many visitors stay much longer than planned. The old-style hostel accommodation offered is simple but comfortable (bring your own food), and lying in bed at night listening to the howling wind, one gets a vivid idea of just how isolated Icelandic farmers have been through the centuries.

Inland from Húsey, the Ring Road follows the **Jökulsá á Dal** river, which flows 150km (93 miles) from the Vatnajökull icecap before hitting the central deserts en route to Lake Mývatn. Until recently, this was east Iceland's most powerful river. Today, it's a trickle of its former self following the completion of the contentious Kárahnjúkar project in 2009, which stemmed the flow with three huge dams upstream.

West of the farm **Hofteigur**, look out for the rise of Goðanes overlooking the river south of the highway: this was supposedly once a temple of Thor, and sacrifices were held nearby. Today there are ruins below the hill, of indeterminate age.

The rough Route 923, which turns south off the Ring Road along the Jökulsá á Brú, first passes the farm **Klaustursel**, which sells handicrafts and keeps a small herd of reindeer for summer visitors to pet. The unusual-looking bridge here is the country's oldest, a former American railway bridge rebuilt over this glacial river in 1908. Around 16km (10 miles) further along the road, turn left onto the even rougher Route 910 and drive another 12km (7½ miles) to reach the farm **Aðalból** ❻, one of Iceland's most remote highland farms, set in country related to the much-beloved *Hrafnkels Saga*.

The story tells of Hrafnkell Hallfreðarson, a power-hungry chieftain who lived at Aðalból and worshipped Freyr, the Norse god of fertility and fruitfulness. Hrafnkell dedicated his favourite horse, Freyfaxi, to the god, swearing that he would kill anyone who rode him without permission. When one of his shepherds innocently did so, Hrafnkell stood by his sacred oath, hunting him down and chopping open the poor fellow's skull. A blood feud resulted in Hrafnkell being outlawed at the Alþingi and ambushed by the victim's cousin, Sámur – who, rather than killing Hrafnkell, maimed him horribly by stringing him up with a rope through the Achilles tendon and seized his lands. The horse that had

TIP

Without your own transport, the only way to reach Borgarfjörður-Eystri is by hitching a ride with the postman. The mail van leaves Egilsstaðir every weekday at noon for the switchback ride over the mountains to the village. The truck also serves as the local post office once it arrives.

BELOW:
Húsey offers space to roam.

Delicate flora at Hallormsstaðarskógur.

caused all the trouble was flung into a pond and drowned.

At this stage, Hrafnkell decided that Freyr was little practical use as a deity and abandoned his worship. Appearing to turn over a new leaf, he slowly rebuilt his fortune at a nearby farm. Of course, Hrafnkell was only biding his time: six years later, he took his revenge, descending on Sámur with a band of warriors and driving him from the East. According to the Saga, Hrafnkell then lived happily ever after. Some ruins from Viking times have been found at the farm Aðalból, but saga fans will mostly have to use their imaginations.

Also south off the Ring Road, Route 901 and then Route 907 lead to **Sænautasel** (open June–mid-Sept daily 9am–10pm). This picturesque turf farmhouse was abandoned after a volcanic eruption in 1875, but is now lovingly restored and serves pancakes (*flatkokur*) to passersby. This area partly inspired Halldór Laxness's masterwork, *Independent People*.

The great Icelandic forest

South of Egilsstaðir stretches the pencil-shaped lake of **Lögurinn ❼**. Over 100 metres (330ft) deep, the lake is said to be home to the Lagarfljót serpent. Sightings of this strange creature have been recorded since the 14th century. It appears on the lake, according to written documents and eyewitnesses, in different forms – as a snake, dragon, seal, horse or even in the shape of a house.

On the eastern shore is the country's largest forest, **Hallormsstaðarskógur**, a place revered by Icelanders, for whom trees are a rarity. Nearly all of the woods were protected from grazing animals between 1905 and 1927, and now cover an area of 740 sq km (285 sq miles). In 1903 a nursery was established to grow different kinds of native and foreign trees. Since then it has distributed some 12 million plants. An arboretum was formally opened in 1993, and now contains around 70 tree species from around the world. The reafforestation programme (using tough plants from Alaska and Siberia among others) has created optimism that other parts of Iceland might return to their pre-Viking state of being "covered by woods from mountain to shore". Shaded by the surrounding trees, **Hallormsstaður** is a popular spot for Icelandic holidaymakers (there is a camping ground and an Edda hotel).

A little further towards the end of the Fljótsdalur valley is the farm Hrafnkelsstaðir, where the hero of *Hrafnkels Saga* lived after he had been maimed. At the southern end of the lake, **Valþjófsstaður ❽** farm is where the beautiful carved wooden church door, dating back to AD 1200 and on display in the National Museum in Reykjavík, used to hang. The box-like modern church now on the site sports a shiny new replica. Nearby **Skriðuklaustur** (open daily June–Aug 10am–6pm, May and early Sept noon–5pm; charge) was the site of a monastery from 1493 until the Reformation; finds from an ongoing archaeological dig are displayed inside the quirky black-and-white house that now stands on the site. This was designed in 1939 for the author Gunnar Gunnarsson, well known for his novels in Denmark and Germany. Gunnar later presented the house to the Icelandic state for use as a cultural centre and writers' retreat. In 2008, Skriðuklaustur became one of four

visitor centres for the newly-created Vatnajökull National Park.

North of Lögurinn, a steep hour-long walk leads to the "hanging falls" of **Hengifoss ❾**, the third-highest of Iceland's waterfalls at 110 metres (360ft).

Hiking country

A rough four-wheel-drive road runs south of Lögurinn to **Mount Snæfell ❿**, the 1,833-metre (6,013ft) peak that dominates the valley. Further on are the **Kverkfjöll** mountains at the northern edge of the icecap. Special buses run from Egilsstaðir to the hut at the base of Snæfell in summer. The mountain is an ancient primary volcano, surrounded by colourful rhyolite. If you are in good shape, the hike from the hut up to the peak, which stands about 800m (2,600ft) above sea-level, takes about 4–6 hours. The hut warden can provide all the necessary information.

For those who want to spend more time exploring the area, a popular long-distance walk is between Snæfell and Lónsöræfi – taking from 3 to 7 days, depending on how long is spent at each stop. This is a spectacular hike

Wooden sculpture at Borgarfjörður-Eystri.

BELOW: Hallormsstaðarskógur, Iceland's largest forest.

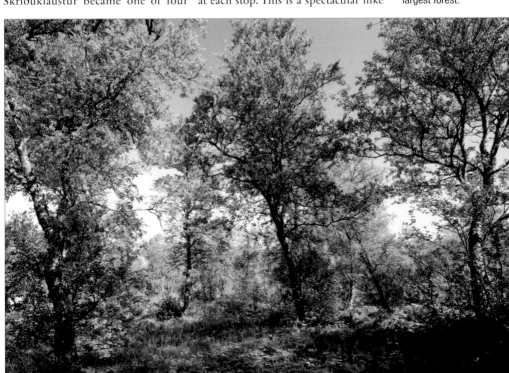

TIP

Boat trips (tel: 478 8119) to Papey island run from Djúpivogur (mid-May–mid-Sept). Papey is about 30 minutes away, and the whole trip, including a guided walk on the island, usually takes about 4 hours. This undulating island of tussocky grassland and marshes is just 2 sq km (¾ sq mile) in size and a favourite breeding spot for many species of bird, especially puffins who are drawn here by the low sandy cliffs in which they make their burrows.

BELOW: the stone and mineral collection at Stöðvarfjörður.

in an uninhabited wilderness. Multi-coloured rhyolite rocks can be found in many places, while impressive canyons and ravines cut through the land. There are plenty of flowers in early summer, and reindeer herds can sometimes be seen along the way. It is essential to have a good, up-to-date hiking map and to contact the local tourist information centre (in Egilsstaðir) to obtain all necessary information about the route, including a weather forecast and the state of rivers and streams. Do not attempt the walk alone – much of it is remote and mist and ice are common hazards.

Starting from Snæfell hut it is best to organise a lift in a four-wheel-drive towards Vatnajökull glacier. From here it is possible to walk over the **Eyjabakka-jökull** glacier, a tongue of Vatnajökull (you will need crampons) towards the hut at **Geldingafell**. From there the next hut to head for is at **Kollumúli**. The hut is run by the local Travellers' Association and situated by the tranquil lake **Kollumúlavatn**. It is a good idea to spend two nights here and use a whole day for exploring the surroundings,

perhaps hiking down into the **Víðida-lur** valley. The next stage of the walk is through the haunting rock formations of **Tröllakrókar**, down the steep slopes of **Leiðartungur**, and towards the Múlaskáli hut. The last day's hike takes you to the crest of **Illikambur**, from where most people arrange in advance to be picked up.

Following the fjords

The Ring Road runs directly south of Egilsstaðir, although many prefer to take the slower but better-paved and more scenic route hugging the coast. The start of the coast road runs through a steep river valley lined by pencil water-falls at regular intervals – each would be a marvel in other countries, but in Ice-land they are just part of the backdrop. **Reyðarfjörður** ⑪ is the first of many quiet fishing villages along this part of the coast, magnificently situated at the base of the steepest fjord in the East. The town itself only came into being in the 20th century and was the centre of Iceland's biggest environmental row *(see page 106)* when a huge aluminium smelter was built here between 2004–8. Of interest to visitors is the **Icelandic Wartime Museum** (open June–Aug daily 1–6pm; charge), which documents the billeting of 3,000 Allied soldiers on the village in World War II.

From Reyðarfjörður, Route 92 runs north along the coast to **Eskifjörður** ⑫ (population 1,000). Its **Maritime Museum** (open June–Aug daily 1–5pm; charge) is housed in the village's oldest building, dating from 1816, and con-tains exhibits on the fishing and whal-ing industries in the East Fjords. Nearby, **Randulfssjóhús** is a 19th-century herring-salting shed where you can taste dried shark and hire rowing boats.

Further along Route 92, **Neskaup-staður** ⑬, with a population of 1,500, enjoys a remote position on the far side of Iceland's highest mountain pass: it's literally at the end of the road. From May to mid-September, boat trips sail from Neskaupstaður around the head-land into near-deserted **Mjóifjörður**, past the highest sea-cliff in Iceland.

Heading south along the fjords from Reyðarfjörður, the road is squeezed between the choppy North Atlantic and steep mountains – their twisted peaks are usually shrouded in a haunting mist, making this look like troll country. The small villages of **Fáskrúðsfjörður**, **Stöðvarfjörður**, **Breiðdalsvík** and **Djúpivogur** ⑭ all pass in quick succession. It is worth making a stop in **Stöðvarfjörður** to visit the sparkling **stone and mineral collection** (open May–Sept daily 9am–6pm; charge) amassed by Petra Sveinsdóttir over a long lifetime; and those wanting to visit the nature reserve of Papey Island (*see below*) will need to catch the boat from Djúpivogur.

On the Ring Road southwest of Djúpivogur, heading towards Höfn, is the farm of **Stafafell**, which offers accommodation to travellers and has become a popular base for hikers making day trips into the surrounding river valleys. It has a small church with some interesting artefacts. Nearby is the large and peaceful **Lón** lagoon.

The surrounding area of **Lónsöræfi** is renowned for its wild and dramatic landscape, where deep valleys and chasms have been carved among the mountains by the glacial river Jökulsá. There are plenty of fine hiking trails throughout the area. Using Stafafell as a base, there is a relatively easy day hike, taking about four to six hours. It starts by taking the path up the mountain above the farm, and from there through the **Selárdalur** valley down to the colourful Hvannagil gorge. The trail carries on along the stream at the bottom of the gorge, towards the river Jökulsá, and ends on a track, passing a few summer-cottages, before returning to Stafafell.

Papey Island

The uninhabited island of **Papey** ⑮ is clearly visible from Djúpivogur, the departure point for summer boat trips (*see margin, left*). Named after Irish monks ("papar"), who are said to have lived here before the Settlement, the island was occupied from the 10th century until 1966, when the last farmers moved to the mainland. The remaining buildings are retained as summer houses, along with their tiny wooden church which is chained to the ground to prevent it from blowing away in the fierce winds. Today the island is a nature reserve, home to seabirds (including 30,000 puffin pairs) and a large breeding colony of eider ducks. ❑

Taking advantage of Iceland's short summer.

RESTAURANTS AND CAFÉS

Café Nielsen
Tjarnarbraut 1, Egilsstaðir
Tel: 471 2626
A snug little café and restaurant serving a good choice of light lunches, including the usual fish and lamb dishes. **$$**

Frú Lúlú
Egilsbraut 19, Neskaupstaður
Tel: 470 1930
This antique-filled and jolly coffeeshop offers good soups, pungent salads, tapas dishes and rhubarb icecream. **$**

Hótel Aldan
Norðurgata 2, Seyðisfjörður
Tel: 472 1277
Renowned for miles around for the quality and tastiness of its Icelandic ingredients – reindeer, guillemot, fish, whale – this chi-chi hotel restaurant is a must. Be sure to reserve a table, particularly when the Norröna ferry comes into port. **$$$**

Hótel Framtíð
Vogaland 4, Djúpivogur
Tel: 478 8887
Housed in an old timber

building dating from the early 1900s, this cosy and intimate restaurant is a good choice for fresh fish. Ask about the excellent value dish of the day, which includes a hearty helping of soup and bread. **$$–$$$**

Hótel Hérað
Miðvangur 5, Egilsstaðir
Tel: 471 1500
Top-notch cuisine in an elegant restaurant attached to the main hotel in Egilsstaðir. The Hérað is a popular place, so book in advance.

Its wide-ranging menu includes an East Fjords speciality: succulent reindeer steaks. **$$$**

Kaffi Lára
Norðurgata 3, Seyðisfjörður
A good choice for cakes, coffee and sandwiches at this pleasant café down by the Seyðis-fjörður waterside. **$**

The price guide is for the average price of dinner per person, without wine:
$$$ Over ISK4,500
$$ ISK2,500–4,500
$ Under ISK2,500

THE INTERIOR

Home to Iceland's wildest, most extreme scenery, the vast, empty interior can be accessed by a number of routes suitable only for four-wheel-drive vehicles

Reykjavik

During the Age of Settlement few Viking colonists braved the desolation of the interior. Only outlaws, banished from their society – and thus from the fertile coast – took refuge in its chilly expanses. By the 13th century, however, some paths had been created through the Central Highlands as short cuts to reduce the journey time when travelling from north to south. Today, 800 years later, the vast region of the interior is still almost totally uninhabited.

This large, empty region is Iceland's premier attraction for adventurous travellers. Nowhere else in Europe is so remote from civilisation, or offers such a range of scenery, the most dramatic Iceland has to offer: broad icecaps which split their sides into great glacial tongues; volcanoes of every size with extensive fields of block lava and pumice; freezing deserts and endless outwash plains of black sand. There are two main routes that go right across the interior: the Kjölur and the Sprengisandur. Other routes offer further opportunities for exploring this unique area.

In the southeast of the interior in the pristine land immediately to the north of Vatnajökull icecap, the recently constructed dam at Kárahnjúkar has divided public opinion and led to the biggest

debate Iceland has ever seen on environmental protection *(see page 106)*.

Challenge of the wild

There are serious logistical problems to be overcome before visiting the interior. Roads are reduced to mere tracks, most passable only in four-wheel-drive vehicles. The interior routes are open only in the middle of summer and even then snowfalls and blizzards can still occur. There are years when some tracks never open due to severe weather.

The weather is unpredictable and

Main attractions
HVERAVELLIR
ALDEYJARFOSS
LANDMANNALAUGAR
ÓFÆRUFOSS
HERÐUBREIÐ &
  HERÐUBREIÐARLINDIR
ÖSKJUVATN / VÍTI CRATER
KVERKFJÖLL MOUNTAINS

PRECEDING PAGES: a geothermal photographer greets the rising sun at Hveravellir.
LEFT: Aldeyjarfoss. **RIGHT:** close-up of basalt rock formations at Aldeyjarfoss.

The Interior

20 km
20 miles

camping is the main form of accommodation, although there are a few huts
operated by the walking-tour groups Icelandic Touring Club (Ferðafélag Íslands)
and Útivist. Located in key areas, like the
Sprengisandur and Kjölur, facilities are
very basic but feel luxurious after several
nights in a gale-battered tent.

Modes of transport through the interior vary from the buses that operate
between Reykjavík and Akureyri via
the Kjölur route in summer (*see pages
300, 307 and 315–6 for details*) to the
latest high-tech 4x4 or beaten-up Land-
Rover, to mountain bikes and walking.
If you are bringing your own transport,
extreme care is required in preparation.
You must take everything you will need
with you, including all food and water,
and in some cases fuel, and to be aware
of how to deal with the punishing terrain and weather conditions (*see also
pages 103–4, 317–19*). Because of the
dangers, many travellers opt to embark
with one of the adventure-tour operators based in Reykjavík. These use short
wheelbase, four-wheel-drive coaches for
tours ranging from day excursions to
longer-term camping trips. For the latter, the vehicles are heavily modified,
often to include a kitchen and a full
complement of picnic tables and chairs.
An alternative form of adventure tour is
traversing the interior on horseback.

The Kjölur route

The Kjölur route (F35), based on an
ancient byway used in Saga times, is
one of the main links across the interior,
passing between the Langjökull and
Hofsjökull icecaps. A four-wheel drive
is advisable but other vehicles are sometimes seen on the southern part of the
main track which begins at the majestic
Gullfoss waterfall in the southwest (*see
page 177*) and runs northwards to the
Blöndudalur valley. The first part of
the journey, to the hot springs of Hveravellir, is on a road of gravel, stones and
rock. Beyond Hveravellir, the route dete-
riorates as the track becomes muddy.
Nonetheless, in comparison with other
interior routes, the Kjölur has always

been relatively well travelled (historically, its grassy stretches were important
grazing areas for travellers on horseback), and today all of the main rivers
on the F35 are bridged.

Into the interior

Leaving Gullfoss, the grassland on the
plain above the falls soon changes to
lichen-dotted stones. There is a steady
drop in temperature as the landscape
becomes increasingly bleak and uninviting. On the skyline the only relief is the
snow-sprinkled mass of **Mount Bláfell**
(1,204 metres/3,950ft).

Before Bláfell there is a ford across the
River Sandá and a track (F335) branch-
ing off to the left. This detour from
the main route, taking several hours as
a round trip, goes to the large glacial
lake **Hagavatn ❶** and the icecap of
Langjökull. As the track bumps its way
towards the edge of the ice, it crosses a
once volcanically active fissure several
miles in length. All that remains today
is a high ridge of black rock with a narrow break that allows access through
to the edge of the glaciers. The final
approaches to the icecap are very steep

*A weather station sits
on the distinctly alien
landscape. Fittingly,
NASA scientists have
found a plausible
model for Martian
conditions beneath the
barren surface. The
existence of microbes,
surviving in extreme
conditions at
Grimsvötn, bolsters the
theory of life on the red
planet.*

BELOW:
driving the Kjölur
route.

A welcome signpost in the wilderness.

BELOW: Hveravellir.

due to huge deposits of glacial moraine, and vehicles should be left below. Water gushes out from the top of the moraine where lake Hagavatn has formed. Standing on the edge of the moraine, buffeted by the cold wind, there is a view of the lake, edged in ice, and, way below, the sweeping plains of black sand that are blown southward and enrich the agricultural land beyond Gullfoss.

Back on the main Kjölur route you head towards a second, even larger glacial lake, **Hvítárvatn ❷**. Skirting around the bulk of Mount Bláfell to the east, the track descends to the **River Hvítá**, crossing four or five tributary streams and small rivers. A spectacular view opens up across desolate dark tundra towards the distant blue glaciers of Langjökull icecap and Hvítárvatn lake.

On the horizon lies another icecap, **Hofsjökull**: the conflicting winds from the two icecaps create swirling dust clouds in between. From the bridge over the Hvítá, there is a clear view to the lake. Small icebergs can usually be seen in the water, and on the far shore towers the outlet glacier from which they originated. A good base for a

more extended exploration of the area is the Touring Club hut at **Hvítárnes**. Beyond, the brown dusty plain turns to gravel and then a great black stretch of volcanic clinker, with mountains and glaciers always on the horizon.

The track soon crosses the southern stony slopes of the small mountain, **Innri-Skúti**. As well as affording a panoramic view over the **Jökulfall** river valley to the Hofsjökull icecap and Kerlingarfjöll mountains, the slopes are particularly rich in tundra plants. Most are no more than tiny specks that eke out an existence sheltered between the rocks. Small pink cushions of moss campion compete with white mountain avens and other alpines for space. Long, severe winters, followed by short, relatively warm summers mean that the growth of these tundra plants is very stunted. Dwarf willows grow barely centimetres above the ground; as soon as they grow above this height, they become bent over by the constant wind.

The track detour (F347) to **Kerlingarfjöll ❸** is well signposted as it dips down into the Jökulfall river valley. The first stream you reach is easy to cross;

for the second, Blákvísl, a slow, steady drive across the water is recommended. Nearby is a small airstrip. These are dotted throughout the interior for emergency use but this one also allows access to **Árskarð**. Until recently this was a ski school, but the warming climate has led to its redevelopment as a mountain resort/hiking area. Facilities here are uncommonly good for the highlands, with sleeping-bag accommodation, a campsite, café-restaurant, petrol, electricity and hot tubs.

The Kerlingarfjöll region itself is an excellent climbing area with superb views of Hofsjökull, many deep ravines and well-vegetated slopes. The mountain peaks, rising to 1,400 metres (4,600ft), are made of rhyolite, making a stark contrast to the dark plains of Kjölur. In a succession of small gorges, sulphur and boiling water vent to the surface – particularly eerie when there is a mild drizzle in the air and great clouds of steam rise out of the myriad small fissures in the ground. Boiling pools have splashed mineral-laden waters across rocks, colouring them green, red and yellow. These mountains can be a very

cold place to camp and there are occasional snowfalls even in August.

Returning to the main Kjölur route, you will see the table-mountain **Kjalfell** (1,008 metres/3,307ft). To the northeast of it, on a low lava ridge, is **Beinahóll** ("hill of bones"). In 1780 four men from Reynistaður farm in Skagafjörður perished here in bad weather with a flock of sheep. Because of this incident, most travellers over Kjölur for the next hundred years chose to pass on the west of Kjalfell, instead of using the main track to the east of the mountain.

A warm oasis

Hveravellir ❹, 100km (60 miles) from Gullfoss, is an oasis within the cold desert. The hot springs here are very different from those at Kerlingarfjöll. Deep pools of brilliant, near-boiling blue water are lined with white silica; all around are small mud pools of black, brown and red minerals. Hissing jets of steam emerge from tall rocky cones, while a number of springs run gently down the slopes. The deposits of silica and sulphur cover the ground like great sheets of glass with fine traces of yellow.

The Icelandic playwright Jóhann Sigurjónsson (1880–1919), a resident of Copenhagen, wrote a very successful play about the lives of the outlaw Eyvindur and his wife Halla, who lived at Hveravellir. In 1917 the play was turned into a film.

BELOW LEFT: plaque at Beinahóll, the "hill of bones". **BELOW:** the mineral-streaked mountains of the Kerlingarfjöll region.

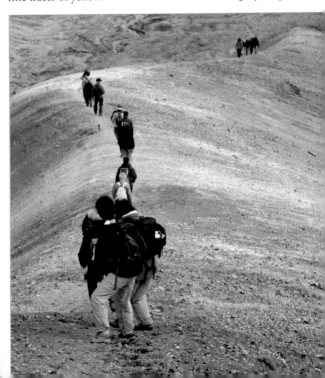

TIP

Scheduled buses run between Reykjavík and Akureyri via the Kjölur route daily between mid-June and early September. Departure from both cities is at 8am. From Reykjavík, buses arrive at Hveravellir at 1.30pm, and then on to Akureyri for 5.30pm. Heading south from Akureyri, Hveravellir is reached by 11.15am. All buses stop at Gullfoss and Geysir. See www.sba.is for more information.

BELOW: perfect reflections in a Landmannalaugar lake.

Hveravellir is another relatively comfortable highland hub, due to the presence of two touring huts with ever-available hot water, a campsite, summer café, small shop and petrol station. Some of the blue pools are as near as the natural world comes to a jacuzzi. With the air temperature near freezing, bathing is possible in one of the outlet pools located by the car park. Among the peculiar hot springs in the area are **Bláhver** and **Öskurshólshver**, the latter being so noisy in earlier times, that it reminded 18th-century travellers in Hveravellir of a screaming lion. Another is **Eyvindarhver**, named after the 18th-century outlaw Fjalla-Eyvindur, who is said to have boiled his meat in the spring. Ruins of the outlaw's shelter can be found nearby on the edge of the lava. Born in 1714, Eyvindur became a thief. In his early thirties, he went into self-imposed exile in the mountains for over 20 years. He met and married Halla Jónsdóttir, and the couple set up home at Hveravellir, where they were gradually joined by a gang of thieves. On one occasion, though, Halla was captured and taken away. One night, as the kid-nappers camped in Borgarfjörður in West Iceland, the exhausted guards fell asleep. Next morning Halla was gone. The swiftest horse was also missing and so were the provisions. Clear footprints of two horses led to the mountains – Eyvindur had come in the night to free his wife.

From Hveravellir a rough track runs north, meeting up with the hard road at the Blöndudalur valley 110km (68 miles) away. En route, the shallower parts of the winding **River Seyðisá** attract water birds, such as phalaropes, which churn up the bottom by walking in circles to dislodge small animals for food. Much of the water comes from the two icecaps and on a clear day the views are magnificent.

Sprengisandur route

The route through the Sprengisandur area can be reached in several ways from the north of Iceland. Although it is easier to reach than the Kjölur route, a four-wheel drive is still necessary. There are three main ways to reach the start of the route proper, all of which converge at or near Laugafell at the edge of the Sprengisandur. After making the crossing through the interior, the main route reaches the beautiful and remote area around Landmannalaugar, where it is well worth taking the time to go hiking, before continuing down to the south coast.

Reaching the Sprengisandur

The most easterly way into the interior takes Route 842 then F26 through the Bárðardalur valley via Goðafoss. A scraped road soon degrades into a rough track, which climbs past the beautiful waterfall of **Aldeyjarfoss** with its tall basalt columns. On clear days there are spectacular views across the Ódáðahraun towards Askja. The shield volcano of Trölladyngja, part of the Gæsavatnaleið route, is clear on the horizon to the south.

The more central F821 goes from the end of the Eyjafjörður valley. Passing the abandoned farm of Nýibær, where there used to be a weather station, the road continues to Laugafell.

The third, most westerly, route to the Sprengisandur is via Route F752 through the Vesturdalur valley which

starts in Skagafjörður. The jeep track begins by the farm of **Þorljótsstaðir** which was abandoned in 1944. The track crosses **Orravatnsrústir**, wet grasslands covered with cottongrass and sedge, around the two lakes of **Reyðarvatn** and **Orravatn**. The area is extremely marshy, with large hillocks covered with low-growing bushes. In the centre of the area is a small hill, **Orrahaugar**, where there is a refuge hut. Shortly before this route joins Route F821 near Laugafell it crosses the **Austari Jökulsá**, a huge glacial river fed by several streams and rivers from the Hofsjökull glacier. The river used to be a great obstacle to those travelling this route, but there is now a bridge at **Austurbugur**.

A cold desert

At **Laugafell** **⑤**, on a ridge leading northwest from the mountain of the same name (879 metres/2,900ft) there are several warm springs, which reach 40–50°C (104–120°F), and a warm bathing pool. Various kinds of grass flourish around the springs. Close to the tourist hut, there is a small trough, most likely man-made, containing warm water.

Motorcycling, with a suitable bike and equipment, can be a good way of seeing the interior.

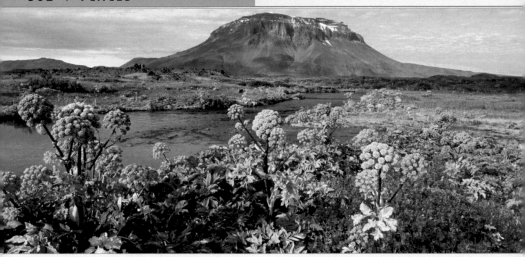

Flowers among the Lava

Unfairly, Iceland is often called "barren". True enough it's hardly a riot of flowers, fields and forests; but mosses, lichens and flowering plants are in their element here

Well over half of Iceland's area is wasteland. Visitors arriving at Keflavík Airport often think they could be on the moon when they look out on the treeless lava fields and the dark mountain slopes beyond. This impression is, however, misleading. While Iceland has next to no trees and the ones that exist are usually restricted in height (a waggish visitor once remarked, "if you're lost in an Icelandic forest, stand up"), there is plenty of compensation. Mosses, lichens and flowering plants flourish all over the country. And even in the barest highland sections, an occasional bloom takes root.

Birch, Iceland's most widespread tree, generally takes the form of a relatively low-growing shrub, often in dense copses and thickets. In the rare locations where it can grow straight and tall, the birch may reach 10–12 metres (30–35ft). Afforestation efforts have introduced many foreign tree species, particularly evergreens, so mixed glades and woods are now seen in many parts. Iceland's largest forest is at Hallormsstaður *(see page 288)* in the east.

Botanists believe that half of Iceland's plant species are survivors of the Ice Age, while around 20 percent have been introduced, deliberately or by chance, since humankind's arrival in the 9th century.

The local vegetation has been characterised as oceanic sub-arctic in character. About one-third of the plant species are of the arctic-alpine type. Many species of sedges and rushes are found in marshes and bogs; cottongrass (common and Scheuchzer's), which flourishes in wetlands all over the country, was formerly used to provide wicks for fish-oil lamps which were the main form of lighting.

In addition to its 490 vascular plants (31 of them rare enough to be protected by law), Iceland has no fewer than 600 different mosses and liverworts. Mosses are generally the first plants to take root on lava fields, preparing the ground for later colonisation by grasses, ferns and later trees. One of the most interesting species among Iceland's flora is the misnamed *Bryoxiphium norvegicum*, sword moss. Though named "norvegicum," sword moss has never been found in Norway, and was first identified at Lake Kleifarvatn in 1928. Found in the US, Mexico and parts of Asia, it is unknown anywhere else in Europe apart from in northeast Greenland.

Food for the table

About 755 lichens and 550 forms of higher fungi are known in Iceland (a lack of local lichenologists and mycologists mean that true numbers are unknown). Very few of Iceland's mushroom species are harmful to eat, and none is deadly poisonous, so mushroom-picking is a popular autumn pastime. Courses in mushroom identification are held from time to time, generally culminating in field trips to gather mushrooms under expert supervision.

Berry-bearing plants such as the crowberry, blueberry and bog whortleberry are common on heathlands. In the autumn families often travel out into the country in search of the biggest, juiciest berries. ❑

ABOVE: an unlikely splash of colour.

According to an old story a woman named Þórunn, daughter of Jón Arason, Iceland's last Catholic bishop, brought her family to stay here in the 15th century during the Black Death, and made the pool with her own hands. Near Laugafell the gravel expanse of the **Sprengisandur** truly begins with magnificent vistas eastwards to **Vatnajökull** and the smaller icecap of **Tungnafellsjökull** and westwards to Hofsjökull. A number of river crossings later, the blue tongues of glaciers come into view. A track forking to the east leads off the gravel plain to **Gæsavötn**, a small yellow-green oasis and crystal-clear lake amid the dark dramatic landscape. Beyond lie the Gæsavatnaleið and Askja routes.

At **Nýidalur** ⑥, close to the geographical centre of Iceland, stand several huts – invariably a welcome sight. Wardened during the summer months, they have occasionally been cut off for a few hours by snow and bad weather. But, whatever the climate outside, the atmosphere inside is always congenial, with travellers habitually swapping tales and sharing food. There is a small campsite on the only patch of green in the area,

but even in the middle of summer high winds and near-freezing temperatures make camping a desperate option.

The dusty track south crosses the mountain of **Kistualda** (790 metres/2,600ft), with panoramic views, before continuing to **Þórisvatn** ⑦ (Iceland's second largest lake) through a landscape of glaciers and black gravel plains. Just beyond the lake and on the main track is a veritable metropolis in this desolation: the **Hrauneyjar Highland Centre** at Hrauneyjafoss, where there is a petrol station, a café-restaurant and a guest-house (its summer-only neighbour **Hotel Highland**, 1.5km (1 mile) down the road, is the interior's only hotel). With the development of new hydroelectric schemes, several lakes (not shown on all maps) can be seen close to the fork in the main track southeastwards to Landmannalaugar.

On to Landmannalaugar

There is a steady increase in traffic south of Hrauneyjafoss en route to Landmannalaugar. The greatest change here is in the colour of the scenery. Instead of the dark Sprengisandur gravel, gaudy green

Cycling can be extremely hard going anywhere in Iceland, let alone in the interior. Poor surfaces, strong winds and rain make these routes challenging for even the most experienced cyclists.

BELOW: shopping, but not as we know it, in the Mountain Mall lorry, Landmannalaugar campsite.

Bighorn sheep.

mosses now coat the ancient rhyolitic rocks. The hills are bright yellow, green and red, dotted with deep blue lakes, creamy brown outwash plains and snow patches lying on grey Rhacometrium mosses. Shortly before Landmannalaugar a side road to the east leads to the edge of **Ljótipollur** (the "ugly puddle"), a picturesque explosion crater which has colourful sides and some greenish water at the bottom.

Exploring Landmannalaugar

Hot springs form the nucleus of **Landmannalaugar ❸**, and steam rises from every corner of the valley. Volcanic activity in the last 10,000 years has been restricted to a few northeast to southwest fissures. The youngest, the **Veiðivötn** fissure, created lava formations and other craters, including Ljótipollur, extending about 30km (21 miles) to the north.

This is a highly popular centre for tourists and there are several camping areas, but in midsummer the main site near to the hot pools, used for swimming, tends to become crowded. Landmannalaugar lies near the outskirts of the **Torfajökull**

volcanic district. Warm and cold springs at the foot of the lava flows make it a true "paradise in the desert". **Laugahraun**, the lava above the tourist hut, was deposited in a relatively recent eruption, probably at the end of the 15th century. The streams of geothermal and spring water, coming from under the lava-wall, mix to make streams and pools of an ideal temperature for bathing.

Landmannalaugar is part of the **Fjallabak Nature Reserve** and forms a good base for the many walks in the area. The bedrock of Fjallabak dates back about 8–10 million years. The varying and delicate colours of the mountain peaks that predominate here are due to their composition of rhyolitic rock. With the cold climate and frequent sandstorms, vegetation is scarce, although willow grows on the dry lava sands, and cotton grass in the marshes. Interglacial rhyolite lava can be found in **Brandsgil**, which is only about an hour's walk from the hut at Landmannalaugar.

Other popular hikes are to the summit of **Bláhnúkur** (940 metres/3,100ft), formed by sub-glacial rhyolites, and to the fumaroles of **Brennisteinsalda** –

BELOW: Landmannalaugar provides a good base for hikes in the area.

these walks take between one and two hours each. Sub-glacial activity has also produced some hyaloclastite ("móberg") mountains such as **Loðmundur** and **Mógilshöfðar**.

There are trout in most of the lakes around Landmannalaugar, including Ljótipollur and Frostastaðavatn. Arctic char have also been added to some lakes in the area.

Slightly longer walks in the area include a five or six hour hike to the summit of **Háalda** (1,090 metres/3,600ft) and a walk around Frostastaðavatn taking two to three hours. The major trek in this area is the 53km (33-mile) Laugavegur Way to Þórsmörk in the Southwest, which takes four or five days if you are reasonably fit. It is best attempted only between mid-July and early September. The scenery encompasses lava flows, rhyolite hills and spectacular views over glaciers. Along the way there are overnight huts at Hrafntinnusker, Álftavatn and Emstrur. Many people extend the walk to finish in Skógar on the coast; the 2010 eruption at Fimmvörðuháls affected this section of the trail, but a new route has been marked.

Returning to the coast

Travellers are faced with several routes from Landmannalaugar. It is possible to take a track southwestwards on routes 26 or 32 to join up eventually with the Ring Road near the south coast. Perhaps the most dramatic, however, is southeast to **Bláfjall** and eventually the coast. Although improved, the track here still provides adventure in the form of numerous river crossings, many of which require long periods of wading down the rivers to check their depth. Again only four-wheel drives should attempt these crossings due to deep water and possible quicksand.

Before Bláfjall there is a track off to the gorge and waterfall of **Eldgjá** ❾ (the "Fire Fissure"). Eldgjá is the most extensive explosion fissure in the world. It is a 40km (25-mile) -long volcanic rift, reaching from the Mýrdalsjökull glacier to the mountain **Gjátindur** (950 metres/3,100ft). The most impressive part is the northern end, where it measures 600 metres (2,000ft) wide and 200 metres (660ft) deep. A part of it is supposed to have been formed in a violent basalt eruption around AD 934.

Crossing a river in a four-wheel-drive. For a list of do's and dont's see page 318.

BELOW: colourful rocks on the Ljótipollur crater, in the Fjallabak Nature Reserve, Landmannalaugar.

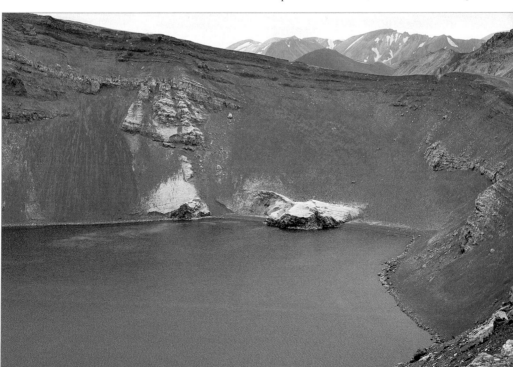

The Landnámabók (Book of Settle ments), *compiled probably in the 12th and 13th centuries, tells of a number of settlers from the British Isles, some of whom themselves may have been descendants of Norwegians. The exact numbers will never be known but of significance is the virtual absence of words of Celtic origin in the language. These are limited to a few place names, such as Papey and Dímon and personal names such as Kjartan and Njáll.*

BELOW: natural patterns in the Fjallabak Nature Reserve.

There are indications that the fissure is related to the volcano Katla, which is under the ice of Mýrdalsjökull glacier (*see page 181*).

Cascading into the rift is the famous waterfall of **Ófærufoss**. It used to have a much-photographed natural arch of basaltic rock which formed a footpath over the lower cascades. The arch, which featured in the Icelandic film *In the Shadow of the Raven*, collapsed in 1993 due to heavy snow and flooding. The hilly region around Bláfjall is a popular walking area. Ancient lava flows are carpeted with mosses and lichens, while innumerable streams and small waterfalls pour out of rocky fissures, only to disappear again under broken lava and cushions of moss

The Askja route

This track through the interior is more difficult than the Sprengisandur and Kjölur routes, and even four-wheel drives are sorely put to the test. Most tracks are marked by yellow poles or cairns of stones and, with reference to good maps, navigation is fairly straightforward.

The track (F88) that leads off Route 1 (the Ring Road) to the east of Lake Mývatn is marked by several makeshift signs warning against two-wheel drive vehicles attempting to go any further. It travels for some 64km (39 miles), following close to the glacial river **Jökulsá á Fjöllum**, before reaching the mountain of Herðubreið. To begin with, the view west across the Ódáðahraun plain is quite intimidating. A flat expanse of black gravel and pebbles (*grjot*), which is made up from the country's largest lava flow, stretches almost to the horizon.

The going is hard due to the severe corrugations in the track. A small range of black hills has to be negotiated, whose summit offers a spectacular view of the Jökulsá – a vast, braided glacial river. Patches of black sand become more frequent with pockets of stabilising lyme gras and ancient, twisted frames of dwarf willow are testimony to the harshness of the environment. Among the dark gravel lie balls of primordial-looking grey lichens; under stones protected from the wind sit small brown moths, barely moving, the only visible sign of animal life.

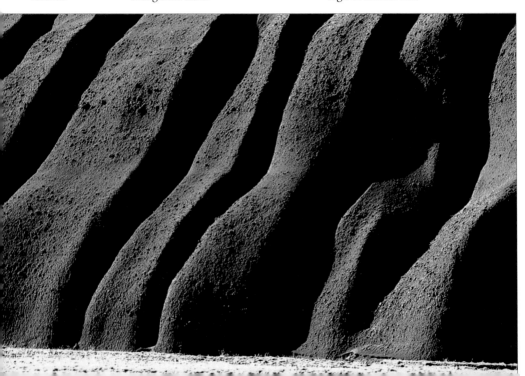

The track twists and turns eventually towards the edge of the River **Lindaá**, a tributary of the Jökulsá, and the first major river crossing. Along the river banks are great carpets of the pink-flowered arctic river beauty, contrasted against the black sand.

A black landscape

The track undulates considerably for the next 20km (12 miles) as it climbs and descends an extensive lava field. The bare rock is covered at times with patches of sand and pumice. The mountain of **Herðubreið** ⓾, 1,682 metres (5,518ft) high, gradually comes to dominate the view as it rises above the surrounding plain. On a cloudy day the upper reaches of Herðubreið are often hidden from view, which only adds to the mountain's gloomy splendour.

For centuries Herðubreið was held to be impossible to climb. The first attempt was made by the English traveller Richard F. Burton in 1872. Accompanied by a local farmer from the Mývatn area, Burton had to turn around, because of rockfalls, shortly before they reached the top. First to get to the top of the mountain were the German geologist Hans Reck and the Icelander Sigurður Sumarliðason in 1908.

For safety's sake, those who intend to climb the mountain should check in and out with the warden in the hut at **Herðubreiðarlindir**, who can also supply in-depth information about the route (allow around 12 hours to get from the hut to the summit and back). A helmet is recommended due to falling rocks and scree.

Herðubreiðarlindir is a wonderful oasis in the middle of black sands and lava fields. It is rich in vegetation and water springs, which appear from under the lava. Ruins of an ingeniously fashioned shelter made by the 18th-century outlaw Fjalla-Eyvindur can be found here. He spent one winter here, which he claimed was the worst time of his long exile, since he had no warm water and was forced to live on raw horse-meat all winter long. The Jökulsá á Fjöllum nearby becomes a violent glacial torrent, creamy brown with rock flour and running between banks of dark lava.

The journey from Herðubreið to Askja is another 35km (21 miles), much

BELOW LEFT: a waterfall negotiates the tortuous volcanic landscape.
BELOW: the icy summit of Herðubreið.

of which is across the yellow pumice fields of **Vikursandur**. The soft honeycombed segments of pumice, originally produced by the eruption of Víti in 1875, have been blown by the wind into small yellow dunes, contrasting with the dark block lava beneath. Storms in this area can make travelling very hazardous.

To the north of Askja lies the centre of the vast **Ódáðahraun** ("ill deeds lava field") which, at over 3,000 sq km (1,080 sq miles), is the world's largest lava flow. This vast area remained unexplored for centuries and was thus seen as mysterious, giving rise to tales of extensive outlaw settlements. Organised travel and exploration did not begin until the early 19th century.

A forbidding caldera

Mount Askja ⑪ is not the neat cone that it appears on the horizon. Seen from closer up, it is a 45 sq km (16 sq mile) caldera of black lava, cream pumice screes and white snow. Low cloud often clings around the summit, which is located amid the sprawling **Dyngjufjöll** massif. A narrow track winds around the base of Askja, through the

Öskjuop pass to a small parking area. A walk leads through the outer walls of Askja into the huge crater, where the great jagged **Vikraborgir** lava field was created as recently as 1961. A deep inner crater is partially flooded with steaming water and marks the site of the 1875 eruption.

Öskjuvatn, a lake several kilometres across, is the deepest in Iceland at 220 metres (721ft). Its water has collected in a deep depression that developed following a tremendous volcanic explosion in the Askja caldera in 1875. This eruption was the first in the Dyngjufjöll mountains to be scientifically researched. At the beginning of 1875 powerful and consistent earthquake shocks were felt in the surrounding area. At the same time, an increasing volcanic cloud was seen over the mountains. Four men from the Mývatn district took it upon themselves to venture in the middle of the winter south to Dyngjufjöll, where they discovered craters in the southeastern corner of Askja. They found three slag cones, two of them active, little or no new lava, but the ground had subsided a good deal, and deep cracks had developed in the vicinity of the craters. After the men returned, the eruptions continued and came to a climax at Easter. Then there was an enormous volcanic explosion that spread a thick layer of grey pumice over a great part of the eastern countryside, devastating many farmsteads and damaging others. This explosion has been traced to the Víti crater, but others in the area were probably also active at the same time.

First to arrive at Askja on 16 July (after trekking across the Vatnajökull icecap) was an Englishman, W.L. Watts, accompanied by two guides. He discovered a deep depression with a circumference of about 8km (5 miles), filled with gaping fissures and seething hot springs, spewing steam and water high into the air. A black column of smoke was rising out of the Víti crater, scattering clay dust in all directions. Because of the tremendous volume of smoke, it was difficult for Watts and his guides to get a clear view of the crater. Throughout the summer of 1875 there were considerable outbursts in Askja, causing volcanic ash to fall in the closest rural districts.

In 1907, a small team of German scientists, the ill-fated Knebel expedition, came to study the area. One of its members, Hans Spethmann, who was collecting samples in the mountains, returned to camp to find that his companions Walter von Knebel and Max Rudloff had vanished. The next year, Knebel's fiancée, Ina von Grumbkow, travelled to Askja with the geologist Hans Reck. Their attempts to throw light upon the disappearance of Knebel and Rudloff proved fruitless, although it is thought that the men probably drowned in the lake.

The last eruption of Askja began at the end of October 1961 and lasted for just over three months. The lava flowed from five craters, now named Vikraborgir, covering a great part of Öskjuop, the entrance to the caldera.

Onward from Askja

From the route between Herðubreiðarlindir and Askja there is a signposted side track (F910, then the F902) to the magnificent **Kverkfjöll** ⑫ ("Nook Mountains") at the northern edge of Vatnajökull. Close to the centre of the

Temperature conditions are extreme.

BELOW LEFT: speleologist Johnny Martinez supervises the course of sulforhodamine in the upper river of Kverkfjöll. **BELOW:** bubbling hot pool at the main entrance to the Kverkfjöll ice cave network.

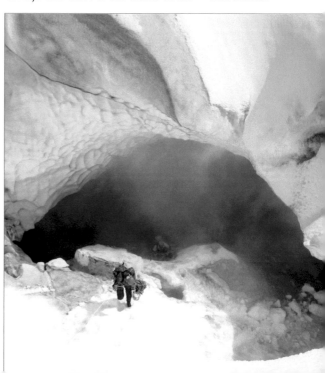

The old 120km (72-mile) Gæsavatnaleið route from Askja to Tómasarhagi was immortalised in Desmond Bagley's thriller Running Blind. *The way that the book's hero Alan Stewart drove in his Land-Rover has changed little since then except for the bridging of the River Tungnaá at the end. It may be difficult, but at least you're unlikely to have a hail of bullets at your back, as Stewart had.*

BELOW: a sight-seeing plane flies over the deep crevasses of the Vatnajökull icecap.

range is the second-highest volcano in Iceland, rising to 1,860 metres (6,102ft). It is split from north to south by a steep and rugged glacier named **Kverkjökull**, which has burrowed out a deep valley, leading to an almost entirely ice-filled caldera. Kverkfjöll has erupted several times in recorded history, although it is less notable for its volcanic activity than for its geothermal nature. A valley named **Hveradalur** ("hot spring valley") cuts southwestwards into the mountains at a height of 1,600 metres (5,250ft). The traveller who hikes into the valley will be rewarded with the entire spectrum of yellow, red and green nuances that characterise *solfatara* areas. Vapours rise everywhere from fumaroles and bubbling mud pits, and in the northeast where the valley is at its narrowest, it is almost blocked off by vapours from the largest vent. The valley is more than half-way surrounded by a brilliant white névé glacier, and at its southwest end there is an oval lake with greenish-blue ice walls. On a clear day, there is a magnificent view over Ódáðahraun wasteland to the mountains rising up above the high plateau. Beautiful ice caves have been discovered in the area. A tourist hut can be found north of Kverkfjöll, and another one high in the mountains.

The Gæsavatnaleið route

Running southwest from Askja, two tracks connect the Askja route with the more westerly one that runs through the Sprengisandur.

The original Gæsavatnaleið route (an unnumbered track) skirts the southern edge of the volcano **Trölladyngja**, very close to the Vatnajökull icecap. It is exceptionally hard going in places, but is the more interesting of the two. It is essential to have a tough four-wheel-drive vehicle and experience of fording rivers. Count on an average speed of no more than 10kmph (6mph). The second route (F910) is the easier of the two, although again you will need a suitable vehicle and 4WD experience, plus patience and respect. It takes a longer journey around the northern edge of Trölladyngja.

The first obstacle is common to both routes, although it applies to a longer section of the old track, after the newer road veers northwards. Spring melt-water floods from the Vatnajökull ice-cap, bringing with it black volcanic sand. This outwash plain runs for many kilometres towards Askja. Late on warm summer days and after heavy rain, melt-water comes roaring out of Dyngju-jökull glacier, creating wide rivers that flow all over the sands east of Urðarháls, an old glaciated volcano. These rivers are called Síðdegisflæður ("Evening morasses") and their sinking sands can be dangerous for all motor vehicles – avoid them at times when water levels are likely to be high.

The old track, marked at intervals with yellow poles, reaches the ice-cap at the forbidding black glacier of **Dyngjujökull** ⑬. Close inspection reveals that the ice is covered in black volcanic ash. Up above is the tufa mountain **Kistufell** (1,446 metres/4,750ft). In September 1950 the Icelandic aircraft "Geysir" crash-landed on Bárðarbunga in Vatnajökull. The successful rescue operation had its headquarters on Kistufell.

Navigation becomes more treacherous

on both routes when they cross the difficult boul-der-strewn sides of **Trölladyngja**, the greatest shield volcano in Ice-land, measuring 10km (6 miles) in diameter and rising to about 600m (2,000ft) above the sur-rounding area. The weather here can be cold and wretched, and blizzards are commonplace in summer, but the soli-tude of the wilderness is awe-inspiring.

After hours of slow driving across block lava spewed out by a succession of volcanic craters, the two tracks rejoin on the edge of the Mid-Atlantic Ridge. above the Sprengisandur plain. This is also where the meltwater from the ice-caps collects in a succession of rivers, giving you more experience of 4WD fording before you reach the small oasis of **Tómasarhagi** ⑭, with a junction of braided rivers, beneath the glacier **Tungnafellsjökull**.   ❏

Admiring the view from Dyngjujökull across to Kverkjökull.

BELOW: glacial streams flowing through the vast gravel plain of Sprengisandur.

✵ INSIGHT GUIDES TRAVEL TIPS

ICELAND

TRANSPORT

GETTING THERE AND GETTING AROUND

GETTING THERE

By Air

All international flights arrive at Keflavík airport, 50km (31 miles) from Reykjavík. After every flight arrival a bus transports passengers to the BSÍ bus station about 1.5km (1 mile) from the centre of Reykjavík. The journey takes about 45 minutes and costs ISK1,950: buy tickets from the ticket machine or ticket booth next to the airport exit. If you require an onward minibus connection from the BSÍ bus station to your Reykjavík hotel, the extended journey costs ISK2,500.

Icelandair is the main airline serving Iceland, operating from both Europe and North America. When booked in advance, a single ticket from the UK (see below for departure airports) to Iceland costs from £95. In summer it is essential to book well in advance to secure the lowest fares. Icelandair regularly reviews its destinations and although the following list was correct at the time of publication, it is well worth checking that your airport is still served by the airline when planning your trip. In the UK, Icelandair serves London Heathrow, Manchester and Glasgow; in mainland Europe, Amsterdam, Copenhagen, Frankfurt, Helsinki, Oslo, Paris and Stockholm; and in North America, Boston, Halifax, Minneapolis, New York, Orlando, Seattle and Toronto. Book online at www.icelandair.co.uk or www.icelandair.com.

Iceland Express, currently the only budget airline operating flights to Iceland, has daily year-round departures from London Gatwick and several departures weekly from London Stansted, as well as Alicante, Berlin Schönefeld, Copenhagen, Friedrichshafen and Warsaw. At the time of writing, during the summer, the airline also flies to New York and Winnipeg, and to a further 15 European destinations. It operates direct flights between Copenhagen and Akureyri in northern Iceland from June to August. The airline reviews its destinations every year and looks set to continue adding new routes to its ever-expanding network. Check the latest schedules and book online at www.icelandexpress.com. Iceland Express operates fluctuating pricing and fares are generally cheaper the earlier you buy.

Icelandair

Iceland: Ticket office, Hotel Loftleiðir, Reykjavík. Reservations, tel: 50 50 700, email: sales@icelandair.is, www.icelandair.is
UK: Adam House, 2nd floor, 1 Fitzroy Square, London W1T 5HE. Reservations, tel: 0845 758 1111, email: uk@icelandair.is, www.icelandair.co.uk
US: 1900 Crown Colony Drive, Floor 1, Quincy, MA 02169. Reservations, tel: 1-800 223 5500, email: america@icelandair.is, www.icelandair.com, www.icelandair.us or www.icelandair.ca

Iceland Express

UK call centre, tel: 0118 321 8384, www.icelandexpress.com

British Airways

Reservations, tel: 0844 493 0787, www.britishairways.com
Air Iceland, the domestic airline (see panel opposite) also operates flights from the Faroe Islands and Greenland.

Stopovers

Icelandair offers a free stopover in Iceland of up to 7 days for people travelling between Europe and North America. This may not always apply to the cheapest internet fares; if in doubt check with the airline.

By Sea

The Faroese shipping company, **Smyril Line**, operates a ferry service to Iceland between April and September. The ship *Norrøna* sails from Esbjerg or Hanstholm in Denmark to Seyðisfjörður in eastern Iceland, calling in at Tórshavn (Faroe Islands). Routes and schedules are complicated and change according to the season. For the latest information see the Smyril Line website. Passenger and vehicle fares are expensive and it is almost always cheaper to fly to Iceland and then hire a car.

Faroe Islands: Yviri við Strond 1, PO Box 370, FO-110 Tórshavn, Faroe Islands, tel: 298 345900, email: office@smyril-line.fo, www.smyrilline.com

Iceland: Smyril Line Ísland, Stangarhylur 1, 110 Reykjavík, tel: 570 8600, email: info@smyril-line.is, www.smyril-line.is.

If you are planning to bring your own car to Iceland by ferry, see *"Bringing your Vehicle" on page 318.*

GETTING AROUND

For the independent traveller, a first visit to Iceland can seem a daunting prospect. Getting to Iceland, both by air and ferry, can prove to be a major expense, although for travellers from the UK flights have become significantly cheaper in recent years, and domestic air travel is relatively inexpensive. When you get there, however, car hire is relatively expensive – four-wheel drive is even more costly but a necessity for the highland routes.

Many independent travellers opt for a travel package. Tour operators offer a wide range of options from a simple fly-drive or flight and bus or air pass deal to a week in Reykjavík or a full-board hotel, farmhouse or camping tour. It is often cheaper to take a package of some sort.

Arrival and Departure

Almost all travellers arrive in Iceland at Keflavík Airport. All Faroe Islands and Greenland flights land at Reykjavík Airport and the odd international flight lands at Akureyri, in the north of Iceland. Arriving by sea, Smyril Line's *Norrøna* ferry docks at Seydisfjörður, in the east of the country, and cruise ships also visit Reykjavík and Akureyri.

The "Flybus" transfer coach meets all incoming flights and takes about 45 minutes to cover the 50km (31 miles) by road from Keflavík to Reykjavík's BSÍ bus station. From here, an onward transfer service is provided to the major hotels. Buses S1, S3, S6 and 19 run regularly from the bus station to the centre of town throughout the day and evening.

For returning to the airport, the Flybus leaves the bus station two hours and fifteen minutes before flights leave Keflavík. Arrange pick up

Domestic Air Routes and Prices

So-called "Net offers" are available on most Air Iceland flights which, when booked in advance, help to secure the best price for any particular flight. It is always worth checking with the airline before paying for a full-price ticket since they may be able to offer an alternative fare or departure.

at your hotel reception desk; buses are provided from other major hotels to connect with the Flybus. Many people flying out of Iceland combine the journey to Keflavík with a visit to the Blue Lagoon. Most tours to the Reykjanes peninsula let you get off at the airport for afternoon flights.

By Air

Air Iceland, also known in Icelandic as Flugfélag Íslands, is Iceland's main domestic airline, although it also operates flights between Iceland and Greenland. Most of Iceland's main towns are linked by air to Reykjavík.

Currently, there are flights from Reykjavík to Akureyri, Ísafjörður, Egilsstaðir and the Vestmannaeyjar. From Akureyri flights operate to Grímsey, Þórshöfn and Vopnafjörður. The smaller **Eagle Air** (Flugfélag Ernir) operates flights from Reykjavík to Bíldudalur and Gjögur in the West Fjords, Sauðárkrókur and Höfn. All domestic flights to and from Reykjavík use the central city airport, rather than the international airport at Keflavík. In winter, when many roads are blocked by snow, flying is simply the only way to get around. Icelandic pilots are reputed to be among the most experienced in the world because of the variety and frequency of extreme conditions that they fly in. Reservations are advisable on all routes, especially in the summer months:
Air Iceland (Flugfélag Íslands): Reykjavík Airport, tel: 570 3030, www.airiceland.is
Flugfélag Ernir (Eagle Air): Reykjavík Airport, tel: 562 2640, www.ernir.is.

By Bus

Bus travel in Iceland is efficient but not cheap. It can in fact work out more expensive than flying on most of the longer routes. From Reykjavík, long-distance buses depart from the **BSÍ Bus Terminal** at Vatnsmýrarvegur 10. In summer, buses depart daily for destinations around Route 1 (the Ring

The cheapest internet fares are as follows: **From Reykjavík to:** Akureyri ISK9,130; Egilsstaðir ISK10,465; Ísafjörður ISK9,130; Heimaey ISK7,020; Höfn ISK13,900; Sauðárkrókur ISK11,700; Bíldudalur ISK11,700; Gjögur ISK11,700.
From Akureyri to: Grímsey ISK7,295; Vopnafjörður ISK8,760.

Road) and elsewhere. On some routes, brief stops are made at tourist attractions en route.

Because of road conditions and distances, some destinations, such as Egilsstaðir in the east, require an overnight stop in Akureyri or Höfn. On other routes, for example to the West Fjords, services are less frequent. BSÍ also operates scheduled **bus tours** in summer, some with a guide but mostly unguided, to places of interest, including Þingvellir, Gullfoss and Geysir, Þórsmörk, Landmannalaugar and Eldgjá (all daily) and across the central highlands over the Kjölur (daily) and Sprengisandur routes (three weekly).

Full details of bus operators, routes and schedules are available online and in the "Iceland On Your Own" booklet, published each year and available from the BSÍ bus station, tourist offices and tour operators.

Timetables and prices are available from **BSÍ Travel**, Vatnsmýrarvegur 10, 101 Reykjavík, tel: 562 1011, e-mail: bsi@bsi.is, www.bsi.is.

Main Bus Routes

Below are the scheduled main BSÍ bus routes, frequency, journey times and approximate cost during summer months:
Reykjavík–Akureyri: daily (6 hours), ISK10,400.
Akureyri–Mývatn–Egilsstaðir: daily in summer, otherwise Mon, Wed, Fri, Sun (3 hours 45 mins), ISK7,400.
Egilsstaðir–Höfn: daily in summer only (3 hours 40 mins), ISK6,900.
Höfn–Reykjavík: daily in summer, otherwise Tue, Fri, Sun (8 hours 30 mins), ISK12,200.
Reykjavík–Stykkishólmur: daily in summer, otherwise Mon, Tue, Thu, Fri, Sun (2 hours 30 mins), ISK4,900.

The BSÍ website, www.bsi.is, provides full details of many bus routes in English and is a good starting point for planning journeys by public transport.

Bus Passes

For information on bus tickets and passes, contact BSÍ *(see above)*.

There are several bus passes that are well worth considering. The **Full Circle Passport** (ISK33,000; ISK50,000 if the West Fjords are included) which allows one full circuit around the Ring Road following the same direction, with no time limit other than those set by road conditions (this particularly applies to routes to/from the West Fjords). You can stop off as often as you like. Another useful pass is the **Highlights Passport** which offers unlimited travel to some of Iceland's top attractions, including Gullfoss, Geysir, Þingvellir, Landmannalaugar, Þórsmörk, Skaftafell, Akureyri and Mývatn. It also includes transport across the interior by both the Sprengisandur and Kjölur routes. The price of this pass depends on the length of its validity; it is available from 7 days (ISK37,600) to 15 days (ISK65,000).

Combined bus and air travel tickets – **Air/Bus Rover** tickets – permit a round trip including some of the highland bus routes and offer a small discount. You can purchase them abroad through many of the tour operators.

By Ferry

Iceland has a number of small offshore islands dotted around its highly indented coastline. A few are inhabited because in past centuries they offered easy defence against enemies as well as good fishing. Sea birds too were an important supplement to the diet and their droppings fertilised the grassy soil, making the land ideal for farming. Scheduled ferry services link these islands with towns on the mainland; services are less frequent from September to May *(see panel, below)*.

Hitchhiking

If you have unlimited time and patience and are prepared to carry a tent and plenty of food, and walk where necessary, then hitchhiking will get you round the Ring Road and on some of the more travelled minor roads. However, bear in mind that the sparse traffic on Icelandic roads often consists of visitors and locals on holiday, with little space to spare in their vehicles. There is hardly any long-distance commercial traffic, and you may find that most rides are from locals on a trip to the nearest shop.

Hitchhiking is reasonably safe, and though quite reserved, most Icelanders do speak some English. Once the ice is broken they may go out of their way to help and provide fascinating snippets of information about their country. If you plan to hitch on the highland routes be prepared for a long wait – on some routes you may only see one or two vehicles a day.

Cycling

For the mountain-bike enthusiast, Iceland might seem an obvious choice. There are miles of empty rugged mountain tracks, and even the main roads can hardly be called busy. However, there are snags: accommodation and shops are far apart and virtually non-existent in the highlands, so carrying a heavy load is unavoidable; high winds, sandstorms and driving rain can make the cyclist's life a misery; if you damage your bike, you may have to resort to a bus to get you to a repair shop. It is fair to say that most Icelanders regard foreign cyclists as clinically insane.

But Iceland is growing in popularity for cyclists, and a number of tour operators offer biking holidays with support vehicle back-up.

The international airlines charge a fee for carrying bicycles, of around US$35/70 for each leg of a European/North American flight. When booking,

---

Scheduled Ferry Services and Prices

Landeyjarhöfn–Heimaey: (Vestmannaeyjar): In July 2010, the new harbour Landeyjarhöfn, 30km (19 miles) southeast of Hvolsvöllur, was opened. From here, a ferry service runs to Heimaey and back four times daily Mon–Wed, and five times daily Thur–Sun. The journey takes 40 minutes. Price: one way, ferry only ISK1,000 for adults, ISK1,500 per vehicle up to 5 metres (15ft). Reservations are essential for vehicles, at least 30 mins prior to departure. For information and bookings, contact **Eimskip**, tel: 481 2800 or 525 7700; www.herjolfur.is. There are bus connections from Reykjavík to the new harbour for each sailing, which set off around 2½ hours before each ferry departure: for details contact BSÍ, tel: 562 1011.

Árskógssandur–Hrísey: From Mar–Oct, the ferry *Sævar* sails daily every 2 hours each way 7.20am–9.30pm (outside those months there's a reduced service). The journey takes 15 minutes and costs ISK1,000

round trip. A bus service is available from Akureyri on summer weekdays. For information and bookings contact tel: 695 5544 or see www.hrisey.net.

Dalvík–Grímsey (via Hrísey): The *Sæfari* sails Mon, Wed and Fri, leaving Dalvík at 9am, arriving in Grímsey 3 hours later and departing from there at 4pm. There is a special bus service from Akureyri, leaving at 7.55am and picking up passengers when the ferry docks on its return. Price: one way, ferry only ISK3,240. Contact **Landflutningar-Samskip**, Ranarbraut 2b, 620 Dalvík, tel: 458 8970, email: jonarnar@samskip.is. www.landflutningar.is/saefari.

Stykkishólmur–Flatey–Brjánslækur: The car ferry *Baldur* sails twice daily from mid-June–mid-Aug from Stykkishólmur at 9am and 3.45pm, returning from Brjánslækur at 12.15pm and 7pm. Once daily Sun–Fri in other months (plus Saturday sailings in late May/early Jun), departing from Stykkishólmur at 3pm (11am on Sat). The journey

takes 2½ hours, and all summer sailings call at Flatey Island (check with the ferry company if you wish to visit Flatey in other months). If you wish you can stop over in Flatey and catch a later sailing. Price: ISK3,950 for adults, ISK1,975 for 16–20 year-olds, under 16s free. Cars up to 5 metres (15ft) long cost ISK3,950 one way. Reservations must be made for cars. Connecting buses run from Brjánslækur to various places in the West Fjords in summer only. For information and bookings, contact **Sæferðir**, Smiðjustígur 3, 340 Stykkishólmur, tel: 433 2254, email: seatours@seatours.is. www.seatours.is.

Ísafjarðardjúp–Jökulfirðir–Hornstrandir: from Ísafjörður there are regular scheduled ferry services to various locations in this part of the West Fjords in the summer. They vary in departure days and length, and each leg of the journey has a different price: for schedules and prices, call **Vesturferðir**, tel: 456 5111, e-mail: westtours@westtours.is; www.vesturferdir.is.

make sure you specify that you are taking a bike and preferably pack it in a specially designed bicycle box, available from bicycle shops. Around Iceland you can transport your bike on the buses for ISK2,000 if there is space available, but you may be asked to remove pedals and wheels. Iceland does not have many specialist cycle shops, but for repairs most villages have a *verkstæði* (workshop).

Useful Addresses

Icelandic Mountain Bike Association, P.O. Box 5193, 125 Reykjavík, tel: 562 0099, e-mail: ifhk@fjallahjolaklubburinn (ensure subject line is "Cycling in Iceland"), www.fjallahjolaklubburinn.is

Bike shops in Reykjavík:
• GÁP, Faxafeni 7, 108 Reykjavík, tel: 520 0200.
• Hvellur, Smiðjuvegur 30, 200 Kópavogur, tel: 577 6400.
• Útilif, Kringlan 4–10, tel: 545 1506.
• Verslunin Markið, Ármúli 40, 108 Reykjavík, tel: 553 5320, www.markid.is

Bike hire and repairs in Reykjavík:
• Borgarhjól, Hverfisgata 50, 101 Reykjavík, tel: 551 5653, www. borgarhjol.net
• Kría Cycles, Hólmaslóð 4, 101 Reykjavík, tel: 659 1595, www. kriacycles.com (repairs only)
• Reykjavík Bike Tours, 101 Reykjavík, tel: 694 8956, http:// icelandbike.com (rental and tours)
   Some places around Iceland hire out bikes; make enquiries at hotels and campsites. Cycling is popular around Lake Mývatn: Hotel Reynihlíð and the Hlíð and Bjarg campsites have a reasonable selection.

Reykjavík Transport

Reykjavík's city centre is tiny in comparison to its sprawling suburbs. You can easily wander through the narrow streets clustered around the harbour and lake on foot and cover most points of interest in a morning.

By Bus

Many hotels and guesthouses, as well as the main youth hostel and camping site, are outside the centre, so it makes sense to use the excellent public bus system run by the Reykjavík bus company **Strætó**. Most services operate 6am–midnight Mon–Sat with a reduced service on Sunday. At peak times buses run at 10–20 minute intervals and at 30-minute or one-hour intervals in the evenings and at weekends. Bus stops are marked "Strætó" and a flat

Reykjavík Welcome Card

The Reykjavík Welcome Card is valid for unlimited travel on city buses, and admission to swimming pools and municipal museums (including the National Museum, Culture House and the Reykjavík 871+/-2 Settlement Exhibition). It is available for 24, 48 or 72 hours and costs ISK1,500, 2,000 and 2,500 respectively. The cards may be purchased at the Tourist Information Centre at Aðalstræti 2; at the Reykjavík City Hall; hotels, guesthouses and the City Youth Hostel and campsite; bus terminals and museums.

fare is charged with no change given. If you need to change buses, ask for a transfer ticket *(skiptimiði)*, which is usually valid for 75 minutes. If you plan to use the buses a lot, it is worth buying either a Reykjavík Welcome Card *(see panel above)* or pre-paid tickets, which give a small discount, available along with a route map between the two terminals at Lækjargata and Hlemmur. For bus information, tel: 540 2700.

By Taxi

Hailing taxis on the street is a hit and miss affair. It is easier to go to one of the taxi ranks around town or ring the taxi firms directly:
Hreyfill-Bæjarleiðir, tel: 588 5522 or 553 3500
BSH, tel: 555 0888.
BSR, tel: 561 0000.
Borgarbílastöðin, tel: 552 2440. The majority of taxis seat four passengers but some larger vehicles seating up to seven people are available on request. If you have unusually large or long items of luggage, ring **Sendibílastöðin,** tel: 553 5050, and ask for a transit van *(sendibíll)*. These are often less expensive than a taxi but are only licensed to carry one or two passengers plus the luggage.
   Tipping taxi drivers is not customary in Iceland. All taxis are metered and if you require a receipt ask for a *nóta*. Most drivers speak some English. The busiest time for taxis is after midnight on Friday and Saturday nights, when it can be virtually impossible to find one.

Driving

Rules of the Road

Iceland drives on the right. It is mandatory to drive with headlights on at all times; the use of seat belts, both front and rear, is also mandatory. Drink driving is a serious offence – just one can of lager takes you over the legal limit. Priority, unless otherwise indicated, is given to traffic from the right; when in doubt, give way.
   Speed limits are 50kph (30mph) in urban areas and 30kph (20mph) in residential areas. On gravel roads outside urban areas the limit is 80kph (50mph), and 90kph (60mph) on paved roads.
   From November–May, snow tyres or studded tyres are mandatory; all rental cars will be fitted with them.
   By law, driving off marked roads and tracks is prohibited. The high latitude and cool climate means the growing season is very short: four months in the lowlands but only two months in the highlands. As a result, damaged vegetation takes years, sometimes decades, to recover. Particularly at risk are marshlands and mossy areas where deep ruts caused by vehicles leave huge scars. The very fine, loose soil is vulnerable to erosion and damage is likely to accelerate the process.

Driving Conditions

Though road conditions in general fall below the standard of their European and North American counterparts, Route 1, also known as the Ring Road, which goes around the island, together with minor roads in settled districts, present no major problem to the normal two-wheel drive car in summer. Most of Route 1 is now paved, as are many of the minor country roads, particularly in the south and west of Iceland. A tunnel under the Hvalfjörður fjord, near Reykjavík, was opened in 1998 and markedly improved communications in the southwest of the country. The price for passing through is ISK900 one way for a normal family car.

Unpaved sections of road can become pot-holed and rutted, unpleasantly dusty in dry weather and muddy when it rains, but are still perfectly passable. Where the surface is loose gravel, it is vital for vehicles to slow down for oncoming traffic. In fact, you should always drive on gravel surfaces with great caution; there have been a number of fatal accidents involving tourists in the past few years.

For travelling around the coast, a two-wheel drive is perfectly adequate. Anyone contemplating a trip to the interior is entering a different league. Four-wheel drives are essential, and even then you should travel in teams of two or more cars (note that insurance companies will not cover hire cars taken into the interior).

For the jeep enthusiast Iceland is a playground of unbounded delights, its many rugged mountain tracks and unbridged rivers a challenge for even the most experienced. Travel through the uninhabited highlands also requires extreme caution; year after year unwary visitors (and Icelanders) undergo the unpleasant and sometimes fatal experience of their vehicle overturning in a seemingly innocuous river or the less serious but still frequent occurrence of getting stuck in sand. Fording rivers requires the utmost care.

Highland routes generally open the first week in July and close at the end of August, but this varies from year to year and route to route. A map is published every summer showing which highland routes are open and is constantly updated throughout the season. It is forbidden to attempt these routes

before they are opened. The Ministry of Tourism publishes a brochure on travels in the Iceland highlands which is available free from many travel agencies and tourist information centres. Details of road conditions, updated every few minutes for all routes in Iceland, can be found on the internet at www.vegagerdin.is (tel: 1777).

For more information about mountain roads and the best routes to travel in the highlands, tel: 522 1000.

Motorcycling in Iceland

The weather is rarely perfect but, nonetheless, Iceland – in summer at least – is a magnificent destination to explore by motorbike. If you are staying on the main roads then a standard road bike is fine; however a trail or enduro machine will open up the interior and the numerous gravel or dirt roads elsewhere. It is important to realise, though, that there are no fuel stations away from the main settlements and the Ring Road: if you are venturing into the interior you will need to plan accordingly. The gravel and dirt roads can be treacherous, and fast-flowing rivers need to be forded (*see panel below*). For this kind of adventure, it is advisable to avoid travelling alone.

If you don't want to bring your own bike (on the ferry or by air), you can hire motorcycles from, or sign up for a tour with, the finely named **Biking Viking** (www.bikingviking.is, tel. 588 3220). **Blue Mountain Adventure Tours** (www.bluemountain.is, tel. 578 7860) also rent bikes and run enduro tours.

Bringing your Vehicle

Given the high cost of hiring vehicles in Iceland, it may seem an obvious choice for Europeans to bring their own vehicle. However, remember that road conditions are not good, and unless you drive only at low speed, your suspension may suffer. Flying stones from passing vehicles are likely to damage your paintwork, whatever speed you drive. The constant vibrations from rutted and potholed roads may also damage your vehicle, not to mention the copious quantities of dust that will enter every nook and cranny. Nevertheless many visitors do bring their own car, year after year, without suffering major damage. *See page 314 for details on car ferries to Iceland.*

On arrival in Iceland your vehicle may be inspected to ensure that it is roadworthy. You will need to produce the following documentation: a passport, driving licence, car registration document and a green card or other proof of auto insurance while in Iceland. A temporary importation permit will then be issued for the duration of your stay, which may not exceed one year. Other conditions for temporary import of vehicles are that the vehicle must be imported by the owner only or anyone having legal possession of it (eg through hiring); the vehicle must be brought to the

Crossing Rivers by Four-wheel Drive

Many rivers, particularly if glacial, can vary enormously in flow. Heavy rainfall or a warm sunny day can treble their flow in hours. Generally, in warm weather, the flow is highest in late afternoon and lowest in early morning.

If the river looks deeper than knee height, stop before crossing and look for the best place to ford, checking the flow in several places. With sediment-laden glacial rivers it is difficult to judge the depth. Narrow crossings are the deepest, wider crossings will be shallower, especially on straight stretches. On bends, the deepest water is usually on the outside. Where there is an

obvious fording place, where the water enters a calm phase forming a pool, the water will be shallower on the downstream side.

Watch out for large boulders, swept down into the fording place by strong flow, or sand – both should be avoided. If it is necessary, and safe to do so, wade first, using a safety rope. If in doubt, do not cross. Wait for another vehicle, get a second opinion, and help each other through. Keep in first gear, in low ratio if available, and drive slowly and steadily without stopping. If there is a strong current, try to cross by heading downstream to avoid fighting against the current.

country when the owner arrives, or within one month of arrival the vehicle must be used by him, his spouse or a hired chauffeur; the vehicle must not be lent, sold or hired; and the vehicle must be re-exported within the stipulated time period. Fuel may only be imported in the vehicle's fuel tank. Full details can be obtained from the Icelandic Directorate of Customs (www.tollur.is).

Use of mudguards is compulsory to minimise stones being thrown onto oncoming vehicles on gravel roads. It is advisable to buy a grille for the front of the car to protect headlights from damage. Before leaving home try to make sure your vehicle is completely dust-proof and ensure that any luggage stored on the roof is adequately protected against both dust and water.

Hiring a Vehicle

You can hire anything from a small car to a 40-seater coach in Iceland, depending on your needs and group size, but prices are high (less so outside the peak tourist season). Four-wheel drive vehicle hire is very expensive. It is almost always cheaper to arrange car hire online before you travel; try searching for cheap car hire through price-comparison websites such as www.travelsupermarket.com or www.comparecarhire.co.uk. You could also consider arranging vehicle hire with one of the tour operators abroad who offer a package that includes flights

and car hire.

When arranging your rental, check what the rates include. The majority of rates advertised are for up to 100km (65 miles) per day. Prices double for unlimited mileage, if that is available. Also check to see whether the hefty 25.5 percent VAT, a collision damage waiver or the highly recommended fully comprehensive insurance are included in the daily rental price.

If you wish to hire locally, the following companies offer a full range of vehicles:

ALP Car Rental, at Reykjavík City Airport, Reykjavík, tel: 562 6060, e-mail: alp@alp.is, www.alp.is

Atak Car Rental, Smiðjuvegur 1, Kópavogur, tel: 554 6040, e-mail: atak@atak.is, www.atak.is

Avis, Knarrarvogur 2, Reykjavík, tel: 591 4000, or at Keflavík Airport, plus other sites around the country *(see website)*, e-mail: avis@avis.is, www.avis.is

Hertz/Icelandair, Reykjavík Airport, 101 Reykjavík, tel: 522 4400, or at Keflavík Airport, plus other sites around the country *(see website)*, e-mail: hertz@hertz.is, www.hertz.is

National/Europcar, Reykjavík Airport, 101 Reykjavík, tel: 568 6915; Tryggvabraut 12, 600 Akureyri, tel: 461 6000, plus other sites around the country *(see website)*, e-mail via website www.nationalcar.is

Many hire companies offer one-way rentals, allowing you to drive from Reykjavík to Akureyri, for example, and then return by air. Provided you stick to roads designated for the category of

vehicle, assistance will be provided in the event of breakdown. Hire nothing but a four-wheel drive for a trip across the highlands. It is worthwhile going over your intended route with the rental company to check what roads are allowed for your type of vehicle.

Petrol

Petrol is quite expensive in Iceland, and is roughly the same price everywhere across the island. Regular, super and unleaded petrol and diesel fuel are available in towns, villages and even in remote country districts, but not always at frequent intervals.

Before leaving a town or village it is always a good idea to check how far it is to the next petrol station. In uninhabited areas there is no petrol available and you will need to take spare fuel tanks with you. Remember that petrol consumption is particularly heavy on the rough interior routes. Petrol stations also stock basic spare parts and most have toilets and either a cafeteria or a restaurant available.

Petrol stations usually open daily at 7.30, 8 or 9am and close any time from 7.30–11.30pm, with shorter opening hours on Sundays. Shell petrol stations marked "Select" are open 24 hours. After-hours petrol can be bought at station pumps – these are labelled *sjálfsali* (self-service) and they usually accept both cash and most major credit/debit cards, or the service station's own prepaid cards.

Driving in Reykjavík

Reykjavík is still small enough for drivers not to experience serious traffic jams, though the city centre – particularly Miklabraut – can often get congested during rush hour. Negotiating the inner city by car can also be tricky since there are a lot of narrow and one-way streets. The best compromise is to park in one of the numerous car parks on the fringe of the inner city, and then walk into the centre.

Most car parks close during the night; their hours are clearly stated on the ticket machine upon entering. Note that you must pay at the vending machine before returning to your car. Payment at street parking meters and in metered parking lots is mandatory from 10am–6pm on weekdays and 10am–1pm on Saturdays. Parking varies in price, with the more central P-1 zones costing the most - around ISK200 per hour. Parking fines are a hefty ISK1,500–2,500, depending on the zone in which you have committed your traffic violation.

A CCOMMODATION

HOTELS, GUESTHOUSES, HOSTELS & CAMPING

Making Bookings

Like many things in Iceland, accommodation is relatively expensive when
compared to mainland Europe. Rooms
are always clean, but guests,
particularly those accustomed to US
hotels, are sometimes heard to
comment on the small size of hotel
rooms. Reykjavík's high-end
accommodation has all mod-cons, but
elsewhere facilities and services can
be simple; and almost all Icelandic
buildings have thin walls.

The growth in tourism heralds an
increasing number of hotels. Most
accommodation outside Reykjavík and
other towns is only open June–Sept. It
is advisable to reserve accommodation, especially during July and
August. Note, you can often find good
discounts with early or online bookings.
Rates can be 30 percent lower Sept–
Apr. You should be able to find space to
bed down at camp sites but even youth
hostels are usually fully booked during
the peak summer period.

Most forms of accommodation,
except camp sites, can be booked
through tour operators in your own
country; better rates can often be found
this way. Links can also be found on
the website of the Icelandic Tourist
Board (www.visiticeland.com).

There is no publication that covers
accommodation for the country as a
whole, but some organisations (eg
Hostelling International, Icelandic Farm
Holidays) publish annual brochures
listing details of their accommodations;
further information is given below
under the relevant sections.

Hotels usually accept payment by
credit card, but payment for guesthouses, farms, hostels and camp sites
is generally by cash only.

Hotels

International-style hotels with a full
range of facilities are mainly found in
the Reykjavík and Akureyri areas.
Elsewhere, they are few and far
between. Top prices in Reykjavík are
over ISK50,000 for a twin room in a
luxury hotel, with en-suite shower or
bath, and breakfast included. Most
international-style hotels have good
facilities for disabled people.

Icelandair Hotels is the country's
highest-quality chain, with seven hotels
around the country. Prices for a double
room with en-suite bath/shower (not
including breakfast) range from
ISK28,000–40,000 in high season,
but you can secure lower prices by
booking early online. tel: 444 4000,
www.icelandairhotels.com.

The **Fosshotel** chain has 10 hotels
and a guesthouse in various locations.
Prices for a double room with en-suite
bath/shower (including breakfast)
range from ISK27,000–35,000 in high
season. They do not generally have
facilities for the disabled. Again, best
deals are to be had online. tel: 562
4000, www.fosshotel.is.

Tourist-class hotels offer fewer
facilities but most have rooms with
private shower/bath and a restaurant.
They are to be found in Reykjavík and in
towns around the country and are open
all year round. Prices are usually
somewhat less than those of the
international-style hotels and facilities
for the disabled tend to be lacking.

In summer 13 of Iceland's schools,
universities and conference centres
open as "summer hotels", operating
under the **Hotel Edda** chain. They offer
comfortable accommodation, generally
in rooms with a basin but without a
private shower/toilet. Prices start from

ISK11,000 for a twin room with shared
facilities. Breakfast costs around
ISK1,000. Most have their own restaurant. tel: 444 4000, www.hoteledda.is.

Guesthouses

These are usually small, often family
run, and offer basic bed-and-breakfast
accommodation. Prices vary, but start
at around ISK12,000, including
breakfast, for a twin room. Guesthouses are good bet for those travelling
on a budget, with facilities generally of
a high standard, and invariably clean.
In most cases, however, the rooms do
not have private baths, nor special
facilities for the disabled. In the peak
season book well in advance.

Private Homes

Because of the shortage of hotel space
in the height of the summer, some
families offer bed-and-breakfast
accommodation in their own homes,
mostly in the Reykjavík area. Bookings
can be made through local tour
operators. Private lodgings in Reykjavík
can be booked via the Official Tourist
Information Centre, Aðalstræti 2, tel:
590 1550, e-mail: info@visitreykjavik.is.
Prices are similar to those given for
guesthouses.

Sleeping bags

Anyone interested in saving
money should bring their sleeping
bag with them. As well as being
essential for mountain huts and
some hostels, many farmhouses
and guesthouses offer "sleeping
bag accommodation" at a
reduced rate.

Farm Guesthouses

Over-dependent on sheep-farming, many farmers have been encouraged to branch out into tourism. Farms around the country offer a variety of services to visitors from bed-and-breakfast and sleeping-bag accommodation, to self-catering summer houses (as they are known locally), rented on a weekly basis. Excursions on horseback, fishing and other activities can be arranged. Not all are working farms.

Farm guesthouses are listed in the Icelandic Farm Holidays booklet, available through tourist offices across the country, tour operators, which also handle bookings, or directly from **Icelandic Farm Holidays**, Síðumúli 13, tel: 570 2700, e-mail: ifh@farmholidays.is; www.farmholidays.is.

Due to the weakness of the króna, Icelandic Farm Holidays will only set their prices in euros. Prices start at €32 per person for sleeping-bag accommodation (without breakfast), €47–57 per person in a twin including breakfast. There is an extra fee of €22 for a single. Cottages cost €85–145 per night in summer, depending on the facilities and number of people they sleep; they cost less in winter.

Travelling via farmhouses is highly recommended for anyone interested in really getting to know Iceland. Many of the farms are in unique, sometimes remote locations, and staying on a working farm gives an insight into the country's ancient rural lifestyle.

Pre-paid accommodation vouchers are available, which offer some discount and allow you to keep your itinerary open. However, remember that in high season, it is quite likely that there may not be accommodation available when you want to use your voucher. If you opt for sleeping-bag accommodation you may get your own room, although not all farms provide this service. Many farms offer kitchen facilities for cooking, and almost all will cook guests' meals if given notice. Prices for meals vary from farm to farm.

Each farm has its own character and range of services, so careful perusal of the Icelandic Farm Holidays booklet is recommended. Reservations at the individual farms can be made by telephone, or simply drop in at any farm where the IFH sign is displayed.

Youth Hostels

There are 34 youth hostels around Iceland, situated in towns, villages and farming districts. All offer sleeping-bag accommodation, usually in 2–6-bed rooms, and family rooms. A duvet is usually provided, but you will need to hire bed linen from the hostel, or use your own sleeping-bag or bedclothes. All hostels have guest kitchens, and some offer meals if booked in advance. Hostels are open to people of all ages and in Iceland you do not have to be a member of the IYHF (International Youth Hostels Federation) though prices are slightly lower for members.

In July and August it is advisable to pre-book hostels with the **Icelandic Youth Hostels Association**, Borgartún 6, 105 Reykjavík, tel: 575 6700, e-mail: info@hostel.is; www.hostel.is; or directly with the individual hostels, whose contact details, opening times and facilities are listed in the association's "Hostelling in Iceland" brochure. Sleeping-bag accommodation costs ISK3,100 per person a night at the hostels, or ISK2,500 for association members. Breakfast costs around ISK1,000.

Mountain Huts

Marked on maps by a triangle, you find mountain huts in uninhabited areas. Some are overseen by local associations, but the majority are owned and maintained by: **Ferðafélag Íslands** (The Iceland Touring Association; ITA), Mörkinn 6, 108 Reykjavík, tel: 568 2533, e-mail: fi@fi.is, www.fi.is **Útivist**, Laugavegur 178, 105 Reykjavík, tel: 562 1000, e-mail: utivist@utivist.is, www.utivist.is

Some huts are accessible by road but others are intended solely for hikers. Some are small, sleeping six to eight persons and have no facilities; others sleep over 100 and offer cooking facilities and flushing toilets. Most have wardens in summer. It is always wise to pre-book the huts as they fill quickly in hiking season and in winter are often locked (a key can be obtained from the ITA office). All huts are uncatered, so bring supplies. Non-members pay ISK2,000–4,300.

Camping in Reykjavík

Reykjavík Campsite
Laugardalur, Sundlaugavegur 34
Tel: 568 6944
Email: info@reykjavikcampsite.is
www.reykjavikcampsite.is
Located behind the youth hostel at the edge of Laugardalur valley, next to the city's largest swimming pool. The camp site offers cooking and laundry facilities. Things get busy in the summer and pre-booking is advisable for larger groups. **$**

Note, basic huts, owned by farming communities and used during the annual sheep round-up in September are often marked on maps as *Kofi*. Many will be kept locked at other times of the year and are not intended for use by tourists.

Emergency Huts

Located on mountain passes, remote stretches of road and along uninhabited coasts, these orange-painted huts are stocked with food, stove, blankets and a radio. They are, by law, only for emergency use.

Camp Grounds

Camping is allowed in most places in Iceland, though on private or farming land it is subject to the owner's permission. Within national parks and conservation areas, it is only allowed at designated areas.

Official camp sites are found in most towns and villages, at national parks, nature conservation areas, places of natural beauty and some farms and community centres. The standard varies. Expect to pay about ISK900 per person per night depending on facilities. A leaflet listing camp grounds is published by the **Icelandic Tourist Board**, Geirsgata 9, 101 Reykjavík, tel: 535-5500, www.visiticeland.com.

*Hotels are listed in alphabetical order within location.
Towns and cities are listed in book order.*

REYKJAVÍK

City Centre

Centerhotel Arnarhvoll
Ingólfsstræti 1
Tel: 595 8540
E-mail: arnarhvoll@centerhotels.is
One of the city's newest
hotels, Arnarhvoll is cool,
clean, and has stunning
views across the bay. Five
minutes' walk from the bar-
and-restaurant action on
Laugavegur. **$$$$**

Centerhotel Klöpp
Klapparstígur 26
Tel: 595 8520
www.centerhotels.is
Pleasant hotel right in the
middle of town. The nearby
Centerhotel Skjaldbreið
(Laugavegur 16, tel: 595
8510) is run by the same
company. **$$$$**

Fosshótel Barón
Barónsstígur 2–4
Tel: 562 3204
E-mail: sales@fosshotel.is
In addition to its normal
hotel rooms, Barón also has
self-catering apartments,
close to the main shopping
street and Hlemmur bus
terminal. Standard rates for
one-/two-bedroom
apartments are ISK36,000/
39,000 per night.

Guesthouse Baldursbrá
Laufásvegur 41
Tel: 552 6646
E-mail: baldursbra@centrum.is
One of the best
guesthouses in the city, run
by a German-Icelandic
couple. The service is
friendly and hospitable and
there is a hot tub in the
back yard. **$$**

Guesthouse Svala
Skólavörðustígur 30
Tel: 562 3544
E-mail: guesthousesvala@
guesthousesvala.com
A stately old residence
tucked away on a street
renowned for its unique and
quirky shops, Svala has cool
white rooms with modern
touches, such as flat-screen
TVs. **$$$**

Hótel Borg
Pósthússtræti 11
Tel: 551 1440
www.hotelborg.is
The city's first hotel, right in
the old town centre. Beautifully renovated in modern
style, with nods to its Art
Deco heritage. **$$$$**

Hótel Holt
Bergstaðastræti 37
Tel: 552 5700
www.holt.is
Luxury hotel in central Reykjavík, tastefully decorated
throughout with Icelandic
works of art. It is also well
known for having one of the
finest ranges of whiskies in
the country. **$$$$**

Hótel Leifur Eiríksson
Skólavörðustígur 45
Tel: 562 0800
www.hotelleifur.is
Rooms are small, but staff
are friendly and the hotel
has a prime location, right
opposite Hallgrímskirkja
church. **$$$**

Hótel Óðinsvé
Óðinstorg 11
Tel: 511 6200
www.hotelodinsve.is
A charming hotel on a quiet
street in the heart of the
city. All rooms have tasteful
Scandinavian decor, but
deluxe rooms with split
levels are the business.
$$$$

Hótel Reykjavík Centrum
Aðalstræti 16
Tel: 514 6000
www.hotelcentrum.is
Built above Reykjavík's
oldest (Viking) house, there
is nothing archaic about this
airy modern hotel. Comfort-
able rooms with the city on
the doorstep. **$$$$**

Luna Hotel Apartments
Spítalastígur 1
Tel: 511 2800
www.luna.is
Restored 1920s' town
house in a quiet central part
of town, with tasteful and
stylish apartments. Studio
apartment ISK14,900 per

night, large two-room
apartment ISK38,500.

**Reykjavík Downtown
Youth Hostel**
Vesturgata 17
Tel: 553 8120
E-mail: reykjavikdowntown@hostel.is
Hostelling International
Iceland opened a second
Reykjavík hostel in 2009.
This smart addition is
central, with sunny staff,
spacious rooms, free Wi-fi
and a clean, green ethical
stance. **$$**

Room with a View
Laugavegur 18, 6th floor
Tel: 552 7262
www.roomwithaview.is
Luxurious furnished
apartments, which sleep up
to seven people. Over half of
the rooms have a balcony
and, yes, as the name says;
a great view. Sizes and
prices vary, from ISK13,000
per night for an apartment
sleeping two to ISK53,900+
per night for a five-room
apartment.

**Salvation Army
Guesthouse**
Kirkjustræti 2
Tel: 561 3203
E-mail: guesthouse@guesthouse.is
The cheapest guesthouse in
Reykjavík. There are no frills
but this hostel-style place is
neat and clean and the
central location is excellent.
There are facilities for
cooking on the ground floor.
$

Three Sisters Guesthouse
Ránargata 24
Tel: 565 2181
threesisters@threesisters.is
A splendid alternative to a
hotel room, these cosy
studio apartments near the
harbour come with bed-
rooms and kitchenettes. **$$**

South of the Centre

Hótel Loftleiðir
Reykjavíkflugvöllur
Tel: 444 4500
www.icehotel.is

Owned by Icelandair and
located at Reykjavík
airport. Modern and
comfortable with an
excellent restaurant.
Situated close to the
Öskjuhlíð nature reserve
and Perlan, a brisk
25-minute walk to the
centre of town. **$$$$**

Radisson Blu Saga Hotel
Hagatorg
Tel: 525 9900
www.radissonblu.com/sagahotelreykjavik
A top-class hotel not far
from the city centre and next
door to the University
Theatre, home of the
Iceland Symphony
Orchestra. Excellent
facilities and the fine
restaurant has wonderful
panoramic views over
Reykjavík and beyond.
$$$$

East of the Centre

Fosshótel Lind
Rauðarárstígur 18
Tel: 562 3350
E-mail: sales@fosshotel.is
A modern hotel on the
outskirts of the old centre,
close to Hlemmur bus
terminal. There are very
good facilities for the
disabled, and free parking.
$$$$

Guesthouse 101
Laugavegur 101
Tel: 562 6101
www.iceland101.com
This is one of the few
guesthouses offering good
facilities for the disabled.
On the main shopping street
just a short distance from
the Hlemmur bus terminal.
$$

Hótel Cabin
Borgartún 32
Tel: 511 6030
www.hotelcabin.is
Standard rooms are very small, but they are great value for Reykjavík. Upper-storey rooms have fine views of the ocean and mountains beyond. About a 20-minute walk from the town centre. **$$**
Hótel Reykjavík
Rauðarárstígur 37
Tel: 514 7000

www.hotelreykjavik.is
Helpful staff and a friendly atmosphere raise this place above the average business hotel. The city centre is within easy walking distance, and Hlemmur bus terminal is just down the road. **$$$$**

Laugardalur

Grand Hótel Reykjavík
Sigtún 38
Tel: 514 8000

www.grand.is
Comfortable hotel with full facilities, located close to the Laugardalur swimming pool. Spacious rooms and excellent service. **$$$$**
Park Inn Island
Ármúli 9
Tel: 595 7000
E-mail: info.reykjavik@rezidorparkinn.com
The immediate surroundings are not picturesque, but this decent-value three-star hotel is close to attractions

in Laugardalur, such as the geothermal pool. The best rooms have sea views and handy kitchenettes. **$$$**
Reykjavík City Youth Hostel
Sundlaugavegur 34
Tel: 553 8110
E-mail: reykjavikcity@hostel.is
Well-run hostel with good facilities. Situated on the fringe of Laugardalur, next to the open-air swimming pool. Good bus connections nearby. **$**

THE REYKJANES PENINSULA

Hafnarfjörður

Hafnarfjörður Guesthouse & Campsite
Hjallabraut 51,
by Víðistaðatún Park,
Hafnarfjörður
Tel: 565 0900
www.hafnarfjordurguesthouse.is
A cheaper, quieter alternative to Reykjavík, this hostel-style guest-house and campsite over-looks a little sculpture park. The trip to the capital takes about 30 minutes by bus. **$**

Keflavík

Flug Hótel
Hafnargata 57, Keflavík
Tel: 421 5222
E-mail: flughotel@icehotels.is
Up-market hotel, mainly for airport passengers, with restaurant and bar. All rooms are en-suite. **$$$$**
Hótel Keflavík
Vatnsnesvegur 12–14, Keflavík
Tel: 420 7000
www.hotelkeflavik.is
Comfortable hotel near the airport with various services on-site and restaurants

nearby. The hotel runs a much cheaper guesthouse at no. 9. **$$** (guesthouse) **–$$$**
Njarðvik FIT Youth Hostel
Fitjabraut 6a
Tel: 421 8889
E-mail: airport@hostel.is
Rather in the middle of nowhere, this is nevertheless the HI hostel closest to Keflavík international airport. Basic but good ratio of kitchens to guests. **$**

Blue Lagoon

Northern Light Inn

Blue Lagoon Road, 240 Grindavík
Tel: 426 8650
www.nli.is
Located at the Blue Lagoon, this large, family-run bungalow hotel offers a free pick-up from Keflavík international airport. **$$$**

THE SOUTHWEST

Hveragerði

Hótel Eldhestar
Vellir, Hveragerdi
Tel: 480 4800
www.hoteleldhestar.is
As well as offering riding tours, Eldhestar horse farm has a lovely one-storey wooden eco-hotel attached. Rooms are comfortable, with direct access to the garden, and there are log fires in the communal areas. The hotel has full disabled access. **$$$**
Hótel Örk
Breiðumörk, 810 Hveragerði
Tel: 483 4700
www.hotel-ork.is
A large business-style hotel with comfortable rooms that do their job. The outdoor pool with water slide will appeal to families with children. **$$$**

Fluðir

Guesthouse Syðra-Langholt
845 Flúðir
Tel: 486 6574
www.sydralangholt.is
Based in a family farm south of Flúðir and open all year. Campsite and horse-riding tours also available. **$**

Geysir

Hótel Geysir
Haukadal, 801 Selfoss
Tel: 480 6800
www.geysircenter.com
Small hotel just a stone's throw from the famous geysers, with lodging in cosy cabins. Horse-riding and quad-bike tours offered. **$$$**

Hella

Guesthouse Árhús
Rangarbakkar, 851 Hella
Tel: 487 5577
www.arhus.is
Open year-round, these 28 little wooden huts can be hired with or without bedlinen. Camping also available, on the banks of the Ytri-Ranga River. **$$**

Hvolsvöllur

Hótel Hvolsvöllur
Hlídarvegur 7,
860 Hvolsvöllur
Tel: 487 8050
www.hotelhvolsvollur.is
Comfortable small hotel near the Saga Centre, handy for the new ferry service to the Westman Islands. **$$$**

Skógar

Hótel Edda
Skógar, 861 Hvolsvöllur
Tel: 444 4830
www.hoteledda.is
One of Iceland's 13 budget

PRICE CATEGORIES

Prices are for a double room per night in high season
$$$$ Over ISK 25,000
$$$ ISK 19,000–25,000
$$ ISK 12,000–18,000
$ Under ISK 12,000

Edda hotels, close to Skóga-foss waterfall and Skógar Museum. All rooms have shared bathrooms. Sleeping-bag accommodation available. Summer only. **$$**

Þórsmörk Valley

Þórsmörk Hut

Hostelling International Iceland, Borgartún 6, 105 Reykjavik
Tel: 552 8300
E-mail: thorsmork@thorsmork.is
Hostelling International Iceland now manage the busy huts and crowded camp site inside the popular Þórsmörk Nature Reserve, where there is bunk space

for around 120 people. **$**

Vík

Hótel Edda Vík
Klettsvegur, 870 Vík
Tel: 444 4000
www. hoteledda.is
An 'Edda Plus' hotel, meaning its clean but basic

rooms have ensuite bathrooms and TVs. Summer only. **$$$**
Vík Youth Hostel
Suðurvíkurvegur 5, 870 Vík
Tel: 487 1106
E-mail: vik@hostel.is
A bustling little youth hostel, based in a white house uphill on the edge of town. **$**

VESTMANNAEYJAR

Heimaey

Guesthouse Hvíld
Höfðavegur 16
Tel: 481 1230
www.simnet.is/hvild
A very good-value budget guesthouse. **$**

Hótel Eyjar
Bárustígur 2
Tel: 481 3636
www.hoteleyjar.eyjar.is
Hotel containing 10 well-appointed apartments right in the centre of Heimaey. **$$**

Hotel Þórshamar
Vestmannabraut 28
Tel: 481 2900
www.hotelvestmannaeyjar.is
A fairly up-market hotel with a lower-priced guesthouse attached. **$$–$$$**

THE SOUTHEAST

Kirkjubaejarklaustur

Hótel Klaustur
Klausturvegur 6, 880
Kirkjubæjarklaustur
Tel: 487 4900
Email: klaustur@icehotels.is
A comfortable all-year hotel in this historic small town, close to the *Kirkjugólf* – basalt that looks like a paved church floor. **$$$**

Höfn

Fosshótel Vatnajökull
Lindarbakki, 781 Höfn
Tel: 478 2555
Email: sales@fosshotel.is
Average rooms and service, but the USP here is the hotel's proximity to the glorious Vatnajökull icecap, 10 kilometres (6 miles) from Höfn. **$$$$**

Nýibær Youth Hostel
Hafnarbraut 8, 780 Höfn
Tel: 478 1736
Email: hofn@hostel.is
Old house near Höfn harbour. Rooms with bunks. **$**
Smyrlabjörg
Suðursveit, 781 Hornafjörður
Tel: 478 1074
www.smyrlabjorg.is
This farm offers simple ensuite doubles in a

purpose-built annexe, half-way between the Jökulsárlón glacial lagoon and Höfn. **$$**

SNÆFELLSNES AND THE WEST

Borgarnes

Hamar Youth Hostel
Borgarbraut 9, 310 Borgarnes
Tel: 695 3366
Email: borgarnes@hostel.is
Set in a beautiful farmhouse at the golf club northeast of Borgarnes, with views over nearby Borgarfjörður and the Skarðsheiði mountains. **$**

Hraunsnef Country Hotel
Norðurárdalur, 311 Borgarfjördur
Tel: 435 0111
www.hraunsnef.is
Located just off Route 1, 3 km (2 miles) north of Borgarnes. A pleasant, purpose-built guesthouse, which also has summerhouses for hire. Closed Jan. **$$**

Reykholt

Fosshótel Reykholt
320 Reykholt
Tel: 435 1260
Email: sales@fosshotel.is
A former boarding school converted into a hotel with its own restaurant. **$$$$**

Búðir

Hótel Búðir
Búðir, 365 Snæfellsnes
Tel: 435 6700
www.budir.is
Destroyed by fire in 2001, Búðir was rebuilt and is now one of the most romantic hotels in Iceland. The elegant restaurant is renowned for its fish and game dishes. **$$$$**

Arnarstapi

Guesthouse Snjófell
Arnarstapi, 355 Snæfellsbær
Tel: 435 6783
www.snjofell.is
Value-for-money guest-house with good cooking facilities and sleeping-bag

accommodation. Tours onto Snæfellsjökull glacier leave from here. Open from Easter to the end of September. **$**

Stykkishólmur

Hótel Breiðafjördur
Aðalgata 8, Stykkishólmur
Tel: 433 2200
E-mail: info@hotelbreidafjordur.is
A friendly, central hotel close to the harbour. **$$**

Hótel Stykkishólmur
Borgarbraut 8, 340 Stykkishólmur
Tel: 430 2100
www.hringhotels.is

Comfortable hotel with
tremendous views over this
pretty town.
$$$

**Stykkishólmur Youth
Hostel (Sjónarhóll)**
Höfðagata 1, 340 Stykkishólmur
Tel: 438 1417

E-mail: stykkisholmur@hostel.is
Large, comfortable hostel in
the Old Town.
$

THE WEST FJORDS

Isafjörður

Gamla Gistihúsið
Mánagata 5, 400 Ísafjörður
Tel: 456 4146
www.gistihus.is
A sweet-and-sunny guest-
house in the middle of the
Old Town, with shared bath-
rooms. Also has sleeping-
bag accommodation. **$**
Hótel Ísafjörður
Silfurtorg 2, 400 Ísafjörður
Tel: 456 4111
www.hotelisafjordur.is
Right in the town centre.
Standard rooms are
average; it's worth paying
extra for deluxe. The
highlight is the good
restaurant with its fine fjord
views. The owners also run
the summer-only Edda
Hotel. **$$-$$$**

Reykjanes

Hótel Reykjanes
Tel: 456 4844
www.rnes.is
Spectacular views across
the fjord from a utilitarian
hotel, with shared
bathrooms. The high point is
the 50-metre swimming
pool, fed by hot spring
waters. **$**

Breiðavík

Gistiheimilið Breiðavík
Breiðavík
Tel: 456 1575
www.breidavik.is
This isolated sheep farm,
with views over Breiðavík
bay, provides friendly, basic
accommodation and is
handy for the Látrabjarg bird

cliffs. Summer only. **$$**

Hólmavík

Gistiheimilið
Borgarbraut 4, Hólmavík
Tel: 451 3136
www.borgabraut4.is
Guesthouse with self-
catering and sleeping-bag
accommodation available.
Wonderful views. **$**

Djúpavík

Hótel Djúpavík
Djúpavík, 524 Árneshreppur
Tel: 451 4037
www.djupavik.com
In the remote village of
Djúpavík, this former hostel
for women workers
(Djúpavík was once a fish-
processing centre) has been

renovated and now makes
for a typically quirky
Icelandic farm-stay. **$**

Flókalundur

Hótel Flókalundur
Flókalundur, Vatnsfjörður
Tel: 456 2011
www.flokalundur.is
Close to Brjánslækur (ferry
to Stykkishólmur), with a
good restaurant and slightly
dated rooms with facilities.
Summer only. **$$**

HÚNAFLÓI AND SKAGAFJÖRÐUR

Blönduós

Geitaskarð Farm
Langadal, 541 Blönduós
Tel: 452 4341
www.geitaskard.com
Farmstay just outside
Blönduós, near the ring
road. **$-$$**

Sauðarkrókur

Hólar i Hjaltadalur
Hólar i Hjaltadalur,
551 Sauðárkrókur
Tel: 455 6333

E-mail: booking@holar
Cabins and rooms are
available during the
summer. **$**

Hofsós

Sunnuberg Guesthouse
Suðurbraut 8, 565 Hofsós
Tel: 453 7310
E-mail: gisting@hofsos.is
Offers basic rooms, some of
which are en-suite. **$-$$**

Hvammstangi

Ósar Youth Hostel
Vatnsnes, 531 Hvammstangi
Tel: 862 2778
E-mail: osar@hostel.is
Farmhouse hostel located in
a peaceful spot by the sea;
good for bird life. **$**

Siglufjörður

**Siglufjörður Youth
Hostel (Gistihusið
Hvanneyri)**
Aðalgata 10, Siglufjörður
Tel: 467 1506
www.hvanneyri.com

A stately hotel in Siglufjörður's boom days, this
touchingly ramshackle old
building is now managed by
Hostelling International
Iceland. Rooms with shared
facilities. **$**

AKUREYRI AND SURROUNDINGS (INCLUDING GRÍMSEY)

Akureyri

Akureyri Youth Hostel
Stórholt 1, 603 Akureyri
Tel: 462 3657
E-mail: akureyri@hostel.is
Busy hostel, a fair distance
from the centre of town. It's

advisable to book ahead in
summer. **$**
Guesthouse Gula Villan
Brekkugata 8, 600 Akureyri
Tel: 896 8464
www.gulavillan.is
Pleasant family-run
guesthouse

in the town centre, with a
second house acting as an
overflow at busy times; also
has sleeping-bag
accommodation. **$-$$**
Guesthouse Sólgarðar
Brekkugata 6, 600 Akureyri
Tel: 461 1133

TRANSPORT

ACCOMMODATION

ACTIVITIES

A – Z

LANGUAGE

Small but comfortable guesthouse in the town centre, which also has sleeping bag accommodation. **$–$$**

Hótel Akureyri
Hafnarstræti 67, 600 Akureyri
Tel: 462 5600
www.hotelakureyri.is
In a quiet spot just outside the town centre, with views out to the fjord. **$$$**

Hótel Kea
Hafnarstræti 87-89, 600 Akureyri
Tel: 460 2000
www.hotelkea.is
A very reliable hotel in the centre of town. Shares restaurant and reception with the Hótel Harpa. **$$$$**

Dalvík

Fosshótel Dalvík
Skíðabraut 18, 620 Dalvík
Tel: 466 3395
www.fosshotel.is
This bright-yellow hotel offers newly renovated rooms, most with private facilities. There's a restaurant, and a guest kitchen for self-caterers. **$$$**

Syðri-Hagi Farm
Árskógsströnd, 621 Dalvík
Tel: 466 1961
E-mail: sydrihagi@hotmail.com
Farm accommodation near the ferry to Hrísey. Wonderful views over the fjord. **$–$$**

Hrísey

Guesthouse Brekka
Brekkugata 5, 630 Hrísey
Tel: 466 1751
www.brekkahrisey.is
Comfortable but small guesthouse with restaurant. **$–$$**

Grímsey

Guesthouse Básar
Tel: 467 3103
E-mail: gaga@simnet.is
Next to the airstrip, with standard rooms and sleeping-bag accommodation. **$**

Gullsól Guesthouse
Tel: 467 3190
Simple rooms above the harbourside giftshop and café. **$**

LAKE MÝVATN AND THE NORTHEAST

Fosshóll / Laugar

Fosshóll Guesthouse & Restaurant
Bárðardal, 645 Fosshóll
Tel: 464 3108
E-mail: fossholl@nett.is
In a beautiful setting right next to the Goðafoss falls between Akureyri and Mývatn. Also has camping facilities.
$$–$$$

Fosshótel Laugar
650 Laugar
Tel: 464 6300
E-mail: sales@fosshotel.is
Still serving as a boarding school in winter, this hotel is well located for exploring the area between Mývatn and Akureyri. Sleeping-bag accommodation available. Summer only.
$$–$$$$

Reykjahlíð / Mývatn

Bjarg
Tel: 464 4240
E-mail: ferdabjarg@simnet.is
Large, well-equipped campsite beside the lake. A few rooms available in the main house.
$–$$

Eldá
Helluhraun 15, 660 Reykjahlíð
Tel: 464 4220
www.elda.is
This guesthouse operates at two more locations around Reykjahlíð with a choice of comfortable rooms. **$$**

Hlíð
Hraunbrún, 660 Reykjahlíð
Tel: 464 4103
A busy campsite with (noisy!) sleeping-bag accommodation. **$**

Hótel Reynihlíð
Reynihlíð, 660 Reykjahlíð
Tel: 464 4170
http://reynihlid.is
The biggest and classiest hotel in an extremely popular area. Essential to book ahead – it gets very busy in high season.
$$$$

Skútustaðir Farm
Skútustaðir 2b, 660 Reykjahlíð
Tel: 464 4212
www.skutustadir.info
Based on the southern side of the lake, slightly away from the crowds. **$$**

Húsavík

Fosshótel Húsavík
Ketilsbraut 22, 640 Húsavík
Tel: 464 1220
E-mail: sales@fosshotel.is
Open all year, this friendly hotel is centrally located. Standard rooms are a little tired; superior rooms are newer and better. **$$$$**

Guesthouse Árból
Ásgarðsvegur 2,
640 Húsavík
Tel: 464 2220
E-mail: guest.hus@simnet.is
A comfortable, if dated, old guesthouse in the middle of town. **$$**

Hóll Farm
Kelduhverfi, 671 Kopasker
Tel: 465 2270
E-mail: hrunda@ismennt.is

Ideally located for visiting the Jökulsárgljúfur area of Vatnajökull National Park. Horse hire available. **$–$$**

Kaldbaks Kot
Kaldbakur, 640 Húsavík
Tel: 464 1504
E-mail: cottages@cottages.is
These snug wooden cottages, overlooking the sea one mile from Húsavík, make the perfect base for self-caterers. **$–$$**

Þinghúsið Hraunbær
V. Laxa i Aðaldal, 641 Húsavík
Tel: 464 3695
E-mail: thinghus@simnet.is
Renovated old community house in a tranquil rural setting, 25km (15½ miles) south of Húsavík. Summer only. **$$**

THE EAST FJORDS

Egilsstaðir

Egilsstaðir Guesthouse
700 Egilsstaðir
Tel: 471 1114
www.egilsstadir.com
Characterful old farmhouse with tasteful rooms, situated on the shores of Lake Lagarfljót. **$$$**

Gistiheimilið Eyvindará
Eyvindará II
700 Egilsstaðir
Tel: 471 1200
www.eyvindara.is
Cute wooden chalets, 10 brand-new guesthouse rooms and a warm welcome. **$$**

Hótel Hérað
Midvangur 5-7, 700 Egilsstaðir
Tel: 471 1500
E-mail: herad@icehotels.is
Smart, newly renovated business-class Icelandair hotel in the middle of town, with good restaurant. **$$$**

Seyðisfjörður

Hótel Aldan
Norðurgata 2, 710 Seyðisfjörður
Tel: 472 1277
www.hotelaldan.com
Split across two sites:
'Snæfell' is more basic, the
'Old Bank' is a gorgeous
boutique hotel (rare in
Iceland). $$$–$$$$

Borgarfjörður-Eystri

Guesthouse Borg
720 Borgarfjörður-Eystri
Tel: 472 9870
E-mail: gistingborg@simnet.is
Basic hostel-style beds/
sleeping-bag space, with
guest kitchen and lounge;
excellent walks are

possible nearby. **$**

Mount Snæfell

Snæfell Hut
Ferðafélag Fljótsdalshéraðs
(Fljótsdalur touring club), 700
Egilsstaðir
Tel: 860 1393 (summer)
863 5813 (winter)
E-mail: ferdafelag@egilsstadir.is
GPS: 64°48.250 N/15°38.600 W
Mountain hut and camp
site with a full-time warden
in summer, hot showers
and WC. A good base for
walks in the Snæfell area.
The same organisation
runs the Geldingafell and
Egilssel huts on the
Vatnajökull east traverse
route. **$**

Reyðarfjörður

Fjarðahótel
Búðareyri 6, 730 Reyðarfjörður
Tel: 474 1600
www.fjardarhotel.is
A modern, comfortable
hotel next to the post office
on the main road in
Reyðarfjörður. **$$**

Breiðdalsvík

Hótel Bláfell
Sólvöllur 14, 760 Breiðdalsvík
Tel: 475 6770
www.blafell.is
A well-priced hotel,
constructed in a chalet-
style, that benefits from
cosy communal areas.
$$

Djúpivogur

Berunes Youth Hostel
Berunes 1, 765 Djúpivogur
Tel: 478 8988
E-mail: berunes@hostel.is
Accommodation in the old
farmhouse is a slice of pure
Iceland, and there are more
rooms in a newer building. **$**
Hótel Framtíð
Vogaland 4, 765 Djúpivogur
Tel: 478 8887
E-mail: framtid@simnet.is
Accommodation here varies
enormously: Framtíð offers
camping, sleeping-bag
space, simple hotel rooms,
apartments and summer
houses. Elegant restaurant
with tasty fish dishes, too.
$–$$$

THE INTERIOR

The Kjölur route

Hveravellir Huts
Svínavatn community
Tel: 894 1293
www.hveravellir.is
GPS: 64°51.910 N/19°33.150 W
Very busy huts, used by
groups travelling the Kjölur
route. With relaxing
geothermal pool. **$**

Sprengisandur

Guesthouse Hrauneyjar
Sprengisandur Route (F26), 851
Hella
Tel: 487 7782
www.hrauneyjar.is
GPS: 64°11'48,56 N/19°17'07.31 W
On the Sprengisandur route,
this guesthouse has basic
rooms. Attached service

station and camp site. **$**
Laugafell Huts
Ferðafélag Akureyrar (Touring Club
of Akureyri)
Strandgata 23, 600 Akureyri
Tel: 854 9302, 462 2720
E-mail: ffa@ffa.is
GPS: 65°01.614 N/18°19.923 W
Heated huts north of
Hofsjökull ice field.
Accommodate 35. **$**
Nýidalur Huts
Ferðafélag Íslands, Mörkinn 6,
108 Reykjavík
Tel: 568 2533,
860-3334 (summer only)
E-mail: fi@fi.is
GPS: 64°44.130 N/18°04.360 W
A good base for walks and
cycling in a desolate location
on the Sprengisandur route.
Camping available. Room
for 120 people. **$**

Landmannalaugar

Hólaskjól Hut
Tel: 487 1447
GPS: 63°58.849 N/18°31.319 W
Mountain hut near Eldgja
on Fjallabaksleið. Basic but
comfortable and not usually
busy. Great walking and
cycling nearby. **$**
Landmannalaugar Hut
Ferðafélag Íslands, Mörkinn 6,
108 Reykjavík
Tel: 568 2533,
863 1175 (summer only)
E-mail: fi@fi.is
GPS: 63°59.600 N/19°03.660 W
Large crowded hut, with 75
beds plus a busy camp site.
Start of the Laugavegur
hiking trail (Landmanna-
laugar-Þórsmörk). Club
members have priority. **$**
Sveinstindur Hut
Útivist, Laugavegur 178
105 Reykjavík
Tel: 562 1000
www.utivist.is
GPS: 64°05.176 N/18°24.946 W
Basic but new hut in a
traditional design, east of
Landmannalaugar. Makes
an excellent base for walks
off the beaten track. **$**

The Askja route

**Herðubreiðarlindir Hut
(Þorsteinsskáli)**
Ferðafélag Akureyrar (Touring Club

of Akureyri)
Strandgata 23, 600 Akureyri
Tel: 854 9301, 462 2720
E-mail: ffa@ffa.is
GPS: 65°11.560 N/16°30.390 W
An old but comfortable hut,
with room for 30 people. **$**
**Kverkfjöll Hut
(Sigurðarskáli)**
Ferðafélag Fljótsdalshéraðs
(Fljótsdalur touring club), 700
Egilsstaðir
Tel: 863 9236 (summer),
863 5813 (winter)
E-mail: ferdafelag@egilsstadir.is
GPS: 64°44.850 N/16°37.890 W
A comfortable mountain
hut with a full-time warden
in summer, hot showers
and WC. Ideal base for
walks in the Kverkfjöll area.
$

PRICE CATEGORIES

Prices are for a double
room per night in high
season
$$$$ Over ISK 25,000
$$$ ISK 19,000–25,000
$$ ISK 12,000–18,000
$ Under ISK 12,000

TRANSPORT

ACCOMMODATION

ACTIVITIES

A – Z

LANGUAGE

A CTIVITIES

THE ARTS, NIGHTLIFE, FESTIVALS, SHOPPING, OUTDOOR ACTIVITIES AND CHILDREN

THE ARTS

Music

Iceland is a nation of music lovers, as witnessed by the vast number of concert recitals given over the course of a year and by the numerous choirs active in the country over the winter months.

Reykjavík is renowned for its ever-evolving contemporary music scene: new heavy-metal, indie, rock and experimental bands are born every week, some dying like gadflies after a short day in the sun, some going on to win international fame. Gigs tend to take place in tiny cafés and tucked-away bars: *Grapevine (see panel below)* will give you the best inroads into the music scene, or try to visit in October, when the eclectic five-day Iceland Airwaves takes place in venues across the city.

The Iceland Symphony Orchestra,

which has gained widespread international acclaim, holds concerts from September to early June only. Not to worry if you're here outside those months: a vibrant music scene kicks in at the beginning of the summer, both in and outside of Reykjavík. Below is a listing of the main musical events and classical venues, year-round.

Venues in Reykjavík

Iceland Symphony Orchestra, University Concert Hall, Hagatorg (opposite Hótel Saga), tel: 545 2500, e-mail: sinfonia@sinfonia.is, www.sinfonia.is. Weekly concerts Sep–Jun with international guest artists. The orchestra is due to move to the brand-new waterfront Icelandic National Concert and Conference Centre in January 2011.

Iðnó Theatre, Vonarstræti 3, tel: 562 9700, www.idno. is. This renovated theatre hosts various types of concerts during the summer, anything from jazz to piano and theatre music recitals.

Jazz at Jómfrúin, Lækjargata 4, tel: 551 0100. This restaurant serves excellent Danish-style open sandwiches and has free jazz recitals on Saturdays from 3–5pm during the summer months.

Nordic House, Hringbraut (by the university campus), tel: 551 7030, www.nordice.is. Hosts concert recitals year-round.

Sigurjón Ólafsson Museum, Laugarnestanga, tel: 553 2906, www. lso.is. A yearly concert series with recitals every Tuesday evening mid-July– August.

International Organ Summer, Hallgrímskirkja church, tel: 510 1000, www.listvinafelag.is. Concerts in Hallgrímskirkja church are organized by a group of music lovers. In summer these are organ concerts.

Venues outside Reykjavík

Contact the Tourist Information Centre in Reykjavík for information on dates and bookings for the following events:
Kirkjubæjarklaustur Chamber Music Festival, Kirkjubæjarklaustur, www. klaustur.is. This yearly festival takes place for one weekend in early August, in beautiful surroundings, with national and international musicians.
Summer Concerts at Akureyrarkirkja. Annual Sunday concerts, held in June in the church in Akureyri.
Reykholt Festival, Reykholt, www. reykholtshatid.is. A renowned three-day classical concert festival held in the last week of July, which attracts high-calibre international musicians.
Skálholt Summer Concerts Festival, Skálholt Church, www.sumartonleikar.is. The church at this ancient bishopric in the southwest hosts a yearly concert series on weekends in July and August.

Sources of Information

That a country with a population of 318,000 has three professional national theatre companies, a thriving film industry, a national ballet, opera and symphony orchestra and hosts an annual international arts festival is itself remarkable. Add to this the two-dozen or so museums and galleries in Reykjavík and over 50 others throughout the rest of the country, internationally acclaimed opera singers, world-famous rock bands and a world-class female pop star –

can anywhere else match Iceland for variety and intensity of cultural activity in such a small community?

Tourist information offices have copious amounts of information about current cultural events and productions. The free monthly booklet *What's On in Reykjavík* contains extensive event listings, (as well as maps, bus schedules, descriptions of walking tours and more), as do the free tourist newspaper *Grape-vine*, and the back pages of daily newspaper *Morgunblaðið*.

The focus tends to be on baroque music with musicians from around the world. Admission to all events is free. **Blue Church Concert Series**, Seyðisfjörður church, www.blaakirkjan.is. A series of Wednesday-evening concerts are held in this picturesque church in July and August.

Theatre, Ballet and Opera

Iceland offers up exceptional theatre with actors and directors of international calibre. All productions at the main professional theatres are in Icelandic, but often they are stagings of famous works with which tourists will be familiar. Theatres close in July and August.

Opera and dance, of course, transcend the language barrier. The Icelandic Opera is a world-class professional company, featuring top performers. The Icelandic Dance Company has in the past few years focused exclusively on modern dance. It is made up of both Icelandic and international dancers and has toured extensively abroad. Opera and dance performances are staged from September to March.

Venues in Reykjavík

The Icelandic Dance Company (based at the Reykjavík City Theatre), Listabraut 3, tel: 588 0900, www.id.is
The Icelandic Opera, Ingólfsstræti, tel: 511 6400, www.opera.is
National Theatre of Iceland, Hverfisgata 19, tel: 585 1200, www.leikhusid.is
Reykjavík City Theatre (Borgarleikhúsið), Listabraut 3, tel: 568 5500, www.borgarleikhus.is

Venues outside Reykjavík

Venues for cultural events outside the capital include:

Akureyri Theatre Company, Hafnarstræti 57, Akureyri, tel: 460 0200, www.leikfelag.is. Open Sept–June.
Hafnarfjarðarleikhúsið, Strandgata 50, Hafnarfjörður, tel: 555 2222, www.hhh.is.

NIGHTLIFE

Since the early 1990s Reykjavík at night has been transformed from a sleepy provincial city to one of the hottest venues in Europe, with as lively a nightlife – in the bars and clubs clustered in the tiny city centre – as you will find anywhere. Many locales which masquerade as perfectly civilised cafés during the day transform into rip-roaring bar rooms in the evening. But most places don't even begin to get going until after 11pm – Icelanders drink at home before going out to party, as bar prices are high. If you are intent on serious drinking come prepared – a half litre of draught beer costs around ISK700 in most places.

In most cafés and night spots, the clientele is young and dress is casual. For upmarket Reykjavík establishments you have to dress smartly, as for night clubs.

Drinking

Iceland has strict rules about buying and drinking alcohol. You have to be at least 20 years old to buy alcohol and you may be asked to show proof of your age. Visitors wanting a regular tipple should bring in their full duty-free allowance, because all alcoholic drinks are very expensive in Iceland.

Wines, spirits and beers over 2.25 percent alcohol are only sold at state-controlled outlets, ÁTVR shops (Vín Búð). Light beer can be bought in general supermarkets.

Pubs, Bars and Cafés

Opening hours were extended in 2000, with pub/club owners permitted to keep their places open pretty much as long as they liked. This was partly to help alleviate the congestion on the streets that took place when the legal closing hour was 3am. These days Reykjavík's weekend nightlife doesn't really get going until after 1am. Many pubs and bars are open Sun–Thur 6pm–1am and Fri–Sat 6pm–5am.

For individual listings, see *Places* chapters (*Reykjavík, page 159, and Akureyri, page 247*).

FESTIVALS

Diary of Events

February

Þorrablót: Although there is no fixed day for Þorrablót, most communities celebrate it in February. Essentially an occasion to eat, drink and be merry, Þorrablot has its roots in a long-forgotten pagan ritual. A feast of Icelandic delicacies, including the dreaded rotten shark (*hákarl*) and singed sheep's heads, is washed down with Brennivín (the local caraway-seed-flavoured spirit) and plenty of song and dance. If you are in Iceland in February it is well worth enquiring if there is a Þorrablót scheduled. Many are private affairs but those in the smaller villages are open to all, though must usually be booked in advance.
Sunshine Coffee: Or many of the remote fishing villages situated in the steepsided West Fjords, real winter starts when the sun ceases to rise above the mountains and even in fine weather the village is in perpetual shadow. The sun is often absent for several months but when its first rays hit the village again, everyone celebrates with sunshine coffee.

March

Bolludagur, Sprengidagur and Öskudagur: The Monday before Shrove Tuesday everyone bakes *bollur*, a kind of pastry eclair filled with cream, hence the name Bolludagur. Shrove Tuesday is called Sprengidagur (Explosion Day) and traditionally a hearty meal of salted lamb and split peas is served. On Ash Wednesday, or Öskudagur, children collect money for sweets and delight in pinning small cloth bags – in the old days, they

Cinema

Icelanders are avid cinema-goers and the greater Reykjavík area has an amazing number of screens considering its small size. Most films are from the US though a certain number of Icelandic and European films are also shown. All films are advertised in the daily press and shown with the original soundtrack, sub-titled in Icelandic. Cinema listings can also be found at www.kvikmyndir.is. There is a large film festival in Reykjavík every year. Other towns throughout Iceland have cinemas and smaller villages show films once or twice a week.

Cultural Festivals

Contact the Tourist Information Centre in Reykjavík *(see page 341)* for details on the following events:

Dark Music Days: Late January. Run by the Composers' Society, with emphasis on new Icelandic music.

Reykjavík Arts Festival: First held in 1970, this three-week festival takes place every year in May/June. It features music, theatre, visual arts, opera and ballet, and attracts national and international artists; tel: 561 2444, e-mail: artfest@artfest.is, www.artfest.is.

Reykjavík Gay Pride: Over the second weekend in August, the city is bedecked with rainbows as thousands of people gather to watch the annual Gay Parade, which processes from Hlemmur bus station down the length of Laugavegur into town. www.gaypride.is.

Reykjavík Jazz Festival: An annual event in August, with acclaimed international jazz performers; www.reykjavikjazz.com.

Reykjavík International Film Festival: A 10-day festival held every September/October. A range of mainstream and experimental works – a must for film buffs; tel: 411 7055, e-mail: riff@riff.is, www.riff.is.

Reykjavík Culture Night: Held on a Saturday in late August. The city centre turns into a cultural mecca, with every venue utilised. Musical events are staged in shops, poetry readings in cafés, street theatre flourishes and self-appointed performers set up wherever they can. The night culminates with a fireworks display; pubs and cafés are open extra late and are packed until the small hours.

Iceland Airwaves: This exuberant five-day international music festival in mid-October showcases Icelandic, American and European bands. Every venue across the city is utilised, as locals (and visitors) grab the chance to party hard before the full force of winter hits the city.

celebrated with singing, dancing and general festivities. For more information, contact the Tourist Information Centre in Reykjavík.

December

Christmas and New Year's Eve: Celebrations begin on 24 December when many people attend mass before going home to a festive dinner, gifts and dancing around the Christmas tree. New Year's Eve's celebrations are more outdoor-based, consisting of huge bonfires and an explosion of fireworks at midnight.

SHOPPING

In the past Iceland tended to attract tourists for whom shopping was not on the travel agenda, mostly because the main attraction was the landscape, but also because prices were considered ridiculously high – at best foreign visitors might purchase some woollen goods. But things have changed. Although the 2008 economic crisis was atrocious news for Icelanders, today's weak *króna* means that tourists can buy Icelandic goods at reduced rates, at least compared to those of a few short years ago.

It's still not bargain-basement. Icelandic products are marketed at those who believe in paying for style and quality, and Icelandic taxes remain extremely high. However, do note that most shops offer visitors a tax refund *(see panel, opposite)*, which reduces the price of goods by 15 percent. Geographically, the capital is also very shopper-friendly, with shops concentrated in a relatively small area.

What to Buy

Books

There are many fine books on Iceland aimed at the visitor and almost all are available in English. Many can be bought abroad through tour operators

used to contain ashes – to the backs of unwary strangers.

April

First Day of Summer: In a country where winter seems to drag on interminably, celebrating the first day of summer in April (usually on the third Thursday in the month) seems a little premature. Even so, there are big festivities in Reykjavík.

June

Sjómannadagur (Seafarer's Day): The first Sunday in June is the greatest celebration of the year in many fishing villages. Often a holiday for the whole village and always for seamen, there are rowing and swimming races and a chance for the young and not so young to test their skill and strength in contests from tugs of war to sea rescue. A fun-filled and lighthearted occasion, generally stretching across the whole weekend, with lots going on.

Independence Day: Iceland's national day is celebrated on 17 June, the day in 1944 when the country declared full independence from Denmark and also the birthday of Jón Sigurðsson who contributed more than any other Icelander to the struggle. The greatest celebrations are in Reykjavík, with parades, street theatre and music, side shows and dancing, but the day is a festive occasion throughout the country.

August

Verslunarmannahelgi: The first weekend in August is a long weekend all over Iceland with everything shut on the Monday. Icelanders take to their cars and head out of town to camp in the wilds or join in one of the organised events that are held throughout the country. These range from teetotal family festivities to loud rock festivals. Just to avoid the crush, most visitors will probably want to miss out popular destinations for Icelanders at this time. On the same weekend, Heimaey, in the Vestmannaeyjar (Westmann Islands), celebrates its own Þjóðhátíð festival commemorating the day in 1874 when Iceland got its constitution. Bad weather prevented the islanders from reaching the mainland so they celebrated independently and have done so ever since. The occasion draws Icelanders from all corners of the country to a huge outdoor camp for a weekend of music, song and dance and a fair amount of drinking.

September

Réttir: During the month of September farmers set off on horseback to round up their sheep, who have grazed freely in the highlands over the summer. When the sheep are brought down to the lowlands they are herded into pens and sorted. The end of this major event in the farming calendar is

How to pay

Icelanders use credit/debit cards to pay for even the smallest items. Most visitors can easily do the same, but check with your bank before travelling to ensure your cards will work in Iceland and to notify them of your visit so the cards will not be frozen by the bank's fraud department.

who also run a book and map service (see *Tour Operators, page 341*). Books published outside Iceland are much cheaper to buy abroad.

Ceramics

If the rather garish lava ceramics are not to your taste, shop around. Pottery in Iceland tends to be artistic rather than functional, so expect to pay accordingly. There are some fine potters producing unusual pieces. Often they will sell their own work in their studio, or will be members of an artisans' co-operative (see panel, page 332, for details).

Clothing

With such a northerly latitude, Iceland has become something of an expert producer of outdoor and hiking wear – prices are high, but the clothes are as tough and weatherproof as a salty old seadog, and look good too. Reykjavík also has a fair share of high-end boutiques full of smart, sculpted women's clothing – designers such as Andersen & Lauth, Birna, ELM, GuSt and Spaksmannsspjarir epitomise the Icelandic look.

Food

If you can protect your luggage against the smell, pack some dried fish. It weighs nothing, keeps for ever and may amuse your friends. Eat it with lashings of butter. Smoked trout and salmon also keep quite well. If you like *skyr (see page 120)*, take some home – you can make your own culture in the same way as yoghurt and it freezes well. A wide range of Icelandic foods is sold at the duty free shop at Keflavík Airport for departing passengers.

Music

For traditional Icelandic music, try the album *Íslensk alþýðulög* (Icelandic Folk Songs). There are also fine classical recordings by the Iceland Symphony Orchestra, particularly of works by late composer Jón Leifs (listen before buying – his music is intense and not for everyone), as well as by other Icelandic classical musicians. Of course, Björk and Sigur Rós are Iceland's biggest musical exports, but the modern music scene is ever-changing and new bands appear all the time. Reykjavík's helpful music-store staff will give recommendations and let you listen to the latest releases; or for variety look out for the *Made in Iceland* compilation CDs, which contain a great selection of Icelandic tunes.

Sheepskin goods

These are expensive but the quality is excellent. Hats, slippers and gloves sell for approximately ISK4,000–7,000.

Woollen Goods

The Icelandic sheep is an almost pure breed descended from the animals brought over by the first settlers. Its fleece is of an exceptional quality and produces a wool that is durable and naturally water resistant, yet soft and warm. It is this wool that is used to make the handknitted sweaters with traditional patterns around the yoke.

A simple cottage industry has grown into one of the country's major agricultural exports, and though the traditional sweaters are still hand-knitted, most woollen goods are now machine-made. A handknitted medium weight sweater costs around ISK10,000; however, if you buy the wool, circular needles and pattern (available in several foreign languages) you can knit yourself one for under ISK6,000.

For handknitted sweaters it is worth trying some of the farms in the Icelandic Farm Holidays network. Sweaters on sale here are usually cheaper than those in the shops and they will be authentically homemade and handknitted.

Where to Shop

In the centre of the Rekyavík, most of the tourist shops are in and around Hafnarstræti and Austurstræti, though Laugavegur, leading out of the centre, is home to the majority of the fashion shops; and Skólavörðustígur, which branches off Laugavegur at a sharp diagonal, is good for gifts and crafts.

In the suburbs are two large malls, Smáralind and Kringlan, which house most of the usual European high-street chain stores. The biggest, Kringlan, has 150 shops and is easy to reach – it's just a 15-minute bus-ride from the city centre.

Tax-free Shopping

All non-residents (other than Icelandic citizens) are entitled to a VAT refund on goods purchased in Iceland if the value of the goods exceeds ISK4,000 in one shop, and if the goods are going to be taken out of the country. You have to pay the full amount, VAT included, in the shop but then ask for your VAT refund at the cash register. The shop assistant will fill out a special Tax Free form – keep this safe, along with your purchase receipt.

For a cash refund, take the form to the tax refund desk at the Kringlan or Smáralind shopping malls, at the main tourist office in Reykjavík, or at the airport (be prepared to queue). Alternatively, you can fill in the form with your credit-card details and then post it in a special "Iceland Refund" envelope, and the amount will then be refunded direct to your card. The refund will amount to approximately 15 percent of the purchase price.

If the amount that is to be refunded exceeds ISK5,000 on a single purchase, you will need to show the goods to customs when leaving the country and receive a customs stamp before claiming your refund. (Woollen goods do not need to be shown.)

For more information on refunds see the free *Shopping in Iceland* brochure that is available in most shops; or check online at www. eurorefund.com/iceland.

Commercial Galleries in Reykjavík

The following galleries mostly feature sales exhibitions:

Gallerí Fold, Rauðarástígur 14, tel: 551 0400; www.myndlist.is. Diverse selection of paintings, prints and sculptures, with frequent exhibitions and quarterly auctions. Mon–Fri 10am–6pm, Sat 11am–4pm, Sun 2pm–4pm (closed Sun in July and Aug). Also in Kringlan mall, tel: 568 0400. Open in mall hours.

Gallerí Jens, Kringlan Mall, tel: 568 6730; www.jens.is. Jewellery designed and crafted by Icelandic artists, the unique styling drawn from the Icelandic landscape. Open in mall hours.

Kirsuberjatréð, Vesturgata 4, tel: 562 8990. Unique and beautiful crafts made from such

unconventional materials as fish skin and pigs' bladders. Mon–Fri 10am–6pm, Sat 11am–3pm.

Kogga, Vesturgata 5, tel: 552 6036. Ceramics by one of the country's foremost potters. Mon–Fri 9am–6pm, Sat 10am–2pm.

Listvinahús, Skólavörðustígur 41–43, tel: 551 2850. Iceland's oldest ceramics workshop. daily 10am–6pm in summer, Mon–Fri 10am–4pm winter.

Textílkjallarinn, Lokastígur 28, tel: 551 3584. Hand-printed and painted textiles. Bedcovers, sheets, scarves and more, made of cotton, satin, silk and wool. Mon–Fri noon–6pm, Sat 11am–3pm, or by arrangement.

Shops in Reykjavík

Try the following for a wide variety of gifts, woollen goods, ceramics, crafts and jewellery:
Íslandia, Kringlan shopping mall.
Kraum, Aðalstræti 10.
Rammagerðin, Hafnarstræti 19.
For books try:
Eymundsson, Austurstræti 18.
Eymundsson, Skólavörðustígur 11.
Íða, Lækjargata 2a.
For photographic equipment:
Hans Petersen, Ármuli 38.

Opening Hours

Shopping hours vary in Iceland – some smaller shops in the centre of Reykjavík may open only for a few hours on Saturdays, for example, or not open at all. By contrast some shops stay open late every day of the week, particularly book and record stores. Most shops are open Mon–Thur 9am–6pm, Fri 9am–7pm and Sat 10am–noon or 4pm.

Shops in the Kringlan mall are open Mon–Wed 10am–6.30pm, Thur 10am–9pm, Fri 10am–7pm and Sat 10am–6pm. Some of the shops are open 1–6pm on Sundays, particularly in winter.

Most branches of the big Icelandic supermarket chains (Hagkaup, Nóatún, Krónan) stay open daily until 8pm and 9pm; budget supermarket Bónus has shorter opening hours, generally closing by 6pm; 11–11 supermarket branches open 11am–11pm; but confusingly the 10–11 supermarket chains are usually open 24 hours. Many corner shops, selling sweets and basic groceries, stay open until 10pm or later. In the countryside, some supermarkets in the Samkaup

chain, notably those attached to petrol stations, may stay open until 8 or 10pm. In the evenings basic groceries, snacks and confectionery are sold at a *sjoppa* (kiosk).

OUTDOOR ACTIVITIES

Angling

Unlike many countries, Iceland has clean waters, and salmon runs have not been disturbed by sea fishing. Excellent fishing is therefore available but at a very high price, which varies according to river and facilities available. Permits can cost an incredible ISK15,000–100,000 per day, and sometimes even more. The other snag is that most rivers have to be booked months, if not years, in advance. For further information contact:
Angling Club of Reykjavík, Háaleitisbraut 68, Reykjavík, tel: 568

6050, e-mail: svfr@svfr.is, www.svfr.is.
National Angling Association, Hagatorg, 107 Reykjavík, tel: 553 1510, www.angling.is.

Trout fishing can often be arranged on-the-spot and at a reasonable price. Many of the farms in the Icelandic Farm Holidays booklet (see *Farm Guesthouses, page 321*) offer trout fishing. An open voucher system is available for some of the farms in this network.

Sea angling can be arranged from many fishing villages and coastal farms and can be combined with a boat trip to offshore islands, or whale-watching excursions. This is usually best arranged directly with hotels and farms.

Iceland's waters are disease-free, so all equipment coming into the country, including waders and boots, must be disinfected *(see Customs Regulations, page 337).*

Bird-watching

Iceland is renowned for its birdlife and is home to some of the largest breeding colonies in the world. A variety of cliff-nesting species can be seen at Látrabjarg in the West Fjords *(see page 224)*, and sea birds, including puffins and arctic terns, can be seen all around the island. Lake Mývatn *(see page 261)* is a major breeding ground for ducks and other water birds, while the large areas of glacial-sand wasteland to the east and west of Skaftafell *(see page 199)* are home to huge colonies of great and arctic skuas. Bird-watching tours can be arranged through agencies both in Iceland and abroad *(see Tour Operators, page 341).*

Golf

With 65 courses, golf is thriving in Iceland. Most courses have just nine holes, however there are fifteen 18-hole courses including those in: Reykjavík (Grafarholt and Korpa), Hafnarfjörður (Keilir), Garðabær (Oddur), Hella, Keflavík (Suðurnes), Vestmannaeyjar and Akureyri. For further information contact: **Golf Federation of Iceland/ Golfsamband Íslands**, Engjavegur 6, Reykjavík, tel: 514 4050, www.golf.is.

The major golfing event in Iceland is the Arctic Open, which takes place in June each year and is open to professional and amateur golfers alike. Hosts to the event are the **Akureyri Golf Club**, 600 Akureyri, tel: 462 2974, www.arcticopen.is. A complete package including flights, accommodation and admission charges can be booked through tour operators abroad.

Hiking

For walking off the beaten track and variety of scenery Iceland is unsurpassed. Hiking in Iceland is very popular with Icelanders and foreigners alike and both facilities and variety of hiking trails have improved tremendously since the early 1990s.

The most popular marked long-distance trail runs from Landmannalaugar south to the coast at Skógar and takes four to five days. Known to the locals as "Laugavegur", which is also the name of Reykjavík's main shopping street, the route is scenically stunning but well trodden, though venture off the track and you

are unlikely to encounter another soul. There are huts along the way, owned by Ferðafélag Íslands and Útivist, but it is advisable to take a tent as well in case the huts are full, as they do become very crowded in summer. In winter, huts are generally kept locked, so it is necessary to pick up a key first in Reykjavík to gain entry.

In June 2008, Europe's largest national park, Vatnajökull, was created, by joining together the Jökulsárgljúfur and Skaftafell national parks with a large protected area. In practice, little has changed on the ground for ramblers, as much of the protected area is taken up with the inaccessible icecap itself. In the Jökulsárgljúfur area, a two-day walk follows the length of the spectacular gorge from Ásbyrgi to Dettifoss, with camp sites en route. Skaftafell is Iceland's most popular protected area, with good walking paths and varied glacial and forested scenery. Within Þingvellir National Park and protected areas such as Mývatn, there are marked paths suitable for day hikes.

Another area that is attracting growing numbers of backpackers is Hornstrandir, in the extreme northwest. A series of indistinct and mostly unmarked trails link the fjords and bays of this rugged, uninhabited area. Hornstrandir is linked to Ísafjörður by a scheduled summer boat service.

The East Fjords district from Borgarfjörður-Eystri southwards and

Iceland from the Air

Sightseeing flights from Reykjavík airport offer a unique view of areas such as the Tindfjallajökull and Eyjafjallajökull glaciers (overflying the site of the 2010 eruption), Grímsey Island and Vestmannaeyjar *(see Sightseeing Air Tours, page 342)*. Trips can be arranged directly with the air company Eagle Air Iceland, Reykjavik Airport, 101 Reykjavik, tel: 562 4200; e-mail: info@ eagleair.is, www.eagleair.is.

Lónsöraefi in the southeast both offer challenging and varied wilderness hiking.

For some the ultimate challenge is to traverse Iceland's interior, following one of the highland tracks that run north to south. In clear weather the views are stunning, but much of the route is over bare sand and stone desert with little variation in terrain or scenery. Far more interesting hiking is often to be found in the areas immediately bordering the settled districts. The Kjölur and Sprengisandur routes are tough but highly rewarding to part hike. Take a map, compass and overstock on food just in case – routes are largely unmarked and it may take you longer than expected.

Hiking Maps

National parks and some nature conservation areas produce leaflets, including maps and hiking times. These are often more accurate and up-to-date than the general map series *(see Maps, page 338)*. Maps of Hornstrandir, Landmannalaugar and Þórsmörk areas mark paths but should be used with caution – the Hornstrandir map, for example, does not mark cliff faces! Always use these maps combined with the general map series.

Horse-riding

The sturdy Icelandic horse is a pure and unique breed, descended from stock brought over by the first settlers from Norway in the 9th century. No horses have been imported for 800 years so the breed has remained pure. It has adapted to the demands of harsh weather and rough terrain and is ideally suited to local conditions.

The Icelandic horse still plays a vital role in the autumn round-up, when farmers throughout the country

Safety for Hikers

All safety rules apply, doubly so when hiking in uninhabited areas or crossing rivers: fatal accidents are not uncommon among foreign travellers. Wherever possible seek the advice of local people at farms, mountain huts and national park wardens' offices and leave details of your intended route. Remember to inform people when you have arrived back safely.

Venturing off the beaten track is only for properly equipped hikers with considerable wilderness experience. Many of the BSÍ and other highland bus services will take hikers into remote areas and if pre-arranged, will pick up again further along the route, several days later. Obtain all you need for a trip beforehand, including sufficient food. Water is not always available, particularly in the cold desert region

of the Ódáðahraun. Even if you find water, you may have to filter it to remove the fine particles of rock in the glacial rivers. In case of problems, rescue is often difficult. Wardened huts and most vehicles have radio communications and can summon aid in an emergency.

When crossing rivers on foot face upstream and link arms with other members of the party to steady your-self, forming a wedge shape. Glacial rivers can flood after heavy rainfall or on a warm summer day. They can be very dangerous and if in doubt it is always best to wait until the flood subsides, often in only 12 hours.

Along uninhabited stretches of coastline, at regular intervals, are emergency huts for shipwrecked seamen. These huts are equipped with radios and are not for hikers' use except in a real emergency.

Whale-watching

Whale-watching has been growing steadily in popularity in Iceland in recent years, and a number of whale-watching tours are now offered across the country.

Of all the cetaceans in Icelandic waters, the minke whale is most often spotted of the larger species, with killer whales, sperm whales, fin whales, humpbacks and even blue whales sometimes seen. Harbour porpoises and white-beaked dolphins are also common along the coast. The best place for seeing whales is in the north of Iceland, around Húsavík.

The best times for whale sightings are late spring and summer and you do not always have to be on a boat to see them: sometimes just looking out to sea from the shore will reveal a whale's back breaking the surface.

The following agents operate whale-watching tours:

Bátaferðir, 620 Dalvík, tel: 771 7600; www.bataferdir.is

Elding, Ægisgarður, 101 Reykjavík, tel: 555 3565; www.elding.is
Gentle Giants Whalewatching, Húsavík, tel: 464 1500; www.gentlegiants.is
Hvalalíf – Life of Whales, Suðurbugt, Old Harbour, 101 Reykjavík, tel: 562 2300; www.hvalalif.is
North Sailing Whale-Watching, Hafnarstétt 11, 640 Húsavík, tel: 464 7272; www.northsailing.is
Viking Tours, Suðurgerður 4, 900 Vestmannaeyjar, tel: 488 4884; www.vikingtours.is.

set off for the highlands on horseback to gather their sheep. Mostly, however, horses are used for recreation and riding is a popular sport among Icelanders. Farms all over the country offer anything from a one-hour ride to a seven-day trek. The majority of these can be booked in advance through tour operators abroad *(see pages 341–2)*.

Prices start at ISK3,000 for an hour's ride. On long treks food and lodging is included; price per day is ISK12,000–15,000. Information on stables can be obtained from the Tourist Information Office, Reykjavík, or from: **Icelandic Farm Holidays**, Síðumúli 2, Reykjavík, tel: 570 2700, www.farmholidays.is.

Ice Climbing & Glacier Walks

In summer guided day-walks on the glaciers from Skaftafell (part of the Vatnajökull National Park) can be arranged with two groups based at the visitor centre: the Icelandic Mountain Guides, tel: 894 2959, 478 2559, www.mountainguide.is; and newcomers the Glacier Guides, tel: 659 7000, www.glacierguides.is. For more ambitious expeditions contact the following organisations: **Icelandic Alpine Club/Íslenski Alpaklúbburinn**, Skutuvógur 1G, 104 Reykjavík, tel: 868 8754, e-mail: info@isalp.is, www.isalp.is **Öræfaferðir**, Hofsnes-Öræfi, 785 Fagurhólsmýri, tel: 894 0894, www.oraefaferdir.is (winter tours.)

Kayaking

Kayaking is an excellent way to experience the tranquility of Icelandic waters, and get up close to bobbing seabirds and the occasional seal. Several companies offer kayaking tuition and guided tours. For very gentle child-friendly outings on a lagoon in Stokkseyri, southeast of Reykjavík, contact Kayak Tours, tel: 896 5716, www.kajak.is. Two other companies also offer family trips plus longer guided sea-kayaking tours for more adventurous travellers. In Ísafjörður in the Westfjords, contact West Tours, tel: 456 5111, www.vesturferdir.is; and in Seyðisfjörður in the Eastfjords, contact Hlynur Oddsson, tel: 865 3741.

Skidooing

An essential means of communication on remote farms in winter, skidoos (snowcats) are increasingly used for recreation. It is an exhilarating sport that has to be experienced.

In summer, trips run daily from Höfn to the Vatnajökull icecap, from where you can join a one- or two-hour guided excursion by skidoo. A full-day trip is also possible but must be booked in advance through **Glacier Jeeps** Glacier Tours, 780 Hornafjörður, tel: 478 1000, e-mail: glacierjeeps@simnet.is, www.glacierjeeps.is.

If you have a four-wheel-drive jeep, you can take the track up to the glacier (off from the Ring Road at Smyrlabjarg) – an experience in itself.

For excursions onto Snæfellsjökull glacier, contact **Ferðaþjónustan Snjófell**, Arnarstapi, 355 Ólafsvík, tel: 435 6783, e-mail: snjofell@snjofell.is, www.snjofell.is.

Skiing

Facilities and conditions for skiing fall far short of the Alps or North America. Snow is most consistent in the north. In the south, bad weather, even lack of snow, often closes the slopes for days on end.

Cross-country Skiing

Both Bláfjöll and Hlíðarfjall have marked cross-country ski trails but most people will probably want to head off on their own. This is safe in the farmed lowlands; venturing into uninhabited areas is only for the properly equipped and fit. Some tour operators offer cross-country skiing excursions *(see Tour Operators, page 341, for details)*.

Downhill Skiing

On a clear, calm weekend the whole of Reykjavík seems to head out of town and there can often be long queues for the lifts. Skiing is one of Iceland's bargains – a day ticket costs around ISK2,200 and children pay half price. The best facilities are in Reykjavík and Akureyri but other towns also have skiing areas and shorter drag lifts.

Reykjavík

Bláfjöll, one of the main skiing areas, is about half an hour's drive from Reykjavík. Scheduled buses depart from the Mjódd bus terminal on the eastern outskirts of Reykjavík once a day. The track to the ski slopes is open to private four-wheel-drive vehicles.

The lifts are open 2–9pm Mon–Fri and 10am–5pm at weekends. There are 15 lifts, and boot and ski hire is available. There is no overnight accommodation but a cafeteria serves snacks and drinks. For up-to-date information on conditions and opening times, tel: 530 3000, or check the website www.skidasvaedi.is.

Akureyri

There is more reliable snow and similar facilities at the Hlíðarfjall skiing area, just above Akureyri, which has six lifts and a café. Buses leave the city bus terminal once a day. The opening times of the slopes vary greatly from week to week in season, and from year to year depending on snowfall. For up-to-date information, tel: 462 2280.

Spectator Sports

Most Icelanders are avid sports fans and handball, football and basketball are all popular. Football is a summer sport, while handball and basketball, being indoor sports, are played year round. In all three sports Iceland has excellent players under contract to well-known teams abroad. Most international matches take place in Reykjavík and international and national games are advertised in the press. For information contact: **National Olympic and Sports Association of Iceland/Íþrótta-og Ólympíusamband Íslands**, Íþróttamiðstöðin, Engjavegur 6, 104 Reykjavík, tel: 514 4000, e-mail: isi@isi.is, www.isi.is.

Boxing is banned in Iceland, but Glíma, a form of wrestling from settlement times, is still practised. Contact Glímusamband Íslands at the National Olympic and Sports Association of Iceland.

Possibly Iceland's best-known spectator event is chess; the country currently has 11 grand masters. Chess tournaments are regularly held in Iceland.

Riding clubs hold races and other events throughout the summer.

The Reykjavík Marathon takes place in August each year and includes the marathon, half marathon, 10km race and a 3km fun run. For information and registration contact the Reykjavík Marathon Office, Engjavegur 6, 104 Reykjavík, tel: 535 3700, e-mail: marathon@marathon.is, www.marathon.is.

Swimming

If Iceland has a favourite national sport, it surely has to be swimming. The country's vast geothermal resources account for the selection of great pools throughout the country: just about any place with a population over 500 will have one. These range from the ultra-modern pools in the Greater Reykjavík area to the more primitive examples, such as the mineral-water pool at Lýsuhóll on the Snæfellsnes peninsula, which comes complete with an algae-covered bottom.

In Reykjavík, just about everyone will have their own favourite pool. The Laugardalur swimming pool is perennially popular, though many locals complain that it is too big, favouring the smaller-scale Vesturbæjarlaug in the west end of the city, or the small but modern facilities on Seltjarnarnes instead.

Those with small children might prefer the recreation-centre-like facilities of Árbæjarlaug pool, with its hot-pots, spouting fountains, water slides and reclining jacuzzi seats (see Children's Activities).

White-water Rafting

Rafting has steadily gained in popularity as a sport and there are now a number of tour operators offering a wide variety of such trips (see page 341). Main rafting areas include Skagafjörður in the north and the Hvítá river in the southwest.

CHILDREN'S ACTIVITIES

Facilities for Children

In Iceland, children are greeted with enthusiasm and welcomed at hotels, and in restaurants and homes. Many restaurants provide baby chairs and children's portions. Tourist Menus give free meals to children of five and under and a 50 percent discount to those aged 6–12. Hotels, if notified in advance, will provide a cot but families with a baby would be advised to bring their own carry cot. Children aged four and under will often stay free if not occupying a separate bed, but where an extra bed is required a reduction for the child is usually given.

Places to take Kids around Reykjavík

There are a number of places of special interest to kids in the Reykjavík area. Some cost money, others do not; a case in point is the **Tjörn** in central Reykjavík, which on weekends normally attracts hordes of children and their families to feed the ducks and geese.

Ábæjar Museum, Kistuhylur 4, tel: 411 6300, www.minjasafnreykjavikur.is. Open summer daily 10am–5pm. This open-air museum on the eastern edge of the city contains 20 traditional old Icelandic buildings, brought here from various sites around the country. There are frequent craft demonstrations, a café, and plenty of space for kids to run around. Bus no. 19 from Hlemmur bus station stops closest to the museum.

Reykjavík Zoo & Family Park, Laugardalur Valley, tel: 575 7800, www.mu.is. Open daily summer 10am–6pm, winter 10am–5pm. When the kids tire of looking at the seals, foxes, reindeer, horses, cows, pigs and all the other animals, they can head over to the Family Park. There they can try their hand at operating little electric automobiles, pull themselves across a man-made lake on a raft, climb in a Viking-ship replica and much more. There is a large grill, which can be used to grill hotdogs bought from the snackbar. The seals are fed twice a day: at 11am and 4pm; feeding times for other animals are listed by the main gate. Entry price: children (5–12 years) ISK500, adults ISK600, free for under fives. Ride prices: 1/10 tickets ISK220/2000.

Swimming Pools; just about any and all will do. The best ones for kids are the Árbæjar pool, Fylkisvegur, tel: 567 3933, with its outdoor/indoor pool, hot pots, water slides for big and little kids, whirlpool, sauna and solarium; and the Laugardalur pool, Laugardalur valley, tel: 411 5100, which has a very large children's pool and a big water slide.

A – Z

A HANDY SUMMARY OF PRACTICAL INFORMATION, ARRANGED ALPHABETICALLY

Admission Charges

Although Iceland is not the cheapest country to visit as a tourist, admission charges for museums and galleries are generally quite reasonable. Expect to pay around ISK600–700 for entry into most museums around the country. Some attractions, such as the National Gallery in Reykjavík, do not charge admission. In some instances, an entry ticket for one museum will give free entry or reduced entry to another (if they are operated by the same organisation – ask locally).

During the winter months, there is often a charge for checking in a coat when entering a bar or smart restaurant. This is not a strict admission charge but if you refuse to pay you will be denied access.

Budgeting for Your Trip

Following the 2008 financial crisis and the devaluing of the króna, Iceland is much cheaper for foreign

visitors. However, a small population and high import costs still conspire to make most items and services more expensive than you will be used to paying at home. Accommodation prices change significantly according to the season: they are up to one third lower outside the main tourist summer season.

A sit-down lunch in a restaurant costs from ISK1500 (but look out for cheap lunchtime buffet deals), and dinner from ISK2500. Alcohol is expensive, with a glass of beer costing around ISK700 and a bottle of wine upwards of ISK1000. It's a good idea to bring your maximum duty-free allowance with you from home.

Reykjavík's city bus service is good value, with bus tickets costing ISK280. Taxis are costly – the meter starts running as soon as the vehicle pulls up to your hotel, and a trip from Reykjavík to the international airport costs around ISK14,000 (compared to the Flybus ticket price of ISK1,950).

Generally, if you visit during the summer, stay in decent hotels, eat out in restaurants most nights and undertake a few activities, you should expect to pay upwards of ISK25,000 per person per day, based on two people sharing. However, it is possible to cut costs by staying in guesthouses or youth hostels and eating the odd meal in a restaurant – for this, you should reckon on about ISK10,000–15,000 per day. Camping and self-catering will cost around ISK4,000 per day.

Climate

Influenced by the warm Gulf Stream and prevailing southwesterly winds, Iceland's temperate oceanic climate is surprisingly mild for the latitude (63–66°N). Reykjavík's average January temperature is similar to that of Hamburg, -0.5°C (31°F), though the July average is a cool 11°C (52°F). Because the Gulf Stream influences the south and

CLIMATE CHART
Reykjavik

- ☐ Maximum temperature
- ■ Minimum temperature
- ∿ Rainfall

west of the country, there are marked regional differences in climate. This is also due to the prevailing winds and the position of mountain ranges.

The north, east and interior experience colder winter temperatures but warmer summers, and markedly less precipitation. The south side of Vatnajökull can see up to 10 times the annual 400mm (16 inches) of rain of those areas north of the glacier. This is quite evident in the vegetation cover on lava flows. In the northeast, lava dating back thousands of years is still bare, while in the south a 200-year-old flow is covered with thick spongy moss.

Iceland's most ubiquitous element is wind. The Icelandic language allows for at least eight different degrees of wind, from *logn* (calm) to *rok* (strong gale), and you can expect to encounter most of them during your stay. Finding shelter is not generally a problem in the settled lowlands, but for the hiker or cyclist, a storm in the central highland deserts or glacial outwash plains may mean hours, even days, of unimaginable misery. The soil whipped up by such winds can blot out the sun, covering the land in a brown haze.

Crime and Safety

Iceland is one of the world's safest countries. Of the few people in prison, most are drugs offenders. Public

Weather Information

The Icelandic Meteorological Office provides recorded weather bulletins in English; tel: 902 0600, then choose 1 on a touch-tone phone (this service is not available from all telephones). For a weather forecast on the internet, go to www.vedur.is/english.

places are well lit. Violent crime is virtually non-existent, bar the odd domestic dispute and drunken brawl. The latter is most likely on Friday and Saturday nights, when the city's youth takes to the streets of central Reykjavík on a (mostly good-humoured) drunken spree.

Though Icelanders are relaxed when it comes to security, for the visitor all normal precautions apply. Pickpocketing and street crime are rare, although Reykjavík has a few drug addicts and alcoholics who steal to fund their habits. Petty theft does occur in swimming-pool changing rooms (always leave valuables at the pay desk) and in bars and nightclubs. In the event of theft or loss, contact the nearest police station, where you will be required to fill in a statement. A copy is invariably required to claim on your travel insurance.

Customs Regulations

Visitors aged 20 and over are allowed to bring in 1 litre of spirits up to 47 percent alcohol content and 1 litre of wine up to 21 percent alcohol content. Six litres of beer may be brought in instead of either the wine or spirit allowance.

Visitors aged 18 and over may bring in 200 cigarettes or 250 grams of tobacco. As alcohol is expensive, it is worth bringing your full allowance. If you do not use it yourself, it will make a very welcome gift.

You may bring in 3kg (6lbs 9oz) of food up to the value of ISK18,500 free of duty, but the import of uncooked eggs, raw milk products and uncooked meat, including salami, bacon and uncooked ham, is prohibited.

On entering or leaving the country, if you are carrying more than €10,000-worth of Icelandic currency, you must declare it to a customs official.

Angling gear that has been used outside Iceland, including boots and waders, must be disinfected by a vet before being taken into the country. Bring a certificate from the vet stating that this has been done, otherwise your equipment will be disinfected by Icelandic customs at your own expense. It is also forbidden to introduce any animal into Iceland without permission from the Ministry of Agriculture. A lengthy quarantine period is required for all animals.

D isabled Travellers

Smaller hotels and guesthouses in Iceland rarely have elevators, and the narrow doorways and small rooms of

Emergencies

For police, ambulance, the fire brigade or other emergency situations, call 112.

many buildings in Reykjavík's old town can make wheelchair access to restaurants and shops difficult. However, wheelchair access is available at most of the major purpose-built hotels. Larger department stores, as well as the Kringlan Mall, are accessible to wheelchair users.

Rough terrain and a lack of developed facilities mean wheelchair access to Iceland's natural wonders is rare. There are paved paths at Geysir, Gullfoss and Þingvellir National Park. For information on vehicles for hire suitable for disabled persons, contact one of the tour operators or tourist information offices, or see the Sjálfsbjörg website (below). Highland buses for wheelchair users are available on request.

The ferries Baldur and Herjólfur have good facilities for the disabled. All airlines serving Iceland can accommodate disabled passengers.

For further information , contact Sjálfsbjörg, the Association of the Disabled in the Capital Area, tel: 550 0360, e-mail: mottaka@sjalfsbjorg.is, www.sjalfsbjorg.is.

E lectricity

The electric current in Iceland is 220V AC 50 HZ. 50Hz (cycles). To use North American and Japanese electrical devices in Iceland, you will require a voltage converter.

Icelandic electrical plugs are of the European two-pin type, so UK visitors and those from outside Europe will require a plug adapter for their electrical devices.

Embassies

Australia: Australian Embassy in Copenhagen, Denmark, tel: (+45) 70 26 36 76, www.denmark.embassy.gov.au
Canada: Túngata 14, tel: 575 6500, www.canada.is
Ireland: Honorary Consul in Reykjavík, Mr David Thorsteinsson, tel: 554 2355, e-mail: davidcsh@islandia.is
UK: Laufásvegur 31, tel: 550 5100, http://ukiniceland.fco.gov.uk
US: Laufásvegur 21, tel: 562 9100, http://iceland.usembassy.gov

The Icelandic Foreign Ministry has a full list of diplomatic representatives on its website: www.utanrikisraduneyti.is.

Etiquette

Shyness towards visitors may be mistaken for coldness, but Icelanders are by nature hospitable, innately curious and great socialisers. Family ties are strong in this small, closeknit society, and Icelanders are quick to establish family connections when introduced by delving into each other's genealogies.

If you are invited to an Icelander's home, it will most likely be for coffee, often accompanied by copious quantities of cakes and biscuits. The younger generation may be more likely to invite you for dinner; in this case a small gift – wine or flowers, for instance – is appropriate though not essential. It is customary to shake hands when greeting and leaving, and Icelanders always remove shoes before entering anyone's home.

Smoking is strictly prohibited in public buildings.

Iceland uses the old system of patronymics, once common throughout Scandinavia – very few Icelanders have surnames. Instead a child takes his father's first name, to which is added "son" or "dóttir" (son or daughter) as the case may be. Thus, if a father named Magnús has a son, Jón, and a daughter, Kristín, their full names will be Jón Magnússon and Kristín Magnúsdóttir. And as Icelandic women never change their names on marriage, their mother too will have a different name. A child may also take the mother's name by law, though this is less common. If the identity of the father is not established, the child may take the mother's or grandfather's name.

Icelanders always use first names and visitors will be expected to follow suit. The concept of titles, except for ministers of religion, is unknown. The exception to this is on formal letters when Herra (or Hr.)

Magnús Jónsson or Frú Kristín Jensdóttir would be a correct form of address on the envelope.

In the telephone directory, all entries are listed under first names. If the prospect of sifting through pages and pages of Jón Jónssons is daunting, many entries also give the person's profession (in Icelandic) as well as the address.

G ay Travellers

Iceland has a tolerant attitude towards gays and lesbians. It has the world's first openly gay prime minister, and passed a gender-neutral marriage bill in 2010.

For information and advice contact: **The Gay and Lesbian Association/ Samtökin '78**, 4th Floor, Laugavegur 3, 101 Reykjavík, tel: 552 7878, e-mail: office@samtokin78.is. Open daily 1.30–5.30pm; Monday and Thursday evenings there is a library and a coffee bar, open 8–11pm. **Samtökin '78** also have a website: www. samtokin78.is.

There is more information about the gay scene in Iceland at www.gayice.is.

H ealth and Insurance

Iceland is a very healthy country. Nonetheless, all visitors should have adequate medical insurance, though an agreement exists between Iceland, the UK and Scandinavian countries for limited health insurance coverage of its residents. Travellers from those countries should obtain the European Health Insurance Card (formerly the E111 form) before leaving home. No vaccinations are required for visitors, unless you are arriving from an infected area. Tap water is glacier-clean and delicious.

In Reykjavík, for medical help call the **National Hospital** (Landspítali Háskólasjúkrahús) on 543 1000, weekdays 8am–4pm. A doctor is on call after those hours, and at weekends. In case of serious illness or accidents, there is also a 24-hour casualty department in Fossvogur; telephone 543 2000, or phone an ambulance directly on the emergency number 112.

For non-emergency medical treatment outside normal hours the **Medical Centre** (Læknavaktin), Smáratorg 1 (in Kópavogur), is open Monday–Friday 5pm–11.30pm and Saturday–Sunday and public holidays from 9am–11.30pm. Their helpline (tel: 1770) is open Monday–Friday 5pm–8am and 24 hours at weekends. They can provide advice by

telephone, direct you to the nearest place with after-hours care, or send a doctor to your accommodation.

Emergency **dental care** is available, tel: 575 0505 for information about dentists on duty.

Most pharmacies (apótek) are open normal business hours (9am–6pm). However, Lyfja at Lágmúli (daily 7am–1am) has longer opening hours.

I nternet

Virtually everyone in Iceland has internet access at home. Hence, there are very few internet cafés across the country. A free guest computer is often available in the lobby of hotels and guesthouses. Libraries usually have bookable internet access for a small fee (usually no more than ISK200–300 per hour). Tourist offices, where they exist, usually also have one or two terminals for internet use. Once again there's usually a nominal fee, similar to that in libraries. Most cafés and bars in Reykjavík have Wi-fi, so if you are travelling with your own laptop, you can access the web for the price of a coffee.

Useful websites about Iceland include the following: www.icelandinfocus.com A good source of geographic information about Iceland. www.icetourist.is The definitive travel website of the Icelandic tourist board. www.icelandreview.com A daily news digest of events in Iceland. www.vedur.is/english The all important daily weather forecast for all areas of the country.

L eft and Lost Luggage

Hotels, guesthouses and hostels will often store luggage free of charge for guests; if you lose something while out and about, the lost and found office in Reykjavík is at Hverfisgata 113, tel: 444 1000; open Mon–Fri 8.15am–4pm.

M aps

Visitors can obtain a useful (and free) tourist map of the country and city plan of Reykjavík, which is adequate for general planning purposes and orientation but not for actual touring, from tourist information centres, airports, bus terminals and accommodation throughout Reykjavík and the rest of the country.

More detailed maps can be bought from tourist offices and all larger

Lost Credit Cards

Credit-card issuers strongly recommend that you take the emergency credit-card telephone number in your home country with you when going on holiday. However, if you lose your credit card, you can phone the following numbers for initial assistance: **Visa**, Álfabakki 16, Reykjavík, tel: 525 2000. Emergency (24 hours) tel: 525 2200. **MasterCard/EuroCard/Diners Club.** Emergency number (in Denmark): (+45) 3673 7373. (24 hours). **American Express.** Emergency number (in the UK): (+44) 20 7365 4846.

bookshops in Iceland, as well as at many fuel stations, or before you travel from the Ferðakort website www.ferdakort.is. For general touring purposes the **Insight Fleximap** (1:910,000) has a laminated finish ideal for withstanding Iceland's wind and rain. The 1:500,000 touring map **Ferðakort Ísland** is excellent, as is the 1:200,000 **Ferðakort Ísland Vegaatlas (Road Atlas)**. There are four new touring maps available that cover the country at a scale of 1:250,000: **Westfjords and North Iceland; West and South Iceland; Northeast and East Iceland;** and **the Highlands.**

Large-scale 1:100,000, 1:50,000 and 1:25,000 maps of areas of particular interest to visitors, such as Þórsmörk/ Landmannalaugar, Húsavík/Mývatn, Skaftafell, The Golden Circle, Vestmannaeyjar and Hornstrandir, are also available. But a word of warning: the accuracy of such maps, especially when marking footpaths and cliff faces, falls far short of maps in other countries. A general map series on the same scales also covers all areas of the country but some sheets are still under preparation or out of print.

Media

Newspapers and Magazines

English-language newspapers and magazines are on sale in Reykjavík, one or two days after publication. They can also be found in public libraries (*bókasafn*).

The magazine *Iceland Review* (www.icelandreview.com) is published in English with informative articles and great photographs. The *Reykjavík Grapevine* is an irreverent, free

English-language newspaper containing articles, reviews and listings, which publishes around 18 issues per year and is available wherever there are tourists.

Of the Icelandic-language media, the daily newspaper *Fréttablaðið* has the largest circulation (about 90,000) – it is distributed free, and is relatively lightweight in both content and size. *Morgunblaðið*, the longest-established daily, has excellent coverage of foreign affairs, reflecting an isolated nation's desire to keep pace with the world. *DV*, the main tabloid, publishes on Monday, Wednesday and Friday.

The free monthly listings booklet *What's On in Reykjavík* is available at the tourist office.

Television

The government-owned Sjónvarpið and the commercial channel Skjár 1 are the two main TV channels in Iceland. Also broadcasting are Omega, a Christian station; and several subscription-based pay-TV channels. Alongside homegrown programmes, you will find foreign films, serials and documentaries, mostly imported from the US. These are usually subtitled in Icelandic, save for children's programmes which are dubbed. Satellite TV is available by subscription in Iceland, giving direct access to international news and entertainment channels including CNN and the BBC.

Money

The monetary unit is the Icelandic króna (ISK; plural: krónur), divided into 100 aurar. Notes are in denominations of ISK5,000, 2,000, 1,000 and 500. Coins are in denominations of ISK100, 50, 10, 5 and 1.

At the time of writing, the króna had recovered some of its value after the disastrous 2008 crash, but exchange rates were still favourable for foreign visitors. In May 2010 the exchange rate was ISK190 to the pound sterling, ISK128 to the US dollar and ISK164 to the euro. It is possible that Iceland will adopt the euro in 2011.

You can bring in unlimited foreign currency in the form of travellers' cheques or bank notes and up to €10,000-worth of Icelandic currency. However, it is rarely worth purchasing Icelandic króna abroad, as you usually get a poor exchange rate; moreover, following the crash, it is now quite difficult to buy króna outside Iceland. Similarly, you should

change back all unused króna before leaving Iceland (this can be done at the airport departure lounge) and you may need to produce receipts of exchange transactions from foreign currency or travellers' cheques to króna. Icelanders use cards much more readily than cash, even for very small purchases; visitors may as well do the same.

Exchange Facilities

The simplest way to obtain Icelandic króna is to find an ATM cash machine – plentiful in Reykjavík and other Icelandic towns. Banks will change foreign currency or travellers' cheques – US dollars, sterling and euros are all easily exchanged. Some tourist shops will accept payment in euros and US dollars, but usually at unfavourable rates.

Hotels usually exchange travellers' cheques and banknotes for guests, at a rate slightly below the bank rate, depending on the availability of cash in the till.

Outside normal banking hours 24-hour exchange facilities are available at Keflavík Airport: look for **Landsbankinn** in the arrival hall for arriving passengers; on the second level for departing passengers.

Credit Cards

Credit cards are used everywhere in Iceland, with the most ubiquitous being Visa and MasterCard/EuroCard. American Express, JCB and Diners are far less common.

Cash advances are available on Visa and MasterCard/EuroCard from all banks, savings banks and automatic cash machines displaying the respective logos.

Debit Cards

Visa, Delta, Maestro/EDC and Electron debit cards are widely accepted. Cash may be obtained against these cards in all banks and automatic cash machines displaying the relevant logos.

VAT refunds

Foreigners making purchases in excess of ISK4,000 are entitled to a partial VAT refund when they leave Iceland. For full details, *see Tax-Free Shopping on page 331*.

Opening Hours

Banks are open Monday–Friday 9.15am–4pm, but rural branches may have limited opening hours. All banks have a few branches with extended opening hours, particularly in shopping malls such as Kringlan. All offer foreign exchange services.

Offices open Monday– Friday 9am–5pm. Most post offices open Monday–Friday 9am–4.30pm.

Museum opening times vary. They are usually open from 10am or 11am until 5pm or later in high season. Outside Reykjavík, many museums only open from June to August; so if you are travelling out of season but have set your heart on seeing a particular collection, ensure that the museum has not closed for winter.

Cafés throw open their doors between 10am–6pm. In Reykjavík, many cafés become bars after 6pm, remaining open until 1am Sunday– Thursday and anywhere between 3am and 6am Friday–Saturday. Restaurants have short, sedate hours: usually from 11.30am– 2.30pm and 6–10pm or 11pm.

Off-licences (liquor stores) vary greatly, with many outside Reykjavík only opening for a couple of hours a day. *For detailed information on shop opening hours, see page 332.*

P hotography

Crystal-clear air and long hours of daylight create ideal conditions for photography, and enthusiasts will probably take many more photos than they plan to. If your camera can be fitted with one, don't forget to use a UV/skylight filter when photographing outdoors. All photographic equipment, memory cards, and processing is expensive, so bring your own or purchase it at the Duty Free Shop at the Keflavík airport, though memory cards for digital cameras are readily available. If you do have to buy film in Iceland, bear in mind that outside Reykjavík slide film, in particular, may be hard to get hold of.

Postal Services

Post offices *(Íslandspóstur)* are found in all major towns and villages and some country districts. The postal system is efficient with letters taking two to six days to reach Europe or North America. Letters are sent by either priority (A) or economy (B) service, but delivery time abroad is not noticeably different between the two services. Air-mail letters or postcards to Europe cost ISK165 (A) or ISK140 (B); to other areas they are ISK220 (A) or ISK155 (B). You can buy stamps from post offices. Some shops that sell postcards also stock stamps. The Central Post Office has a philatelic section, and stamp collections are also sold at souvenir shops. Icelandic stamps often show native birds and natural phenomena, making an unusual and affordable gift to take home. Poste Restante is available at post offices throughout the country. Mark letters clearly with the surname in capitals or underlined.

Post offices are generally open Monday–Friday 9am–4.30pm. The **Central Post Office** on Posthússtræti 5 (near Laugardalur) in Reykjavík is open Monday–Friday 9am–6pm, June, July and August Saturday 10am–2pm.

Public Holidays

January New Year's Day/*Nýársdagurinn* (1st).

March/April Maundy Thursday, Good Friday, Easter Monday; First Day of Summer/*Sumardagurinn fyrsti* (third or fourth Thursday in April).

May Labour Day (1st); Ascension (sixth Thursday after Easter); Whitsun (eighth Monday after Easter).

June Independence Day (17th).

August *Verslunnarmannahelgi* (first Monday).

December Christmas Day (25th), Boxing Day (26th). Christmas Eve and New Year's Eve are half-day holidays.

R eligious Services

Just under 79 percent of Icelanders belong to the Evangelical Lutheran Church, about 3 percent are Roman Catholics, 4 percent are atheists, and various denominations account for the remaining 14 percent of the population.

Reykjavík has a number of churches that hold regular services on Sundays and in the week. Churches in central Reykjavík include: **Hallgrímskirkja**, Skólavörðuholt, tel: 510 1000;

Dómkirkjan (the cathedral), Kirkjustræti 16, tel: 520 9700; Landakotskirkja (**Catholic cathedral**), Hávallagata, tel: 552 5388 (celebrates Holy Mass in English on Sundays at 6pm); **Fríkirkjan** (Free Church), Fríkirkjuvegur 5, tel: 552 7270.

Outside Reykjavík there are Lutheran churches in all towns and villages and on many farms as well, though services may not be held every Sunday in rural districts. Apart from main **Akureyrarkirkja** (tel: 462 7700), Akureyri also has a Catholic church at Eyrarlandsvegur 26.

Student Travellers

Student discounts are rarely, if ever, advertised, but is worth asking at museums to see what is available.

T elecommunications

The Icelandic word for telephone is *sími*. Public telephone kiosks are something of a rarity in Iceland so making a telephone call demands ingenuity and perseverance. Restaurants, roadside service stations, swimming pools and hotels sometimes have coin-box telephones, taking ISK10, 50 and, usually, 100 coins. Most call boxes will also accept phonecards – available from post offices. Call costs vary according to the time and day of the week, and the distance that you are telephoning. Try to avoid calling from your hotel room – hotels often charge three times the official rate.

Direct dialling is available to most countries – to call internationally from Iceland, first dial 00 followed by the country code. Country codes and international dialling procedure in English are listed in the telephone directory. For international directory enquiries dial 115.

All Icelandic telephone numbers have seven digits, with no area codes. The international code for calling Iceland from abroad is 354. Fax services are available from post offices around the country and many hotels also offer this service to guests and sometimes to non-residents. The main tourist information office in Reykjavík has telephone and fax facilities, available to visitors.

Time Zone

Iceland is on Greenwich Mean Time (GMT)/Coordinated Universal Time (UTC), but no daylight saving time is applied. This means that in summer it is one hour behind London, four hours ahead of New York and seven hours ahead of California. In winter, it is on the same time as London, five hours ahead of New York and eight hours ahead of California.

Tipping

Tipping is not customary in Iceland and is not expected.

Toilets

Public toilets are a rarity. It is better to make use of the facilities at your accommodation or at a bar or café.

Tour Operators

A wide range of travel packages are offered by tour operators in Iceland and abroad. Itineraries range from short coach-based sightseeing tours to longer camping tours and activity holidays – including horse-riding, whale-watching, hiking, river rafting, snowmobiling and mountain biking. Those who prefer a roof over their head but do not mind roughing it a little could try sleeping-bag accommodation holidays. Winter packages offer cross-country skiing, snowmobiling and jeep touring.

Outside main towns with tourist offices, it is worth asking at your hotel for details of local tours. Some operators offer a special service for schools and universities. Local tourist offices usually offer sightseeing tours ranging from one morning to several days.

Tourist Offices

Reykjavík: Tourist Information, Aðalstræti 2, 101 Reykjavík, tel: 590 1550, e-mail: info@ visitreykjavik.is, www.visitreykjavik.is. Open 1 June–15 Sept: daily 8.30am–7pm; 16 Sept–31 May: Mon–Fri 9am–6pm, Sat 9am–4pm, Sun 9am–2pm.
Nordic Visitor – Iceland, Laugavegur 26, tel: 511 2442, www.icelandvisitor.com. Open June–Aug daily 9am–10pm, Sept–May Mon–Sat 10am–6pm.
Akureyri: Tourist Information Centre, Hof Cultural Centre, Strandgata, 600 Akureyri, tel: 553 5999, e-mail: info@visitakureyri.is; www.visitakureyri.is. Open mid-June–Aug: Mon–Fri 7.30am–7pm; Sept & early June: Mon–Fri 8am–5pm, Sat-Sun 10am-2pm; Oct–May: Mon–Fri 8am–5pm.

For more detailed information contact the Icelandic Tourist Board or tourist information offices.

Tour Operators in Iceland

Arinbjörn Jóhannsson, Brekkulækur Farm, 531 Hvammstangi, tel: 451 2938, e-mail: brekka@nett.is. A company offering unique holidays in northwest Iceland. Especially notable are a 10-day Icelandic-style Christmas/New Year celebration and a spring hiking tour in May to observe nature's awakening. Also does horse-riding (*see page 342*).

Guðmundur Jónasson Travel, Borgartún 34, Reykjavík, tel: 511 1515, e-mail: gjtravel@gjtravel.is, www.gjtravel.is. A diverse range of tours including horse-riding and river rafting.

Hotel Reykjahlíð, 660 Mývatn, tel: 464 4142, e-mail: reykjahlid@islandia.is, www.reykjahlid.is. Based next to Lake Mývatn, this hotel offers jeep tours to hard-to-reach areas in the northeast, including the Askja Caldera, Herðubreiðarlindir nature reserve, Dettifoss and the surrounding national park, and Lofthellir ice cave. Tours generally run from June–September.

Iceland Excursions (Gray Line), Hafnarstræti 20, 101 Reykjavík, tel: 540 1313, e-mail: bookings@grayline.is, www.icelandexcursions.is. Day tours from Reykjavík to the west and southwest of the country, including whale-watching, the Blue Lagoon and glacier tours.

Iceland Total/Iceland Travel, Skútuvogur 13A, 104 Reykjavík, tel: 412 4444, 585 4300, email: info@ icelandtotal.com, www.icelandtotal.com, www.icelandtravel.is. Both part of the Icelandair group, these sister companies seemingly offer every kind of tour imaginable: with trips to all parts of Iceland and a variety of adventure tours.

Icelandic Farm Holidays, Síðumúli 2, Reykjavík, tel: 570 2700, e-mail: ifh@ farmholidays.is, www.farmholidays.is. Specialising in farm holidays and farmhouse accommodation, including self-drive packages.

Nonni Travel, Brekkugata 5, Akureyri, tel: 461 1841, e-mail: nonni@ nonnitravel.is, www.nonnitravel.is. This travel agent can arrange trips around Akureyri and nearby areas including Mývatn and Grímsey, plus jaunts to Greenland and the Faroe Islands lasting from three days to three weeks.

Reykjavík Excursions, BSÍ Bus Terminal, 101 Reykjavík, tel: 580 5400, e-mail: main@re.is, www.re.is. This bus company is one of the oldest and largest organisers of day trips around the west and the southwest, with the possibility of incorporating activities such as horse-riding.

Snæland Grímsson, Langholtsvegur 115, 104 Reykjavík, tel: 588 8660, e-mail: snaeland@snaeland.is; www.snaeland.is. Hiking tours, group tours, day excursions, winter excursions, jeep safaris and more.

Adventure Tours

A number of tour operators specialise in adventure tourism, such as river rafting, glacier tours, kayaking, winter excursions and mountain climbing. Many larger tour operators may also offer such trips as part of their regular programme.

Activity Tours, Vegamót, 560 Varmahlíð, tel: 453 8383, e-mail: info@activitytours.is, www.activitytours.is. White-water rafting in the Skagafjörður region of north Iceland. Three rivers, which are graded according to difficulty.

Blue Biking, Stekkjarhvammur 60, 220 Hafnarfjörður, tel: 565 2089, e-mail: bluebiking@simnet.is, www.simnet. is/bluebiking. Made-to-measure bicycle tours for groups. All the necessary equipment is provided.

Glacier Jeeps Glacier Tours, 780 Hornafjörður, tel: 478 1000, e-mail: glacierjeeps@simnet.is, www.glacierjeeps.is. Snowmobiling onto the Vatnajökull ice-cap, sailing on Jökulsárlón glacial lagoon and ice-walking on a glacier. Protective gear provided.

Ice Travel, Álftaland 17, 108 Reykjavík, tel: 588 5555, e-mail: ice@ icemail.is, www.icemail.is. Individual/group tours, expeditions. Snowmobile and jeep safaris, glacier tours, helicopter tours, river rafting etc.

Iceland Excursions (Gray Line; *see above*). In addition to a plethora of bus tours, this large tour operator arranges jeep and ATV trips, snowmobiling, glacier hikes, ice climbing and more.

Icelandic Mountain Guides (Íslenskir Fjallaleiðsögumenn), Vagnhöfði 7b, 110 Reykjavík, tel: 587 9999, e-mail: mountainguides@mountainguides.is, www.mountainguides.is. An association of

Tourist Offices Abroad

USA: tel: 212-885 9700, mailing address: 655 3rd Ave, Suite 1810, New York, NY 10017-5617, www.goiceland.org
UK: There is no tourist office in the UK; for information on the internet, visit www.icetourist.is

mountain and trekking guides with years of experience, which offers the usual day-long activity tours (glacier walks, horse-riding etc), plus a range of rugged multi-day hikes and treks for experienced walkers and/or climbers. Can also custom-design tours for individuals and groups. **Mountaineers of Iceland**, Skútuvogur 12E, 104 Reykjavík, tel: 580 9900, e-mail: ice@mountaineers.is, www.mountaineers.is. Offers super-jeep tours off the beaten track.
Öræfaferðir, Hofsnes-Öræfi, 785 Fagurhólsmýri, tel: 894 0894, e-mail: info@oraefaferdir.is, www.oraefaferdir.is. Located in south Iceland, the people on this farm specialise in tours of the Hofsnes-Öræfi region: from gentle coastal trips and bird-watching walks, to ascents of Hvanndalshnúkur (Iceland's highest mountain) and ski mountaineering expeditions.

Hiking Tours

Two local outdoor organisations – the Iceland Touring Association (Ferðafélag Íslands) and Útivist – offer guided backpacking tours and day walks. For more on hiking, *see page 333*.

The backpacking tours are graded according to level of difficulty and accommodation is usually in mountain huts. Participants must bring their own food and equipment. Both organisations are practically national institutions and are extremely popular with Icelanders. Consequently, these tours provide an excellent way to meet the natives. The downside is that the tours are guided in Icelandic, though the majority of guides do speak English as well.
Iceland Touring Association (Ferðafélag Íslands) Mörkinn 6, 108 Reykjavík, tel: 568 2533, email: fi@fi.is, www.fi.is. Founded in 1927 and offers various hiking and cross-country skiing tours with mountain hut accommodation. Trips usually depart from the ITA's Reykjavík office, but check when booking.
Útivist, Laugavegur 178, 105 Reykjavík, tel: 562 1000, e-mail: utivist@utivist.is, www.utivist.is. Hiking tours to Þórsmörk and other south Iceland locations, with camping and mountain hut accommodation. Trips usually depart from the BSÍ bus terminal in Reykjavík, but check when booking.

Horse-riding Tours

The Icelandic horse is a delightful creature: small, sturdy, sure-footed and good-natured. It has five different gaits, including the *tölt*, a fast, smooth trot. Since the 1980s the Icelandic horse has become increasingly popular worldwide, and many foreign Icelandic-horse lovers come to Iceland especially to ride the horse in its natural environment. Besides, experiencing Iceland on horseback is utterly exhilarating. A number of tour operators specialise in horse-riding tours of long or short duration. *(See also page 333.)*
Arinbjörn Jóhannsson, Brekkulækur Farm, 531 Hvammstangi, tel: 451 2938, e-mail: brekka@nett.is. Based in the northwest of Iceland. A variety of longer and shorter horse-riding tours, including winter excursions to observe the northern lights and starry night sky.
Eldhestar (Volcano Horses), Vellir, Ölfus, P.O. Box 90, 810 Hveragerði, tel: 480 4800, e-mail: info@eldhestar.is, www.eldhestar.is. Offers short and long riding tours, riding camps, lessons and special holidays including tours to the National Equestrian Meets.
Íshestar (Icelandic Riding Tours), Sörlaskeið 26, 220 Hafnarfjörður, tel: 555 7000, e-mail: info@ishestar.is, www.ishestar.is. Organises diverse riding tours of various lengths, including visits to the annual sheep round-up, driving herds of horses and historical trekking routes across the beautiful Icelandic interior.
Polar Horses, Grýtubakki 2, 601 Akureyri, tel: 463 3179, e-mail: polarhestar@polarhestar.is, www.polarhestar.is. A family-run outfit offering tours with such intriguing names as "Riding with the Elves". Also organises tours to the National Equestrian Meet and farm holidays with daily riding tours incorporated.

Sightseeing Air Tours

Flugfélag Vestmannaeyja, (Westman Islands Airline), Vestmannaeyjar airport, Vestmannaeyjar, tel: 481 3255, e-mail: eyjaflug@eyjaflug.is, www.eyjaflug.is. Aerial sightseeing around Vestmannaeyjar.
Mýflug Air Service, Reykjahlíð airport, tel: 464 4400, e-mail: myflug@myflug.is, www.myflug.is. Offers sightseeing flights around Lake Mývatn from the airfield behind the Hlíð campsite. On a clear day the 20-minute flight over the lake is stunning. They also fly over Krafla, the Jökulsá Canyon, and the central highlands to Askja and Kverkfjöll. A minimum of two to three persons is usually needed to go ahead with the flight.
Atlantsflug, Skaftafell Airport, Skaftafell (Vatnajökull National Park), tel: 899 2532, e-mail: info@atf.is, www.atf.is. Offers sightseeing flights over the glacial tongues streaming from the Vatnajökull icecap, and over the highland interior.

Tour Operators Abroad

UK
Dick Phillips, Whitehall House, Nenthead, Alston, Cumbria CA9 3PS, tel: 01434 381440, www.icelandic-travel.com. Iceland specialist for self-reliant types interested in hiking, cycling and mountaineering. Information and book and map service. Special arrangements made for school and university groups.
Discover the World, Arctic House, 8 Bolters Lane, Banstead, Surrey SM7 2AR, tel: 01737 214250, email: travel@discover-the-world.co.uk, www.discover-the-world.co.uk. A comprehensive travel and information service for Iceland. Hotel tours, camping and sleeping-bag accommodation tours, activity holidays, fly drive and independent travel arrangements, bus and air passes. Also offers winter activity holidays and a book and map service. Special arrangements made for school and university groups.
Icelandair, Adam House, 2nd floor, 1 Fitzroy Square, London W1T 5HE, tel: 0844 811 1190, email: uk@icelandair.is, www.icelandair.co.uk. Icelandair's in-house travel agency. Offers a broad range of escorted and unescorted programmes for groups and individuals year round, including fly-drive packages and stopovers.
Sherpa Expeditions, 131a Heston Road, Hounslow, Middlesex TW5 0RF, tel: 020 8577 2717, 9788, e-mail: sales@sherpa-walking-holidays.co.uk, www.sherpa-walking-holidays.co.uk. 9- or 15-day escorted walking tours through the Markafljót valley in the Torfajökull region.

USA
Distant Journeys, P.O. Box 1211, Camden, Maine, 04843, USA, tel: 888-845 5781, e-mail: journeys@distantjourneys.com, www.distantjourneys.com. Hiking and walking tours in the Fjallabak nature reserve.
Icelandair Holidays, 1900 Crown Colony Drive, Quincy, MA 02169, USA, tel: 1 800 223 5500, e-mail: america@icelandair.is, www.icelandair.com. Icelandair's in-house travel agency *(see UK entry, above).*

V isas and Passports

The normal entry stamp in your passport is valid for a stay of up to three months, and your passport must be valid for a further three months beyond your proposed departure date. You may be asked to produce evidence of funds to support yourself and an air or ferry ticket out of the country. If you wish to extend your stay after arrival, this can be done at the main police station in Reykjavík at Hverfisgata 115, or at police stations around the country.

If you intend to work in Iceland, you will need a pre-arranged job and a residence and work permit which your prospective employer applies for before you enter the country. Residents of the European Economic Area (EEA states) may stay in Iceland for up to three months without having an air or ferry ticket out of the country and may also look for work.

Residents of the following countries may enter Iceland using their personal identity card: Austria, Belgium, France, Germany, Italy, Liechtenstein, Luxembourg, The Netherlands and Switzerland.

W eights and Measures

Iceland adopted the metric system (SI) in 1900, so all distances and weights are in centimetres, metres, kilometres, litres, grams, kilograms, metric tonnes etc.

What to Bring

Although the 2008 financial crash has made Iceland more affordable for visitors, it is still expensive: the cost of importing goods, and a 25.5 per cent VAT rate on some items, means that you may pay more than at home. Bring everything for your stay in the way of clothing, medicine, camera film and other equipment. If you plan to backpack around the country, it is worth bringing in your duty-free food allowance (3kg/6.6lb, up to ISK18,500 in value) in the form of dried foods. Freeze-dried products are costly and virtually unavailable outside specialist shops in Reykjavík.

Iceland's freak wind gusts have been known to wreak havoc at campgrounds – a summerweight tent will not survive. If you bring your own

tent, make sure you are able to repair bent poles, broken guy ropes and holes in canvas. Bring heavy-duty tent pegs; lightweight aluminium pegs may not be enough.

What to Wear

In summer, light woollens or a fleece, and a wind- and rainproof jacket or coat are essential, along with something for warmer days (wearing layers works best in Iceland's changeable summer weather). If you plan to travel around the country, go walking or head into the uninhabited interior, you must dress accordingly. Your best investment for Iceland will be a quality rain/wind jacket and leggings together with a thick sweater (or a fleece, which will still insulate when wet), scarf, hat and gloves. For footwear, bring a thick-soled pair of walking shoes or trainers. Even if you don't plan to do any serious hiking, a pair of lightweight hiking boots is a good idea – many of Iceland's most visited sights are reached on foot via uneven paths.

Bring swimwear for Iceland's numerous geothermal bathing pools.

Icelanders are very clothes-conscious, which is reflected in Reykjavík's fashion shops. If you plan to eat out at one of the city's better restaurants, you should dress up. Although most pubs are casual, people do get dressed up to go to smarter bars, and a few clubs maintain a policy of no jeans or trainers.

For travel in Iceland between October and May, conditions can be severe. Although prolonged cold spells are rare, temperatures as low as -20°C (-6°F) can occur and, with the wind chill factor, it can feel very much colder than that. So, any visitor planning to travel outside the Reykjavík area in winter must be well kitted out.

When to Visit
Spring

April and May can be good times to visit Iceland, although it is still cold and most highland and interior routes are closed to standard vehicles. Long daylight hours, few tourists and the beginning of the whale-watching season are all reasons to visit at this time of year.

Summer

Summer in Iceland is a brief affair. By June the lowlands are snow-free and the land bursts into colour. Between

mid-May and the end of July there is almost perpetual daylight. July signals the opening of the highland routes and travellers take to their vehicles in a frenzy of activity. By mid-August the nights are cooler, and the tourist season draws to a rapid close.

Mid-June to mid-August sees the warmest, though not necessarily the best, weather. Most people visit at this time and accommodation can be hard to find. However, if you travel off the beaten track, you will still find plenty of open space.

The first half of June and last two weeks in August see less tourist traffic and often have fine weather, though nights can be chilly. Most campsites, summer hotels, tours and excursions only operate from June through August.

For birds and flowers the first half of summer is undoubtedly better, but if you want to get into the highlands don't travel before mid-July. You can catch the midnight sun in June in the north of Iceland but the northern lights do not start to appear until the cooler and darker nights of late August.

Autumn

September 1st signals the end of summer and tourist operations start winding down. The Edda chain of hotels return to their normal operations as boarding schools, universities and conference centres during the winter.

However, farms and other hotels will welcome business and if you have brought a tent, camping presents no problems. Many of the highland routes are passable with care throughout September – the added dimension of autumn colours and a dusting of snow on the mountain ranges can make this one of the most beautiful months.

Winter

Reykjavík is gaining in popularity as a winter-break destination, and a number of tour operators offer bargain packages out of season. Hotels, most museums and some excursions operate all year in Reykjavík. Some bus routes and most flights operate year-round but schedules can be disrupted by weather. If you plan to hire a vehicle in winter, a four-wheel drive is a must. Car rental firms and hotels have special winter rates.

Some tour operators offer winter activity holidays with travel by jeep, snowmobile or on cross-country skis (see Tour Operators, pages 341–2).

TRANSPORT

ACCOMMODATION

ACTIVITIES

A – Z

LANGUAGE

LANGUAGE

UNDERSTANDING THE LANGUAGE

About Icelandic

Icelandic is one of the Nordic family of languages and most closely resembles Norwegian and Faroese. Remarkably, the Icelandic spoken today has not changed greatly from the language of the early Norse settlers (see page 91).

For the foreigner, Icelandic is daunting, but most Icelanders, particularly the young, speak English fluently, as well as Danish, Norwegian or Swedish. German and French are less widely spoken, but also taught at school. Icelanders are by nature quite reticent with foreigners and not easily drawn into conversation but it will be worth it. If you can pick up a few phrases of Icelandic, it will be appreciated.

Pronunciation Tips

Stress falls naturally on the first syllable of a word. The following examples of pronunciation are for guidance only – many Icelandic sounds do not exist in English.

Vowels and Consonants

Ð / ð pronounced 'th' as in the
Þ / þ pronounced 'th' as in thing
a as in hard
á as in how
e as in get
é as in yet
i or **y** as in thin
í or **ý** as in been
o as in ought
ó as in gold
ö as in first
u as in hook
ú as in fool
ae as in fight
au between the sounds in fate and oil, as in the French feuille
ey/ei as in day

fn is pn as in open
g when followed by i (except at the start of a word) is y as in yet
hv is kf as in thankful
j is y as in yet
ll is tl as in bottle
r is always lightly rolled
rl is rtl as in heartless
rn is tn as in button
tn and **fn** when at the end of words are almost silent.

Geography

The following lists show common elements in place names, the English translation and an example.

Á	**river**
Hvítá	**white river**
Borg	**rocky crag**
Dimmuborgir	**dark crags**
Brekka	**slope**
Brekkulækur	**slope stream**
Dalur	**valley**
Fljótsdalur	**river valley**
Drangur	**column**
Drangavík	**rock bay**
Eldur	**fire**
Eldfell	**fire mountain**
Eyja	**island**
Flatey	**flat island**
Fell	**mountain**
Snæfell	**snow mountain**
Fjall	**mountain**
Bláfjöll	**blue mountains**
Fjörður	**fjord**
Hafnarfjörður	**harbour fjord**
Foss	**waterfall**
Gullfoss	**gold falls**
Gígur	**crater**
Lakagígar	**cow stomach craters**
Gil	**ravine**

Jökulgil	**glacier ravine**
Heiði	**heath**
Hellisheiði	**cave heath**
Hellir	**cave**
Sönghellir	**song caves**
Hlíð	**hillside**
Reykjahlíð	**smoky hillside**
Hóll	**hill/hillock**
Vatnsdalshólar	**lake valley hills**
Holt	**hill**
Brattholt	**steep hill**
Hraun	**lava**
Ódáðahraun	**ill deeds lava**
Höfði	**cape**
Höfdabrekka	**cape slope**
Höfn	**harbour**
Þórshöfn	**Thor's harbour**
Jökull	**glacier**
Vatnajökull	**lake glacier**
Lækur	**stream**
Varmilækur	**warm stream**
Laug	**hot spring**
Laugarvatn	**hot spring lake**
Lind	**spring**
Hvannalindir	**angelica springs**
Lón	**lagoon**
Jökulsárlón	**glacier river lagoon**
Mýri	**marsh**
Mýrdalsjökull	**marsh valley glacier**
Nes	**peninsula**
Snæfellnes	**snow mountain peninsula**
Reykur	**smoke**
Reykjanes	**smoky peninsula**
Sandur	**sand**
Mýrdalssandur	**marsh valley sand**
Skarð	**pass**
Kerlingarskarð	**troll wife's pass**

Skógur	**wood**	*Sveppir* **Mushrooms**	**Sorry** *Fyrirgefðu*

Skógur	**wood**
Skógafoss	**wood falls**
Staður	**place**
Egilsstaðir	**Egil's place**
Strönd	**coast/beach**
Hornstrandir	**horn peak coast**
Tindur	**peak**
Tindfjöll	**peak mountains**
Tjörn	**pond**
Störu-tjarnir	**big ponds**
Vatn	**lake**
Hvítárvatn	**white river lake**
Vík	**small bay**
Reykjavík	**smoky bay**
Vogur	**inlet**
Kópavogur	**seal pup inlet**
Völlur	**plain**
Þingvellir	**assembly plains**

At the Restaurant

Most restaurant staff speak some English or other Scandinavian languages. The words and phrases below will help you order from simpler menus.

Ég ætla að fá… **I would like…**
Áttu til…? **Have you got any…?**
Meira… **More…**
Ekki meira takk **No more thankyou**
Mjög gott **Very good**
Ég er grænmetisæta **I am vegetarian**
Reikninginn, takk **The bill, please**

Matseðill **Menu**
Forréttir **Starters**
Súpa **Soup**
Brauð **Bread**
Smjör **Butter**
Sósa **Sauce**

Kjötréttir Meat Dishes

Kjöt **Meat**
Lambakjöt **Lamb**
Nautakjöt **Beef**
Svínakjöt **Pork**
Kjúklingur **Chicken**
Hangikjöt **Smoked lamb**

Fiskréttir Fish Dishes

Fiskur **Fish**
Ýsa **Haddock**
Lúða **Halibut**
Rækjur **Prawns**
Lax **Salmon**
Silungur/Bleikja **Trout**

Grænmeti Vegetables

Kartöflur **Potatoes**
Franskar **Chips**
Blómkál **Cauliflower**
Grænar baunir **Peas**
Rauðkál **Red cabbage**

Sveppir **Mushrooms**
Gulrætur **Carrots**
Rófur **Turnips**
Salat **Salad**

Eftirréttir Desserts

Ís **Ice-cream**
Kaka/Terta **Cake**

Drykkir Drinks

Te **Tea**
Kaffi **Coffee**
Mjólk **Milk**
Sykur **Sugar**
Appelsínusafi **Orange juice**
Bjór **Beer**
Pilsner **Low-alcohol beer**
Hvítvín **White wine**
Rauðvín **Red wine**
Vatn **Water**

Useful Words and Phrases

The Icelandic language does not have an equivalent to "please". The phrase *Gerðu svo vel* is employed to invite a person into a house, to the table or to begin eating. It also translates to "here you are" when giving something to somebody. On a public notice "please" is *vinsamlegast*. For example, "please take your shoes off", a common request when entering a home or changing room is *vinsamlegast farið úr skónum*. When leaving the table or saying goodbye after a meal or drinks it is customary to thank the host by saying *Takk fyrir mig*.

Hello/good morning *Góðan dag*
Good evening *Gott kvöld*
Goodnight *Góða nótt*
What is your name? *Hvað heitir þú?*
My name is… *Ég heiti*
How are you? *Hvað segirðu gott?*
Fine, and you? *Allt fínt, en þú?*
Fine *Allt fínt*
Alright *Allt í lagi*
Goodbye *Bless*
Yes *Já*
No *Nei*
Thanks *Takk*
Thank you very much *Takk fyrir*
Yes please *Já takk*
No thank you *Nei takk*
May I have… *Má eg fá…*
When? *Hvenær?*
Today *Í dag*
Tomorrow *Á morgun*
Yesterday *Í gær*
In the morning *Fyrir hádegi*
In the afternoon *Eftir hádegi*
Cheers! *Skál!*
How much does *Hvað kostar*
this cost? *þetta?*
Come! *Komdu!*
Excuse me *Afsakið*

Sorry *Fyrirgefðu*
I do not understand *Ég skil ekki*

Signs

Toilet *Snyrting*
Gents *Karlar*
Ladies *Konur*
Open *Opið*
Closed *Lokað*
Danger *Hætta*
Forbidden *Bannað*
Campsite *Tjaldstæði*
Entry *Inngangur/Inn*
Exit *Útgangur/Út*
Parking *Bílastæði*
Schedule *Áætlun*
Airport *Flugvöllur*
Blind summit (road sign) *Blindhæð*
Jeep track *Jeppavegur*
Police *Lögreglan*
Hospital *Sjúkrahús*
Health Centre *Heilsugæslustöð*
Doctor *Læknir*
Dentist *Tannlæknir*
Bank *Banki*
Post Office *Póstur*
Chemist *Apótek*
Co-op store *Kaupfélag*
Swimming pool *Sundlaug*
Mechanic/garage *Verkstæði*

Numbers

Núll **zero**
Einn **one**
Tveir **two**
Þrír **three**
Fjórir **four**
Fimm **five**
Sex **six**
Sjö **seven**
Átta **eight**
Níu **nine**
Tíu **ten**
Ellefu **eleven**
Tólf **twelve**
Þrettán **thirteen**
Fjórtán **fourteen**
Fimmtán **fifteen**
Sextán **sixteen**
Sautján **seventeen**
Átján **eighteen**
Nítján **nineteen**
Tuttugu **twenty**
Tuttugu og einn **twenty one**
Þrjátíu **thirty**
Fjörutíu **forty**
Fimmtíu **fifty**
Sextíu **sixty**
Sjötíu **seventy**
Áttatíu **eighty**
Níutíu **ninety**
Hundrað **one hundred**
Tvö hundrað **two hundred**
Þúsund **one thousand**
Milljón **one million**

TRANSPORT
ACCOMMODATION
ACTIVITIES
A – Z
LANGUAGE

FURTHER READING

General

Cod: A Biography of the Fish that Changed the World by Mark Kurlansky, Vintage, London 1999. Highly acclaimed, fascinating account of a fish and an industry so vital to Iceland.

The English Dane by Sarah Bakewell, Vintage, London 2006. Readable biography about Jørgen Jørgensen, the "Dog-Days King", one of the strangest characters ever to set foot in Iceland.

A Guide to the Flowering Plants and Ferns of Iceland by Hörður Kristinsson, Mál og Menning, Reykjavík, 2005. Written by the former Professor of Botany at the University of Iceland, this is a comprehensive, easy-to-use full-colour identification guide organised by flower colour and characteristics.

Icelandic Food & Cookery by Nanna Rögnvaldardóttir, Hippocrene Books Inc., 2002. Icelandic cookbook, for a literal taste of Iceland.

Icelandic Bird Guide by Jóhann Óli Hilmarsson, Iðunn, Reykjavik 2000. A practical guide to identifying Icelandic breeding birds, visitors and vagrants, including a section on identifying eggs and fledglings.

Last Places: A Journey in the North by Lawrence Millman, Houghton Mifflin, 1990. An extremely funny travelogue, which exactly pinpoints the attraction of cold, bleak landscapes.

Letters from Iceland by W.H. Auden and Louis MacNeice, Faber and Faber, 2002. Irreverent letters and poems sent by the two poets on a 1936 journey to Iceland, still fascinating and funny today.

Ring of Seasons by Terry Lacy, University of Michigan Press, 2001. A good all-round overview of Icelandic history and culture from the perspective of a foreign resident.

Literature

Angels of the Universe by Einar Már Guðmundsson, Mare's Nest, London, 1995. This acclaimed novel won the Nordic Council's Literary Award in 1995. A disturbing and moving tale of a young man's slide into schizophrenia, based on the life of the author's

brother. Also released as a film.

The Atom Station by Halldór Laxness, Vintage (Random House), 2004. A wonderful dark comedy with a political slant by Iceland's late Nobel laureate.

The Blue Fox by Sjón, Telegram Books, 2008. A short, strange fable by playwright, poet and sometime-Björk-collaborator Sjón.

Devil's Island by Einar Kárason, Canongate Books, 2000. Pithy novel about the clash between poverty-stricken Icelanders and flashy American culture in 1950s Reykjavík.

Independent People by Halldór Laxness, Vintage (Random House), USA, 1997. The classic story of a man's struggle for independence, symbolic of the Icelandic nation, which helped to win its author the Nobel Prize for Literature.

Tainted Blood by Arnaldur Indriðason, Vintage, London 2005. A fascinating murder mystery featuring Reykjavík detective, Erlendur, and his team who

investigate a man's murder with help from Iceland's Genetic Research Centre. (Also published under the title **Jar City**, the name too of its successful cinematic release.)

Treasures of Icelandic Verse by various authors, Mál og Menning, Reykjavík, 1996. An anthology of various Icelandic poems, with both the original and the translation.

Troll's Cathedral by Ólafur Gunnarsson, Mare's Nest, London, 1996. The story of a family beset by violence.

Many of Iceland's **Sagas** have been translated into English and other languages; particularly readable are Egils Saga, Laxdæla Saga and Njáls Saga, which are all published under the Penguin Classics label.

The Sagas of the Icelanders, translated by Robert Kellogg and also published by Penguin Classics, includes 10 sagas and seven shorter Old Norse tales.

Send Us Your Thoughts

We do our best to ensure the information in our books is as accurate and up-to-date as possible. The books are updated on a regular basis using local contacts, who painstakingly add, amend and correct as required. However, some details (such as telephone numbers and opening times) are liable to change, and we are ultimately reliant on our readers to put us in the picture.

We welcome your feedback, especially your experience of using the book "on the road". Maybe we recommended a hotel that you liked (or another that you didn't), or you came across a great bar or new attraction we missed.

We will acknowledge all contributions, and we'll offer an Insight Guide to the best letters received.

Please write to us at:
Insight Guides
PO Box 7910
London SE1 1WE
Or email us at:
insight@apaguide.co.uk

Other Insight Guides

More than 120 **Insight Guides** and **Insight City Guides** cover every continent, providing information on culture and all the top sights, as well as superb photography and detailed maps. In addition, **Insight Smart Guides** present comprehensive listings in a snappy, easy-to-find way, held together by an A–Z theme and with a street atlas showing major attractions, hotels and public transport; while **Insight Step By Step Guides** deliver self-guided walks and tours.

Companion Insight Guides include Norway, Sweden, Finland, and Scandinavia.
Step-By-Step guide to Copenhagen.
Smart guide to Copenhagen.

ART AND PHOTO CREDITS

AKG London 54, 55, 111, 125
courtesy Blue Lagoon 160, 164
Bryan and Cherry Alexander 95B,
122, 196, 221, 254T
Art Archive 28TL, 57
AWL Images 142,
Corbis 29MR, 44, 65, 191L,
214/215, 222T, 240T, 249T,
250/251, 261, 307R, 309L/R
Julian Cremona 128R
courtesy Decoding Iceland 72
Mary Evans 26M, 45, 175, 209
APA Ming Tang Evans 2/3, 3B,
4BL/T, 6MR, 7M/ML/MR/T, 8BL/
BR/T, 9T, 10/11, 12/13, 16, 17, 18,
22, 60, 62, 66, 67, 69, 70, 77, 79,
81, 84, 86, 88, 98, 113, 114, 119R,
136, 137B/M/T, 144L/R/T, 145/T,
146, 149R, 150, 152L/R/T, 154T,
155, 156/T, 158, 161/T, 163,
166/167, 168, 169, 170T, 171,
173/T, 176, 177, 178T, 179T, 180,
181, 182/183, 185L/R, 186/T,
187T, 188T, 189/T, 191R, 192/193,
197, 199, 204/205, 206, 207,
209T, 211, 212, 217, 219, 220T,
222, 223, 224, 225, 228/229, 230,
231, 233/T, 234L, 236/237, 240,
241, 243L/R/T, 246, 261, 262/T,
263, 264L/R, 266/T, 270/271,
272, 273, 274T, 275, 276, 277/T,
278/T, 279/T, 280/281, 282, 283,
284, 285/T, 286, 287/T, 288L/R/T,
289/T, 290, 291, 312, 320, 327,
332, 336, 340, 343, 344
Fotolia 253, 254, 297T
Getty Images 12/13, 28TR, 29B,
73, 75, 91, 110, 120/B, 186, 190,
257, 314
Dave Gingritch 299L
Bragi Gudmundsson 19, 20, 187
Hrafn Gunnlaugsson 36
Catherine Harlow 265
Blaine Harrington 143, 153T
Rudy Hemmingsen 183, 211T,
244/245, 300/301, 305
Hafdis Hilmarsdottir 303
Iceland Tourism/ Ragnar Th.
Sigurosson 6T, 102, 105, 196, 198,
200

Iceland Tourism/Ingi Gunnar
Johannsson 76, 101, 103,
108/109, 112, 130/131, 132/133,
314T, 328, 335,
Icelandic Tourist Board 80, 100,
104, 106B/T, 162, 172, 176T, 197,
246T, 305T, 319,
Istockphoto 7B/TR, 124, 178, 252,
256, 292,/293, 297, 299R, 304T,
307L
APA Britta Jaschinski 4BR, 9L, 40,
78, 118, 121, 134/135, 148T,
149L/T, 153/T, 157, 234R, 247,
317, 329, 331, 338
Sigburg Johanesdottir 304
Hilmar Thor Johannsson 298T,
308T
Hans Klüche 149
Kobal 74
Bob Krist 64, 82/83, 90R, 119L,
148, 188, 216, 219T, 306
Courtesy Arni Magnuson
Foundation 87
Ragnar Axelsson/Morgunbladid
301T, 310
Asdis Asgeirsdottir/Morgunbladid
213
Kristinn Ingvarsson/Morgunbladid
99
Arni Saeberg/Morgunbladid 156
Kjartan Thorbjornsson/
Morgunbladid 237, 244T
NHPA 123, 126, 128L
PA Photos 255
Tony Perrottet 26B/T, 68/69,
175T, 245T
Photographer's Direct 6BL
Photolibrary 28B, 115, 236, 265T
Lance Price 32R, 34, 151T
APA/Tom Le Bas 210
Bruce McAdam 295
National Museum of Iceland 5 53,
89
Cathleen Naundorf T62
Nikos Photography 179
Rex Features 63
Ljósmyndasafn Reykjavíkur 27T
Hasse Schröder 21, 24/25, 96/97,
258/259
Jacob Sigurosson 85

TIPS Images 294, 302
Topfoto 61
Werner Forman Archive/Stofnun
Árni Magnússon Institute 37
Werner Forman Archive/ National
Museum Reykjavík 38
World Picture News 107T
Sara Yeomans 308

PHOTO FEATURES

92/93:
APA Ming Tang Evans 92/93, The
Árni Magnússon Institute 92BR/
TL, National Museum of Iceland
92BL, 93BL, AKG London 93TR,
Werner Forman Archive 93BR

116/117:
Bob Krist 116/117, Keith Skelton
116M, APA Ming Tan Evans 117B,
Corbis 117T, Icelandic Tourist
Board 117B, Rudy Hemmingsen
117M.

202/203:
APA Ming Tang Evans 202/203,
203B/M, Hasse Schröder 203T,
Photographer's Direct 202B, Tony
Perrottet 203ML

226/227:
Arni Saeberg/Morgunbladid
226/227, G Bernard/NHPA 227M,
Laurie Campbell/NHPA 226BL,
227BL, Jim Bain/ NHPA 226BR,
Andy Rouse/NHPA 227BR

268/269:
APA Ming Tang Evans 268/269,
269B/M, 269B, Icelandic Tourist
Board 269M/TR

Original Cartrography:
Cosmographics; updated by Apa
Cartography Department
© 2011 Apa Publications GmbH & Co.
Verlag KG (Singapore branch)

Production: Tynan Dean

INDEX

ÖRFIRISEY

Höfn

Viðeyjarsund

VESTURBÆR

Myragata

Grandagarður

Geirsgata

Vesturgata

Öldugata

Tungata

Kaþólska kirkjan

Sólvallagata

Garðastræti

Suðurgata

Hafnarhús
(Reykjavik
Art Museum)

Kolaportið
Market

Harpa
(Concert Hall and Conference Centre)
(under construction)

Tryggvagata

Austurstræti

AUSTURVÖLLUR

Kirkjustræti

Alþingishúsið

Ráðhús
Reykjavikur

Vonarstræti

Iðnó

Dómkirkjan

Tjörnin

HÓLAVALLAGARÐUR

Þjóðarbókhlaðan

Þjóðminjasafn
Íslands
(National
Museum)

Háskóli Íslands
(University of Iceland)

Keflavik

Sæmundargata

Skothusvegur

Suðurtörn

Tjarnargata

Fríkirkjuvegur

Frikirkjan

Listasafn
Íslands
(National
Gallery)

Hljómskálinn

HLJÓMSKÁLAGARÐURINN

Hringbraut

Þorfinnstjörn

Skeljagata

Gamla Hringbraut

Baldursgata

Bragagata

Njarðargata

Laufásvegur

Bergstaðastræti

Bjarkargata

Kalkofnsvegur

Ingólfsstræti

Skúlagata

Sólfar
Suncraft

Rauðarárvik

Höfði Hou

Borgartun

Mie

Þjóðmenningarhúsið

Þjóðleikhúsið

Stjórnarráðið

Hverfisgata

Laugavegur

Klapparstígur

Skólavörðustígur

Pósthússtræti

Lækjargata

Þingholtsstræti

Nýlistasafnið
(Living Art Museum)

Grettisgata

AUSTURBÆR

Bergþórugata

Frakkastígur

Vitastígur

Hverfisgata

Barónsstígur

Snorrabraut

Egilsgata

Hallgrímskirkja

Safn Einars
Jónssonar

Landspítalinn
(National Hospital)

Vatnsmýrarvegur

Umferðamiðstöðin BSÍ
(Coach Terminal)

Hlemmur

Sundhöll Reykjavíkur
(Swimming Pool)

Austurstræti

Stórholt

Háteigsvegur

Flókagata

Langahlíð

NORÐURMÝRI

MIKLATÚN

Miklabraut

Eskihlíð

Kjarvalsstaðir
(Reykjavik Art Gallery)

Bólst

Mávahlíð

Stakkahlíð

Ha

Sidurgata

Njarðargata

Norræna
Húsið
(Nordic House)

Þorragata

Innanlandsflugvöllur
(Domestic Terminal)

Einarsnes

SKILDINGANÉS

Hotel
Loftleiðir

Reykjavikurflugvöllur

Flugvallarbraut

Vallarvegur

Hlíðarfótur

Perlan
(Pearl)

Sögusafnið
(Saga Museum)

Öskjuhlíð

Goshver
(Geyser)

Bústaðavegur

Vesturhlíð

Fos

Reykjavikurflugvöllur

Skerjafjörður